LECTURES & ADDRESSES

ON

MEDIAEVAL AND MODERN HISTORY

STUBBS

HENRY FROWDE, M.A.

PUBLISHER TO THE UNIVERSITY OF OXFORD

LONDON, EDINBURGH, AND NEW YORK

SEVENTEEN LECTURES

ON THE

STUDY OF MEDIAEVAL

AND

MODERN HISTORY

AND KINDRED SUBJECTS

DELIVERED AT OXFORD, UNDER STATUTORY OBLIGATION
IN THE YEARS 1867—1884; WITH TWO ADDRESSES
GIVEN AT OXFORD AND READING

BY

WILLIAM STUBBS, D.D.

Bishop of Oxford and Chancellor of the Most Noble Order of the Garter and Honorary
Student of Christ Church; Late Regius Professor of Modern History; LL.D.
of Cambridge, Edinburgh, and Dublin; Doctor in utroque jure, Heidelberg;
A Member of the Court of the Victoria University, and an Honorary
Member of the Imperial University of S. Vladimir of Kieff, and of
the Royal Bavarian, Prussian, Irish and Danish Academies;
Correspondent of the Academy of Moral and Political
Sciences of the Institute of France; And Knight
of the Prussian Order pour le Merite

THIRD EDITION

Oxford

Oxford
PRINTED AT THE CLARENDON PRESS
BY HORACE HART, M.A.
PRINTER TO THE UNIVERSITY

Printed in England

PREFACE

IF I were asked what is my reason for printing these lectures, I might be at a loss for an answer. They are not printed by request, or because they seem to me worthy to be preserved, or because they are likely to be useful reading, or because they supply a want. It may be that they owe their present form to the fact that the love of correcting proof-sheets has become a leading passion with the author.

Some part of the volume may be readable, some part useful: it may be that the useful part is hard reading, and the readable part trifling, but I will give myself, unphilosophic as it may be, the benefit of a doubt. The lectures were written under the pressure of statutory compulsion, and against the grain. I know, by sad experience, how often the best lecture, the best sermon on which I have most prided myself—eloquent, lucid, learned, logical—has gone the way of all fireworks. There is a chance that something may be said for work elicited by forcible pressure, under weariness and vexation, against stress of time, under statutory obligation and a conscientious sense of duty.

ᛈ The statute under which these lectures were delivered was a burdensome statute to me ; it would not be so to every professor, but the discomforts of working under it could only be explained by experience : and the statute itself is now a thing of the past. The feeling of compulsion, the compulsion to produce something twice a year which might attract an idle audience, without seeming to trifle with a deeply loved and honoured study, was so irksome that never once, in the course of my seventeen years of office, did I think that there would come a time when I could look back on this part of my work with pleasure or grateful regret. And I fear that this will be only too obvious to any one who tries to read this book. But I have said more than enough about it; and I will content myself with adding that the following are only a selection from a larger number of exercises delivered under the same conditions. Most of the omitted lectures have seen the light in other places. The second lecture of 1867 was made part of the Introduction to the second volume of Roger Hoveden, in the Rolls Series. The lectures of 1868 and 1874, on Anglo-Saxon literature and monastic history, formed part of a plan which I finally discarded after the restoration of Professor Earle to the Anglo-Saxon Chair, and, by themselves, do not seem to justify publication. Those for 1869 on Comparative Constitutional History, and for 1871 on Scottish Constitutional History, would have required a larger apparatus of notes, and more labour of revision, than I could at present afford, to qualify them for a permanent form, and are as a matter of necessity excluded. The lectures for 1870 form the Introduction to my *Select Charters*; those for 1873 were utilized as the seventh chapter of the *Constitutional History*; those for 1875 as the fourteenth chapter; and those for 1872 in the preface to the second volume of the Memoriale of Walter of Coventry.

W. CESTR.

DEE SIDE, CHESTER:
May 17, 1886.

THE Lectures contained in the present volume were first published in a collective form in 1886, two years after I had ceased to hold the office which had involved their production and given them such dignity as they had. The lapse of fourteen years ought to be sufficient to enable me to get my own professional personality into focus, and perhaps also to get the work of my term of office into perspective. I am very glad that a third edition of the lectures is required, and would take the opportunity of making a few remarks on both these points.

And of the first, first. In the careful reading of the proofs for this edition, I find myself, although carried back to some extent into a conviction of the rudeness and crudeness of some of my work, still profoundly convinced of the truth of the principles which I held thus long ago on the study of History. Whatever more I have learned has generally strengthened, and has never weakened, the convictions of my first and last public lectures, or my profession of faith made in those others which were specially devoted to the methods and conclusions of the study. Further, the few hard things that I thought I had to say, I tried not to say hardly, and have not to retract : the kind words that I was glad to say have borne kindly fruit. If I spoke severely of the casual criticisms of casual critics, they have had their revenge in deciding that my writings are not literature : perhaps that is enough. I do not remember that the thought occurred to me at the time, that I was expected to have a style that would qualify me to meet the criticisms of those to whom for the moment belongs the adjudication of what is or is not literature, to determine in fact the fashion of the uniform of the Man of Letters. I had worked hard, and was working hard, and have worked hard since—never finding work anything but happy, however much I might desire the rest that comes like to-morrow. The nineteen volumes of texts and prefaces which I had edited in the Rolls Series, my four volumes of *Constitutional History*; the three volumes of joint-work on the Councils; the contributions to, and reading of the sheets of, Dr. Smith's two great *Dictionaries of Christian Antiquities and Biography*, with a good deal of mechanical labour, as on Lechler's edition of Wycliffe's *Trialogus*, and Dr. Pusey's issue of *Torquemada on the Immaculate Conception*, with two or three minor diversions of the same kind—these things constitute my claim to the title of a qualified, if not skilled operative in the field which had opened before me, and which indeed I should have chosen if other influences had not superseded the necessity of making the choice. It was as a worker that I said what I had to say—I am and have been, all through, what I was called in company with Hallam in an examination paper last year, a horny-handed son of toil—and experience of work has confirmed me in my beliefs. That is as much as I need say now.

Of course I have plenty of reminiscences that would, I conceive, be as interesting to my old friends as theirs are to me; and my life and office have brought me into relations with many, at home and abroad, whose pleasant ways and sympathies are far deeper in my remembrance than any points in which we have differed. I do not think that I have been quarrelsome, or that there is much that I need ask to have forgiven. Work has led on to work, and the fruit of patience in the old field has contributed some result of experience to the new. My auguries, which were never prophecies, in the anticipation of improvement in our plans of teaching, in the progress of the study at home in Oxford, have had some fulfilments; not the least in the education of men who have made and are making their mark in public life, not only as teachers, but as servants of God in Church and State, judges, senators, ministers, bishops, editors, and

even cabinet ministers. Least of all, perhaps, was I lucky
in anticipating for myself some opportunity, such as I indicated
in my last Public Lecture, of continuing and completing
some work that I had begun; that hope the care of a great
diocese very soon showed me must be given up: I need not
recur to it. But in all else my faith has been justified; so
much I may fairly claim, I should not like to be thought to
take credit for more.

But this is my second point—I was *felix opportunitate
operis.* I came back to Oxford in 1866 at the moment of
the great expansion of study, and had the initial advantage
of the experience of those teachers who had fought their way
through the times of discouragement. Some of these are
still at work at Oxford; some, like the Bishop of London
and the Dean of Durham, have found, with me, some exercise
for other sets of nerves and sinews in other fields of work;
some have been long at rest, one of whom I may name, as
for especial example, C. W. Boase, the value of whose
labours as a teacher cannot be overrated: although he left
behind him no book but his College Register, he yet left
a memory of tutorial effort and industry which is monu-
mental in the minds of his associates. But it is not within
the experience of many ex-professors to get into the glass of
memory such men as Freeman and Froude, who, although
both of them my seniors, took up the work after me. When
in my inaugural lecture I tried to sum up in a couple of
lines, to which I still adhere, my appreciation of my illustrious
predecessor, who is still alive and strong, it certainly did not
occur to me that I might live to pronounce, even such an
éloge as I can now offer, on two great men destined to be
my successors. I had not anticipated, at the time of my
appointment to Chester, that Mr. Freeman would care to

take the professorship, and accordingly, when Mr. Glad-
stone consulted me about the choice of a successor, I
named the present Bishop of London. But that very day
it was announced that Mr. Freeman would accept the post,
and that was settled. And what can I say of him now but
that he was the most faithful and kindest friend, truly
sympathetic, and more than appreciative—however much
we differed in view or varied in our choice of method and
field of work? He was a really great and finished scholar,
and one in whom a peculiar fineness of judgement—for which,
early in our acquaintance, our friend A. W. Haddan specially
pointed him out to me—was curiously combined with a
certain vivacity of combative energy that seemed at once
to invite attack and insure defeat. I think that his influence
as professor was rather more obvious in the promotion of
research than in the educational aspect of his study. His
work outside the lecture-room, especially his very remarkable
beginning of his *History of Sicily*, was as thorough and
devout as one can imagine. But his early death cut off
a long hope of the development of historical study in every
direction under his able hand.

With Mr. Froude it is needless to say that I had much
less in common; but notwithstanding an occasional point of
provocation, such as was his ideal picture of clerical un-
veracity, we were very good friends; and I never had any
hesitation in expressing my belief in his sincerity as a writer,
or my admiration for the beauty of his style and his power
of stimulating interest. His tenure of office was too short,
but was long enough to give him opportunity and temptation ; he was an inspiring teacher, and he proved his love of
the work in the resumption of the discipline in which so long
ago he had won his spurs.

And now the work is in the hands of one of whom I could not speak too highly, if I had a right to speak at all ; who, like my predecessor, occupies a position of general authority, which must come within the speculative grasp of the historian of the future.

Under these leaders, and with the help of the strong helpers who helped me, the History School at Oxford has, as I am glad to bear witness, developed, specialized and differentiated, and at the same time has spread, through the action of its successful pupils, through the length and breadth of Britain. Hand in hand with Cambridge under Sir John Seeley and Lord Acton, our workers have undertaken and have gone no small way towards the accomplishment of the ideal which charmed me, and laid deep and broad foundations for a great future. But this is not my perspective : only I have stood and waited.

In the present edition I have added two quasi-popular addresses on the study, which contain a few remarks that I wish to put on record, and which may serve to my juniors as examples of what may be said, or perhaps not be said, to mixed companies. I had tried my prentice hand on the sort of thing in the 'Early Plantagenets' and earlier still in some lectures in Essex, which, in their small way, were a first lesson in lecturing, on Constitutional History. I had taken up the subject on the invitation of Dr. Shirley. I fear that these will not deserve, and I hope that they will escape, criticism.

Some fault has been found with me, as having been unbecomingly impatient of the conditions under which my Oxford Lectures were delivered, and the pressure of the statute under which I worked. That statute was, I am glad

to say, altered in my last year, and I the only one of the list
who had to, and did, actually work under its provisions during
my whole period of office. It is a thing of the past; and the
frequent references which in the Lectures are made to its
compulsory clauses, might very well have been omitted in the
edition. But when they were first printed, I simply revised
the proofs of the copy as delivered, and it is scarcely worth
while to remove them now. My dislike to compulsory
functionary utterances must be allowed to bear, as it may
well deserve, its punishment without any more solemn
profession of repentance than I gave in my last Public
Lecture.

W. OXON.

CUDDESDON PALACE:
July 20, 1900.

CONTENTS

I

INAUGURAL

(Feb. 7, 1867.)

THE giving of an Inaugural Lecture is an occasion which compels and may well excuse a little trepidation. The speaker, although he is wisely restrained by academic decorum from courting or fearing the thunder, propitious or otherwise, of right or left, cannot divest himself of the feeling that he is really about to take the omens of his future success, and cannot but be anxious to make, if he possibly can, a promising beginning. This is especially the case when he is called upon, as I am now, for the first time in his life, to address an academic, I may even say an educated, audience. He has not learned the tone of authority which befits the professorial character: it is no mere matter of form for him to deprecate adverse criticism; he feels that he must introduce himself, in a way that is of necessity painful both to his self-respect and to his modesty, to an audience from whom he has at least as much to learn as he can ever hope to teach them. I can indeed hardly use the word teach without reservation. I am so sensible of the greatness of the field, the variety of the instruments, the infinite multitude of the workers employed on the subject to which my labours in this place are to be devoted, that I am afraid even to advertise myself as a teacher, and would rather be looked on as a helper and trainer in a school in which every man has to learn his own lessons.

B

For I am thoroughly convinced that the purpose which is answered by the study of Modern and Mediaeval History is twofold; it is at once the process of acquisition of a stock of facts, an ignorance of which unfits a man from playing the very humblest part as a citizen, or even watching the politics of his own age with an intelligent apprehension; and it is an educational discipline directed to the cultivation of powers for whose development, as it seems to me, no other training is equally efficacious. It is but natural that I should speak thus of a study which has been to me the pleasure, rest, and comfort of a somewhat busy and anxious life, to whose teachings I feel myself indebted for whatever power of judgement, critical experience, or speculative equity, if I may be allowed to use such a form of words, I am conscious of possessing. I wish to undervalue no other system of training, no other field of inquiry, but I speak of this as I love it, and as, if a sound purpose of doing with my might what my hand has found to do can be any pledge of honest and effectual work, I trust those who will apply themselves to it with my assistance will come to love it and profit by it as well. But as I shall have, no doubt, to say more than enough about myself before I finish this lecture, I will proceed now, in that desultory way which the nature of an inaugural lecture necessitates, to say something about my founder and my predecessors; and, having done that, to enlarge somewhat on the place which our study has among the pursuits of this University, the method of training, and the end which I propose to myself in the work that lies before me. I have pleaded guilty to a natural trepidation, I have acknowledged that what I have to say will be desultory. I think that the circumstances account for both, and trust to you for an equitable consideration.

The Professorship of Modern History was founded in the year 1724 by King George I; a prince of whom those who would say the worst must allow that he was an honest and harmless sovereign, whilst a professed panegyrist would most wisely content himself with saying that his reign is the commencement of an era during which the happiness of the kingdoms he ruled, their progress in knowledge, political intelligence, wealth, domestic and social comfort, have increased in a ratio unprecedented and unparalleled: during which the exertion of English influence in the councils and contests of the world has been effective beyond precedent and parallel, and has been used, if not always in the most enlightened way, always for the end and for the cause that seemed to be just and right. The process of events, and the action of various systems of politics, have in a great measure served to alter the views which at the time were taken of the wars of the last century and of the early years of the present. We have learned some of us to approve, and more perhaps to acquiesce in, proceedings which our fathers looked on as in the last degree unrighteous and intolerable. The days in which men go to war for an idea, and accept subjugation because they cannot afford to be sentimental, can safely smile at the errors of statesmen and the short-sightedness of kings, to whom justice and honesty were still justice and honesty, although disguised in the mock solemnities of dynastic shadows. But we will not deny either to kings or to peoples the credit of zeal for what they believed to be right, and the glory they had, so far as it was real, of counting no cost too great to be incurred for what they saw to be the cause of order and of society. They fought, as they believed, for their own existence and ours.

George I, whatever may have been his personal faults, and however little adapted he may have seemed in his own days, or may seem now, to fulfil the ideal character of kingship in a free and enlightened people, comes on the stage of English History as the representative of a principle which has been found to answer, and as the inaugurator of a period of national prosperity. So far, at least, we have no cause to blush for our founder. But as our founder, I think we may look at him more closely. The house of Brunswick has always had the reputation for the good sense to patronize literature, and especially historical literature. Not to seek for precedents so far back as Henry the Lion, who superintended the writing of the annals of his country in the twelfth century, it will perhaps suffice to give a general reference to the enormous number of historical books which, during the sixteenth, seventeenth, and eighteenth centuries, issued under ducal patronage from the presses of Helmstadt, Hanover, and Göttingen. George himself had been the patron of Leibnitz, of Jo. George Eccard, Burckhard Gotthilf Struve, and Johann Lorenz von Mosheim, whom I name rather as familiar to English ears than as standing alone in their peculiar studies. One of his first measures, when his accession to the crown of Great Britain had increased his influence in Europe, was to interest himself in behalf of Leibnitz and Muratori in their attempts to draw, from the archives of the jealous republic of Venice, materials for their gigantic undertakings in the same line. At Cambridge, again, he appears as purchasing and bestowing on the University the invaluable MS. Collections of Bishop More, which have helped to make the Public Library there one of the most useful and famous historical libraries in Europe. Whatever may have been the king's purpose in these several measures, we may safely, I think, affirm that it was not a mere political or official object which determined him when, in 1724, he wished to confer a mark of favour on Cambridge and to hold out an olive-branch to Oxford, to give to his sister foundations the same character of professorships of Modern History. Leibnitz was the most learned man he had ever seen, and perhaps Leibnitz's learning was most intelligible to George I in the shape of the

Annales rerum Brunsvicensium. Nor should I omit to mention what, in the opinion of their most adverse critics, ought to be a redeeming point in the later Hanoverian princes. George II refounded and reformed the Chair which I have the honour to fill; under George III began those long and at last successful investigations into the archives of the kingdom and the treasures of our great public libraries, which are now but beginning to bear a promise of abundant interest: under George IV, as king of Great Britain and Hanover, was begun the great series of Monuments of German History, the editor of which was once wont to call himself Historiographer of the Most Serene Guelfic house, and of which the king of Hanover was a patron to an extent double of that of Prussia, and nearly equal to the patronage of all the rest of the German Courts; a great work which has made Hanover its home, and for the possession of which our Library here is indebted to the munificence of king George V.

It is hardly, I think, necessary to look further than the king himself for the influence under which the foundation was first projected; the exact time and the declared purpose of the completion of the design may have been determined by others. It is possible that Walpole or Stanhope may have been the adviser; it is by no means improbable that bishop Robinson, who has been looked upon as the founder of the eighteenth-century school of English diplomacy, may have been consulted as to those details of the plan which were intended to afford to the students of the Universities the means of a diplomatic education. I am sorry to say that I have been unable to find any satisfactory evidence on the subject. I have indeed heard it positively affirmed that bishop Robinson drew up the scheme which took effect the year after his death; and I should have been glad to believe it was so, for bishop Robinson was a benefactor of the Church to which I owe my own education, and the College which has munificently contributed a large portion of the endowment of the professorship. But until more evidence is attainable, I cannot speak with confidence. The influence of either Stanhope or Robinson would account for the particular intention with which the foundation was completed; whilst that of Walpole, if it were used, would hardly have taken any other than a utilitarian direction. It is to the prominence with which this particular intention is put forward that, in conjunction, I think, with a general distaste to accept a benefaction from the duke of Brunswick, the ungracious reception which the new foundation met with at Oxford is to be ascribed. For the University not only acknowledged the receipt of the king's letter in a most contemptuous way, forwarding their letter of thanks by a bedell, but when, by due pressure and by the example of Cambridge, compelled to send a formal answer by a deputation to the king, clothed it in such words as showed that the introduction of the new study was looked on as an unwarranted interference with the educational government of the place; clearly it was no part of the intention of Oxford in 1724 to educate able servants for the house of Hanover.

For the study of History Oxford had hitherto been no unkindly school. The period of literary activity which had succeeded the Restoration had been greatly indebted to Oxford scholars. The names of Bishops Nicholson, Tanner, and Kennett, of Atterbury, Wake, and Gibson, although in these days they are chiefly known, if known at all, as antiquaries or controversialists, mark a period of historical exertion second to none either in the importance of its researches or in the value of their results. Cambridge began the modern study of English History with Parker, Oxford followed up briskly with Savile and Camden, Selden, Gale, Fulman, and Fell; men who, if they did not pretend to shine as Historians, are entitled to the eternal gratitude of all students, and appreciated at least that true and fundamental canon of composition that the materials for History must be provided before History can be written. From Oxford, or from the studies of Oxford men, proceeded nearly all the great collections of English Historians; and the old school of students was now well represented by Thomas Hearne. But at the time when this professorship was founded this class of men were either withdrawn, like Tanner and Kennett, to other work, or relegated by their own political sympathies and Whig liberality, like Hearne and Baker, to the comparative uselessness of literary retirement. Nor, I think, were the ministers of the crown very careful as to the hands in which they placed the engine of education, from which so much might have been hoped. To speak with the utmost respect of my early predecessors, I do not find that they were men to whom the study of History, either English or foreign, is in any way indebted, until we come down to Dr. Nares at the beginning of the present century. They probably owed their position to their political connexions or to literary eminence of other kinds. It is no wonder that under the circumstances the place of History among the studies of the University became worse rather than better, or, like that of Moral Philosophy, was lost altogether.

Passing on from Dr. Nares, of whom I speak with all gratitude, remembering well, as many of the elders amongst my hearers can doubtless remember likewise, the days when his weighty volumes were almost the only available sources of information for later history: we come to the great name, never to be pronounced without reverence even by his opponents, of the man whose sincerity, energy, and power of training, made him the prime mover of this generation. What Arnold might have done for the study of History in this place, had his time been given to it or been prolonged sufficiently to produce any appreciable effect on it, may be estimated by the effect of his work on other branches and in other places of education. I say it with diffidence, rather because I fear your criticism than because I have any doubt of the truth of the assertion, I believe that the one thing which Arnold wanted to perfect the balance of his admirable judgement, and to direct the current of his overflowing sympathies, was that experience of critical difficulties and moral incompatibilities which becomes practically, to the devoted student of History, a training in itself. Of Dr. Cramer I can say little. He was well furnished as a scholar and a most accomplished man : his contributions to literary history are exceedingly valuable : but his time here was short; he was not a young man when he undertook the office : he had other cares which took him away from Oxford. Most of all perhaps during the time of his holding this office all the thinking men of the University were engrossed in controversies on matters interesting, most interesting to all, in which, however much a historical training might have profited them, it was too late to forge their weapons when they were in the midst of battle. Of the two professors who preceded me, I must not, need not, say much : you are far better able than I am to appreciate their work here : but I may say that none of you can more sincerely than I do admire the learning, acuteness, earnestness, and eloquence of Professor Goldwin Smith : learning, acuteness, earnestness, and eloquence never more signally admirable than when employed, as we have so often rejoiced to see them employed, on the behalf of Christian Truth against philosophic sciolism.

The circumstances under which I return to Oxford and begin my work here are, for many reasons, most encouraging ; so encouraging as to afford, I think, some grounds of apprehension that the responsibility is heavier than I ought to have undertaken. In no respect does the Oxford I find

on my return contrast more favourably with the Oxford I
left sixteen years ago. At that time the professorship of
Church History had been founded, and was filled by one
[Robert Hussey] who was undoubtedly the founder of the
modern study of that subject in Oxford. I mean the study
of the history of the Church as a whole, not from points of
controversy to supply weapons for the discomfiture of opposing theologians, but as the life of the Christian Church itself,
the whole history of the body of which the modern nations
claim in their spiritual character to be members. But the
theological exigencies of the time had so far narrowed the
field of inquiry that it was practically restricted to the first
three centuries, or at the outside to the period embraced
under the topics of the general councils. The attempt which
he made to extend the range by introducing the study of the
Venerable Bede as a textbook was, as you are aware, foiled
by the impossibility of getting together a lecture on a matter
that was neither connected with the controversies of the day,
nor required to be known by candidates for holy orders.
The College libraries then as now afforded abundant resources for any student who would take up the subject for
himself, but my grateful recollection of the first acquaintance
made with Hearne, Dugdale, and Prynne, in Christ Church
Library, is inseparably connected with the reminiscence of
the amused, and I am glad to remember approving, surprise,
with which Dean Gaisford took me unawares at my note-
book. It is possible that the rooms of the Architectural
Society in Holywell were the school in which a taste for
mediaeval history, at least, was insensibly acquired.

The introduction of new studies into the course of
University training was viewed with apprehension by many :
some perhaps of us who are now here were inclined to waver
between a mistrust of innovations which seemed likely to
break down the traditionary character of our education and

the desire of welcoming a study of all others the most germane to the true and perpetual genius of Oxford. I may now, I suppose, say it without offence : I think that the distrust of the new studies, at all events of the study of Modern History, was owing quite as much to the management of their advocates as to the conservative habits of the opponents. I am not sure that either party would have admitted, or indeed would now admit, what, to adopt a proper professorial tone, I may say is certain, that whilst of all studies in the whole range of knowledge, the study of law affords the most conservative training, so the study of Modern History is, next to Theology itself, and only next in so far as Theology rests on a divine revelation, the most thoroughly religious training that the mind can receive. It is no paradox to say that Modern History, including Mediaeval History in the term, is co-extensive in its field of view, in its habits of criticism, in the persons of its most famous students, with Ecclesiastical History. We may call them sister studies, but, if they are not really one and the same, they are twin sisters, so much alike that there is no distinguishing between them. Men who are bent on seeing only differences and ignoring points of agreement refused to see that in 1850, and I dare say refuse to see it still.

So much, however, has changed and changed rapidly in sixteen years ; so many old friends have sought new fields of work, so great changes have passed over the moral and intellectual atmosphere of Oxford, that one is prone to forget that in truth the precedent era from 1830 to 1850 was itself only a transient phase, and not to be looked on as stamping for ever the character of the University. I for one can rejoice in looking back on those days, and I can look forward with hope and sympathy to what is before us in these respects. If I regret the absence of some things that were pleasant in the old life, at least I can appreciate much of

that which promises to be the charm of the new. Happily
removed for all these years from Oxford controversies, and
I am glad to say that in the humblest way I have not had a
finger in them, I can still clothe the old life with that glad-
ness which for most men gilds the recollection of undergraduate days. But the world did not stop with me when I
left Oxford, and I trust, if God shall spare me, to work with
a good heart as long as it is called to-day.

I rejoice then to find on my return the School of Law
and Modern History occupying a well-defined and still improving position, and bestowing honours which the men most
honoured in the other contests of the academic arena are
glad not only to win but to work for. The Modern History
School has thriven with very little nursing; and it needs but
a glance at the class lists to show that there has been and
continues to be, I will not say abundant promise, but actual
work done in the cause of historical study by those who have
distinguished themselves in our examinations. It is not
invidious to mention the names of some who have challenged
public criticism by their books, and have not merely shown
in them the usefulness of historical training, but conferred
lasting benefits on the students that follow them. The Law
and Modern History School helped at least to train my
excellent colleague, the Chichele Professor, for his labours;
and it has helped to give us from Mr. Kington an English
life of Frederick II, from Mr. Bryce a monograph on the
Western Empire, which have already taken their place as
standard books on our shelves. But far more than this has
been done by the direction into the same channel of a considerable part of the more industrious teaching power of the
Colleges, so that there is now a strong and, I hope, an
increasing, staff of College tutors, whose time and mind are
devoted primarily to the cultivation of this study. With
these my occasional visits here as examiner have put me into

communication, and the association with them in their work
is to my mind one of the happiest incidents of my present
position.   I would, indeed, that this thought had been without the drawback that, at the very moment of my return, I,
in common with the whole of the rest of the University,
should have to lament the loss of one [Dr. Shirley], noble,
good, and wise far beyond his years, who had watched and
worked for the development of this study from the day of its
introduction to Oxford, whose labours and influence were
ever used for good and for everything that was good, whose
early promotion and effective character had marked him out
as the man who was to do great things for the University
and the Church of God in this age.   Seldom has so much
promise, seldom have so great earnests of great work been
so sadly or so fatally blighted: we cannot look that his place
can ever in all respects be so filled that there will not still be
much, very much, to desiderate; for it is not Oxford alone
that laments him, nor the cause of Historical study only
with which he had identified himself both here and throughout the literary world.   But I will not touch on questions
beyond the scope of my present consideration.

Besides the very advantageous position which, without
nursing, I repeat, our study has attained here, in men, books,
and honours, the immense treasures of historical lore which
are now being poured liberally from the great storehouses of
record throughout Europe, but most especially in England,
form a feature of the present time that promises to renew
the youth of the Historic Muse.   The great Continental collections of Historians are growing slowly but substantially;
the German collection, begun in 1826, nearly rivals the
French one a century its senior; the Sardinian Government
had one of its own, which we may hope will not be
smothered for the sake of more ambitious plans; the Vatican
itself, under the kindly influence of a German Oratorian, has

begun to thaw from its old reserve. Last and greatest, our own national work under the direction of Lord Romilly has in eight years proved itself more than a worthy rival both in bulk and workmanship of the older repositories. And not to speak of the collection of Historians, of which from my own connexion with it I am obliged to speak with modesty and reserve, the extracts and abstracts of public and private documents found in our Record offices and in those of Spain and Venice are rapidly filling our libraries with cases of stout green volumes from which the history of the most eventful of our years is being rewritten, and which will soon involve the necessity of a new Macaulay as they have already brought into being a new Burnet and a new Robertson.

From this sudden breaking-up of the fountains of historical refreshment I dare not augur what results may follow, or what new worlds may be opening for other generations to exercise their logical acuteness and their historical per-spicacity upon. We have our work set, in a literary point of view, in arranging, and bringing into bearing on one another, the masses of information that are threatening to overwhelm us. Happily, there is no lack of helpers; the great German hive of historical workers is busy as we are on our archives; such and so close are the ties which now, owing to the facilities of travelling and communication, the abundance of libraries and the accessibility of records, the extension of literary and investigative sympathies, and, I am happy to think, the extinction of literary jealousies, are now binding the historical scholars of Europe, that I think and hope that the day is coming when, although we may not cease to quarrel with and criticize one another, there will be a great republic of workers able and willing to assist one another; not working for party purposes, unfettered by political preju-dices, and although as strong partizans and politicians as ever, anxious above all to find the truth, and to purify the cause that each loves best from every taint of falsehood, every inclination to calumny or concealment. I confess that it is towards this consummation that my dearest wishes as a student of History are directed; and that I anticipate with the greatest pleasure the prospect of being instrumental and able to assist in the founding of an historical school in England, which shall join with the other workers of Europe in a common task; which shall build, not upon Hallam and Palgrave and Kemble and Froude and Macaulay, but on the abundant collected and arranged materials on which those writers tried to build whilst they were scanty and scattered and in disorder. The time cannot be far off when all the records of the mediaeval world which are in existence will be in print either in full or in such abundant abstracts as will be thoroughly trustworthy representations of their contents; when every great Library will contain copies of them all, and when every town will contain a great Library. The seed sown by the old Record Commission, by presenting copies of their publications to the municipal corporations and principal provincial libraries, marks an era, as antiquaries well know, in the development of antiquarian study and the preservation of archaeological treasures. We may hope to see the same principle extended now, and although the chief labours of the historian must continue to find their place in his own study, as no library can supersede the need of books at home, still no man may be obliged to keep all his ideas in chronic effervescence and all his hopeful discoveries in a state of tantalizing suspension, in the hope that once a year he can visit the Bodleian or the British Museum. For that day of many students, many books, many libraries, and many readers, I look with confidence; in the meantime I do hope and trust that my work here, although this may not be its primary aim or its most successful use, may help in a humble way to educate workers for the good time coming.

For I desire to introduce myself to you, not as a philosopher nor as a politician, but as a worker at history. Not that I have not strong views on politics, nor short and concise opinions on philosophy, but because this is my work, and I have taken it up in all sincerity and desire of truth, and wish to keep to my work and to the sort of truth that I can help on in the inquiry; because you have plenty of politicians and plenty of scholars to whom, if they wish to have it, I certainly will not begrudge the name of philosophers. I suppose that it is truth we are all seeking, and that though the sorts of truth are distinct and the ways that we work in are very different, when we have found what we seek for we shall find all our discoveries combine in harmony; and I trust and believe that the more sincerely, the more single-heartedly we work each of us, the nearer we consciously come to the state where we shall see the oneness and glory and beauty of the truth itself. So that the theologian, the naturalist, the historian, the philosopher, if he work honestly, is gaining each for his brother, and being worked for each by his brother, in the pursuit of the great end, the great consummation of all. We may all speak humbly, the theologian because of the excellence of his subject, the rest because of the vastness of our field of work, the length of our art and the shortness of our life; but we cannot afford to speak contemptuously of any sort of knowledge, and God forbid that we should speak contemptuously or hypercritically of any honest worker.

The subject-matter of Modern Historical inquiry has peculiar advantages for the training of the powers most constantly in exercise in a practical generation. Compared with the study of Ancient History it is like the study of life compared with that of death, the view of the living body compared with that of the skeleton. The student of Ancient History has his advantages; he can speculate on his skeleton, he can penetrate more deeply into the framework of ancient society, so far as his materials allow him ; he can handle the different parts and form his political hypotheses as it pleases him, according to the various ways in which his skeleton can be put together ; he is little troubled by the fear of new facts, or new developments making their appearance suddenly to put to flight his calculations ; he has all the existing materials for his investigation before him, or within easy reach; he has for the geographical area of his work a portion of the earth and its peoples that has had, since the roll of its own historians was closed, little to do with the active work of the world. He can work out principles at his will; he can educate his taste and analyse and experiment to the very ne plus ultra of critical subtilty. But the principles he works out, and the results of his criticism, are alike things that give the world no new knowledge, or exercise no direct influence on the interests of real life. And in this is one of the great incidental uses of classical training as an engine of education. You have in its languages and histories and philosophies, the most elegant, the most compact, the most ingenious systems on which the mind of man can be exercised ; and you have them in such isolation, so set apart altogether from personal or party or national or scholastic propensions, that the lessons to be drawn from them are for the most part as safe, as un-exciting, as far removed from the heart and interests of life, as any proposition in mathematics.

In Modern History, on the contrary, you are dealing with the living subject : your field of examination is the living, working, thinking, growing world of to-day; as distinguished from the dead world of Greece and Rome, by the life that is in it, as it is in geographical area and in the embarrassing abundance of the data from which only in their full integrity it is safe, or ever will be safe, to attempt to philosophize. England, France, Germany, the East, regions that have but a shadowy existence in the background of the

pictures in which living Egypt, Rome, and Asia stand before
us, after thousands of years of death, in the bright colouring
and life-like grouping of yesterday; these are the area in
which the modern historian seeks and finds the interests of his
pursuit. Italy, the common ground of the sister studies, the
strange borderland between light and darkness, in which
alone the past seems to live and the present for the most
part to be a living death, has a double existence that fits and
unfits her for the free handling of either.

And in this new and modern and living world there has
been since the era began, such a continuity of life and
development that hardly one point in its earliest life can
be touched without awakening some chord in the present.
Scarcely a single movement now visible in the current of
modern affairs but can be traced back with some distinctness
to its origin in the early Middle Ages; scarcely a movement
that has disturbed the world since the invasion of our barbarian ancestors but has its representative in the chart of law
or thought or territory to this day. Not a dynasty that is
trembling out its little span of days now but represents in its
shattered tottering throne some great hero, some great heroic
movement, that has won the gratitude of the mediaeval world.
Not a country revolutionized and levelled until it hardly knew
itself, until it scarcely remembered the names of its rivers and
mountains, has been able utterly to obliterate the boundaries,
or the customs, or the affinities of its old divisions. The
dynastic traditions of Europe are rooted and grounded in
the distant past : the principle of nationalities, new in its
fashion of announcement and most unlucky in its prophet,
is rooted and grounded in a past more distant still ; the
principle of freedom, in their effect on which only the
dynastic and national ideas have their true political value,
rests on a yet more ancient foundation, but on one that
is peculiar to the modern field of study, for it was brought

c

into the world and proclaimed and made possible by the Church.

It is Christianity that gives to the modern world its living unity and at the same time cuts it off from the death of the past. The Church in its spiritual work, the Church in its intellectual work, the Church in its work with the sword, or with the plough, or with the axe; the soul and spirit of all true civilization, of all true liberty, of all true knowledge; the Church in its work of evil, in the abasement of its divine energies, in the vile fetters of priestcraft, in the blind paroxysms of popular fanaticism, in the strange varying fortune that allies Ireland with Rome, Scotland with Geneva, setting father against son, and husband against wife, the herald of peace with a sword; such an influence so wide in its extension, so deep in its penetration, so ancient in the past, and in the future eternal, could by itself account for the unity, the life of modern history: the life, the soul of a body which thrills at every touch. The student cannot handle his subject-matter as he can a skeleton; if he is a true student he knows himself to be at work among living influences, some active, some slumbering, but all of which are so vital and so entangled that he cannot move without making some one feel, or without being himself affected in his process and in his judgement by the system of which he is himself a part. Modern History is the history of ourselves, of the way in which we came to be what we are, of the education of our nation, of the development of our government, of the fortunes of our fathers; that caused us to be taught and governed and placed as we are, and formed our minds and habits by that teaching, government, and position; and as for the soul, that other portion of us—unchanged by education, government or fortune, unchanged and untrained in the development and education of the world, unchanged except by the Spirit of God beginning at the beginning in every

one that is new-born of Him—that gift in which almost
alone we trace the unity of our nature with that of the
ancient world, in its waywardness, and short-sightedness, and
self-will, what can all history tell us other or more than this,
how God sent light into the world and men loved darkness
rather than light, how they have perverted, but not closed
the way of eternal life ?

But if the student of Modern History finding himself at
work among such subjects misses the facility with which
Ancient History may be handled, he has the advantage to
begin with, that the interest of his own department is un-
flagging and inexhaustible : every day adds a new development of the old elements; he feels that he is living in his
subject, it is living all around him. And this being so, he is
conscious that he is working with a different set of mental
powers from those which he works with on the old world; I
speak under correction, for I do not pretend to look at the
subject as a question of psychology, simply for the moment
as one of education. It is in a manner analogous to a
training for association with men in the world ; the student
must look for Truth, and work for Justice, but he must work
for such truth and justice as is attainable. He must not, as
in Ancient History, amuse himself with principles however
valuable or however generally applicable, because he has to
deal with rights : his inquiry is more into laws than into
principles, more into facts than into laws. He must act as
a judge, not as a philosopher ; all the better judge for being
somewhat of a philosopher, but never in the philosopher
forgetting that he is a judge. And as in practical matters
we, ordinary men that is, are seldom called upon to act as
judges except in questions where our own sympathies or
interests are concerned, the faculty to be trained is the
judgement, the practical judgement at work among matters in
which its possessor is deeply interested, not from the desire

of Truth only, but from his own involution in the matters of which he is to judge.

I think that there are few lessons more necessary for men to learn, not merely who are going to take to public life, but who are going to live and move as men among their fellows, than these :—that there are few questions on which as much may not be said on one side as on the other : that there are none at all on which all the good are on one side, all the bad on the other, or all the wise on one and all the fools on the other ; that the amount of dead weight in human affairs, call it stupidity or what you will, is pretty equally divided between the advocates of order and the advocates of change, giving to the one party much of its stability and to the other much of its momentum : that intolerance is no prerogative of heterodoxy, nor tolerance the inseparable accompaniment of the conscious possession of truth, a condition which might of all others the best afford to be tolerant, the most merciful and pitiful of error : that all generalizations, however sound in logic, are in morals and practical matters ipso facto false ; that there is no room for sweeping denunciations, or trenchant criticisms in the dealings of a world whose falsehoods and veracities are separated by so very thin a barrier : to learn that simple assertion however reiterated can never make proof : that a multitude of half-believers can never make faith : that argument never convinces any man against his will : that silence is not acquiescence : that the course of this world is anything but even and uniform : that such by-words as reaction and progress are but the political slang which each side uses to express their aversions and their propensions ; above all, that no material success, no energy of development, no eventual progress or consolidation, can atone for the mischief done by one act of falsehood, treachery or cruelty. Most of these lessons are truisms. Yes, but there are no truisms in facts : there are no truths which may not be stated as truisms, but there are no truths which a sound judgement can be warranted in despising.

When the student comes to apply these lessons to the judgement of the characters and events of the history that he is studying, and to carry his experience of the past into the present, he finds, if his study has taught him facts as well as maxims, that the great necessity of practical judgement is patience and tolerance, and that the highest justice must rest content for a time to see many things continue wrong that cannot be righted without a greater wrong.

The stock of information from which the student draws these practical lessons is itself the matter on which in the further stages of present history he is called upon to exercise them. He has a part to play in the politics of his own age: he must have made himself acquainted with the national identity of nations, the rights and claims, the sins and punishments and probations of dynasties; the origins and accretions of parties; the growth of the influences to which their owners give the name of principles. The stock of information accumulated is only secondary in importance to the habits of judgement formed by the study of it. For we want to train not merely students but citizens; and citizens of the great communities—the church and the civilized world; to be fitted not for criticism or for authority in matters of memory, but for action. And so it is not views of men and states that are to be taught them, but the power of judging that is to be cultivated, and the information on which that power is to be exercised that is to be imparted, and the faculty of accumulation to be directed to good and pure sources. It is not to make proselytes to one system of politics or another that the work of education is to be directed; a university is no political club or propaganda; I desire to use my office as a teacher of facts and of the right habit of using them.

And to do this we must begin at the right end, work from the past forwards, not backwards from the present.   Our students ought not to go into the world a prey to newspaper correspondents : they ought not to go into public life ready to be moulded to the political views of the first clique that may catch hold of them.   So far as the fundamental principles of politics go, that is indeed impossible, for men are born most certainly with constitutional inclinations, some to order and others to change; and the power of the earliest education is exerted to direct those inclinations into channels most in accordance with the views of the educators : so by attraction or repulsion, by reaction or by hereditary succession, not by the lessons of books or views of philosophers, young men's sides are taken in life before they know it.   But there is still far more in common between the wise and sound of opposing parties than there is between the sound and the corrupt of the same ; between the thinkers of opposite parties and the thinkers and the fools of the same.   We should teach both sides to teach themselves.

Am I to be understood as stating the purpose of the study of History to be the production of scepticism in politics ? Surely not.   Rather I maintain that there is so much of good in both the opposing views that good men are pretty equally divided between the two ; and that there is so much, I will not say evil, but questionable and debateable, that thoughtless and interested men make their capital of, that thoughtless and interested men are equally divided too ; and so much that is obvious to the meanest sense, that stupidity and intolerance are in much the same proportion.   What we want to see is men applying to history and politics the same spirit in which wise men act in their discipline of themselves : not to cease to be partisans, not to cease to hold and utter strong opinions, but to be as careful in their party behaviour and in their support of their opinions, as they are in their behaviour in social circles, their conversation in social life. The first object of the true politician, as of the true patriot, is to keep himself and his party true, and then to look for success : to keep himself and his party pure, and then to secure victory : to abolish meanness and corruption where he has influence, rather than to make capital by denouncing it where his denunciation can only provoke a retort. The sound politician, on whichever side he may be and however thorough he may be, believes that his scheme of politics is the one in which the benefit of his country is most entirely involved, and he wishes the position of his country to be impregnable; to be impregnable it must be sound : if his party represents to him his country, his party must be sound, and it concerns him much more closely to purify his own ranks than those of his enemy. Success is certain to the pure and true : success to falsehood and corruption, tyranny and aggression, is only the prelude to a greater and an irremediable fall.

If our students go from us with the certainty of this lesson impressed on them, with information to guide and cultivated power enough to form judgement, we, whatever our private convictions may be, may rest assured both that our own duty has been done, and that the best has been done for the world in which they are to act. Politicians, happily, seldom live to see the final outcome of their aspirations; life is too short to witness a constitutional struggle in all its growth, and, as matters approach the compromise, the minds of the actors modify, or new, more moderate, counsellors see in the process of circumstances grounds for receding somewhat from the rigorous line drawn by the less practical design of their elders. So the world moves on in a line straighter than the rules of either party would have made it; and it is well that it is so, the education of a political life is long, and the time for active work in it, for the most part, extremely short.

A good deal of enthusiasm is worn out before the action begins, or else the difference between the result and the design would be intolerable to a sincere believer in his own system.

We must, I repeat, if we are to qualify ourselves for forming a sound judgement on these matters, begin at the beginning. We must not work back from popular prejudices, or from philosophic ideas, or from the prominent subject of to-day. The history of Poland cannot be truly viewed by one who starts from the Partition; the history of Turkey cannot be truly read from the standing-point of the balance of power; that of Germany does not begin, as politicians nowadays join in insisting, from the treaties of Vienna. There are rights that are not turned into wrongs, and wrongs that cannot be turned into rights, by any treaties. There are hopes that cannot, ought not to, be dashed into despair by any pacifications. There are sentiments, if you please to call them so, which depend on long ages of deeply implanted sympathies, of long experience of common suffering and common success, on a firm basis of right and popular love, that may be dismissed by an aggressive politician as emptiness and vanity, but which are the only true basis of free government, the only safe support of thrones, the only true tie of nationalities.

With these things and the deep wide range of facts from which they spring, the student of history must make himself acquainted, and being acquainted he learns to sympathize. Unlike the genealogist and the local antiquary, he does not work back from the particular sympathy to the old foundation, but begins with the beginning and works up to the situation, the sentiment, the sympathy, or the antipathy of the day. Need I adduce the parallel from the sacred sister study? Who ever became a theologian by working back from the doctrinal or ritual questions of yesterday? Nay, who is qualified to give an opinion above that of a newspaper letter-writer on such subjects, who has not begun from the Upper Chamber at Jerusalem and worked his way from the coming of the Day Star, through the gloom and twilight of the ages, towards the bright shining, such shining as it is, of these days, before he ventures to apply the *spectrum analysis* to the doctrinal light of the nineteenth century?

There is a contrary error; the true student has learned that the past is no more a whole without the present than the present without the past; that the past has no claim to infallibility any more than the present, that the past has had no power, no moral right to dispose of the present by a deed in mortmain. To be a slave of old traditions is as great a folly as to be a slave of new quackeries; but the fault is in the slavish use, not in the old traditions nor in the modern nostrums; and the former error is perhaps the less pardonable as it is a sin against greater light.

I am aware that there are great difficulties; if there were not, History would be no matter of study, politics would be no ground of controversy. There is the great question, where does fact end and opinion begin? there is the great question, at what point in the study of modern and mediaeval history does the sympathy of his own day force itself into the judgement of the student? There is the question, can any length of acquiescence turn a wrong thing into a right one; any length of prescription turn an abuse into a right? How far are men bound by the acts of their fathers, or by their own acts when deceived or ill-informed? Then there is the further question, how far is the moralist—righteous, free, unprejudiced as he may be—qualified to answer these questions off-hand? Each application of each question has its own modifying circumstances. I can only say that the man who knows the facts and has formed the habit of judging on them, is better able and more likely to answer them rightly than the man who has not. Some people will call him dogmatic, but he who has read and thought ought to be able to have an opinion, and he who has one of his own will always be deemed dogmatic by the many who take theirs from the newspapers. He is dogmatic if he ventures to express a doubt where the infallible of the time being has laid down a certainty.

To turn for a moment to the general question. I should not like to be thought to be advocating my study on the mere grounds of utility; although I believe that utility, both as regards the training of the study and the information attained in it, to be the highest, humanly speaking, of all utilities; it helps to qualify a man to act in his character of a politician as a Christian man should. But this is not all; beyond the educational purpose, beyond the political purpose, beyond the philosophical use of history and its training, it has something of the preciousness of everything that is clearly true. In common with Natural Philosophy it has its value, I will not say as Science, for that would be to use a term which has now become equivocal, but it has a value analogous to the value of science ; a value as something that is worth knowing and retaining in the knowledge for its own and for the truth's sake. And in this consists its especial attraction for its own votaries. It is not the pleasure of knowing something that the world does not know—that doubtless is a motive that weighs with many minds, a motive to be accepted as a fact, though it may not be worth analysis. It is not the mere pleasure of investigating and finding with every step of investigation new points of view open out, and new fields of labour, new characters of interest ;—that investigating instinct of human nature is not one to be ignored, and the exercise of it on such inexhaustible materials as are before us now is a most healthy exercise, one that cannot but strengthen and develop the whole mind of the man who uses it, urging him on to new studies, new languages, new discoveries in geography and science. But even this is not all. There is, I speak humbly, in common with Natural Science, in the study of living History, a gradual approximation to a consciousness that we are grow- ing into a perception of the workings of the Almighty Ruler of the world; that we are growing able to justify the Eternal Wisdom, and by that justification to approve ourselves His children; that we are coming to see, not only in His ruling of His Church in her spiritual character, but in His over- ruling of the world to which His act of redemption has given a new and all-interesting character to His own people, a hand of justice and mercy, a hand of progress and order, a kind and wise disposition ever leading the world on to the better, but never forcing, and out of the evil of man's work- ing bringing continually that which is good. I do not fear to put it before you in this shape; I state my own belief, and it is well that you should know it from the first.

The study of History is in this respect, as Coleridge said of Poetry, its own great reward, a thing to be loved and cultivated for its own sake. If there are few who do really love and care for history, and I remember with sorrow that such was the remark of Dr. Shirley the last time that I had any lengthened conversation with him, is it not the result of a neglect of the principles which I have tried to express to you as the ideal of the study to my mind? It has not been well used of late years; it has been taught as a task to children; it has been valued only as an instrument to strengthen the memory; it has been undervalued in its true character of mental training; it has been learned to qualify men to make effective speeches to ignorant hearers, and to indite brilliant articles for people who only read periodicals; it has been begun from the standing-point of popular infatuation; it has been begun from the advanced ground of ecclesiastical or political partisanship; it has been made an embellishment for wordy eloquence, a source of subjects for pictorial talent that has evolved grouping, features and circumstances, from its own consciousness; it has been written as a poem, but without the inspiration of poetry, as philosophy without the thoughtfulness or humility of the true philosophic spirit; it has been written for readers already known, counted and pandered to. What wonder that there are few who love it for its own sake, when there are so few who know it as it is!

In this respect, as I have said, I hope and trust that the better time is coming, when the universality of the training and the outpouring of the sources of knowledge will make imposture futile, and adulteration unprofitable. I hope and trust that in that good time our training here will be found to be a part of the true higher training, and the knowledge acquired in it to lead up to the true and highest Knowledge.

II

ON THE PRESENT STATE AND PROSPECTS OF
HISTORICAL STUDY

(May 17, 1876.)

Some things may be said but not printed, some may be printed
and not published; many that are published are not, and need not
be, read. Many more would be better left unsaid. The following
pages contain a good deal that falls within each of these descriptions.
They were written with a full determination that they should not
be printed. Circumstances which need not be detailed have led me
to alter this resolution. Still there is much in them that would
have been said otherwise or omitted if they had been meant for
publication. Some things too are omitted that ought to have been
said. It is obvious that no attempt has been made at completeness
or exhaustiveness of detail. By what I have said or left unsaid, I
trust that I have wounded no one. Certainly all was meant in gratitude
and kindness.

A FEW days ago, in turning over the contents of my old
lecture drawer, I came upon two newspaper cuttings,
which a vanity, pardonable I hope after the lapse of ten
years, had conserved in company with even more perishable
matter. The slips contained the reviews, of the *Pall Mall
Gazette* and the *Saturday Review*, of my inaugural lecture as
Regius Professor of Modern History. The latter of the two
critiques was in itself worth preserving, for it was an early
effort of a dear friend [1] who has since made himself a great
name in the region of historical study. It was an article full
of blessing and good omen, with a sufficient amount of dog-
matism to prove that the writer believed himself entitled to
criticize ; and it contained, with all its precious balm, enough
of the element of blister to produce a wholesome irritation:

[1] J. R. Green.

for the one or two points in the lecture on which I had bestowed especial pains were described as praiseworthy but illusory. The *Pall Mall* review, the authorship of which I never learned, was a kindly article also, giving a fair *résumé* of what I had said, and ending with the remark that, although it was clear from the tone of my lecture that I should take a somewhat clerical view of history, still that was not to be deplored, as in the interests of truth it was desirable that the clerical view should have its own exponent.

The incident suggested to me that I should once more look at the inaugural lecture, and see for myself how the hopes and anticipations of 1866 looked in 1876. I found myself reading over the record of feelings and impressions of ten years ago with as much freshness as if they had been another man's ; and the happy thought struck me of turning my reflexions to account in the form of public lectures. It would relieve me of the puzzling anxiety over which six weeks of spring are wasted every year—what shall I take as the subject of the two solemn statutable lectures imposed upon the unhappy professor, who, without this annual mortification, might be in danger of thinking more highly of himself than he ought to think? It might also seem that, after ten years' occupation of this chair, I might have occasion to review the progress of the study in which I have had so great an interest; and it might also perhaps help me to gauge the amount of interest which the study itself is receiving in Oxford; for a notice that I have something to say about myself, and about those whom I might fairly expect to be present to hear me, would perhaps attract a larger audience than a much more elaborate vindication of St. Dunstan, or an inquiry into the merits of the customs duties as a part of the budget of King Edward I. It is true, I thought, I shall have to say some things about myself; I shall have to blush for my confessions of failure and for my assertions of success; I may, if I am fortunate in my company, have to make some of them blush too. But what is that among friends? and here I know none but friends. There may be some who have a vested interest in stupidity and false criticism, but I am thankful to say that I do not know even their names; and all who take a real and genuine interest in my studies, whether I know them or not, I am proud to look upon as friends with whom I need practise no reticence or concealment. So with your good leave I will dismiss myself first.

The thought that ten of the best years of a man's life have been given to work like this is a very serious one. What have I done? How have I done it? How far have I fulfilled my own hopes? How far have I realized the good wishes of my friends? How have I justified the good opinion of those who placed me where I am? Perhaps it would be more modest if I left it to others to judge and to pass judgement. But I would rather try to report what I have tried to do, and how I have tried to do it, than leave it unsaid. No man is so fit to review a book as the author himself, because he both knows what he meant to say and will be the first to hear and feel what his kind friends the critics would make the world believe that he has said. In the first place, let me say that I have tried to fulfil the promise which I made in my inaugural lecture—'I desire to introduce myself to you not as a philosopher, not as a politician, but as a worker at history.' That I have worked at history is, I think, proved by the bulk of the results: for during the ten years I have completed ten volumes, and nearly an eleventh volume, of the English Historians published by the Master of the Rolls; I have edited the whole of the third volume and assisted in the first and second volumes of the Councils of the English Church; I have published the volume of Select Charters, which has now passed into a third edition, and two volumes of the Constitutional History of England, besides other work edited or passed through the press for practical aid in historical study. I am aware that it is not the bulk, but the character of the work, by which it must ultimately be tried; I can only say that I hope my work has not been unworthy of Oxford, or of England. Judging from the reception accorded to it, I think I should say that it has met with more appreciative and intelligent reception in Germany than in England; and I may add that I believe that I owe to this the honour, and a very great honour I esteem it, of an invitation to take part as a fellow editor in the great series of German Historical Monuments, known for the last fifty years under the name of Pertz, which has now passed into the hands of a commission of which Dr. Waitz is the chief. I am proud indeed to be an instrument, in the humblest way, in repaying the debt which English history owes to German scholarship.

Further than this I shall not speak of my books, except to point out how, by giving a clerical complexion to my work, I have fulfilled the auguries of the kindly critic in the *Pall Mall*. A kindly critic in the New York *Nation*, reviewing the first volume of the Constitutional History, has described the writer as entirely free from political bias, and adds that, 'what is more surprising, he appears to be scarcely influenced by ecclesiastical sentiment or prejudice.' Well, I thought, when I read that notice, here is at last a man who takes a right view of the clerical character. Here am I, steeped, as I fondly believe, in clerical and conservative principles, and yet able to take such a view of matters as scarcely to betray ecclesiastical prejudice or political bias. Seriously speaking, that is just what I wish. I understand the clerical spirit and mind to be that which regards truth and justice above all things, which believes what it believes firmly and intelligently, but with a belief that is fully convinced that truth and justice must in the end confirm the doctrine that it upholds; with a belief that party statements, and highly coloured pictures of friend and foe, are dangerous enemies of truth and justice, and damage in the long run the cause that employs them; that all sides have everything to gain and nothing to lose by full and fair knowledge of the truth. And a clerical view of professional responsibility I take to be the knowledge that I am working in God's sight and for His purposes. If such be a right view, I rejoice to have evidence of my success in realizing it. If it be a mistaken one, well, I will claim credit for good intentions as well as steady work.

I wish that my conscience were equally clear as to the other branch of professorial usefulness—oral teaching or lecturing. On this topic I proposed in my inaugural lecture to set before myself two leading principles : the first was to begin at the beginning—' We must begin at the right end, work from the past forwards, not backwards from the present.' I meant, of course, not merely that I did not intend to read history backwards, which would be a difficult process in lecture, but that I should start from the beginning of the modern period and treat the course of historical progress generally and in natural order, rather than, by choosing topics which owed their importance to the interests of the day, work in the reverse order. I intended, in fact, to trace the gradual development of the modern world rather than to trace back particular points of development to their original germs. I have on the whole followed out that idea, although from time to time I have varied it with a course of analytical lectures. The result has been that, during these ten years I have never got beyond the year 1648. I have gone over the whole of the political history of Europe generally, and over that of England and Germany, with great minuteness, throughout the greater part of that long series of years; but beyond the Thirty Years' War I have not gone. I may add that there were two reasons for this; one, because I found the later history already in very good hands, a favourite subject with my colleague the Chichele Professor, and very well represented by the College Lecturers on History; the other, that my own separate line of study and work lay in the earlier portion mainly, and it would have been somewhat distracting to be treating widely distant periods of history at the same time. A third reason, I am free to confess, was that I had some misgivings as to the usefulness of the later period as a topic of historical education, until the foundation of the earlier knowledge had been well and strongly laid. I have often questioned whether it were indeed desireable to exercise the minds of young men, old enough to have strong political feelings, not old enough to exert a calm historical judgement, on periods of history teeming with the very same influences as those which are at work at this moment; at least before they had had an adequate training in the earlier history and were able to account for the origin and trace the earlier workings of those influences, so as to be able at least to accord an equitable sufferance to those who take a view contrary to their own. My apprehensions have not been shared by other teachers here, and it is well that no misgivings of mine should have acted so as to leave the treatment of modern history in this respect inadequate. I do not decide the matter, but simply state my own reason for holding back.

And this leads me to recur to the other principle upon which I proposed to act, and which struck the imagination of my reviewer as illusory or useless. My idea was and is, that, as mankind is roughly divided between the advocates of order and the advocates of change, and as both classes contain about an equal number of good, bad, and indifferent, of the wise, of the sensible and of the stupid, it was a function of the historical teacher, not to try to make them all think alike or to set himself up as a judge, saying to the one side you are all wrong, or to the other you are all right, but to present to both the facts and courses of events, which are the stores out of which both sides must draw their weapons, in such a fair and just view that they might be safely used by either. Simply, it was not my work to make men Whigs or Tories, but to do my best, having Whigs and Tories by nature as the matter I was to work upon, to make the Whigs good, wise, sensible Whigs, and the Tories good, wise, sensible Tories; to teach them to choose their weapons and to use them fairly and honestly. Well, I still adhere to that view, and every year what I see in public life around me confirms my belief in the truth and value of the principle. How far I have been successful in acting upon it I cannot of course say; but I feel sure that the growth of sound historical teaching would have spared us such national humiliation as we have undergone, during the last few years, in the treatment of the Public Worship Act, the Judicature Act, and the Royal Titles Act. I am quite sure that both the speakers and writers on those subjects would have been very much wiser and more modest men, if they had, I will not say attended my lectures, but passed a stiff examination in the History School: if we could not have made them wiser, we would at all events have made them sadder.

Well, are these statements of principle made merely to cover the sad fact that I have not been a successful lecturer? that I have to join in the professorial chorus of complaint that the professorial and tutorial systems have not yet dovetailed into one another with all the completeness that could be wished? Perhaps it is so. I have sometimes felt a little hurt that, after preparing and advertising a good course of lectures—and I feel no modesty in speaking thus, because I believe that good and thoughtful work will make good lectures—I have had to deliver them to two or three listless men; sometimes I have felt hurt that, in the combined lecture list, when it appeared, I found the junior assistant tutor advertising a course on the same subject, or at the very same hours as my own. But I will allow gratefully that such occasions have been few; I am pleased to remember that my classes, although they have never been very large, have as a rule been very faithful; that the combination system has brought me far more men than, on the most sanguine computation, it could have taken from me; and that I believe the real cause why professorial lectures are less useful than they should be, is the perhaps unfortunate fact that nearly all study in Oxford is directed towards the securing of honours in the Class Lists. Tutors, lecturers, and pupils are all working for the Schools; even the professorial statutes are drawn with a view to usefulness mainly in that direction; nor could any professor, however eminent, expect to get a considerable class to attend eighteen or even twelve lectures a term on any subject that would not pay—if I may use the current language on so solemn an occasion. The result is that, so far as lectures go, the professor has to take his chance of a class among the general run of college lecturers, without that power of commanding attendance which the college lecturers have. It is scarcely surprising that the weaker goes to the wall, and that the professor has to yield his place to younger men who perhaps may themselves owe some portion of their success to what they have learned from him. In saying this, I am not speaking of myself, for it would not be exactly true of me, but on the general question. For myself I am quite ready to accept the consolation and to declare that it is really much better, both for the growth of historical study, and for the development of the educational instrument, that there should be a dozen or fifteen college lecturers working away with large classes when I have only a few stray men, than that I should be lecturing to large assemblies of men who came to me simply because they had nowhere else to go. And I am quite willing that my character as a professor should stand or fall by my other work.

And now let me cease to speak of myself. It will be best perhaps that I should arrange what I have to say in circles; and, taking Oxford first, proceed to remark next on the position of historical study in England generally, and then outside England in Europe and America. Oxford first. There can, I think, be no doubt that the growth of the study of History at Oxford during the last ten years has been continuous and very rapid. I have no hesitation in saying this, because no one will think that I claim any credit for myself in it. The foundation work was done before I became professor, and the principal teachers who helped in the laying of that foundation, are working vigorously now at the superstructure. We have had great losses, I grieve to say, and great gains. I think I will not mention names: your memories will advert at once to the losses; the gains are here to speak for themselves. It is no small ground of congratulation to be able to say that, whilst our losses have not weakened us, our gains have very greatly strengthened us; our position is strong enough not to be shaken by the loss; our study is still in such a growing state as to be able to incorporate and amalgamate or assimilate all new helps. And that result speaks well for us in several ways. In the first place, our corporate strength is much greater. The History teaching in the colleges is not left to the accidental supply of teachers who have an aptitude for the subject in common with all the other subjects of the University course, but every college has its own recognized History Tutor or Lecturer; and these, or most of them, are acting together. Whether in the Board of Studies or in the meetings of combined lecturers, they are able to exert on the

study itself a concentrated influence which tells very effectively on the students who are reading for the Schools. The
objection that might suggest itself to those who do not know
Oxford, that such a corporate union may tend to cramp the
freedom of study and, in preventing desultory or straggling
reading, may discourage independent research, will not hold
here, so long at least as the system of examinations remains
what it is. There is no risk of the History Lecturers ever
forming a clique, or close school of History, as a single
glance at the list of them is sufficient to prove. But in the
second place, the multiplication and association of lecturers
enables us to offer a systematic and continuous reading of
History to the student. Each lecturer will, as time advances,
find out his own strongest period, or his friends will find it
for him; and then the student, who chooses to give his time
to the work, will be able to obtain a thorough guidance
through the several stages of his subject; and the historical
training will be both continuous and complete. And, in the
third place, the opportunity of reading continuously, under a
series of able teachers of different tones of mind and different
schools of thought, will most certainly be a great advantage
to the student who wishes to take History as a real part of
his mental training. I hope and trust that this will always
be the case; and that, although we may be earnest and glad
to work together, we may never be in danger of thinking all
alike, on those topics at least upon which constitutional
opinion and controversial criticism must be content to permit
difference of view. In this aspect the training for the School
of History may become a beneficial training for public life;
and although that is not the sole or the primary object in my
eyes of the study of History here, it is a most important one;
we must try to furnish men who will not be merely good
historians, but good citizens, or, as I said before, good
Whigs and good Tories. And there is another point in

which great advantage may be hoped from the increase and combination of teachers, which I can only just indicate now—I mean the connexion which is to be looked forward to between the University course and the teaching of our great schools and local institutions of education.

Next to the strengthening of the historical staff, the separation of the School of Jurisprudence from the School of History is the most important point of our Oxford history. And this change, although it was anxiously desired by many teachers of both subjects, was not adopted without some serious apprehensions. Whether the joint School, so young as it was, was sufficiently strong to bear the shock of division; whether the supply of teachers would be sufficient; whether each subject by itself was substantive enough to furnish the training for a class examination of high character; whether the separation would not produce a tendency to eliminate History from the Law teaching and Law from the History teaching, were questions which might well cause misgiving. Some of them have been solved in the process of experiment. Both Schools have increased their numbers and raised their standard since the division; as to the supply of teachers, what I have just said as to the increase and co-operation of the History teachers is a sufficient answer for them; the Law professors can, I believe, give a like answer. As to the third point, the substantive value of historical training, opinions will still differ; I for my part have no desire that, as an educational instrument, the History training should take the place of the classical and mathematical training, which must always form the chief part of the school education, and the strongest and favourite work of the University career. But, as a further stage of training, I maintain that the reading of History may claim an equal place with all the other studies pursued here: I believe that a man who has taken a good Class in Moderations would, so far as

mental training is concerned, do wisely in taking up a fresh
subject, especially Modern History. As a piece of professional training for the work of a schoolmaster or a clergyman,
it may not be so, at all events during the present state of
school education; I only allege it as a means of mental
culture. There is, however, a fourth question, which time will
have to answer, and for which time must supply a remedy,
if the mischief comes. It will be a fatal thing for the study
of History here, if the study of Law should ever be quite
eliminated from the History course; and as fatal for the
study of Law if it should ever come to be read on its merely
scientific or on its merely empiric sides. With our present
Law teachers both of these are alike impossible. The lectures
of Sir Henry Maine, Dr. Bryce, and Mr. Holland are to
a great extent historical lectures, and are as great an advantage to the History students as they are to the Law
students. I hope that in a humble sort of way some work
of the other School is found useful to the lawyers. But this
may not always be so. I think that it is a point that will
need watching. The great fault of the old combined School
was that there was no unity about the prescribed reading.
Much of the Law, that was superadded to the History, had
no more real connexion with it than a similar bulk of ento-
mological reading might have had; and the really important historical side of Law was not brought in. I am not
sure that, even now, both Schools would not be benefited by
a more distinct method ; and, whilst I should be glad to have a
section of legal history more definitely and generally made
a part of the History examination, I should very greatly
regret to see the Law Board proceeding further than they
have done in shutting out History from their scheme. But
this is going beyond my last. It seems to me, however, in
connexion with my own study, that the growth of jurisprudence, the history of foreign codes, ancient and modern,

and the connexion between legal and constitutional growth, are, as well as international law, a common ground between the two studies; and I am not inclined to surrender the rights of my School in them any more than I should wish the lawyers to leave them wholly to us. To some extent the relation of the studies is the same as that which subsists between Ecclesiastical History and Theology; each is a very maimed affair without the other. It will not be our fault if the common ground is altogether lost.

Next, to descend from the higher regions to the lower, I would say a word about the Historical Prizes. And in what I have to say, I hope I shall not be understood to cast any slight on the very meritorious essays which have in the last few years received the Arnold, Stanhope, and Lothian Prizes. I have been on each occasion a judge, and have very carefully and anxiously observed the character of the productions sent in. The fact that in several instances the Prizes have not been awarded is a proof that where they have been awarded they have been, in the opinion of the judges, thoroughly well merited. But the experience of these years has not, on the whole, been encouraging. Of the Stanhope I need say little: it is intended to be an undergraduate prize; the style of writing is scarcely of less importance in the estimation of the judges, as guided by the intention of the donor, than is the matter of the essay. For the Stanhope, too, there have always been plenty of competitors and no lack of creditable, very creditable, essays. But for the Arnold, which is a graduates' prize, and for the Lothian, which is common to both bachelors and undergraduates, I am sorry to say that there has not been lately good competition. I speak primarily of the modern side of the Arnold Prize ; the ancient side has been still more unproductive of good work. This lack of competition is not, I am sure, a sign of flagging interest in these studies. It is to be explained by a very obvious circumstance—namely, that urgent desire which at present prevails among the Honour men to get speedy returns for their accumulation of class knowledge. Quick returns are generally associated with small profits; and I cannot help thinking that many men, who rush into tutorial work as soon as they have got through the Schools, would do much better, and make ultimately much greater profit, by continuing their reading, or at all events by blending tutorial work with some literary industry such as writing for the Prizes. It looks rather as if they were afraid that the stores of knowledge which have received the brand of the Examination School might lose their freshness and applicability unless they were immediately put to use in one particular way. I am aware that this is no new snare; and twenty-eight years ago, when I myself was subjected to the temptation, it was hardly less a snare than it is now. But then, as a rule, men went into the Schools younger than they do now; there were fewer Schools and fewer first class men; less ardent competition perhaps among private tutors, and on the whole more leisure for continued reading. There may be other reasons for the result that I complain of. The ignorance with which the Lothian Prize, a handsome prize of £40, open to all graduates and undergraduates up to their twenty-seventh term, has been disregarded, is, to say the least, curious. The subjects proposed, for which I am in a measure responsible, have perhaps not carried on their face the recommendations of general or popular interest; and Foreign History does not of course receive so much attention as English History. But none of these is a satisfactory reason. The view which I have every reason to believe that the founder of the Lothian Prize had before him was, not merely to stimulate historical reading, but really to help to increase the stores of historical knowledge by the production of valuable monographs on points of foreign history.

My own idea of what we should look for is something like the small but most valuable dissertations which are produced in some of the German Universities as exercises for the doctorate. These are the work of men of twenty-three or twenty-four, just the age at which our high-class men graduate; and they are the result of their private reading, approved and authorized, so to speak, by their professors. Within the last few weeks I have received two such essays on subjects mainly of English interest, in fact upon portions of our history which I myself have treated: a tract on the ' Dialogus de Scaccario,' by Mr. Liebermann, of Göttingen ; and one on the capture of Lisbon by the English crusaders in 1147, by Mr. Cosack, of the University of Halle. I mention these, not because I have any credit to claim for them, for I am criticized quite as calmly and unsparingly as any other Englishman may expect to be in German reviews, but because I take them to be a sign of a sort of literary culture which we ought not to be ashamed to imitate. Unlike most of our ordinary historic reviews, they have a permanent value: they are not condemned, as some very good English work of the kind is, to be the padding of popular magazines —the ever uncut leaves that interpose between the two sensational stories by which the magazine lives—but they are put together and stored up for the days when either the writers or some who have profited by the reading of them can use them in more continuous, more consolidated, work. Now it is useless to argue that we cannot do this. Mr. Dicey's Essay on the Privy Council, which took the Arnold Prize in 1860, is a proof that our prize system is not incapable of such success, although it cannot insure it. Dr. Bryce's Essay on the Holy Roman Empire, in 1863, is not exactly a case in point, for it is not a study of some minute fact or institution, but a brilliant sketch of the whole course of one of the great influences which make up modern history;

but not to be invidious, there are other essays which do more or less approach the standard of deep research and sound criticism which I wish to see adopted. I have sometimes thought that it would be a good plan to give a number of alternative theses for such a valuable prize ; but I will content myself with a recommendation that, if any new benefactor wishes at once to encourage critical study and reward research, he should establish a prize for which the competitors should choose their own subject, to be approved by the judges a year before the time fixed for sending in the essays. Such an experiment might fairly be tried. There are, I believe, quite sufficient inducements of a local and personal kind, connected with History, which would draw the intelligent student into much more earnest work than any thesis simply imposed as a test of his powers. Local history, family history, the possession of important documents such as may be found in every country house, and almost every parish register or court roll, open ways of access to historical interest of a varied kind, in which the extent of research may be almost unbounded, in which a critical spirit may be trained and disciplined, and the results of which are sure to be valuable, certainly invaluable to the worker himself. Well, I do not wish to see the Lothian essays devoted to points of very minute history, and it is of foreign history that they are, by the injunction of the founder, to treat; but I think that some latitude in the choice of subjects for prize dissertations might be conveniently adopted, say for college prizes; and if any college will try the experiment, I will gladly serve as a judge for the purpose.

What I have said about the Lothian Prize, its value, and the really important work which, if it were taken up by classmen after they have passed through the Schools, it might be made to insure, will, I hope, have fallen on some ears that will attend to it.

The mention of these prizes leads on to the further point, the encouragement given to the study of History at this moment by scholarships, exhibitions and fellowships bestowed after a competitive examination in History. On this a very few words will suffice, and those shall not be dogmatic or even positive. I would not say a word to discourage the idea, or a word that might seem to show that I wished to determine in my own way the result of the experiment that is being at present tried. But, until public school education, until school education generally, has much more completely assimilated, and found a more comfortable place for historical teaching, I should deprecate any large increase of historical exhibitions for boys coming up to the University. Holding, as I do, that a sound classical training must be the foundation of successful historical study, and sure as I am that nothing but such training can prepare a man to be a good historical teacher, I should not give a historical exhibition to a boy who does not show some promise of taking good Honours in Moderations. In most instances I think it would be better not to give it until Moderations are over; of course, however, I am speaking with a view to the study of History, and not to the pecuniary interests of candidates for scholarships. Example has shown us that it is of little use to hope to promote a study like this by overnursing. One reason, I think, that we have had such success as we have had, is that we have had no such nursing; that the study itself, and such a modicum of honour as could be gained in the Class Schools, has been the main incentive to historical reading here. We are, I am quite willing to allow—nay, I am most anxious that we should remember—but at the beginning of our work; we have very much to do still before the History School of Oxford can take its stand beside the historical schools of Paris, or Bonn, or Göttingen, or Munich, or

Vienna; but having well begun, we have half won our place already.

What I have said of scholarships is in its way true of competitive examination for fellowships. If a college desires simply to acquire a creditable Fellow, a mere historic examination may be as good as any other; if a college desires a good History Tutor, I conceive that the best way to get him would be to subject the History candidates (selected in the first instance on the ground of their Honours acquired in the History Schools) to a sound examination in the work of the Literae Humaniores School, in which teaching power is at present most fully developed. If a college desires to have what is called a man of research, I am not sure but the best way to obtain him would be to choose him without examination. There are not, I believe, many men worthy of such distinction who are not already marked out by work done.

The whole question of research is difficult, the direction as well as the endowment of it. I confess that I do not like the idea of giving a man an income which would by itself be sufficient to make work unnecessary, and telling him to devote himself to research as he pleases. Not to consider cases in which the duty of research would, like other duties heretofore, be eluded—and idle professorships would take the place of idle fellowships—the temptation to desultory research must in every case be very great, and desultory research, however it may amuse or benefit the investigator, seldom adds much to the real stock of human knowledge. We have had enough spent already on self-culture taken for granted. If we would provide for research, it must, so far as History is concerned, be done by paying for results. Let me not be misunderstood. For results I should rather say work done. There are fields of work in History as well as in Natural Science in which experiment is to be treated as result. If a scientific man tries some new and costly combination of chemicals, if a practical gunfounder or shipbuilder attempts some grand and novel scheme of artillery or naval architecture, and, after making careful calculations, fails, his failure is a result for which he has a right to be paid; it is an addition to our knowledge to have learned that such and such combinations do not produce the effect which it was calculated that they would produce. So in historical study I should place among the lawful researches and results, the investigation of foreign libraries, the exploration of un-searched districts for the purpose of collecting inscriptions, the calendaring and cataloguing of manuscripts—all sorts, in fact, of investigations on which it was, *a priori*, reason-ably probable that discoveries would be made; provided such investigations were carried out systematically, provided the work were well done, even if, in that sense of result, there were no result but the discovery that there was nothing to discover. I do not mean to say that the successful re-searcher should be placed on a level with the unsuccessful, although his success would probably be in itself remunerative, and the element of good fortune should not be left out of account.

Well, I should like to see us send an occasional envoy to the Vatican Library, or to the great libraries of the Roman princes; or to send a trained scholar, chosen not by com-petition, but because his peculiar qualifications forced him upon our notice, to watch the explorations at Olympia or at Troy. More generally, however, I think that the endow-ment of research should take the form of payment for actual results. Find your man of research, and set him to the work of research; pay him something by way of retaining fee, which you may safely do when you have caught him, but let the liberal remuneration for work actually produced be the real endowment, be it books written, books edited, coins or manuscripts collected, as the case may be. The further

point, how to reward men of research when their day of
research is over, scarcely belongs to this subject ; for the rule
must be the same, I conceive, in all departments of knowledge : it is a question of pensioning those who have deserved
well of us, not of securing any further addition to the sum of
knowledge.

The rule that we should first find the man of research and
then endow him, not found a chair of research and then find
the man to fill it, applies to another important matter which
is very much forced upon our minds at this moment. And
I must request you to take what I have to say upon it not as
any final conclusion, but as the view which at this moment
presents itself to me as most feasible, but which circumstances may at any time modify. If we are to look on the
measures of change which are at present imminent, as likely
to settle the future of the University for any considerable
number of years, we must look about us and see whether
our staff of historical teachers and searchers is sufficient for
present needs, if it is likely to be sufficient for future needs,
how by careful speculation and economic arrangement we
can best utilize the means which we have a right to expect
under any re-apportionment of academic resources. Now I
am not prepared to allow that our staff of historical teachers
is either sufficient in itself or organized in the best way at
the present moment. I am quite sure that, if our study
advances during the next ten years in anything like the same
ratio in which it has advanced during the last ten years, we
shall need more professors and an organization of teaching,
which, like the present organization of Natural Science professors, may be not so much dependent as we now are on
the tutorial system in the colleges. It is most important to
observe that, if impending changes alter the collegiate system
or affect its available resources, the University will have to
supply a large part of the teaching power, now provided by

the colleges, in the shape of an increased professoriate or sub-professoriate. I should not like to have to make even an estimate now of the staff that we may require in ten or twenty years, and I should very much deprecate any measure which, taking the present as the standard of our needs, should prevent us from securing such development as the occasion for it may arise. At the present moment we want a Professor of Later Ecclesiastical History, to take up the subject at the point at which the department assigned to the Regius Professor comes to an end. We want a permanent chair of Indian History. The labours of our friend the present Indian Reader have shown us how thoroughly that study, the importance of which can scarcely be over-rated by Englishmen, falls in with the current of our University work. I say a permanent chair, because that is a subject of permanent necessity, not a subject like palaeography or numismatology, in which the labours of one good professor may serve for two or three generations, and the endowment of the man is of equal importance with the endowment of the chair or study. It is the belief of a large class of scholars that we require a professorship of English History by itself; and it is certainly desirable that no chance should be allowed of English History being without adequate representation. I think it is unlikely that that should be the case, or that both the Regius and Chichele Professors at the same time should devote themselves to Foreign History; but it might as well be made certain, and English History is a subject which might well employ the energies of three or four professors. I am not, however, an advocate for tying down the History professors to particular branches of the subject; I am sure that each will work best if he is left to devote himself to his own specially chosen department, and that, provided the whole field of teaching be sufficiently well covered, the more freedom that can be given, the better for both teacher and learner.

E

However, whilst with this limitation the permanent chairs may be expected to represent the whole field of teaching, it seems to me most important that for our greater extension we should employ the means which the Board of Historical Studies were among the first to suggest in their answer to the questions of the late Vice-Chancellor, and avail ourselves of the services of professors-extraordinary: that is, as I have begun by saying, find a man who is making himself a great authority and teacher in a special department, and bring him here and make him a professor, not considering whether, when he is gone, we can find another as good to fill his place, but simply taking him as a very good godsend and making the best of him. Of course we should never choose the professor of a worthless subject, but worthless subjects do not often attract the men whose services would be otherwise worth having. Historical teaching, method and criticism, may however be exemplified in very many sections of the great subject: and it might be very well indeed, the general balance being otherwise preserved, to have a professor-extraordinary who would exemplify them, for instance, in the minute working out of the lessons of the reign of Edward III, or of the age of the Reformation, or of the reign of Charles I or Queen Anne. So research might be combined with teaching, the discipline of research might be itself inculcated, and the voice of research be made to attune itself to the work of teaching.

But whether we want a present reinforcement, or content ourselves with looking forward to a probable development, we must not let the opportunity escape. We must not ask too much, but we must ask the University to keep its eyes open to what we believe to be our certain and noble future, and not to make the modesty of our present petitions the limit of her prospective liabilities in our behalf. We must ask her to secure for us a competence for the moment and ample freedom for growth and expansion. As to any definite finality, any perfect and exhaustive division of periods and duties, any theoretically complete staff of professors of History, I confess that I am not disposed to be anxious. If the study flourishes and is not cramped for means, the completeness and the neatness of system will grow as it grows: and we may be content to let it grow so.

In conclusion, that is, of this part of my subject—the condition and prospects of historical education, apart from the general subject of the *bona fide* development of historical study—I should say a word or two about teaching in schools. And this I do with great diffidence, because I have no experience in such work; at the same time I trust that I shall not make any impracticable suggestions. For the growth and development of the study, as an instrument of education, we must look for much help to the public schools and other great feeders of University life. If they find it possible to incorporate it permanently with their course of work introductory to the University career, the men will come up better prepared for such training as we can give them, and so more and more ready to assist in the growth of the growing study. Now although this seems simple enough to say, in reality it involves a great deal. It means not only that the great schools should have History masters who can keep themselves abreast with the rising tide of knowledge, but a constant revision or provision of improved textbooks. It seems to me that the great schools are awake to the necessity, and that the publishers of school books are vying with one another in the production of manuals which will combine the conclusions of the most advanced students with simplicity of plan, and, we may hope, attractiveness in treatment. Only there is no finality to be looked for. We must not expect manuals that, like the old grammars, will keep their places for two or three centuries. Every few years great discoveries are made; the use of the comparative method, long ago applied superficially and partially to History, has now become, owing to its employment in other fields of work, far more valuable and remunerative; and more especially in regard to early periods with respect to which error and misapprehension are the greatest among fairly educated people, and almost ineradicable from otherwise fairly useful textbooks. To take the simple instance, which will perhaps have occurred to some of you : the proved discovery of the forgery of Ingulf's History of Crowland Abbey was a fact that necessitated the revision of every standard book on early English History. It is more than forty years since that discovery, long ago suspected, was proved beyond the possibility of doubt. Yet to this day the Ingulfine leaven remains in our elementary books, nay, in more than elementary books, in standard works of History, from which it is almost impossible to eliminate it ; it remains as a warning light—a wandering marsh-fire—to caution the reader not to accept too abjectly the conclusions of his authority. Even the recently published list of landowners of England, called somewhat fantastically by the leaders of public opinion the new Domesday, contains in its introduction a quotation from Ingulf, made apparently without any suspicion of falseness. But it is not only the name of the writer, but the more subtle influence of conclusions drawn from his fabrications that are to be guarded against : and these lie at the very basis of our popular histories. For school books it is absolutely necessary that such primary errors should be corrected at once ; for it is impossible, at least at present, to suppose that the reading of original authorities can be to any great extent introduced into the scholastic course as is done in Germany. And this will necessitate constant revision.

Another point to be watched is the not unnatural desire of

teachers to attract the minds of boys to the picturesque and dramatic sides of the subject, to the neglect of the greater lesson, the investigation of causes and effects and the connexion of events. I would almost rather that boys were attracted by the reading of Ivanhoe and the Talisman, books which do not pretend to be true, and are full of strange misrepresentations of manners and thought, than by a serious History composed with a view to the picturesque only or mainly. The ivy may conceal the structure of the building far too much for safety. We cannot safely content ourselves with fanciful grouping or imaginary drawing of character and situation. Let us trust the novelist so far. There are novels that may well be trusted so far; Miss Yonge's Chaplet of Pearls, and Dove in the Eagle's Nest, for instance—beautiful and, I think, perfect pictures of manners and reflexions of ideas. We will attract but not educate by such books. Our real education in History must not be less precise or severe than the discipline of language or of natural science; it cannot be valuable if it be desultory.

One point more. If the study of periods of history is to become part of a school education, I trust that due care will be taken not to dwell unnecessarily on, or to choose for exaggerated illustration, those periods which are connected most closely with the questions and controversies of to-day. Of all things in the world, except a controversial woman, a controversial boy is the most disagreeable, the most pragmatic, the most irrepressible, the most aggressive. Now even in the training of children we want to train the judgement. That training is the great educational or disciplinary object of historic teaching, the formative as distinct from the material acquisition that results or should result from it. The judgement must be trained in cooler air and by milder methods than are found in the battle-field of modern politics. Surely boys and girls should be taught elementary History, should be trained in the exercise of the powers that can trace cause and effect in historical narrative, should be given credit for the germs of a critical faculty and helped to cultivate it, before they are plunged into the details of the struggles of puritanism and absolutism, or the deep religious divisions, that for three centuries have separated Christendom into two camps and do so still. Let them learn the history of early England and early France before they are called to exert their tender judgement on the Great Rebellion or the French Revolution. If the teachers had been so taught the experiment would never have been tried.

III

ON THE PRESENT STATE AND PROSPECTS OF HISTORICAL STUDY

(May 20, 1876.)

IN the remarks which I took upon myself to offer in the last Lecture on the present prospects of historical study, I think that I managed to touch upon every point of special interest to Oxford and the educational use of my subject: to touch upon every point, I say, because it was neither necessary nor possible to treat exhaustively of any one. I may have to recur in the present Lecture to some of the more general or more prominent topics, but I propose now to take a view of the broader side of the subject—Historic study and its position in England and Europe, as affected by the work of the last ten years—not with any special view to the educational importance of the work, but generally as a material and substantial branch of human knowledge.

Taking England first; the first point I shall notice is the great spread of the taste for History which has marked the period. This may be tested in two ways. The great number of new books and reprints of old ones, the large editions and re-issues of standard books, school books, and volumes of essays, and the number of reviews of historical books, or short historical articles in magazines and newspapers, are one branch of proof; the more lively interest taken in the preservation of historical monuments, whether in the shape of documents or in that of architectural and antiquarian remains, is another. I am not prepared to say that the last ten years have witnessed the introduction of any entirely new elements in either branch, or that we are not yet a long way off from the state of things which we may wish for, when the publication of a great historical discovery may be welcomed with as much ardour as a new poem or a new book of travels, and when the preservation of public and private memorials will become the care of every family and individual that possesses them, as well as of the nation at large. But we have gone on steadily improving ourselves ; not to speak yet of the important works which have met appreciative readers, I would adduce such points as these : the revival and extension of the work of the learned societies, especially the Camden and Surtees Societies ; the widespread interest taken in the work of the Commission for examining Historical Manuscripts in private hands ; and the Parliamentary discussions on the preservation of Historic Monuments. Each of these three matters may claim an important bearing on the growth of historic culture. In each we see those private and personal influences combined and utilized for good purposes, which too often have been wasted upon mere pomps and vanities, or mere archaeological trifling.

The expansion and extension of genealogical study is a very remarkable feature of our own times. Men are apparently awaking to the fact that there are other families besides those described in the peerage, that those families have their records, played their part in history, furnished the bone and sinew of national action, and left traces behind them which it behoves their descendants to search out and keep in remembrance. There is nothing in this that need be stigmatized as vain and foolish ; it is a very natural instinct, and it appears to me to be one of the ways in which a general interest in national history may be expected to grow. It is an increasing pursuit both in America and in England, and certainly helps, by the promotion of careful investigation and by the publication of recondite memorials, the more complete adjustment of personal and local details. This has no doubt helped largely the work of the Manuscripts Commission; it has enabled the learned societies to attempt larger and more costly works, and has been the portal by which many, destined and qualified to be valuable historical helpers, have entered the field of historic study.

Local history and minute archaeology have been of use in the same way: the Harleian Society has published heraldic visitations; the local societies have printed subsidy rolls and old legal memoranda; old county histories have been republished; little popular county histories are found in every farm-house in the country, where the editors or compilers have contrived, by mingling the *utile* of the directory with the *dulce* of historic memoranda, to stimulate the curiosity of every class.

I have called this a revival, and so it is; these pursuits do not seem to admit of much development, one flourishes and another languishes, as may be traced very clearly in the pages of the Archaeologia; twenty years ago architectural antiquities were the great object of local study, now through a genealogical period we are perhaps working our way to a constitutional one, which I shall be most happy to welcome. I think that just now, when so many of our most ancient institutions, the manorial system and the ecclesiastical and civil judicature of old times, are either falling into desuetude or being ruthlessly abolished, it would be a good work for local zeal to put on record what memory and custom can still supply as to the working of these old institutions. I wish to see a manorial map of England as it exists now or as it existed twenty years ago, reflecting as it must do the condition of territorial power at the time when it became impossible to create new manors, in the reign of Edward I ; reflecting, as it could easily be made to do, the local and dynastic arrangements of parties and families during the fourteenth, fifteenth, and seventeenth centuries, arrangements which still survive, but are destined, by the operation of legal changes, most of them intended to facilitate the alienation of land and to amend the administration of justice, to speedy extinction.

Well, I only adduce these as feeders, so to speak, of the stream of historic interest. Here and there they add a really precious contribution, but chiefly they are valuable as drawing in students to the higher and nobler study. Without them I doubt not we should have our Macaulays and Froudes, our Maines and our Freemans, but without them those writers would have to dispense with nine-tenths of their intelligent and interested readers ; and without their contributions the historians of the grand school would have to content themselves with portrait painting ; they would lose all minute details of character, and background and foreground alike of local colouring. The 'Worthies of All Souls' have shown us how even more directly and more personally the dry stores of the College Treasury can bring us into relation with the great men of old days, and the same plan followed out by the Colleges generally would serve to fill up a great gap in our national history.

But considering the magnitude of the subject, I have said enough about local influences. They prove the increasing interest, but they do not yet prove that interest to be of the most refined and educated character. If we test it by the character of the work it welcomes, we shall perhaps be inclined to put a drag on historic zeal. I cannot help thinking that, although sound historical books find a hearty welcome for the most part, unsound and sensational books, which pretend to the character of history, are too often welcomed quite as heartily. High patronage, as well as large circles of readers, seem now and then to waste themselves on trashy books which owe their circulation to advertising skill or to pretentious claptrap. I cannot of course mention names, but I do not doubt that you can supply them. Now, although this is an unfortunate waste of power and strength, it is not wholly to be deplored: a taste for history must exist before it can be educated, and it will, until it is thoroughly educated, be liable to be misled and waste itself on what is unprofitable. But to whom does it belong to educate and refine it? That place is claimed by the reviewers. But I take leave to say that it is with the reviewers that the improvement should begin; and it is a sad truth that the improvement in reviewing has not yet gone far enough. By reviewing I mean what strictly speaking reviewing should be, and I take leave to say it because, having never been a reviewer, having in fact written but one article of the kind in my whole life, I have been for many years a steady reader of reviews. It is easier perhaps to say, with regard to this point, what we do not want than what we want. We do not want sledge-hammer articles, that demolish an unhappy pretender without attempting to tell us what he pretended or attempted to do; or niggling articles, which enumerate the mistakes and misstatements of a book, ignoring the fact that, with much carelessness of detail, the author has shown a great grasp of knowledge of his subject, skill in grouping and colouring, and power in investing the subject with true and real interest; we do not want reviews in the grand style, which seem to be intended to prove that the writer knows or believes himself to know more of the subject than the author whom he is reviewing. All these sorts of reviews are either injurious to knowledge or useful only by way of advertisement. I need scarcely point out to you that while the reviewer, as a reviewer, is a man of many books and many subjects, the author is generally a man of one book or one subject. Ten to one the most indifferent author knows more of his book (I speak of *bona fide* authors, not of bookmakers) than his reviewer does. In fairness he has a right to demand that his critic should have tried to put himself in his place and looked at the subject from his point; but how very seldom does he find himself so treated. What we want, I take it, in historical reviewing is that the critic should first give a fair account of the work; that he should exhibit, in doing this, just so much superior knowledge as will justify his claim to sit in judgement upon it, and not put in a word for mere display; that he should discuss the subject-matter judicially and as a whole, not confining himself to the portions in which he is presumedly better informed, but gauging the work by the author's standard as well as his own; that he should not dogmatize where the points of difference are matters of opinion—how many a sore heart would have been spared if the critic would have said, 'Here we differ,' instead of saying, 'This is a great mistake'; and finally that, in recounting blemishes, he should not confuse structural with incidental error. I do not recommend German reviews as models for English ones; too often they seem to me to be written by rival competitors in the same field with the author; but as a rule they give more real information as to the work criticized than ours do; and they are more moderate in denunciation.

So much of our reviewing is done in newspapers and critical notes in magazines and quarterlies that this sort of criticism nearly engrosses the name; and the great old reviews are come to be collections of essays, the book supposed to be criticized standing merely in the place of text or thesis to a discourse in which neither book nor author may be mentioned. But the historical value of this sort of essay might be very great; and, as History is of course only one of the subjects that compete for a limited number of places in such periodicals, it has frequently been suggested that we should have a historical review of our own; by 'we,' I mean the students of History who are at work here or in London and elsewhere connected with the two Universities. Such a design has much to recommend it. It would be very becoming to the English School of History to have an accredited organ; it ought not to be beyond our powers and resources to maintain such a journal as is kept alive in many of the smaller universities of Germany; and it would be very useful indeed to have a record of the incidental discoveries, and of the minor studies which every historical scholar makes in the process of his work, many of which are thrown away as soon as the immediate occasion for their use is over, or, being employed as appendices to works already too bulky, remain practically unread and unknown. But there are objections or rather hindrances to such a scheme which have hitherto been sufficient to prevent us from making the attempt. It is very questionable whether we can as yet appeal to a public sufficiently extended, and sufficiently educated, to make the design remunerative to either publishers or contributors: the writers whose work would be most valuable are all of them busy men to whom the writing of two or three articles a year would, if made a matter of *rigueur*, become exceedingly burdensome; and the prospects of any new review in England at this moment can hardly be called encouraging. The older quarterlies have long ceased to provide us with such reading as was found in the *Edinburgh* and *Quarterly* of fifty years ago, when Hallam, Allen, and Palgrave were writing on History. Now and then we have contributions to contemporary history, either from the statesman of the day or from the industrious collector of the gossip of the last generation, which have a value, and will hereafter have a greater. Now and then we have a sound critique on new matter brought out in foreign countries, and careful, well-considered judgements on the re-reading of re-written history. Occasionally, very rarely, when a question of theological or political interest touches upon the more recondite stores of History, we have an industrious examination of ancient sources made subservient to the advocacy of some particular theory. But so far as reviews go, this age is one not of deep study; the articles are read by, and therefore written for, men who care just enough about such matters to induce them to read fifty pages of cleverly arranged, not too exhausting argument. They share the ephemeral character of the rest of our popular literature, and, so long as that ephemeral character is a mark of such productions, it is only courting failure if we attempt to add to the list of competitors one which would find, in the very points which recommend it to the student, characteristics which would repel those whom, I think I may say, we ought to try to attract.

Still I do not despair of the plan; only it will require an amount of devotion as well as an affluence of means, which are not, it seems to me, at present forthcoming. The confession is, when we look at what is done in Germany, or even when we look at what is done by private societies in England, not a thing to be proud of: but the conditions of publishing and the estimation of literary labour in Germany are so different from what they are here, that the comparison is hardly fair, and the best English private and local societies have always made their publications a labour of love to both writer and editor, whilst by their subscriptions they are secured from serious loss. On the whole, I think that if we were to make the effort, it might best be done at first by the agency of a publishing society. Five hundred subscribers, such as sustain the Camden and the Surtees Societies, would launch and keep afloat even a larger plan than has yet been contemplated.

If I were called on to furnish an illustration of the

increased interest felt in historical matters at this day, I
might, I think, allege the curious phenomenon of the republication of the Paston letters. Curious, invaluable, as these
relics are, they are really unintelligible to all but the inner-
most ring of historic students. Their language, their localized
details, their minutiae of family history and illustration of
manners, are without any meaning to nine people out of ten.
Yet they have just been reprinted with a most admirable
apparatus of notes and introductions, in a most useable and
convenient form, for the small sum of one guinea ; a price at
which only a very large circulation can repay the editor for
his outlay, to say nothing of his labour and the expenditure
of stores of carefully gathered knowledge. So far, you may
say, so good ; but when we remember that the demand for
the republication was not the result of awakened historic
interest, or even of curiosity as to what the much-talked-of
letters might contain, but sprang directly from an ingenious
and paradoxical argument on their authenticity written by a
well-known scholar, who was not, I believe, specially interested
in their contents so much as in their external history ; that it
was promoted by the rumour that our greatest judge was
going to investigate their genuineness, and that in the third
place the curiosity so provoked was stimulated and encouraged by the unexpected discovery of new stores of similar
matter—when, I say, we remember these things, we are
bound to confess that the sensational history of the Paston
letters, rather than the really valuable matter contained in
them , has been the chief element in the demand for their
reproduction. However this may be, we bless the accident
and rejoice in the result. However the zeal originated, that
result is according to knowledge.

It is time, however, that I should proceed to mention some
of the more important additions to our historical stores which
have marked the period which I have, desultorily I fear, tried

to embrace in the general scope of my remarks. I can but
mention a few out of many names, and most of those few are
above my unpretending criticism. The last ten years have
seen the production of Mr. Freeman's Norman Conquest,
which, I believe, is well known to us all, and is a monument
of critical erudition and genius in the recreation of historical
life of which Oxford may well be proud. We have seen too
the conclusion, premature and abrupt, of Mr. Froude's great
work, a book to which even those who differ in principle
from the writer will not refuse the tribute of praise as a work
of great industry, power, and importance ; the conclusion
scarcely less abrupt, though not premature, of the great work
of one of the best and greatest men that Oxford has ever
produced, the Lives of the archbishops of Canterbury by
Dr. Hook ; two out of the three most valuable contributions
of Mr. Samuel Gardiner to the Jacobean and Caroline period,
the earnests, as we hope, of still greater contributions yet to
be looked for; the studies of Mr. Brewer on the reign of
Henry VIII included in his volumes of Calendars of Public
Documents, but rivalling in bulk and more than rivalling in
interest the documents themselves ; Mr. Pocock's labours
on the same age in his edition of Burnet and of the early
documentary history of the Reformation ; Professor Rogers'
great work, or beginning of a great work, on mediaeval
economy, the History of Prices ; these are but a portion of
the history work done for England by men trained in the
old Literae Humaniores School of Oxford ; how long will it
be before the new school will have something of the sort to
show ? To the facile pen of an Oxford man we owe the
production of the most popular manual of our history that
has ever appeared, the Short History of the English People.
To the Oxford Press and the labours self-denyingly and
generously tendered of hard-worked tutors we owe the translation of Ranke's History of England.

Of this, as one of the original suggesters and promoters of the undertaking, I may say a word more; for, curiously enough, the boon conferred by this translation has not been adequately recognized. Leopold von Ranke is not only beyond all comparison the greatest historical scholar alive, but one of the very greatest historians that ever lived. Unrivalled stores of knowledge, depth of research, intimate acquaintance with the most recondite sources, have been, in his case, supplemented by everything which could be conferred by a long life, continuous study, close association with the great political actors and thinkers of the greatest part of the most eventful century of the world's history. Scarcely less eminent as the founder of the German School of History than as an historian himself, he has had the singular felicity of living to gather up the results of the labours of the men whom he himself started in the career of study. It seemed to me, and it was the idea in which the work was begun and carried out, that for Englishmen in their own tongue to have from such a man a reading of the most critical period of English history, would be a boon of incalculable value. Not that we regarded him as infallible, not that we looked for him to have the sympathies of an Englishman, but that we did look to have, for a period on which no Englishman can look or speak without prejudice, the evidence of a witness and critic who brought unparalleled qualifications and entire impartiality to bear upon it. The reception of the boon by scholars has been most grateful; that our literary guides have condescended to look on Ranke as one of the ruck of German professors, to treat his work as on the same plane with those of the ephemeral writers whose reputation is so carefully nursed in what is called literary society, does appear to me to be one of the discouraging signs of the times to be set against our more sanguine hopes.

F

To come down to smaller works of a more distinctly educational character; whilst we may regret perhaps that the good example set by Mr. Kitchin and myself in the Clarendon Press Series has not yet been more widely followed, we cannot but regard the competition among the great publishers in producing manuals of history for schools as a most significant mark of growth. Mr. Longman's Epochs, Mr. Freeman's Manuals, Mr. Green's Primers, Messrs. Rivington's Handbooks, all have in common the mark of a purpose to secure skilled labour of the best sort; boys are not to be taught any longer by book-makers. May the omen be fully borne out by the result!

So far, however, I have mentioned no book except those in which we here have a direct and personal interest. We should be ungrateful indeed to leave out of ever so general review Mr. Kinglake's great work on the Crimean War, or Mr. Molesworth's on the History of the Period of Parliamentary Reform; these stand at the head of a list of laborious and able publications, the interest of which depends on the incidents of our own time: to some extent they are attempts to forestall the opinion of posterity, but they are books which, if such books ever are to be written, if the contemporary knowledge and opinion are to be applied to the record of the events to which they are devoted, should be written now before the actors are dead or the public sympathy chilled. So rapid is the progress of political life and opinion that even these great subjects are becoming quickly extinct or lost influences among the crowds of new ones. The Reform History has come to be regarded no longer as a grand revolution, of which its chief agents could predicate perfection and finality, but merely as a single stage in a progress the present velocity of which would have made the projectors dizzy. What shall we say of the Crimean War itself? begun as it was by the wisest men of the nation with the greatest reluctance, but begun because they believed that they ought to keep national promises and to maintain treaties even at the risk of sustaining weak and wicked governments. Why, for all the good that it did, it might never have been fought at all. The treaties that resulted from it are thrown to the winds; the powers that fought it have resumed that natural attitude which treaties might attempt to modify but cannot alter: the crisis that it tried to avert is approaching more quickly and more certainly, and it is reverted to only because in it an experiment which we thought fit to try was tried in vain. The history of our own times does, whilst the events are in progress, seem more important than any history that has gone before; greater interests are seen to be involved, greater armaments brought into the field, more critical changes follow, more startling principles are enunciated; yet after all the proportion of historic incident is scarcely changed. The tide began to roll with greater waves at the Reformation, with higher still during the age of Lewis XIV, deep called unto deep in the upheaval of the French Revolution, and the European wars of 1866 and 1870 have proved that the storms grow wilder as the world grows older. But the results are not, so far as we can see, much more permanent, the rapidity of action keeps pace with the growth of the contending influences, and events which centuries ago would have been regarded as striking the knell of Christendom, form the subject of a hasty telegram which we read and say, It is no more than we expected. But I am not going to philosophize; μὴ γένοιτο. When I say that such books as these are not history, but rather the materials of history, I do not mean to undervalue them, but simply to point by them to the fact that until events have come to be seen in due proportion and in their relative bearing, their full history cannot be written; and the most perfect memoirs will need reduction and review. But at the risk of seeming to pass over even more important matters I must pass on.

It is unfortunate, I think, that English writers confine their attention too much to English and French History; and that the History of further Europe, that of Italy being a partial exception only, is seldom made the subject of research. Carlyle's Frederick II is really the only great work on German or European History which has appeared in England, for nearly half a century, on its merits as a work of History. It will scarcely be claimed for Sir Archibald Alison's valuable works on the period immediately following that of Frederick, that they owe their importance to their character as works of historical research. They were read and are read as any other very interesting book on a very interesting subject, but they do not reach even to the stature of Von Sybel's French Revolution or Lanfrey's work on Napoleon. Carlyle's Frederick is primarily a work of a different sort; although, in the prophetic sight of the writer, that most remarkable book may, at the moment it was written, have borne a conscious reference to events which were still future, but have since most wonderfully illustrated its great theme, the world in general recognized nothing of the sort in it. The author, if he knew himself to be a *vox clamantis* at the time, must have been astonished at the rapidity with which his Gospel of Force triumphed as soon as it had its chance. Some of us shook our heads over it, one great man amongst us, whose place I am proud to occupy, I dare not say to fill, did not hesitate to speak words of summary condemnation; but the doctrine itself was esoteric, the words, like much else of Carlyle's, were φωνᾶντα συνετοῖσιν, but συνετοῖσιν only; to the ears of the many they required the sacred interpreter. Shall I be thought hard if I say that the popularity of Carlyle's Frederick was not an intelligent appreciation; that it was Carlyle's reputation

and manner that made men read it; and that it was for
the Carlyle not for the Frederick that they cared, whilst
they wholly missed the prophet's lesson? Such as it is,
however, Carlyle's Frederick stands alone in recent historic
work.

There may be good reasons for this. The accumulation
of new material for German and Italian history is perplexing
in itself; the Germans and Italians have scarcely begun
to sort it. The materials for Spanish history are only a little
more accessible than before, and accessible only to workers
who are capable of great fatigue, as well as, what few can
pretend to be, already well qualified to make the very utmost
of scanty opportunities. But making allowance for everything that can be allowed for, it is, I think, no credit to us
that since the republication of the old Universal History,
a hundred years ago, we have had nothing like a general
book of historic reference undertaken in England, and that,
with the exception of Carlyle, we have had no first-class work
on German history since Archdeacon Coxe wrote on the
House of Austria. We have had sketches and essays, and
lectures, and articles in encyclopaedias,—one of which at
least, Lardner's Cyclopaedia, furnishes incidentally some very
valuable helps,—but nothing like a comprehensive, well-
considered design, such as for its day the old Universal
History was. This I hope is a *lacuna* which will not exist
much longer. Not that it can be filled up in a day; but that
we have in Heeren and Uckert a model which it will be
no disgrace to us to copy, a great credit to equal or to
surpass.

And this leads me on to that further circle of European
historic study towards which I have been looking at several
points in both these lectures. We ought to be taking
advantage of the great interest with which English history
is now being read in Germany, and, more than that, we ought

to learn from that interest that German history might be quite as remunerative to us as ours is to the Germans. Such has always been my contention. The study of French and Italian history appeals to our fancy, to our ecclesiastical and political tastes, but the history of Germany is bound up with our national and natural identity. And you may depend upon it, in our comparative history we have to receive as much as we have to give. Consider the number of precious contributions that we have received already. Immeasurably the best edition of the Anglo-Saxon Laws, by Schmid; the work of Lappenberg and Konrad Maurer on Anglo-Saxon Constitutional Antiquities; Pauli's exhaustive History of Mediaeval England; Ranke's History of England under the Stewarts; Pauli's History of the Present Century, of which the third volume has just appeared, furnishing by far the most accurate and well-proportioned view of recent history, and anticipating, I do not question it, most of the conclusions of the next generation as to the great men and great events on which we have looked too closely to see them in their due proportion and relations. There is scarcely a nook of our ancient and medieval history which the Germans are not now exploring. To Jaffé we owe the republication, from original texts, of the writings of Aldhelm and Boniface, the first Englishmen who wrote at all. The letters of Alcuin, the great scholar of York and light of learning in the West, have not only been most elaborately edited by Jaffé, Dümmler and Wattenbach, but are being subjected to a minute historical analysis by Professor Sickel at Vienna, an analysis which brings out, and must bring out more and more as it proceeds, the points of international and inter-ecclesiastical intercourse in the critical century of Anglo-Saxon growth. The Roman and the early Christian inscriptions in Britain have found in Dr. Hübner a critic who can not only collect and record and arrange them, but bring them into com-

parison and connexion with the like remains throughout
Europe. Month after month brings me essays and dissertations, as I said before, upon minute points of English law,
chronology, even geography and personal history. What
does this mean? Not surely that those scholars are following
an erratic fancy in trying to perfect their knowledge of
English history, or that they are working without plan or
leading idea. I do not indeed suppose that the scholars and
students of Göttingen and Vienna are doing as Von Moltke
and his agents are said to have done before the war of 1870,
collecting plans, and charts, and itineraries, and models
of fortresses, and raised maps of provinces, whilst they were
training men and officers both at work and play for conquest.
I do not believe that they want to take from us anything, not
even the pride of knowing more of our own history than
they do, or that they want to engross to themselves by conquest the whole domain of historical knowledge. But I am
sure that they have a great object—to increase human knowledge in minuteness of accuracy as well as in breadth and
firmness of grasp; to perfect the instruments of historic
study; to make, perhaps subordinately and subsidiarily,
their exploration of our history throw light on the dark
places, the obscure passages, and flickering popular institutions of their own land. I wish that we should do the same,
that we could and would so study not merely the works of
Waitz, Sohm, Brunner and the Maurers, but the documentary evidence on which those writers have based their
conclusions.

There is very much both of matter and method to be
learned from them. A few months ago a young American
professor who called on me told me that he was lecturing in
one of the great universities of the United States on constitutional law; he had been in doubt where to begin, and was in
fact lecturing on the capitularies of the Frank emperors.

I could not help thinking that, if he was not really wasting his powder and shot upon a class that could not appreciate him, he was doing something that I should like to see done here. And, within a very few weeks after, my aspirations were gratified by finding the Corpus Professor lecturing on the Salian law, going further back, and taking probably a more remunerative subject than my American friend.

Well, perhaps I am prejudiced by my own especial line of study in favour of such speculations, but I will go still further and say that the devotion with which, since the days of Grimm, the local and municipal institutions of Germany have been studied sets us a fine example. The publication of Grimm's collection of Weisthümer has been followed by a great and general exploration of local archives. Now in England we do not possess one single complete and detailed monograph on town life; Drake's Eboracum, published a century and a quarter ago, is perhaps the best, but in the lapse of many years a vast amount of new matter has turned up, by which Drake could be enlarged and improved. Mediaeval London still waits for its constitutional historian. The history of the Cinque Ports, and of the mercantile communities on the coast, lies at the root of our naval history, and contains the germs of our international jurisprudence. On them we have a few law-books which are the peculiar domain of a few legal offices in London; but their history has yet to be explored. Every year perhaps we are drawing nearer, for the discoveries of the Historical MSS. Commission are richer in this than in any other region; but for the successful investigation, for the comparison of materials, and for the systematic use of them, we must look to the association of such labourers as are now in Germany employed on the history of the Hanse Towns. Even the Scottish boroughs are in this particular ahead of us; there is a society

for publishing the records of Scottish burgh life. All the
efforts as yet made in England in that direction have been
the result of local and personal interest excited by merely
antiquarian curiosity.

It is time that this went further. It is time too, as I said
before, not only that we had a feudal map of England before
the manorial boundaries are wiped away, but that we had
a careful collection of manorial customs : such a codification
in fact, as is possible, of the ancient unwritten popular law as
it is preserved in these most ancient shadows and skeletons
of the early life of our fathers. And so I come round to the
point where I digressed.

We may take pattern by the Germans in collecting these
relics, but when we have done so we shall have to bring
them to comparison with the similar German collections
before we can extract the whole lesson that they would convey.
I would not be too sanguine, but I honestly believe that such
a comparison would reveal to us points of contact and diver-
gency as yet unsuspected even by the most careful investigators, and would enable us to reproduce the ancient
society of our common ancestry in a way that would speedily
set at rest some of the most controverted questions of institutional history. In such an investigation we might rely
on the help of the greatest foreign scholars ; and it is a task
to the performance of which every intelligent country gentleman could contribute an appreciable share without stirring
from his own muniment room.

If we turn to France and Belgium, we shall find work of
the same kind going on, which is only second, if it be indeed
second, to the historical industry of Germany. The re-issue
of the Recueil des Historiens de France, of the Gallia Chris-
tiana, and the Acta Sanctorum, proves that the revival is
begun at the right end, from the ecclesiastical side. The reproduction, in the great Patrologia of Migne, of the early

mediaeval historians, as well as the theologians, is an almost portentous fact; one wonders where the readers and students of such collections are to be found, and fears that, after all, such monuments must find their resting-places chiefly on the shelves of the public libraries rather than on the desks of close students. The intermission or retarded issue of the series of *Documents inédits* is perhaps not to be wondered at, when we consider the uncertain tenure of power and the enormous demands made for other purposes on the resources of the recent governments of France; but private enterprise and scholastic co-operation have done much to supply the void caused in this way. The collection of the historians of the Crusades, published under the direction of the Institute, increases and flourishes. The publications of the ' École des Chartes' and of the officers of the National Library supply in their fine criticism and deep research two elements that are somewhat deficient in the other lines of historical work. Local antiquaries and local societies flourish in France as much as in Germany, and the same spirit of restoration and conservation, which is exhibited in the case of historic buildings and other monuments, is conspicuous in the minute reproduction of chronicles and cartularies. At last constitutional history has found a home again in the land of Montesquieu. The History of États Généraux and Parliaments is critically and impartially investigated by men like M. Picot and M. Boutaric. Ancient laws and customs also are found to have a value besides their importance to the scientific lawyer. M. Fustel de Coulanges brings to the study of institutions a philosophic spirit, critical acuteness, and learning which seems not unlikely to have the effect of inducing some of the German constitutionalists to revise or modify their conclusions. And lastly, in the foundation of the *Revue Historique*, the best scholars, in all of these departments, have stretched out the right hand of fellowship

to the workers in other lands, and occupied their place in the
alliance for international knowledge and help in history.
It is perhaps true to say that in the most essential and
characteristic parts of our own national history we have less
interest in France than in Germany; but throughout many
ages French and English history, both external and institutional, are bound together as closely as any two national
histories can be; and that which illustrates the one cannot
but illustrate the other. English writers have long ago
learned that there are other histories worth studying besides
their own: German writers seem to have been late in learning that the Fatherland has a united and continuous history.
France is at last showing that she recognizes the fact that
other lands have histories at all, and that the whole of
mediaeval history is not a mere preparation for the dramatic
glories of the seventeenth and eighteenth centuries. If she
has somewhat to learn from her neighbours, surely we
cannot afford to say that we have not much to learn from
her; much to hope for, and much to be grateful for, in
the co-operation of her scholars.

There are signs too of a harvest and promises of co-
operation in another field which for several centuries has had
little community or sympathy with English students. We
have all probably been surprised, pleased,—may I not say
amused?—by the consequences of the inaugural lecture of
the Professor of International Law; at the chorus of praise
and harmony between Italian and English lawyers which
followed the note struck by him in the mention of Albericus
Gentilis. The very fact that Albericus Gentilis was almost
forgotten in England and had scarcely been heard of before
in Italy, only proves that there was a latent desire of recognition among the Italian literati with which we had
scarcely credited them. Now a very great deal may be hoped
for from an awakened spirit of this kind, more especially

when we remember the enormous mass of historical material which lies ready in Italy for the researches of competent scholars. It would be a waste of words if I were to attempt even to enumerate the treasures which must exist in Rome itself, in the Papal archives, where are, or should be found, the records of that great court of review and international arbitration which the mediaeval see of Rome claimed to hold. Much has no doubt perished, but much must remain; much does remain, as the labours of Theiner have shown, to shed new light on the history of remoter Europe. The Church History of the extreme North, of Norway, Iceland, Sweden, Britain, of the Slavonic lands also, has been already illustrated. What could be more remote or insignificant than the Manx Church? Yet Dr. Munch succeeded in extracting from the Vatican archives matter which settles the main question of her history, on which we had no record. Throughout the middle ages every great event, nay, every small event, that in the remotest way pretended to public interest, was discussed at Rome; every great power had a diplomatic agency there; every leading or aspiring statesman had there an agent and probably a paid patron. It is not only in the records of the great public offices of Rome, but in the libraries of the princely families which furnished so long the cardinals and confidential ministers of the Papal See, that new matter will be found. The researches of Dr. Brady, the printed results of which I have not seen, but some part of which I saw in MS., brought out of the note-books and diaries of the cardinals of the Elizabethan period, not merely some most important personal and chronological details relative to the English episcopate, but revealed an almost unsuspected web of papal intrigue underlying the better known public action of the popes. Where Dr. Brady, who was working with a definite purpose and not very impartial judgement, stumbled on so much that was valuable,

surely much more would be found by a fully equipped
investigator. The prizes of this initial research have not
fallen to English scholars. Rome is a long way off; English
scholars are looked on with suspicion there; even Dr.
Todd was not left to work freely and alone in the Vatican:
English visitors on a holyday have far too much else to do;
the endowment of research has not yet advanced far enough
to send searchers thither. So it was left for Cardinal Mai
to discover and edit the long-lost and long-lamented *Draco
Normannicus*, the poetical biography of the Empress Matilda,
which was printed by him apparently without any knowledge
of its history, but was not published until seventeen years
after his death, and in 1871, owing to a review by Dr. Pauli
in the *Academy*, was introduced to English scholars. It was
a German that discovered, and it is French scholars who are
editing that early French poem on the Crusade of Richard I
which is said, I believe with certainty, to be the original upon
which the Latin author of the *Itinerarium Regis Ricardi*
based his work. Just so it was the labours of Dr. Pertz and
his agents that unearthed the *Historia Pontificalis* of John of
Salisbury among the MSS. of the Bern Library, as he had
espied the long-lost *Encomium Emmae* in the library of the
Duke of Hamilton. No doubt luck is an element in these
discoveries, but a far more powerful element of success was
the educated eye, the larger opportunity, the knowledge how
to look, and what sort of things to look for. I should
not despair of discovering even the lost *Antiocheis*, the
poem of Joseph of Exeter on the first Crusade, when the
Vatican has proved a safe refuge for a Latin poem on
the prophecies of Merlin and for the fragments of Giraldus
Cambrensis.

Let us, it may be said, ascertain our own stores first,
catalogue our own collections, ascertain what really is contained in the vast collections of Sir Thomas Phillipps and

Lord Ashburnham, ransack the muniment rooms of Belvoir and Ripley, and the records of the cathedrals and church courts, before we go to Rome. It is by no means necessary that either should take precedence of the other; but the opportunities for Italian research are enlarging daily, and it is of great importance to catch the chances whilst they are yet new, and engage the co-operation of willing agents before they weary of the work, or fall back into the jealousies and obstructive ways which have so long debarred English students from their treasures.

Whilst we rejoice in the prospect that Italian scholars and scholarship, libraries and charter rooms, are likely to be open to us more generally, we may, I think, congratulate ourselves on having been able to do something for our Northern neighbours. The Icelandic Dictionary and the new recension of the *Sturlunga Saga,* which we have now in hand at the Press under the editorship of our friend Mr. Vigfusson, is surely an earnest of something yet to come. We are not so entirely disinterested in making these offerings to our Scandinavian kinsfolk : true we do not expect to make great discoveries of MS. treasures, although there are far more unlikely places than Drontheim and Upsala; but we hope to attract new friends to the study of our own history and theirs, the common points of external and internal development which the English here have with their kinsmen and the neighbours of their ancient home.

And whilst we look with hope and gratitude to these elder kinsfolk, we look with hope and gratitude too to our more modern cousins across the Atlantic. Why American historians like Prescott, Ticknor and Motley have chosen Belgian and Spanish History as their special field of work, it is not for me to decide. Possibly it is for the best, and the conviction that it is for the best for them to work in fields in which they are less liable to be entangled in the political quarrels, and made obnoxious to the political feelings of their own country and time, may have determined their choice. If an Englishman cannot write without prejudice about the Rebellion and the Commonwealth, much less can an American. But it is, I take it, a misfortune that the earlier English History has not received its share of attention in the United States. Very much of English life was ripe when it was transplanted thither, and belongs as much almost to them as to ourselves. Judging from the letters of friends and the American reviews of English books, I conceive that this is being amended, and that we may soon have reason to rejoice that American acuteness and industry are applying themselves to this region in which they will find so much to profit both themselves and us. The wonderful and successful labours of Colonel Chester in the minuter department of genealogical research, which have produced so noble a book as his Register of Westminster Abbey, may be another earnest of co-operation that will produce good fruits both here and there. We know that we are kinsfolk, that we have thirteen centuries of common Christian History and culture, and a remoter past common to a much larger family: we may hope that with a fair acquaintance with one another we may diverge no more widely, and never have to be ashamed of our connexion.

I must ask you to pardon me for making these remarks so desultory and so discursive, on the solemn occasion of a public lecture. I need hardly repeat that such solemn occasions are not the most congenial portion of my work here. But I have had somewhat to say, and you must take it as I could say it. If another ten years should see me here, solemnly lecturing from this desk, I shall have no doubt to look back on some anticipations frustrated, and to welcome fuller new opportunities which will have presented themselves. But neither occasional disappointment, nor distaste for peculiar parts of my work, will, I may venture to say, damp the ardour of my hopes for the future of historical study here, or my faith in the permanence and development of a great historical school in England, which will look to Oxford as an 'Alma Mater' and 'Fons Scientiarum.'

IV

ON THE PURPOSES AND METHODS OF
HISTORICAL STUDY

(May 15, 1877.)

LAST year, in fulfilment of my statutable obligation to deliver two solemn lectures annually on some subject of modern history or political biography, I took occasion of the fact that I was just completing my tenth year of service as Professor to discuss some of the more obvious phenomena which had, during the preceding ten years, marked the progress of Historical Study in Oxford first and in Europe generally. As is invariably the case when one has written a book or made a speech, subsequent reflexion, after no long time, brings home to one the conviction that, besides saying much that were better unsaid, one has left out very much that ought to have been said if the intention were to be realized with which the discussion was attempted. In this particular instance, I confess, one whole region of my subject was left out of sight: my object, indeed, was principally to view the extension and advance of the study, and it was only incidentally that I felt called upon to say a word here and there on the method and purposes of it. But, judging from the utterances which have recently, both before and after the delivery of those two lectures, fallen from the mouths of some of the most clever and cultivated men of this generation, it would appear that the method and purpose of historical

G

reading were points by no means second in interest to
the external development of the study of history.

These utterances are in themselves valuable as the mature
judgements of men who have at all events known how to
draw from history precious lessons on the subjects on which
they desired to be taught; but they have an additional
value in setting plainly before us, teachers of history, the
views which popular opinion and the men who lead popular
opinion upon educational matters formulate regarding the
pursuit to which we have devoted ourselves. To us a great
many of the statements, as well as of the theories, that find
enthusiastic echoes in mixed audiences, are apt to appear
either truisms, or fallacies, or both. In many of them there
is an apologetic tone which reminds us to some extent
of what we used to hear in common rooms when our
History school was first started, as if the study was one
that needed some vindication as a bona fide study, valuable
in itself and in its results, before it could be allowed to
compete with other older and more organized departments
of learning. And, as usual, when that is defended which
needs no defence, the theories of the advocate produce an
effect diametrically opposite to that which he intended;
he seems to hazard on the strength of some occasional or
adventitious argument the claim which on its own merits is
indisputable. Now far be it from me to attempt even to
gather up or analyse, much less to review, the deliberate and
elaborate utterances to which I have referred. I am not
going to answer or to refute them where they need refuta-
tion, or to use them to strengthen my own theories where
I agree with them : it may be enough to say that many of
them contain good and sound suggestions which recommend
themselves as soon as they are heard ; that others are
familiar as lecture-room words to all who have any experience in teaching ; and that the worst that can be justly

said of any of them is that they prescribe, for the general pursuit of the whole study of History, directions which are valuable in their way in relation to particular portions of it, or for particular purposes for which it may have been undertaken. Instead of reviewing them, then, I shall simply accept them as furnishing suggestions for a brief discussion on points on which it is my privilege to speak, and yours to judge whether what I have to say is worth saying. For I also will claim it as a professorial right to be allowed to utter truisms, and will claim, moreover, as one advantage accruing from our common heritage of error, that, if I utter fallacies, I may have the sympathy of men who know how easy it is, in matters where head and heart are alike engaged, to disparage truth by exaggeration.

Although I am not going to venture on any philosophical arrangement of my topics, or to lay down anything pretending to be a complete theory of the method of historical study, I will begin by saying that there are, as it seems to me, and as I doubt not it seems to you, three different sorts of object or aim in reading History: it may be read for its own sake, it may be learned as a mental discipline, and it may be acquired as a piece of the furniture or apparatus of cultivated life. I have used the words advisedly, for they imply, with diversity of object, diversity of method also. In the first aspect History assumes the dignity of a science, in the second it is a great engine of education, in the third it is in its higher forms a graceful and useful accomplishment, in its lower an indispensable requisite for every-day existence in a civilized country.

The three aims are not by any means incompatible, and the results are of course coincident so far as they go. He who reads History for its own sake gains the educational result in the process, and possesses in the fullest way the stock of knowledge which enables him to read his newspaper, to give his vote, or to pass his opinion on any new book. The man who has gone through the educational training will likewise be able to do these things, besides benefiting by that disciplinary and formative process that qualifies him to give a sound historical judgement on passing events. And it is no small advantage to be able to give an honest, really intelligent vote and to take an interest in a really interesting book. Only, the man who has only read History for the purpose of education has not entered into the fulness of the blessing of the man who reads it for its own sake, and the man who has learned it as he learns French or German from a travelling conversation book, does not gain either the formative effect on the judgement, or the great inheritance of scientific study. These points need no insisting upon; I merely state them to set us clear at starting, and to point out that the method which may be with advantage adopted for one of these purposes will not be applicable for the other two; popular lectures may serve admirably to the third object, but be absolutely useless as regards the second; careful study of isolated periods may suffice for the second, but will not satisfy the instincts that are aroused in the pursuit of the first. But I will not anticipate what ought to come later on.

In the distinction that I have drawn you will no doubt recognize your old friends, the professorial, the tutorial, and the popular view of history. I will so far admit the charge as to arrogate to myself the professorial right to make the first the largest half of my discussion, and devote this lecture to the first point, leaving the other two for the second. But there is a prior question, prior even to the assumption that History should be studied for its own sake: Is it worth studying at all? As I have said, the apologetic tone of many of its advocates renders it necessary that I should at once state why it needs no vindication. If man

is not, as we believe, the greatest and most wonderful of
God's works, he is at least the most wonderful that comes
within our contemplation; if the human will, which is the
motive cause of all historical events, is not the freest agent
in the universe, it is at least the freest agency of which we
have any knowledge; if its variations are not absolutely
innumerable and irreducible to classification, on the generalizations of which we may formulate laws and rules, and
maxims and prophecies, they are far more diversified and
less reducible than any other phenomena in those regions
of the universe that we have power to penetrate.   For one
great insoluble problem of astronomy or geology there are
a thousand insoluble problems in the life, in the character,
in the face of every man that meets you in the street.
Thus, whether we look at the dignity of the subject-matter,
or at the nature of the mental exercise which it requires,
or at the inexhaustible field over which the pursuit ranges,
History, the knowledge of the adventures, the development,
the changeful career, the varied growths, the ambitions,
aspirations, and, if you like, the approximating destinies
of mankind, claims a place second to none in the roll of
sciences.   Arising from one of the first and most anciently
cultivated instincts, the desire to know how we come to be
what we are, and how the world comes to be what it is,
the love of history is certainly second in origin to no other
sort of love of knowledge.   As a search for truth it tries
to investigate matters in which the truth may be more difficult to find than it is in mere matters of observation or
deduction, but surely its difficulty is not an argument for its
disparagement; as a hoarding up of knowledge, it collects
facts and records, the results of which are less exact than
those of strict science, but are not less precious even in the
eyes of the man who would regard them as mere engines of
power.   It is not true that written history is a mere tradition

of falsehoods, assumptions and illogical deductions, of what the writers believed, rather than of what they knew, and of what they wished to have believed rather than what was true; even if it were, it would be no reason why we should not do our best to unmask the falsehood and detect the fallacies. But we have all heard enough of that sort of thing before; there is, in the most exact science that has subject-matter at all, a mixture of the phenomenal and the real: even the falsehoods and misrepresentations of the record serve as a guide to the discovery of the truth of fact, and certainly serve to train the mind to distinguish historical truth.

Agreeing, then, that both for the great extent of its field of view, the grandeur of its subject-matter, the difficulty of its problems, and the value of its results, the study of history is worth pursuing; and that, for its own sake, not merely for its effects as an educational agent, or its usefulness in the business of life,—we may allow that, even for its own sake, it may be studied with some variety of aspect or approach. We may work simply for the love of discovery, that is the exercise of the investigative instinct and the pleasure of over-coming difficulties; or we may work with the beneficent idea of increasing the sum of human knowledge, or of unravel-ling the string which forms the clue to the history of human progress, or of making such generalizations as may constitute the laws of a new historic science. All these, and perhaps some other purposes may be arranged under our first head, because, although some of them may seem subsidiary to larger and wider general designs, they all have in common the belief in the real value of history itself. Of these purposes, the mere gratification of curiosity, even in its highest and most dignified form, ranks first and lowest; and yet without some infusion of it the genuine love of history is out of the question; and the usefulness of it, even in the humble office of providing materials for men who work with a higher purpose and idea, cannot be gainsayed. The mere archaeologist, the mere genealogist, the mere antiquary, are not the parasites of historical study, as they are too often regarded by men who find it easier to borrow than to estimate the results of their researches; they are working bees in the hive of historic knowledge.

And the curious fact that the contemptuous toleration of archaeological research is very often found in the speeches and writings of men who profess to set a high value on the study of original sources, a fact so curious as to lead to the conclusion that the critic is dealing on both hands with unknown quantities, may serve to lead on to the question, what are, and what is the value of the study of, original sources? We hear a great deal about them at the present day; not only are our bookshelves actually broken down with the weight of them, but the exact study of them is becoming a subordinate science with method and rules of its own, and with a great apparatus of material appliances in the shape of palaeographical tests; a science of historical palmistry, if that is the word, that attempts to refer, by distinctions of penmanship, parchment, paper, ink, illumination and abbreviation, every manuscript to its own country, district, age, school, and even individual writer. Truly we may say the study of Geschichtsquellen is not to be approached without clean hands and an open mind. And after the initial investigation comes the criticism; first we have to identify, then we have to value our historical inventory. Both these processes are involved in the study of original sources; it means not merely the reading, or the restriction of reading to, the primary authorities, but the weighing and critical analysis of the primary authorities themselves.

Perhaps you think that I am misusing terms when I speak of analysing primary authorities, but I will explain directly what I mean; only a word first on the interest and value of the processes I refer to. If I were drawing a comparison between ancient and mediaeval and modern history as re-munerative studies, this is probably the first point in which I should claim superior interest for the latter. In ancient history we have wonderful models of thoughtful writing, and ingenious record of primitive tradition, tradition at least that is so far primitive that to us no further analysis is possible. There are exceptional departments even here; recent discoveries in Assyriology and Egyptology are opening up regions of interest which appear to me to be absolutely beyond parallel or comparison; new records of most ancient life which not only lie out of the scope within which cri-ticism, up to the last twenty or thirty years, confined itself, but which must, if they be approached with due reverence and delicacy of touch, reveal a strange and hitherto unread stage of the world's History, and in it the springs of an older cultivation than we have been used to dwell upon, and the links that bind the great civilizations of the Western world with the earliest, but not perhaps less magnificent, civilizations of the East. In these we may hope one day to read a new and clear page of the fair record of human history, of which we have bright but unconnected glimpses in the incidental notices of Holy Scripture. But outside of these, and the study of them is to most of us only in its beginning, the study of ancient History is mainly the study of classical History; and in classical History, splendid as our materials are, they have been in our hands for ages. Every bone of the great skeleton has long been put into its place: criticism upon it is becoming more and more every year the rearrange-ment of the critical material collected long ago, or the recon-struction of the History with all the charm which novel treatment, without novel material, can supply. Unluckily we can only, in a very fragmentary way, trace back, in commenting on Herodotus or Livy, the actual line of tradition by which they received what they report to us; as to Thucydides and Tacitus the chain is less fragmentary, and, of course, in the narrative of contemporary writers we look less for traces of earlier authority than for traces of sympathy and antipathy, personal knowledge and direct authenticity. But, as a rule, we may say the study of ancient classical History lies within a confined area, every manuscript, every inscription, every coin, and every map of which has long been known, into which rash speculation never ventures without having cause for bitter repentance, and in which anything like a new discovery, such as the recent finds at Troy and Mycenae, is so very new, that when it does come to pass no one knows what to make of it. The very definiteness of all connected with this study makes it, for educational purposes, an incomparable discipline. As a study of knowledge for its own sake, as a field of discovery and profitable speculation, as a department in which the sum of human knowledge is likely to be largely increased, I confess I think that it promises perhaps less than the study of later History. As a ground for fresh and remunerative exploration, I am sure it is still less promising.

To return, however, to the original sources. We all know how large a debt modern and mediaeval History owes to the ecclesiastical writers. From the very beginning of the middle ages, Annals, Chronicles, and Histories poured in comparative abundance from the religious houses of England and the Continent, records which serve to check and correct one another at almost every turn, and which, for some of the more dramatic incidents of History, enable us to reconstruct a picture of the event, viewed by different minds from different points and in different lights, in a

perfection which has no parallel at all in ancient history.
Such, for instance, is the picture of the life and death of
Becket; some great scenes in the life of Simon de Montfort;
some portions of the history of the Norman Conquest. I
mention these, not only because they are well known, but
because they lie within the region for our knowledge of
which we are altogether indebted to ecclesiastical writers.
Now these ecclesiastical writers have for the most part
two great points of interest in the direction of research.
All, or almost all, are members of religious houses, and all
are members of a great fraternity in close and direct correspondence. The annalist is the annalist of his monastery
or his cathedral; his monastery or his cathedral has had
a history, has records, charters, a library, a scriptorium for
multiplying copies of records, perhaps a school of annalists
of which the representative man appropriates and assimilates
the labours. He is a member of a great fraternity of news-
mongers; every visitor to the monastery, every pilgrim, every
journey of the abbot or bishop up to parliament, every letter
from abroad, contributes something to the multifarious store.
Such a chronicle as that of Matthew Paris contains every one
of those elements and perhaps more; he was an antiquary,
zealous of the history and fame of his own monastery, skilled
in charters and in everything bearing on its origin and
growth, the position of its estates, and the character of its
inmates: he was a compiler who appropriated and digested
the work of a whole school of earlier annalists; he was
an eye-witness of much that he records of contemporary
history, acquainted with the great men of the day; he
had travelled and learned much, he had stayed at home
and learned more, asking questions of every one who came
down that way. Matthew Paris is an original authority;
but what a fine subject for analysis; what an admirable
corpus for the Kritik der Quellen! Further back you have

what is called the Anglo-Saxon Chronicle; one of the first set of books that was subjected to the process of speculative analysis, now fifty years ago, by a gentleman who dissected it out of his own consciousness. Our Professor of Anglo-Saxon has shown us what may be done in a part of the field of criticism on the Chronicle, by study of a small number of MSS. and dialectic differences. But there is still probably, in the region of Cartularies and Acta Sanctorum, and in the more minute study of other MSS., something to be done even for this. I may perhaps be allowed to point to my own edition of the Dunstan Memorials as showing, not any completeness of treatment, for I do not pretend to have effected that, but the singular variety and peculiar interest of the fields of investigation in which new discoveries may be expected.

This sort of study has two great charms, besides the value of the results; in common, to compare small things with great, with the discoveries of natural science—botany, for instance. In one way we take a historical series of events and work out the known items of the series, and range the persons and places of our action, until we know where to look for the missing links, and go to look for them and find them. Such a success, and every student of original sources working with zeal and modesty may hope for such, is in a small way like that of the astronomer who, when from calculating the perturbations and so on of the heavenly bodies he has inferred the existence of a hitherto unknown planet, some bright evening and with a new improved glass discovers the real planet of which he has been thinking, and sees in it, not only a great new fact of science, but a proof of the correctness of his computations, a substantial reward for his efforts. And the other is that in every such search, be it successful or not, the inquirer, who is wide awake, is sure to come upon material that is even more valuable than what he looks for; makes discoveries that are not less delightful because they are accidental.

Of course it may be said that a great deal of useless knowledge is accumulated in this way; what good can be done, it may be said, by analysing Matthew Paris, and determining how much of his narrative is drawn from ancient charters, or foreign letters, lives of saints, or such stribiligines: it is his historic power and authority that gives them value, not they that give authority to him. Not quite so, I think, and even if it were so, there might be a lesson in the mere proof of the fact; the analysis is necessary for the due estimate of his value as a historian; the writer who can pass such an ordeal where it is possible to apply it, may be trusted where it is not possible to apply it. But I take the higher ground and say, how far can any knowledge be said to be useless? there may be much useless learning, I allow; accumulations of other men's thoughts, and crude heaps of second-hand memories that are alike useless to their owner and to the world. But not real knowledge, not a substantiated fact, however remote it may seem from the interests and uses of the day, or the object of the day. It may serve to complete a chain of demonstration, the necessity of which is not as yet apparent; it may furnish, as an undesigned coincidence, an important element in a discussion yet in its elementary stages. How great is the debt that History owes to the ant-like instincts of collectors of memoranda, the recorders of births, deaths, and marriages, the savers of old letters and old newspapers, of the very things that seemed most useless. If there is any useless knowledge in History, we may say,—as Dr. Maitland said, when people talked of the Dark Ages, they meant the ages that were dark to them,—the uselessness of the knowledge is generally the fault of those who do not know how to use it.

It would be doing great injustice, however, to my subject if I were to lead you to suppose that I regard the great benefit arising from the study of original materials to lie in the gratification of our natural instinctive desire to get to the bottom of a thing. I suppose that such an instinct is given us for some good end, and that that which lies at the bottom of the historical well is historical truth: Truth that defies the all-dissolving processes of criticism, or at least such an approach to truth as may be credited to a record incapable of further analysis. The results of such minute study are the little pebbles of the concrete in which the foundations of the historic superstructure are laid. Every great historian has been his own Dry-as-dust, however much he may, as Carlyle does, point the moral of the lesson of labour with small type and inverted commas; for, I take it, the prophet does not adopt this plan as a means of disguise, but rather to show that to a great extent historical genius consists in an unlimited capacity for taking pains. The man who has, out of independent study, produced such results, has made a contribution, small or great as the case may be, to the great stock of sound material which constitutes real knowledge.

This consciousness may be its own reward; but, as I said before, if the love of history for its own sake goes no further, such ambition ranks among the lowest forms of the historical spirit. We take a real pleasure not only in cutting out our sound and perfect stone, but in fitting it into its place in the building: we wish to increase the sum of human knowledge not only by the accumulation of facts but by following them up and making them a part of history. The botanist is charmed when he finds a new plant, and the astronomer when he discovers a new star, but we scarcely should call the one a botanist or the other an astronomer if he did not straightway go and fit in his discovery into the general system of his science, reunite the missing plant to its kinsfolk in genus, and species and variety, or find out the relation of his star to the rest, and assign it to its group and class in the map of the heavens. And I think that the somewhat compassionate condescension with which archaeological inquiry is now and then spoken of, and the study of original sources also, is owing to the fact that so many inquirers do' stop at some such point: hence it is that people are constantly discovering things which have often been discovered before, and trumpeting as new results of research points of fact that have long been ticketed and set in their places in books where they could easily have found them. The study of original sources is thus taken to mean the study of nothing else; a pursuit accordingly which has no other result than the gratification, by a laborious process, of a curiosity that might have been gratified by reference to a cyclopaedia, or the amount of training, not itself to be despised if it be regarded merely as training, which makes the fact that one has worked out for himself infinitely more precious than one that he has simply looked out in the dictionary.

But I am not speaking now of the educational aspect of the subject. Let it suffice to say, that original sources to be studied remuneratively must be approached with all the apparatus and all the appliances that previous inquirers have accumulated for the illustration of them. If that be not done, we shall share the fate of the astronomer who searches for a new planet with the naked eye, and the mathematician who discovers perpetual motion.

And so we may go on to another point. The student of History, for its own sake, may approach his subject with the desire of adding to the mass of human knowledge by the ascertaining of truths hitherto imperfectly apprehended ; the completing of series of developments, or delineations of character, or the explanations of out-of-the-way regions, or the rehabilitation and analysis of traditions. In these points he has a wide field of interest, and a most remunerative sphere of study in exercise and result.

But here we come upon another primary question, Is all History equally valuable? You may say to me, we have accepted your assertion that no knowledge is useless, except by the fault of the person who possesses it; but it does not follow that all is equally useful or equally valuable in itself. What history is the best worth studying for its own sake? Now to answer that question fully would take a long time, and involve a discussion, not only on the nature of History, but on its co-ordination with other branches of human knowledge, such as moral philosophy and theology, carrying us into regions into which I cannot offer to guide you, and must refer you to the philosophers. But if you will be satisfied with a simple answer, I will say that the true field of Historic study is the history of those nations and institutions in which the real growth of humanity is to be traced: in which we can follow the developments, the retardations and perturbations, the ebb and flow of human progress, the education of the world, the leading on by the divine light from the simplicity of early forms and ideas where good and evil are distinctly marked, to the complications of modern life, in which light and darkness are mingled so intimately, and truth and falsehood are so hard to distinguish, but in which we believe and trust that the victory of light and truth is drawing nearer every day. The most precious Histories are those in which we read the successive stages of God's dispensations with man, the growth of the highest natures, under the most favourable circumstances, in the most fully developed institutions, in the successive contributions which those natures, regions and institutions have furnished to the general welfare of the whole.

But I can hear at least one critic say, Is not this assuming the truth of a doctrine that you are always practically denying, that the very designation of your professorship, your very *raison d'être*, forces you to deny—the Unity of History,

the Continuity of Historic growth, the Education of the
world? Well, if the Unity of History means what I have
said, I certainly believe in it : but that is not the meaning
which is commonly attached to the term, and it is not the
meaning in which I have so often had to do battle with the
idea. The false idea, or that which to me seems practically
misleading in the term the Unity of History, is the acceptance
as a practical rule or maxim that there are no new points of
departure in human history ; that modern life is a continuation of mediaeval, of ancient and mediaeval, history, by a
continuity and unity that is at all points equally important, of
the same consistency in fact. Now this idea has a truth
only in the very highest regions of speculation. Every
human soul has an equal value in the eyes of the Christian
missionary and religious philosopher, but every human life
does not convey lessons of the same practical value to the
social investigator ; every national history does not contribute
equally valuable results towards the general progress of mankind, and so neither does every chronological epoch. That
perhaps we all allow. Why then should not cycles of
history, two, three, or more cycles of history, be allowed to
exist, within which all the really important factors have their
origin and development, and, it may be, work out their full
destiny ; successive great dramas of ages, the interest of
which is self-contained, although there is enough of common
ground between them and those which precede and follow
to give them a simple continuity, and although there is
doubtless in the divine mind one great plan of cosmical
action in which each drama of the human ages serves as a
single act or even a single incident ? Let scripture history,
classical and ecclesiastical history, mediaeval history and
modern history, be read successively and connectedly, so
much the better ; but why deny that classical history and
mediaeval and modern can be advantageously studied apart ?

why confine the thoughts to the points on which they are conterminous, continuous and agreed, to the exclusion of those in which they differ, when it is on the points in which they differ that the great contributions to the real history of man are to be traced? In any other sense than that in which I have attempted to limit it and have accepted it, the Unity of History is either the crotchet of a sciolist, or the dream of a universal philosopher.

For just think how the field of view expands; we can never know one thing perfectly unless we know everything; true, but we can try to learn here and there a thing as perfectly as it can be learned, without knowing everything. In the same sense in which the careful study of ancient history is absolutely necessary to the careful study of modern history, the careful study of the latter is absolutely necessary to that of the former. If you read the second alone, where do you find your causes? If you read the first alone, where do you find your consequences? Just in the same way, it may be said, the external history of man cannot be read without an internal reading of his history; no man can approach History without being a consummate moral philosopher; yet is it so? Then most of the great historians of the world have been great moral philosophers without knowing it. But how can a man pretend to understand the moral conformation of his fellows without knowing their physical conformation? Then the moral philosopher must be an anatomist, and the anatomist a chemist, a botanist and geologist, and the geologist an astronomer; i.e. instead of borrowing, and being content to borrow from the kindred and allied sciences what is necessary for the consistent pursuit of our own study, we must know the principles of all, like the sophists of old, and we all know what that ends in, κακῶς ἠπίστατο πάντα. But my friend says, exaggeration is no argument, an answer which, by-the-by, may tell either

H

way : ancient, and modern and mediaeval history, as you call
them, have the same subject-matter, they are connected by
certain visible and tangible lines of recorded fact, and they
are, as yourself admit, acts of one great drama. Granted :
first then, ancient history has much that is common with
modern in the region of political thought; second then, the
ancient Roman civilization and literature constitute by themselves, and they are but one of many, a sufficient line of
continuity to prove essential identity ; third, but it is enough
for you to admit the continuity of the world's progress.

Now, if I were arguing against the reading of ancient
history in connexion with modern, such an answer would be
complete ; but, as I am merely protesting against the idea
that it is impossible to read modern history from its own
starting-point, I will observe, and content myself with observing, first that there are no doubt political thoughts common
to ancient and modern life ; nay more, that, as has been said,
there is very much that is modern in ancient history and
much that is ancient in modern history; and yet that that
very element of continuity on which the whole discussion
hangs is wanting. There may be, I will not say there is, a
certain similarity of thought in a leading article of *The Times*
and a chapter in Thucydides : the similarity of the circumstances of two political crises may bring out parallels and
coincidences ; Constantinople may be the Athens, Alexander
II the Xerxes of the day, and anyhow the Bosphorus must
be pretty nearly where it was. But the connexion of the
political ideas is one of coincidence and not of continuity ;
there is not even the life that germinates in the grains of
wheat found in Egyptian mummy-pits. Every factor is new,
even the area, the nationality of the actors, the whole idea in
its origin and every stage of growth is new. Or let the area
be the same ; what has modern Greece in continuity with
ancient Greece, but the soil and sky and the, to it, un-

intelligible wreck of ancient magnificence, from which it fails apparently to draw even the ordinary lessons of civilization? what period and region of the whole history of the world conveys a less important lesson than Greece during the Middle Ages of European History? It is scarcely less so with Italy, except for the fact that during a great part of those ages Italy was the centre and stage of Ecclesiastical History, in which, as I shall point out directly, and in which alone, on any large or broad scale, the unity and continuity are to be found.

The vital interest of Mediaeval and Modern History lies in England, France and Germany, as certainly as that of the ancient lies in the East, in Greece and Italy; no small part of that of the future lies in the further Western world. The actors in the mediaeval and modern drama are the new nations, nations that were unheard of before the decline of the Roman empire began, and which inherited from the civilization of that empire only the ecclesiastical culture, not the political system, or even the political map, which that system had laid out. The ideas of mediaeval and modern life are of mediaeval and modern growth, or if connected with antiquity, connected by a new birth of culture, a re-discovery, a re-creation, not a continuous impulse of vitality. Save in the one region, that of the History of Religion, Ecclesiastical History; yet in that also the one great fact of the Christian dispensation, which connects the ancient Hebrew isolation with the great Catholic Church life, is itself as much a break as a link of continuity; so immensely does the new transcend the old, that, in the apostle's words, old things are passed away and behold all things are become new. The Unity and Continuity of Ancient and Modern History is an idea which is realized on a great and intelligible scale in Ecclesiastical History only; and even there the unity is to some extent a unity of ideas, a coincidence of religious and moral motive influences, and not merely of historic continuity. It is in it that the continuity of the Latin civilization, of the Holy Roman Empire and of the Latin language, Roman Law and Latin literature, is traceable, and to it that we owe them. To it, or to influences which it nourished or provoked, we owe the renaissance, that revival of ancient culture the very title of which is a denial of the continuity which its influences seem to claim for it. But I am not going to usurp the functions of a Professor of Church History, and I am very sure that Church History is not the ground on which the doctrine of the Unity of History is supposed by its advocates to take its stand.

One word more ; I do not deny this Unity in the high region of religious History or in the scarcely less comprehensive grasp which the political philosopher may take of Universal Human Life ; nor do I deny it in the minute archaeological investigations in which all particulars great and small have much the same value ; nor do I deny that the student of modern history may gain lessons of immense value from the old. But I do maintain that it is wrong to say that the one cannot be studied without the other ; for the things, persons, ideas, plot and scenery are different in the two ; and more than that, save in the region of Church History, the precious lessons of the two are not those in which the approximate continuity may be traced : the continuity lies in the less important, the great contributions of either to the world's growth lie in the less continuous influences ; in the ancient world in a perished civilization, in the modern world in one in which all the fresh springs are, by God's grace, in the new races.

You will, I hope, acquit me now of any desire to undervalue any kind of culture ; but, put upon our defence, we must maintain the strong point, as it seems to us, of our position ; and it is our duty, as well as our right, to say what we think. Most successful teachers of Modern History have passed through the gate of the ancient lore; but if they would look the truth in the face, they would see that the help which that ancient lore gave to the study of the modern, was first in the discipline of the mind, for which it furnishes an incomparable exercise, and secondly in the wealth of illustration with which it provides them; but the illustrations are not links in a historic chain, and the fact that the discipline of the mind has been beneficial by no means implies that the powers cultivated in the two studies are the same, or the method of the one applicable, without much modification, to the exploration of the other. And this is a point which is scarcely less important than the more ostensible and obvious one on which I have dwelt so long.

The method of historic investigation is different in the two or three regions which we have been comparing. Of that I have said something in reference to original sources, and I may have to say something more in reference to the educational view of Historic study. I will not therefore dwell upon it now; but rest content to base my argument on what I have said; that is, the Unity and Continuity are only traceable in the high regions which belong to other sciences and other studies, or in the lower departments of minute archaeology; it is well to abstract, and well to make our own generalizations in the realms that are common to the two, but it is a poor result if, after fixing our thoughts on the things in which they agree and excluding those in which they differ, we find that we have come to generalizations that might be discovered by intuition and cast away differences in which all that is new and true and precious was inherent.

But thus I come to the region of abstractions and generalizations, and to the old question, How about the science of

History? As I hope I made clear before, I do not intend this lecture to be a systematic exposition of my own views or any one else's; and I certainly do not intend to attempt an analysis of History as the subject-matter of a science or philosophy. I am only trying, if possible, to adjust my own impressions to the maxims of our theoretical instructors, and to say a word or two on subjects which recent discussions suggest. It certainly seems curious that, although the advocates of the Unity and Continuity of History, and the believers in the science and philosophy of History, imagine themselves to be diametrically opposed to one another, the weakness of their respective positions seems to be the same. Both prefer to work out generalizations and collect coincidences, rather than to study the drama in its plot and personnel; both decline to look at the subject, as we might say, all round. It is true that this is a fault of theory rather than of practice: a really good historian may, as we all know, combine an earnest faith in the Unity of History with a power of creating most exact and minute reproductions of periods, scenes and characters; and such an advocate might almost convince us of the truth of his doctrine, because his practice is so completely free from the faults which that doctrine seems to the outside critic to involve. I am perhaps in error too on the other side, in speaking of the Science of History and the Philosophy of History in one breath; for certainly there is a Philosophy of History which is not content with abstractions, but busies itself with following up causes and following out consequences, goes behind the scenes of the drama as well as directs a microscopic vigilance on the stage; and there is a sense in which the Unity of History is itself a Philosophy of History. I will then leave out the Philosophy of History, and finish the lecture with a few words on the theory of a science of History.

Shall I be saying too much if I say at once that one great objection to the very idea of reducing History to the lines and rules of exact science lies in the fact I have already stated, that generalizations become obscurer and more useless as they grow wider, and, as they grow narrower and more special, cease to have any value as generalizations at all? Is not a historical science liable, if it can be elaborated at all, to become on the one hand a mere table of political formulae and on the other a case-book of political casuistry? And, in either case, is it not as a mere political weapon that it is sought for, not as an increase of knowledge, not as an investigation of truth, nor as a study of History for its own sake? And is not the fact that the idea of a science of History finds acceptation, not among practical historians, but among high-paced theorists, a proof that such a possibility belongs to theory and not to practice; that it is aimed at as a new grace for the all-accomplished doctrinaire, rather than as an object to be sought by those who seek after wisdom?

There were days, centuries ago, when the schoolmen fancied that they could bring into class and line all human knowledge, and encroach to some extent upon the divine, by syllogisms and conversions and oppositions. Much precious knowledge those men handed down to us, with much verbiage and false logic; but even they for the most part left History alone. They ticketed every portion of man's moral anatomy, found a rule for every possible case of choice, a reason and a reward for every virtue, and a punishment for every conceivable crime; they turned generalizations into laws, and deduced from them as laws the very facts from which they had generalized. They benefited mankind by exercising and training subtle wits, and they reduced dialectics, almost, we might say, logic itself, to absurdity. I do not undervalue them, because the

great men among them were so great that even such a
method did not destroy them : in reading Thomas Aquinas,
for instance, one is constantly provoked to say, What could
not such a mind have done if it had not been fettered by
such a method?

Such, I imagine, must be the result of every attempt to
substitute abstract reasonings for minute examination of
facts in the study of History.   History repeats itself we
know, parallels and cycles recur, the speculative mind can
evaluate the curve in which political progress moves, trace
the contortions of the unruly spiral, and eschew a cusp as
a historic anomaly.   But the dealings of human wills, in
countless combinations, and circumstances which no theory
can ever exhaustively calculate, are not the field for dogmatic assumption or for speculative classification.   Perhaps
you may think that I am talking at random, that no people
ever were so foolish as to suppose that even an exhaustive
knowledge of past history could enable a man to prophesy;
for such should be the result of a scientific treatment, even
if the subject-matter be akin rather to the subject-matter
of meteorology than to that of astronomy.   It may be so ;
but the idea is not strange.   Experience of life, it is argued,
qualifies us for dealing with men ; knowledge of human
history must qualify us for calculating on the results of even
historical contingencies ; the practical politician can arrange
the factors of his problem so as to work out the solution
beforehand ; the theoretic explorer of History may so
manipulate his factors as to provide for every conceivable
combination.   Again, I say, it may be so ; but not in the
regions of life that are worthy of real study ; vague generalizations may form the stock-in-trade of the political empiric,
but he is an empiric notwithstanding ; readiness of observation and fertility of expedient, political genius, the power
that interprets events and realizes character and motive,

are not the result of abstraction even from universal
reading.

I grant that genius may do great things with poor instruments and out of small materials.   But the scientific
triumphs of genius all imply minute knowledge as well as
the power of grasping the idea.   Owen, from a single bone,
could reproduce an entire archaic animal, the real existence
of which later discovery vindicated : in that great exploit of
scientific genius, there was not only consummate grasp of
the idea but enormous knowledge of mechanical anatomy :
he did not elaborate the beast out of his own consciousness,
nor make a lucky guess; but he looked at his bone all
round, and saw its mechanical capabilities, and realized the
idea which only could explain the possession of such capabilities.   So, to some extent, the historical genius can reconstruct character.   From a very incomplete study of
History Scott could create a Richard, the truth of whose
portraiture careful historical scrutiny seems to assure.   Out
of an enormous amount of material, Carlyle reconstructs
for us Frederick William I of Prussia, a living, moving, tantalizing reality.   In both there is the eye and the hand of
genius, different as is the workmanship, distinct as is the
result.   But although genius can reconstruct character, it
cannot reconstruct events : it flashes its lightning into the
dark, and for the moment we see battles and alliances, life
and death, growth and decline of heroes, cities and nations ;
but it would require many such flashes to produce one permanent impression ; and for even an approach to an understanding of the vision we must go down and map out the
land, photograph the heroes, and classify the populations of
the cities.   Patient study may not have much to do with
genius ; it has less to do with generalizations : but without
patient study genius will flash with no productive efficacy,
and generalizations will become mere formulae, useful neither

to teachers nor to learners, neither to statesmen nor to scholars ; and even with patient study, what results ? Surely that scientific generalizations are but by-play, diversions and amusements, not real lessons : formulae that are convenient for a moment now and then, but quite unsafe as implements of investigation or even as helps for memory : truisms, or fallacies, or both : or if containing truth, or aiming at universality, diluting the truth until it is useless ; assuming a universality of rule which, when it comes to be applied, is met with a universality of exception.

There is a ' One in History ' as a One in Nature, but it is not shown to the man whose idea of science is confined to making his inventory or ticketing compartments of his cabinet, even if the mechanism of his museum be ever so complete, unless he has studied and learned well the conformation and individual histories of the specimens which he attempts to classify. Sometimes men classify the specimens which other men have collected, and claim the character of philosophers without any direct acquaintance with materials at all.

METHODS OF HISTORICAL STUDY

(May 18, 1877.)

IN my Lecture delivered the other day, in the discharge of a duty which, in the case of a Professor who is willing to work, might well be dispensed with, I attempted to arrange some few thoughts on the subject of Historical study which had occurred to me, on some sort of a plan, carefully disavowing however any attempt at complete or even systematic treatment; I used the division of the subject which I then proposed, simply as furnishing pegs on which to hang divers desultory observations. The principle of division which I adopted was merely this; that we should view our subject in three lights; first looking on the study of History as pursued for its own sake, secondly regarding it as an instrument of education or training of the mind, and thirdly regarding it in reference to the ulterior uses to which the results of such study could be most advantageously applied; in other words, the student or professorial view, the educatorial or tutorial view, and the popular or utilitarian view. Without, as I said, attempting any systematic treatment, I made the question of History for its own sake an occasion of saying a word or two on the current ideas touching the study; the investigation of original materials, the doctrine of the necessary unity and continuity of History, and the much-debated possibility of the creation of a science of History, in the sense of science which involves the discovery of general laws and the classification of human wills and events out of which the men of the future may prophesy. I have still the other two heads of my division to trifle with, and, as it is now too late to modify my plan, I can only ask for your tolerant attention, and proceed, in the hope that what I may have to say on the practical work of the subject may be better worth saying than what I said on the theory of it, a speculation on speculations.

The first point to be stated in relation with the second head of discussion has merely to be stated ; supposing that the study of History is useful as an educational instrument, that is, not only as providing stores of knowledge or amassing tools for future use, but as having a disciplinary and formative virtue, what part of the mind is it on which the disciplinary process acts, and what power or virtue may it be supposed to develop by training?   It is perhaps unnecessary for me to say more than this, that I regard the judicial faculty, 'judgement,' as in vulgar unphilosophical language we call it, as that on which historical study produces the most valuable results ; I have so often said this from this desk that I feel shy of repeating it ; but it does not appear to me to be less true than it did the first time I said it.   The study of the early stages of that history in whose later stages we know ourselves to be personally interested, the study of the modern world of which we are parts, as distinguished from that of the ancient world which, except as a matter of culture, is dead to us, affords room for the development of an equitable as well as an unbiassed judgement, which is a great advantage in itself and may be of great practical use in the world.   The exclusive study of the more modern phases of history has a tendency to make men partisans or advocates ; but the study of the periods just a generation or two further removed produces far more effect on the judgement ; and the study of mediaeval History, that is, of the ages in which the things that are precious to us were rooted and sprang up, but had not yet entered into the phases in which controversy is most bitter, or in which the political questions of the day are most directly engaged, has always seemed to me to furnish very good training; to enable us to approach questions in which we are ourselves engaged, with moderate and cautious treatment, to allow some of them to wait for solution, to determine others by the evidence of fact rather than by prepossession, and to let others alone altogether. Ancient History exercises the critical faculty in a comparatively narrow and exhausted field, although, as a matter of training, every student has to go over the field and exhaust its interest for himself before he gets the benefit of what he is reading; mere modern politics, as I have said, furnish training only, and that incomplete training, for the advocate and partisan; the intermediate region is that in which real personal interest may be strongly engaged without much temptation to passionate controversy, and in which therefore the judgement may be best trained for its own perfect development, and for the uses of practical politics when the time for practical controversy and advocacy comes. We learn patience, tolerance, respect for conflicting views, equitable consideration for conscientious opposition; we see how very differently the men of the particular time seem to have read the course of events, which seem to us to have only one reasonable bearing; we see how good and evil mingle in the best of men and in the best of causes; we learn to see with patience the men whom we like best often in the wrong, and the repulsive men often in the right; we learn to bear with patience the knowledge that the cause which we love best has suffered, from the awkwardness of its defenders, so great disparagement as in strict equity to justify the men who were assaulting it; we learn too, and this is not the least of the lessons, that there are many points on which no decision as to right or wrong, good or evil, acquittal or condemnation, is to be looked for; and on which we may say that, as often the height of courage is to say I dare not, and the height of love is to say I will not, so the height of wisdom is to have learned to say, I do not know. I will however leave this point, as it is one on which I may have to say a word under my third head.

The next point after determining the nature of the disciplinary value ascribed to historical study, especially modern historical study, is the question of method. And as I have already said that it does not follow that the best method of studying History in one aspect is the best way of studying it in the other two, I will, for the sake of simplicity, go directly to our own idea of teaching in this place as exemplified in the Examination Statute. That statute was the result of a good deal of consideration and discussion between men of very different views and extent of experience, and I do not know that I should venture to say that it is incapable of improvement; but it has worked well, and any improvement that may be made in it must be made on the lines of its own plan, which seem to me complete. I take it, however, as a peg for more general remarks. The main feature of it is, as you are doubtless aware, the threefold division into, first, a continuous reading of our national History, second, an epochal treatment of a portion of general European History, and thirdly, the special study of some character or period in the original authorities. The plan thus aims at realizing two of the ideas which I discussed the other day, although of course only by way of introduction to the larger fulfilment of the promise; it attempts in the continuous reading of one subject to convey the lesson of continuity, and in the special subject to invite the student to see what original sources are like, and what is the pleasurable work of studying them.

Now I am not quite sure that our way of studying the special subject is exactly the best method of beginning work on original authorities, but it may very well be the best that we can incorporate in a plan of gaining, in a year and a half's reading, a mental training, or the beginning of a mental training that may serve a lifetime. I am not sure that it would not be more true to the idea, to require the student to read a single book and explore its mechanism and materials, rather than to set before him a character or institution and bid him look for illustration for it in a particular set of books; but it must be remembered that the immediate object of the reading is to meet the test of examination, and that it would be almost impossible to examine, on one set of questions, a set of men all of whom had been working from different points; for essay writing it might be invaluable training, but for collective examination it would be unreasonable. I will, then, content myself with remarking that the special subject in the class schools should be regarded only as a starting-point in independent research; a sort of first step in the study of original sources, which we hope may lead on to further and deeper investigation, but which, as it has to serve two purposes, can scarcely be likely to satisfy both; it is a specimen of minute study, and it is a specimen of original reading; but the object of the minute study is not the book, but the hero or the plot of it. It is, however, most encouraging to those who have the future of our History school at heart to know that the treatment of the special subject is always one of the best features of our examination ; that in which the best side of the mind of each examinee is as a rule most distinctly shown. Regarded then as a study of a subject, rather than as a first step into the region of original authorities, this part of our work exemplifies one of two diametrically opposed

methods of reading. And, whether there is or is not
a science of History, and I believe that in the reasonable
and intelligible sense of the word there is such a science,
there is, I am sure, an art of writing History and an art
of reading it; and the educational use of it is an exempli-
fication of the art.

According to this, the reader or the writer may set
before himself two opposite ideas; he may either wish to
produce an historical statue or group of statuary, we may
say, or he may wish to produce a historical picture. In
the former case he has to look out his materials first,
then to construct from the careful view of them an idea
or model of the object which he desires to reproduce, and
then to work out his idea. It is necessary for him to look
at his subject all round, to finish it off completely at every
point, and, while seeking for statuesque unity and perfection,
to make truth and reality the first object. Everything
that in the remotest way bears upon the history of the
person or institution that he is describing, has its special
value; original sources, the verdict of other historians,
tradition, popular conceptions, poetic idealizing; the place
which his object has occupied in the development of historical life, the results which historical experience has
produced or may have produced upon the object; every
species of illustration derivable from archaeology, genealogy,
law, morals, and religious history, will have to be ransacked.
The result will then, if the writer has chosen his subject well,
and with a due estimate of his own powers, be an artistic
unity, a perfect image, true to its author's idea, and, if he
has not let his own idea prejudice him in the manipulation of
his materials, true to the reality, so far as the reality can be
discovered. It is of course in the life-like portraiture of
great men that success of this sort is most frequently achieved,
for it is in the realizing of grand character that the strength

of historical genius chiefly displays itself. But the same method may be applied to an institution that has a well-ascertained growth, and the result in that case will certainly be not less valuable. Still there are certain unities of time, place, and interest, which are more readily united in biography than in institutional history. As valuable History may be so written, so a good deal of History may be so read, in a way, that is, to produce in the mind a perfect image of the character worth studying; nay, the method is more applicable to the reading than to the writing of History, because it is easier for the mind to receive successive images or phases of the one character, than it is for the writer to reproduce them without becoming tedious; the realization in the mind may easily be a regular and orderly development, whilst in the written record of even the best historian it is liable to become a series of postures and attitudes, attended by tricks and mannerisms of style that are unworthy of the serious student.

The second form of our art is analogous to painting, and its result to a picture; it aims at reproducing not a character or a life, but a situation; it requires a background and a foreground, scenery and perspective, as well as unity and symmetry; it studies the relations and positions, the features and habit of each of the persons or groups that the picture contains, and tries to make them true to the eye, whatever they may be to the life. Thoroughness and complete realization is not a requisite of this sort of work quite so much as accurate reproduction. The painter is not, like the statuary, obliged to look at his figures all round; he need not go to the back of his picture, or if he does, he will see nothing : so the historian, who works at a situation, will often satisfy himself if his grouping is true and consistent for the moment which he wishes to seize; and he will not spend much time in trying to show us how the scene comes to be what it is, satisfied

I

that his reproduction is an adequate representation of what
it seemed to be. The result will have its value ; for first, the
work need not be a whit less conscientious because it is less
deep and searching ; and, secondly, because the good work-
man will only try to reproduce scenes that are worth
describing ; the good painter will not waste his genius on
revolting or worthless subjects, and the historian of true
genius will choose for the employment of his genius scenes
from history that may read good and noble lessons to the
world that reads him. Such historical writing is far more
brilliant, if it is well done, than that which I mentioned
first ; but, like everything that is brilliant, it is liable to be
counterfeited. Sensational and picturesque writing satisfies
the popular taste, and sensational and picturesque writing,
adopted as an historical style, is very apt to corrupt and
destroy the more valuable features of painstaking and conscientious truthfulness. Popularity is nowhere a greater
snare than it is in this region of work ; and magazine articles,
and review articles, the romance of History, and historic
scenes and characters, are produced with great facility when
the principal object is to attract the half-educated to read.
But, notwithstanding this, both the writing and the study
of History in this way has a great value, if it enables the
student to realize the situations more vividly, to put himself
in the place, so to speak, of his characters, and to represent
to his mind's eye, for the purpose of forming an equitable
judgement, the several circumstances of the case on which he
is trying to adjudge, in somewhat the same way as that
in which his characters themselves might have seen them.
I should say, then, read history now and then with a view to
the picturesque, but do not read it too much, and do not
read it at second-hand ; do not write it, or dwell too much
on the pictures which are not drawn by the first masters ; try
to reproduce, not to copy.

A third form of the art, which combines and adds to these two, borrows its analogue from the domain of another of the arts, and attempts to read not only character and situation but plot also; and this, I need hardly say, is in result at least very far in value beyond the other two. It involves the complete identification of persons, and the complete realization of relations; of persons identified through long historical careers, and of relations varying from moment to moment during the long periods over which the drama extends. It can perhaps afford better than our second form of the art, to discard circumstances and characters that are not essential to the plot, but it cannot afford to neglect a single circumstance or feature that may be essential to it. The result of such writing is seen in its best form in the history of great institutions, great empires that have had definite periods of growth, duration, and decline; Church History, or different episodes in it; the history of the Roman empire, or of Athens. It has all the unity of the statuesque, and all the vividness of the picturesque, but a continuity of life and argument that are its own. I need scarcely say that to write this sort of history requires the very highest mental powers, as well as patient training and incredible labour. For even the writing of episodes, as we call them, the minor plots of a great drama, the writer must combine qualities of mind that are combined in but few; the clear sight that can apprehend the idea that gives life and truth to the story, and the labour that will apply itself to details as if it were only out of the study of the details that life and truth could come.

But although to write such history may well be beyond the reach of nine hundred and ninety-nine out of each thousand of historians, there is no reason why every man who goes into the schools should not try to read history with a special view to the realizing of the dramatic plan;

and I think that in our present scheme we hold out to the student the clue which he has to follow in order to succeed; for both in the study of the general period, and in that of the continuous history of his own country, he will find the dramatic interest strong and capable of almost infinite illustration. More especially if he can throw himself personally into the action of it; not merely regarding it as an image, or a picture, or a piece of biography, but as part of the growth of his own life, of the laws, history, circumstances, that have helped to make him what he is; acts that have taken place in scenes with which he is familiar, great deeds of war and peace done by the men whose blood runs in his own veins; high aspirations, sympathies and instincts, that he knows are living in his own heart and brain, not merely by imitation or engrafted life, but with continuous, hereditary strength. I would not have him read as a partisan, with the likes and dislikes, the prejudices, the false and artificial antipathies of modern political life, but with the sympathies of an Englishman; I would have my brother Yorkshireman, for instance, learn to look on Fairfax and on Strafford both as men of flesh and blood, with beliefs, sincerities and virtues that bring them very near to us, notwithstanding their antagonism to each other, and the gap that widens daily between us and both of them. I am sure that the more I know of both of them, the more I find that is admirable and loveable in them. But perhaps it is easier to grow enthusiastic here than to maintain judicial calmness; and I will proceed.

There is yet another way of reading and of writing history which demands its place in our enumeration, which, however, can scarcely be regarded as educational, because the historic faculty, whatever it is, must have been already educated before it can attempt to approach the task. To

read and write with the single and simple purpose of collecting, testing, and arranging the facts of history, to discover causes and work out consequences, to determine the
rights and wrongs of questions as they arise, the growth
and decline of institutions as they emerge from and retire
into darkness when their work is done, to build up history
as a treasure-house of knowledge, that may enable the
man who attempts the task to read with like facility the
history of the past and present, to solve the difficulties of
conflicting testimony, and hold the balance of equitable
judgement between conflicting systems; the study, for I must
recur to the first of our three heads, the study of History
for its own sake can scarcely be regarded as a method
co-ordinate with the other three.   But it unites the advantages of all three, and furnishes still more formative and
disciplinary influence of its own.   It is, in relation to its
subject, an end in itself, and is not to be classed among
means and methods; if there be a science, this is the science.
And yet, strange to say, this idea, like the others, is apt
to be lowered and made vulgar by the impatience and intolerance of utilitarian theory; and of all intolerant things,
utilitarian theory, or theoretic utilitarianism, is the most so.
As however I do not wish to use language unnecessarily
strong, I will leave this, and remark upon two other educational theories connected with the subject.

History may be read either backwards or forwards.   That
is, the man who has time for it may begin at the beginning
and read on to modern times; noting every influence in its
origin and effects, the growth and decay, as I have just
said, of institutions, the origin, complications, and counter-
changes of rights and wrongs; and, whether he reads on
a wide scale or on a narrow one, he will, if he lives long
enough, arrive at such a knowledge of the situation of things
at the present day, as will give him a right to make his

opinion heard.   This is the way in which members of Parliament ought to read history; and I take leave to say that, if they would submit to hold their tongues until they have so read it, it would be all the better for the nation and for themselves.

In working thus through the history of our own country, we should come, no doubt, upon many lines of inquiry as to institutions that have long been obsolete, and influences that have no direct representative among the influences of the day; we shall trace the pedigrees of extinct families, and the growth and disuse of worn-out fashions of thought, dress and manners ; but without such reading we cannot trace the origin of existing institutions and influences with anything like a true appreciation of their proportion and relation to national life.   We may, as we proceed, have to discard much that has seemed historical, as having now become archaeological, but we cannot dispense with the recollection that without that obsolete material, that obsolete influence or form, that which has succeeded, survived and continued to flourish, could not have become what it is.   The tree that has stood for centuries bears to the microscopic investigator marks of every winter that has passed over it; it has not cast aside one dead leaf or rotten branch which would not, had it remained, have made the tree something different from what it has become.   I do not advise microscopic minuteness in this study to the neglect of other methods, but I do claim for it a place and a function ; and further than that, I maintain that this synthetic reading of the subject is the best of all ways for those who have time and patience to follow it up. But here we must be cautious, lest having begun to build we be not able to finish ; and having begun to read history at the Norman Conquest, we find ourselves stranded at the battle of Waterloo, or earlier still.   Observing a due scale and proportion of study, much educational benefit will accrue by beginning at the beginning; neglecting the due scale and proportion, the student may find that instead of educating himself to take his place in the world, he has disqualified himself for being anything but a student all his life; no bad thing perhaps, but not an educational result.

The second and reverse method has strong recommendations to other minds; to take the interesting subject of the day and work back to its beginning, following every branch of inquiry that may present itself, but following it chiefly with a view to the leading idea with which you have started. Here too there is abundant exercise for the historic instinct, the desire of getting to the bottom of everything and looking at it all round ; and, regarded as an analytic process, complementary to that synthetic process which I have first stated, some amount of such reading seems absolutely necessary to the education of the student. Still, I question very much whether it is wise to put this idea forward as the best. As the way in which men of modern ways of thinking, and with little time for study, may be invited, tempted to and interested in History, much may be said in its favour, and much has been said on very high authority. But surely it has, unless it be accompanied by some strong corrective, a tendency to educate men for advocates rather than for judges, it leads them into a habit of looking for all that may be said on one side of a subject, rather than for what may be said on both sides; and it certainly leads a man to give to the point from which his investigation started an exaggerated form and influence amongst the earlier competing influences which, as a matter of fact, it has outgrown, or of which it may itself be in some measure a resultant.

The occasional use of this method as a means of study is one thing, the exclusive use of it is another; the use of it as a means of inviting popular attention to history is a third. And it is perhaps in this its third application that it should be regarded with the most favour; but only as a step towards something deeper and sounder. An audience may be attracted by an able lecturer to listen to him on any subject whatever; he takes the subject of the day and works back; Turkey and Russia, we will say. Of course, if his audience is really a popular audience, they bring sadly little information with them to the lecture ; a large proportion probably of the elder hearers can go back as far as the Crimean War, most of the audience will have come into this world of trial since that date. Their ideas of right and wrong will be very much prejudiced by the fact that England took a side in that war, and by the grand principle that whatever England does is right; some may be equally convinced, on equally sound principles, that whatever the Aberdeen ministry—that is supposing them to have heard of an Aberdeen ministry—did must have been wrong : probably some will have imbibed the belief that there is a subtle connexion between Russia and Ritualism, or between Turkey and religious toleration as exemplified in the massacre of orthodox Greek Christians and the protection of Roman Catholics and Protestant Missionaries. Well, furnished with materials, prepossessions, fixed ideas and expectancy, it would be a miracle if they did not come away fully persuaded of their competence to decide on the minutest questions of the last Protocol.

Really it does seem to me that this is beginning at the wrong end, and yet I confess it is extremely difficult to suggest anything that is at once theoretically better and practically possible. If it were only for the fact that these questions of the day are, to so large extent as they are, doubtful and party, doubtful or party questions ; that matters on which our acutest and most honourable statesmen feel bound to take sides diametrically opposed, are by this process subjected to the rough and ready manipulation of men who know nothing about the premises and care nothing about the logical connexion between them and the conclusions, care nothing about the conclusions except in so far as they are the conclusions of a Blue or an Orange lecturer; the fact itself seems to me a *reductio ad absurdum* of historical lecturing. Yet, what is to be done? A little learning is a dangerous thing, but what of total ignorance, what of that ignorance which will not bear to be enlightened unless it is played on by passion or party? How shall we remedy this? Here is a question that extends far beyond the scope of my purpose, for it touches the whole great field of popular education; it is an inviting subject, for we are so distinctly at the beginning of our work in this department that a man of my age may safely propound any nostrum, sure that he will not live to see its absolute uselessness proved by an adult generation of historically trained people.

Let me just say, before I go on to the next and last point of my subject, that popular lecturing on History can be only one, aye, and only a secondary one, of the implements of historical education, if the people of the next generation are to be qualified to use the power which the men of this generation have placed in their hands. The schools, the national schools as well as the public schools, must be made to begin at the beginning; at present the blind are leading the blind; God help us, for we are very near the ditch. Lecturing is of little use, if it does not lead men to read for themselves; in many instances it is worse than useless, if it be made a substitute for self-culture. So too with newspaper education: imagine the state, moral and intellectual, of the man who tries to form his mind by reading the daily journals of England since the beginning of the last Long Vacation. What value will truth and justice have in the eyes of a man who has read history through such a medium? But again I forbear: one word; it has been said, perhaps the story is apocryphal, that one well-known politician of our own day, one too whose judgement would have been well worth having on present events, once said something to the effect that there was more valuable political training in one column of *The Times* than in all the pages of Thucydides; I will venture to say that there are English journals now, claiming a world-wide circulation and assuming to be the very interpreters of history and political morality, in preference to whose lessons I should recommend the student to seek for lessons of history and political morality among the arrowheaded inscriptions of Assyria or the papyri of the Neapolitan Museum.

But I have already run into the third division of my subject: that is the popular view of historic knowledge; the aspect of it in which it becomes merely a tool or a stock of tools capable of employment for ulterior purposes; and the methods of teaching it by which with the least trouble the learner can acquire practically useful information. I call this the popular or utilitarian aspect, because it belongs to the catchpenny theory of human life according to which the value of a thing is just as much as it will bring; the theory that despises science and research, that regards politics as a game between Blue and Orange, that places the interest of Great Britain at the crown and apex of national ambitions, and regards education in general not as the training of the human mind for God's service, a development of powers to His glory and the welfare of our fellow men, but as a means for the acquisition of a certain sum in the funds; the theory that regards human souls as factory hands, and ascribes to Parliament the power of making a false statement true. But although it is the vulgar view of education, and in this extreme a very vulgar view, it is founded upon a truth. There are many things which a mere acquaintance with the facts of history, however that acquaintance may have been gained, enables a man to do better than he would do them without it. There is a knowledge of history for ordinary practical purposes which may be acquired without either the love of the subject or going through the disciplinary study of it by way of culture. And this we must not undervalue, because a very little may be made to go a great way; and it is quite possible for a man to wish to take an independent and right view of public affairs and political duty, who has not, and never had and never can have, a proper education for forming a complete judgement. We respect the man who, when he has to vote on any public question, goes to his books to get up the question instead of voting as the party whip would wish him; we would rather that his education had fitted him to do right at once, that he had studied public questions to begin with, or that he had, by the culture of educational reading, exercised his mind to discern between good and evil; but we do not despise him even if he votes wrong in the end. Even an indifferent Cyclopaedia is better than a paid party agent as a guide in doubtful questions.

Now how can this sort of information be best provided? I do not know of any expedient that has not been at one time or other tried; tried in vain, you say. Not quite in vain, if such expedient has, as I said, enabled a man to do better than he would have done without it. We do not condemn the use of a Ready Reckoner because we think that a tradesman ought to do and would do better without it; it is much safer for his customers than that convenient leaden canon, the rule of thumb; but we do not think that a banker who entirely depends on his Ready Reckoner will ever become Chancellor of the Exchequer. One has known people too who have thought the Encyclopaedia Londinensis a useful sort of reading for Sunday afternoons; no doubt it would enable you, like one of Dickens's heroines, to pass a number of remarkable opinions upon a remarkable number of subjects. But seriously, anything should be welcome that would save a well-intentioned man from the necessity of taking his rule of political conduct from the leading articles of party papers. We have had popular histories and pictorial histories, political Cyclopaedias, and Books for the Million; a whole historical department of the Society for Diffusing Useful Knowledge. Yet it seems as if, even for such work, even where such work would pay, no one has the spirit to undertake it unless he is stirred by something stronger than the desire of being useful, the desire of ventilating some party view or destroying the character of some partisan opposed to him. Imagine a history of England in which the lying story of Hannah Lightfoot appears as an important clue to the difficulties of the reign of George III, and the triumphs of the Commonwealth are regarded as incomplete unless Henrietta Maria can be shown to have been an adulteress. These are extreme cases, because they are cases in which a coarse and violently prejudiced mind has undertaken the task of writing for party purposes; but the infection is not confined to coarse and vulgar minds: it defiles some of the very noblest works, especially historical works, that have ever been written. How can we recommend the man who wants to get up the rights of a case to a history like Macaulay's? how easy must have been the victory of Macaulay's hero if all his adversaries were the pitiful knaves and fools that they appear to him to have been. I am not calling him a slanderer, I do not believe that he was one; or ignorant or careless, for he was most learned and accurate; nor insincere, for he was most sincere; but for all that he was as much a party writer as Clarendon or Prynne, or Burnet, or Collier. And where such a man with such power of portraiture as would make us believe his pictures, if not true, more lifelike and real than if they were true—where such a man with such knowledge, such memory, such transparent honesty of belief in his own version of history, cannot be relied upon, what shall we poor mortals do? If all the advance in historical study is to result only in the better presentation of party views and party arguments; if no one will write even cram-books without cramming his own disproportioned and one-sided theories down our children's throats, it seems as if it were time to turn over a new leaf; reconcile ourselves with party government and organization and cut ourselves off from shams. Let men cease to pretend to exercise or to prepare to exercise conscientious judgement. Divide the world between Blue and Orange, and nail your colours to the mast.

For my own part I do not see why an honest partisan should not write an honest book if he can persuade himself to look honestly at his subject, and make allowance for his own prejudices. I know it is somewhat critical work, and a man who knows himself in one way, may be quite ignorant of himself in another.. I take Hallam as an illustrious example; Hallam knew himself to be a political partisan, and, wherever he knew that political prejudice might darken his counsel, he guarded most carefully against it: he did not claim the judicial character without fitting himself for it; and where he knew himself to be sitting as judge he judged admirably: so admirably that the advanced advocates even of his own views have long ago thrown him over as too timid and temporizing for their purpose. Yet where he was not awake to his own prejudice, in matters for instance regarding religion and the Church, in which he seems to have had no doubt about his own infallibility of negation, how ludicrously and transparently unfair he is!

I do not see any necessity for this. I do not see why a

man should not say once for all, I like Charles I better than
Oliver Cromwell: I like the cause for which Charles believed
himself to be contending better than that for which Cromwell
strove: Charles is attractive to me, Oliver is repulsive:
Charles is my friend, Oliver is my foe: but, am I bound to
maintain that my friend is always right and my enemy always
wrong; am I bound to hold Charles for a saint, Oliver for a
monster; am I bound never to mention Charles without a
sigh or Oliver without a sneer; am I bound to conceal the
faults of the one and to believe every calumny against the
other? If you like, put it the other way, believe in the
great Protestant statesman, treat Charles as the overrated
fine gentleman, the narrow-minded advocate of a theory
which he did not understand, the pig-headed maintainer of
the cause you dislike. You may be a partisan, but can you
not believe that, if you believe your own side of the question,
truth when it is explored will be found on your side? mis-
representation, exaggeration, dishonesty of advocacy will
only disparage the presentment which you desire to make of
your own convictions and your own prepossessions. Nay,
I would go further, and say I should like Charles better than
Oliver even if his cause were less my own than I conceive it
to be. I am ready to stick to my friends and vote against
my unfriends: but why should I shut my eyes to the false
and foolish things that my friends do, or to the noble
aspirations, honesty, and good intentions of those whom I
think wrong in their means and mistaken in their ends.
Yet, as I began by saying, without some infusion of spite
it seems as if history could not be written; that no man's
zeal is roused to write unless it is moved by the desire to
write down. Of course I seem to be stating extreme cases,
but it is extreme cases that make their own advertisements,
and that do the great mischief. Here the study of ancient
history has its great advantage over modern; yet battles are

fought over the character of Tiberius, and the 'lues re-habilitandi' has given a new reading to the history of Marius and Sylla.

The reason which led me to say that even an indifferent book is better than no book at all, that an encyclopaedic history or a popular compendium, or a cram-book, or even a party pamphlet is better than no book at all, because even if it misleads and misrepresents, it deceives a man one degree less than he would be deceived by a mere party agent; because it makes him think, even if the extent of the thinking be that he thinks that he thinks; because it either suggests to him that he ought to form a judicial opinion, or keeps before his mind the duty of inquiry and furnishes him with a starting-point; the same reason that led me to say this of popular books, leads me also to estimate at something more than their intrinsic value the popular lectures, or lecture-system, of which we have recently heard a good deal.

We are told that even a short course of lectures, clearly and interestingly delivered, will be sufficient to put the popular mind in possession of such an elementary know-ledge of history, its course, influences and material lessons, as will enable men to approach the great questions of the day with some useful amount of foresight and theoretic experience.

Now, if I have misstated this prescription, I am very sorry; but I think I have not. I am quite willing to admit that a popular lecture may give information that is better than total ignorance; I am inclined to value highly the inducement to begin real study which a popular lecture may put before the mind of the audience; I am thankful to the popular lecturer, although he may get no further than to rouse the hearers to the sense of the fact that he is talking about things of which they have no comprehension at all; at all events he tells them that there is such a study as History. But I confess that I do not see my way to go much further, unless I may be allowed very much to modify the prescribed idea of a popular lecture. In the first place, as to lectures at all: that such oral teaching is an important part of the discipline of education we are all bound to believe; it is part of the system under which we have all grown up, and in a University course it is that one part of the system which is capable of the most development; an implement which has been growing to perfection by the labours of many generations of tutors and professors. Yet of our best lectures, as well as of our worst, it may be certainly said that that which a hearer carries away with him will be in exact and direct proportion to that which he brings: or that a lecture-system, unless it be added upon and followed up by independent reading, must be a deceptive and even useless system. Of course this is a platitude; but just consider that, if this be true of us, and true of us in those very subjects in which we have been training ourselves ever since we were seven years old, how much stronger is the point of it when it is applied to lecture audiences that have not studied their subject, that have not even the elements of the study made accessible to them before they come, and that have not yet the means of following up the lessons that are then first propounded to them.

I fail to see that elementary lectures—short courses of elementary lectures—can convey anything to the mind of beginners, besides the most elementary teaching. Twelve lectures on the scale and plan of Mr. Freeman's Handbook of Universal History would no doubt contain the marrow and spirit of Universal History; but the working man who could understand them at the first reading would be fit to be Prime Minister after a second course. If, then, elementary lecturing is ever to furnish material lessons to ignorant men, it must, I take it, go on in long and progressive courses, and inculcate both patient hearing and the duty of independent reading. But, secondly, historical lecturing to uneducated people must surely begin by interesting them. And accordingly I would place the plan of lecturing on character and institutions, things in which every Englishman must almost of necessity feel his interest aroused as soon as he hears them, first; before the plan of elementary lectures to the people. Even where they do not see the direct application of the lesson, so offered, to their own circumstances, where there may be no such lesson, and no such application, they may be drawn to further study by a very inadequate exposition of a noble life or of a great battle, or even by an historical survey of some scene with the landmarks of which they are familiar. When they are drawn to history, they will not be likely to wish their elementary lessons to be restricted to twelve or to a single course.

Without then at all disparaging such a plan of elementary lectures, I feel certain that some preparation for it must be otherwise provided; if that is to be by lecture, it must be something more directly addressed to our common humanity than an elementary lesson can be; but I think that it must have begun at school, and that unless it has begun at school it will not do very much good. This is rather a dispiriting view for people who are too old to go to school; but then we are not dependent on lectures altogether; there are books enough and to spare, and the man who wants to learn will find time to read.

The moment however that people have, whether by reading at home or by hearing lectures, got beyond the elementary stage of historical study, my doubts about the expediency of popular lectures cease altogether; and I am glad to say this because, in some of the remarks that I have made, you may have thought me unwisely cynical and inclined rather to discourage effort in this direction. Popular lectures to fairly well-educated people, who have not the time or the opportunity of thorough courses of reading, must be valuable ; and the experiments which have been tried in some of our large manufacturing towns have been successful in a remarkable degree.   I do not shut my eyes to the fact that in such schemes zeal often outruns discretion, that volunteer lecturers are far more likely to spring from the ranks of the unlearned than from the class that has grown old in convincing itself of its own ignorance, and that, as I have said of writing, it may be true of lecturing, the zeal for informing other people may arise from political feeling quite as often as from the benevolent desire of teaching them what is good for them.   It is most unfortunate that such teaching should be one-sided : how one-sided it could be made we learned from the history of Mechanics' Institutes ; now we may hope that the exertions of the town clergy in their local societies are doing something to redress the balance ; and if I could see my way to an administration on sound principles, apart from party organization, and in the hands of competent teachers, of such a scheme as that known as the University Extension Scheme, I should be inclined to hope very great things from it.   I trust that it will be so shortly.

If by these or any other plans we can induce men in authority to make the real teaching of History a part of the training of elementary schools, the first, and by no means the least, step will be taken towards furnishing the next generation of Englishmen with the means of exercising conscientiously, honestly, and judicially, the great political power which is now lodged in their hands.   They will learn how to vote, and how to guard against imposture, exaggeration, and unfairness in their leaders as well as in their opponents. And with real political awakening I shall trust that moral and religious progress will do more than keep pace.   I go further ; if the study of History can really be made an educational implement in schools, it will raise up a generation

who not only will know how to vote, but will bring a judgement, prepared, trained, and in its own sphere exercised and
developed, to help them in all the great affairs of life.
Therefore let us have lectures many and good, books few and
good; but above all school teaching fair, honest, and thorough.

Further I do not think we need look. I do not anticipate
Englishmen ever becoming a nation of researchers. We may
come, more of us, to love investigation for its own sake, and
to love the study of History for the very exercise that it
furnishes to our powers, and for the new regions of interest
which expand before us as we proceed. Such study must
however continue to be the portion of comparatively few, the
few who have leisure, or who have the love in such strength
as to enable them to overcome all obstacles. On them I
trust the coming age will look more kindly than the present;
which has much praise for the mere material lesson, and
worships the statuesque, the picturesque, and the dramatic,
but certainly honours the inquirers, the researchers, with a
scanty meed. It is an old, old story. Some of you may
remember the passage in Saint Augustine's Confessions, the
story he tells of one who was asked how the Deity, being
from everlasting, was employed before the heavens and the
earth were made; the reply was 'joculariter,' the great
doctor tells us, a very pretty repartee, 'Alta, inquit, scru-
tantibus gehennas parabat.' He was preparing, to put it
gently, a limbo for the advocates of research. 'Haec non
respondeo,' says Augustine; but there are people at all
events in one House of Parliament who seem to hold the same
view: one is glad to see that their number is now reduced
to twelve [1].

---

[1] In the Committee on the Oxford and Cambridge Bill (for University
Commissions, April 30, 1877), on clause 15 providing that the Commissioners in making a statute are to have regard to the interests of
education, religion, learning, and research, it was proposed to omit
research from the provision; this was rejected by 172 to 12.

LEARNING AND LITERATURE AT THE
COURT OF HENRY II

(June 11, 1878.)

WE are at present suffering, and may for some little time to come continue to suffer, from a reaction against mediaevalism. I call it a reaction, for I think it is only caused by a recoil from modes of thought, art, and action, which have been pressed beyond reality, or have been pressed too rigorously. There are not wanting signs that even in architecture, in which the greatest and most permanent traces of mediaeval genius are found, the world is growing a little impatient of Gothic buildings, whether as imitative creations or as the claimants of exclusive orthodoxy in their art; in poetry it can scarcely be denied that the Arthurian legend has begun somewhat to pall upon most ears; in ritual or ceremonial worship we see much of which we are tempted to ask whether it has any meaning whatever for nine out of every ten of those who profess to value it. The dear delightful Middle Ages are unfortunately growing into something like a by-word. We are perhaps witnessing the turn of the tide of fashion which set in with Sir Walter Scott, and found its great triumphs under Sir Gilbert; of which, however, all that is real and natural and free will live, whilst that which is forced, unspontaneous and merely imitative, will not long continue to encumber the ground.

If this be indeed the case, it will explain some things that touch the study of History. Three or four years ago I was startled by the remark, which occurred in a review of Mr. Kitchin's History of France in the *Athenaeum*, to the effect that all study of the early periods was thrown away, and that the true interest of history begins only where that history has begun to be illustrated by the genius of Mr. Carlyle. But I was scarcely prepared for the recommendation of my friend Professor Pearson, in his recent report to the Government of Victoria, on the subject of education, that the teaching of history in the Australian High Schools should begin with the year 1700. And why? because the ages that precede are so entirely unlike our own; there were no railways, no large manufacturing towns, no newspapers to speak of, no such relations as now exist between Lords and Commons, no property tax, no taxation by excise, and a good deal of living religion, which religion exercised over the daily lives and political views of men an influence that is scarcely comprehensible at the present day.

Such a theory, it seems to me, would go a long way towards dispensing with education altogether; but the expression of such a theory, if it be the result of anything else than a clever man's crotchets, is a mark of a reaction; and such a reaction as is even painful to one who has spent the best years of his life in attempting to connect the several stages of his country's life and growth; who believes that the age of railways, and excise and newspapers, would never have been had it not been for the free institutions and high ambitions that were nursed through the preceding ages, and that the present condition of the strength of the world is the direct and continuous result of historical growth and historical training.

It is no wonder, I say, that to me, and those who have pursued the same line of study, this tendency should seem very much to be deprecated. I do not for a moment suppose that it is dangerous; all experience, all belief in progress and true culture, encourage me to believe that it is adventitious. If Australia can content itself with the history of England since the reign of Queen Anne, America has found out long ago the mistake of crippling the historic instinct with any such limitation; and American scholars, lawyers, and constitutionalists are working as zealously at the mediaeval forms as are the students of England, France, and Germany. And not only experience of the past and faith in the future, but sympathy with the historical world both past and future, if I may use such an expression, inclines me to a protest. Like the man in Terence, I say 'Humani nil a me alienum puto'; I have a sympathy with the struggles of the struggling ages, with the weariness of the weary ages, with the faith of the ages of faith, with the controversies of the ages of controversy, with the changes of the ages of change, with the light of the ages of illumination, with the darkness of the dark ages themselves. Nay, I am not sure that I may not some day have to profess myself a convert to the Unity of History and the Education of the World. For after all, human life is not essentially changed by railways or excise, or newspapers, or even by the property tax: the people before the flood ate and drank, married and were given in marriage, planted and builded; still Jacob finds his Rachel at the well, and David and Jonathan make their covenant together, and David mourns for Absalom. Natural selection, and the survival of the fittest, have not done away with sin and sorrow, and, whatever evolution may have done in the producing of new types, those new types have not swept away the old. To go beyond and behind the ancients, what else do we find in Egypt, Babylon and Nineveh, in Japan, and in the China of immemorial sameness? And as there is no history in which we do not find a sympathy, there is none in which we may not find a lesson.

But to put aside generalities; the two or three truisms

which I have uttered, and the subject which I have chosen
for these two lectures, are alike suggested by the discussion
which we have seen recently carried on by Mr. Freeman
and Mr. Froude on the subject of Thomas Becket. I am
not going to interfere in a struggle between two such combatants, nor shall I again refer to either of them, but the
opposite lights in which those two champions approach
the common subject, shed some rays on the fashion of
thought which marks not only the two writers, or the two
schools of which they may be supposed to be the disciples, but the two ways of looking at the Middle Ages
which divide cultivated men of the present day. And I
have thought that I might, in attempting to sketch the
literary life of an age, on which so many lights from various
sides are now brought to bear, contribute somewhat, not
perhaps to the true estimation of that age, but to a realization of, and sympathy with, the life of it, without which no
estimation or even understanding of it can be thought
possible.

But the men of whom I am going to speak lived 700 years
ago—700 years; as long a time as separated them from
Hengist and Horsa, or Hengist and Horsa from Alexander
the Great, or Herodotus from the Trojan war; or us ourselves perhaps from the New Zealander, who, on London
Bridge, is to draw the conclusion that Thucydides ascribes
to the τοῖς ἔπειτα and to recognize the disproportion between
our ruins and our glory. It is true; but the only thought
that this suggests to me is that, if the New Zealander finds in
the ruins of the British Museum half as many of the literary
productions of our time as we now possess of the reign
of Henry II, the shades of the Victorian litterati may, in
the Elysian fields of the period, feel a thrill of satisfaction, and say that a great part of their life has escaped
Libitina.

In truth, I would call your attention to a point which I have never seen fully set out; the fact that the same age that originated the forms in which our national and constitutional life began to mould itself, was also an age of great literary activity; of very learned and acute men, and of culture enough to appreciate and conserve the fruits of their labours.

We all know the debt that England owes to the great men of the thirteenth century, to its political, religious, and scholastic life: Simon de Montfort, Grosseteste, Edward I, and the rest; but I do not remember ever to have seen an estimate of the debt that the thirteenth owed to the twelfth, save and except in the recognition of Henry II's constitutional work. I can now only attempt an outline of any such view as is needed for the purpose, but I think that, when I have briefly reviewed the period, you will allow that in other matters besides constitutional, the glories of the latter age were the result of, and not much in themselves superior to, the glories of the former.

I will begin with the king himself, for, as the mediaeval writers were never tired of quoting, 'vulgi turba movetur regis ad exemplar.' Henry II was by his very descent a champion of literary culture. Not to speak of his grandfather, Henry Beauclerc, whose clerkship was very probably of a very elementary sort, he was the lineal descendant of that Fulk the Good who had told King Lothar that 'Rex illiteratus' was 'asinus coronatus.' He shared too those hereditary characteristics which so strongly marked his two uncles, Baldwin III and Amalric I, Kings of Jerusalem. Both of these princes were, according to William of Tyre, good scholars, and both extremely fond of history. Baldwin was the better professor; Amalric the better examiner; Baldwin the more serious and orthodox, Amalric the more superficial; but both were students of history, and given to reading and discussion—discussion which threatened now and then to go beyond the bounds of orthodoxy.

Peter of Blois gives a similar character of Henry, and in words so nearly resembling those of William of Tyre that the two writers notably confirm one another's probability. And in Peter's sketch this feature comes in quite by the way, for he is describing Henry as a great huntsman. 'He has always in his hands bows and arrows, swords and hunting spears, save when he is busy in council or over his books. For as often as he can get breathing time amid his business cares, he occupies himself with private reading, or takes pains in working out some knotty question among his clerks. Your king,' he is writing to the Archbishop of Palermo, 'is a good scholar, but ours is far better; I know the abilities and accomplishments of both. You know that the King of Sicily was my pupil for a year; you yourself taught him the elements of verse-making and literary composition; from me he had further and deeper lessons, but as soon as I left the kingdom he threw away his books and took to the easy-going ways of the court. But with the King of England there is school every day, constant conversation of the best scholars and discussion of questions.'

He had indeed been well taught; notwithstanding the troubled times in which his youth had been trained, he had learned literature at Bristol Castle in the household of his uncle, Robert of Gloucester; his tutor Matthew, who probably was identical with the officer entitled, in a few records of his reign, his chancellor, took him in charge when he was nine and kept him close at work for four years; there doubtless he had the acquaintance of Gilbert Foliot, then Abbot of Gloucester, certainly one of the ablest politicians as well as of the best scholars of the time; whilst, when political affairs allowed it, he might learn somewhat more under the eye of Archbishop Theobald of Canterbury, the patron of Vacarius the lawyer and John of Salisbury the philosopher.

The hereditary taste for history may perhaps, to some extent, account for the considerable number of independent historians who flourished under him; such chroniclers as those known by the name of Benedict of Peterborough, and Roger of Hoveden, bear intrinsic marks of having been royal historiographers; one distinguished officer of the Exchequer, Master Thomas Brown, kept a Roll on which were entered all the doings of the king: Richard FitzNeal, the High Treasurer of the Exchequer, composed a similar book, the Tricolumnis, in which he kept a regular register of Henry's acts and of the public documents of the time. There was, as we shall see presently, a fashion for writing history.

But not only so; Henry was also a lawyer. Very early in his reign we find him, in the Chronicle of Battle, dictating a new form of writ; he heard and decided law suits, he took an active part in devising budgets, he took an independent line on religious toleration, and refused to persecute. All these are signs of general enlightenment; but the man is even better known by his friends. Becket indeed was no great scholar in the early days when the king treated him as an equal and confidential friend, but later in life, when we find Henry choosing for companions such men as Hugh of Lincoln and Baldwin of Canterbury, both of them as remarkable for learning and eloquence as for piety, or even Giraldus Cambrensis, who had a fund of humour and cleverness that is as noteworthy as his extensive reading; or Peter of Blois, who acted for some time as the king's secretary, and, with all his time-serving and self-seeking, was a distinctly learned man in both history and theology, we feel sure that Henry was neither the mere voluptuary that his enemies represented him, nor merely the man of business that his more lasting works prove him to have been.

It has been the fashion to suppose that some literary influences were brought into England from Southern France by Queen Eleanor, and that it was from her that Richard, and perhaps John also, inherited some instincts of the kind. But I confess that, as against the claims of her husband, Eleanor's title to our gratitude depends very much on conjecture, and partly on a confusion between Aquitanian and Provençal civilization. That Eleanor was a clever and cultivated companion for her husband we may accept as a matter of course, and she probably would have some share in the early education of her sons; but they were very soon removed from her influence, and after the year 1173 she probably saw very little of either them or her husband: whilst in England, court or country, her direct influence could never have been comparable with that of the king. As for her judgements in the Courts of Love, I suppose, we may safely relegate them to the regions of romance, and if they were authentic they would not prove much as to her literary culture. But we may, I think, confidently assume that she was a well-educated woman for those days, and that in her long captivity she had something else to amuse herself with besides needlework. A woman who, after twelve years of seclusion, could come out of prison not only fit to take the reins of government during a short interregnum, but able to exercise great influence in European politics until she was nearly eighty years old, must have possessed not merely vitality and ability, but mental resources also of no ordinary character.

However this may have been, some of her children, if not all, were educated with care, and appear as either possessed of learning themselves or as the patrons of learned

men. Henry, the eldest son, was, as we are told, devoted
to arms; if he was not equally accomplished in letters it
was not because such accomplishments were undervalued
by the people whom he was expected to rule. There is
among the letters of Peter of Blois an epistle written in
the name of Rotrou, Archbishop of Rouen, and at the express wish of the Norman bishops, urging in strong terms,
and by cogent examples, the importance of a literary
training for a young prince. Julius Caesar, Alexander the
Great, King David, Constantine, Theodosius, Justinian,
and Leo are pressed into the service. No doubt the advice
was taken; but the stormy career of the younger Henry
does not afford many indications of its results. One book
we know, a book unfortunately lost, was especially written
for his amusement. Gervase of Tilbury, who, many years
after Henry's death, wrote for his grandson, the Emperor
Otto, the Otia Imperialia, tells us that he wrote a *Liber
Facetiarum* for the young king, in which no doubt he
collected the amusing stories of the popes and emperors
that were current at the time, some of which are probably
preserved for us in the pages of Ralph de Diceto. It is
possible that the Otia Imperialia were originally drawn up
for the instruction of the same prince. It is curious, however, that in none of the panegyrics of this unfortunate
boy is any special stress laid on his knowledge of letters,
and it is even possible that the epistle of Archbishop
Rotrou was intended as a remonstrance against the exclusively military training of the heir to the crown; certainly Thomas Becket, to whose care he is said to have
been committed in his youth, would, at that period of his
career, have been better qualified to instruct him in arms
than in letters.

With Richard it was otherwise. In his case we must
certainly allow some amount of literary knowledge and

skill. We may not perhaps credit him with the quotations from the classical poets which the historians of the third crusade put in his mouth, but we cannot refuse to believe those writers when they tell us of the lampoons of the king's own composition which were sung in the camp in contempt of the Duke of Burgundy; and the stream of time, in which so many more precious things have been submerged, has brought down to us some few sirventes or satiric lays that entitle Richard to the name of a trouvere. His education in the south of France no doubt qualified him for such compositions; but his father's foreign dominions may also have furnished him with more valuable instruction. At the schools of Tours his half-brother Geoffrey was educated, and there Richard himself may have obtained the elements of that 'scientia' which is markedly ascribed to him in contrast with his brothers. Of Geoffrey of Brittany we know no more than that he was an accomplished knight. John's reputation for scholarship seems to rest on the fact that he once borrowed a book of the Abbot of St. Alban's. But the real interest of such inquiries does not lie in the question whether such and such kings could read or write, but in the general character of the court which was kept about them; the king might be illiterate, but if the court around him was full of learned men we may safely infer that the central figure was no contemner of learning. Of the king's daughters we know little more than that they were all married to princes who took a conspicuous place among the pioneers of mediaeval culture. Matilda, the eldest, was the wife of Henry of Saxony, who was not only a great conqueror but a great traveller and collector of chronicles; Eleanor, the second, married King Alfonso of Castile, the founder of the University of Palencia; and Johanna, the youngest, William the Good, King of Sicily, who was not only, as we have seen, both an educated man himself, but also the patron of many learned Englishmen.

There was something, however, besides the literary wide-awakeness of Henry and his family that made England and its Court at the time a centre of literary activity. Henry was the most powerful king of the West, and his hand was in the affairs of all the Western kingdoms: and this at the time when international acquaintance was carried on upon the very largest scale. There can hardly have been a period of our history in which the intercourse between England and France was freer or more frequent. The enormous number of letters which passed between England and Rome, every letter, remember, carried by a separate messenger; the stream of pilgrims to the East, and the prominence given in the histories of the time to the adventures of the few that returned; the cosmopolitan character of the clergy, the frequent promotions of English and Normans in foreign churches, and their continued intercourse with their friends at home; the recourse to foreign Universities, and the honours won by English scholars at those Universities, being a constant inducement to others to follow them; the welcome given at the English Court to foreign scholars, and finally, the fact that the English Court was open to all exiles from East or West, North or South; all these served to arouse and keep awake that curiosity about foreign matters which will not be satisfied without the acquisition of learning: so that learning is not sought for itself only, but as a part of the equipment of a man of the world. A little may go a long way under such circumstances, but yet every little helps to make a mickle, and there were many men about, as I shall hope to show you, who were bent on picking up all they could, and to whom nothing came amiss.

To run rapidly over the more prominent examples under each of the heads I have enumerated: in 1155, the first year

of Henry II, there was an embassy from the kings of Norway.
Henry received the envoys, and sent them back with ambassadors of his own and large presents ; and the next year there
was a similar transaction with Sweden.   Here at once opens
up a field of interesting investigation.   Norway and Sweden
were about as far from England as they are now, but they
seem to have been even more neighbourly.   The Norse
settlements in the islands had not forgotten their origin.   The
Bishop of Sodor and Man was expected to seek consecration
at Drontheim.   Just before Henry's accession, the Bishop
of Bergen had visited Fountains Abbey and obtained a
colony of Cistercians for a cell in Norway itself, called, after
that beautiful custom of the order, the House of Light.
Again, in 1164, another Norwegian prelate appears in the
royal accounts as receiving a gift of £3 6s. 8d. ; and again,
in 1182, the Archbishop Eystein, of Nidros, was maintained for
seventeen weeks at the expense of the English Court.   These
two dates synchronize with the Norwegian revolutions under
Magnus Herlingson and Swerre Birkbain, and we thus learn
how the detailed accounts of those revolutions came into
the English Chronicles of Benedict and Roger of Hoveden,
and William of Newburgh : it was at St. Edmund's that Archbishop Eystein was entertained at the king's expense from
August 1181 to February 1182.   And this leads us on to the
recollection that it was the Englishman Nicolas Breakspere
who had been legate of the Roman see for the settlement
of the Scandinavian churches, before he became pope as
Adrian IV, and so liberally bestowed the realm of Ireland on
the king of the English.

The intercourse with Germany under Frederick Barbarossa
was steady and probably continuous ; for although there was
little love lost between England and the empire, and the
Hohenstaufen were always somewhat drawn to France, the
quarrel of Henry with Becket and that of Frederick with

Alexander III so nearly coincided, that there was always a prospect that the two great sovereigns might make common cause against Lewis VII. Hence in 1165 there was a German embassy under the Archbishop of Cologne in London, and the English lords showed their orthodoxy by refusing to meet the schismatic prelate at dinner, although Henry's own envoys at Würtzburg were credibly reported to have given in the national adhesion to the antipope. The marriage of Matilda with duke Henry, his subsequent quarrel with the emperor, Henry's negotiations for the support and restoration of his son-in-law, the long exile of Henry the Lion and his stay in England, gave English society much interest in German politics; so much so, that it is from the English Chroniclers of this period that much of the German history of the time has to be written; and English writers took sides in the Welf and Hohenstaufen quarrel, describing both events and characters with partisan colouring that is rare even in their pictures of home politics. Thus, too, copies of important documents came to be preserved in the English Annals, and we are so led to infer that the relations of the Court, to whose hands primarily these documents must have come, with the recording annalists, were of the closest description ; and we understand how the great Longchamp or Walter of Coutances could send down important dispatches to be copied into the historical collections of Ralph de Diceto. For when we talk of the public and of the court of Henry II, we are not talking of such a vague and abstract idealism as the court and public of the reign of Victoria, made up of society at large at one end and the press and newspaper correspondents at the other, with all that lies between ; the Court is a small body of well-known men, and the public is the aggregate of the clergy and knights who know foreign lands, can speak foreign tongues, and take an intelligent interest in European politics. Not

to dwell, however, on these points; in 1176 there were at
the English Court at Westminster, on the 12th of November,
embassies from Constantinople, and from Frederick I, the
Eastern and Western Caesars, from France, both Rheims
and Flanders, and from Henry the Lion; the same year
the Sicilian envoys came to demand Johanna in marriage
for their king, and the kings of Navarre and Castile applied
to Henry to arbitrate on a great international dispute in
Spain. It is true that on this last occasion there were some
difficulties of interpretation; the English could not understand the Spanish envoys, a fact which seems to indicate
that thus early Spanish Latin had become somewhat rusty,
for of course it must have been in Latin that the negotiations would be conducted; but the difficulty was surmounted
and the arbitration settled; the documents concerning it,
which are totally without interest to the English mind except
in so far as they contained a full pedigree of the Spanish
dynasties, being circulated among the chroniclers of the
time, and so preserved in several authorities.

With Italy and Sicily, owing first to the constant recourse to
Rome during the Becket and other Canterbury quarrels, and
secondly to the sustained connexion with the Sicilian Normans,
which came to its climax in the marriage of Johanna, the
offer of the Sicilian crown to Henry himself, and the contract
of marriage between Arthur of Brittany and King Tancred's
daughter, the relations of the English were very close.

But in fact the diplomatic activity of Henry II throughout
his reign was enormous; all nations of Europe came by
envoys to his court, and his ministers, especially Richard
of Ilchester and John of Oxford, ran about from one end of
Europe to the other. Spain, the most distant in interest of
all, became familiar by the pilgrimages to Compostella and
by the substitution of service against the Moorish infidels for
service against the Turks. Both Henry and his eldest son

purposed, or said they purposed, pilgrimages to Compostella, and it is well known how great was the debt of the infant kingdom of Portugal to English pilgrims. We see, too, how the elaborate surveys of the Spanish coasts found their way into several of our chronicles, so that Spanish geography, scarcely less than German political history, owes something to the English of this period.

To go, however, one step further; the diplomatic intercourse is illustrated not merely by the occasional visits of ambassadors, but by the constant interchange of letters between Englishmen abroad and at home, or between Englishmen and foreigners. Now the subject of mediaeval letter-writing is one on which a very great deal of entertaining discussion might be taken, but I can now only note a few points in this particular connexion.

At first sight, mediaeval letters are disappointing; the amount of sentiment, and especially of religious generalities, seems altogether out of proportion to the amount of news. That arises from two causes: firstly, many of our collections of letters are edited collections, made by the writers, who prided themselves upon their correct Latinity, and published their correspondence rather as literary exercises than as historical memorials; thus, so far from setting special value on the spontaneous unartificial morsels, which are to us the *bonnes bouches* of letter-writing, these men actually cut them out of their codified letters. This may be seen in almost every case in which copies of the original letters can be compared with the revised editions put out by the writers; especially is it the case with Alcuin's letters. Many of the letters of Peter of Blois look as if they had received the same treatment, and in the Becket correspondence the reader is often nonplussed by finding a provoking *etcetera*, which marks the point at which the gossip, or even the serious news, was expunged by the editor.

The other reason is that in very many cases the letters were little more than credentials. The real news was carried by the bearer of the letter, and the real force of the communication was not in the postscript, we may say, but in the postman. Still, we often come upon letters and letter-writers of real interest, and a good man may certainly be known by good letters, although many good men wrote very weak ones. John of Salisbury, among Becket's correspondents, wrote real letters, and those of Richard of Ilchester, preserved among Foliot's, are the writing of a business-like man. Even amidst the wearisome sameness of the Canterbury letters we now and then get a glimpse of life, such as in the letter of Master John from Lombardy, when he explains why he could not write from the Great St. Bernard. 'Pardon me for not writing. I have been on the Mount of Jove; on the one hand looking up to the heavens of the mountains, on the other shuddering at the hell of the valleys; feeling myself so much nearer to heaven that I was more sure that my prayer would be heard. "Lord," I said, "restore me to my brethren, that I may tell them, that they come not into this place of torment." Place of torment, indeed, where the marble pavement of the stony ground is ice alone, and you cannot set down a foot safely; where, strange to say, although it is so slippery that you cannot stand, the death, into which there is every facility for a fall, is certain death. I put my hand in my scrip, that I might scratch out a syllable or two to your sincerity; lo, I found my ink-bottle filled with a dry mass of ice : my fingers, too, refused to write : my beard was stiff with frost, and my breath congealed into a long icicle. I could not write the news I wished.' But this is a digression, and such scraps are not common.

Well, the mass of twelfth century letters is so large that, notwithstanding the drawbacks, they furnish a large contribution to the materials for national, literary, and social history. John of Salisbury, Peter of Blois, Arnulf of Lisieux, Thomas Becket, Gilbert Foliot, the monks of Canterbury, furnish a series of thick volumes, the many-sided interest of which is not easily exhausted. These collections contain news from every part of Christendom; some of them, although only a few, are really news-letters, containing all that the writers could pick up, like the news-letters of later times. All, however, contain evidence by which the literary culture, as well as the political interest felt at the time, may be tested. The citations of the Latin poets which occur so very frequently are amusing, and often amusingly inappropriate. There is something touchingly comic in the monk of Canterbury who will bring in Ovid's Art of Love as a treasury of stock quotations. Lucan's Pharsalia, Claudian, Statius, even Silius Italicus, but Ovid most of all, notably more than Virgil and Horace, seem to have been the storehouse of proverbs. Shall we be so cruel as to say that the frequency with which particular passages are quoted suggests that the writers betook themselves to a Margarita Poetica, a dictionary of quotations, rather than to the authors themselves? No, it is only true in the very penny-a-lining letters of inferior men. Certainly the best writers, like John of Salisbury, could both read and criticize the originals. But again I am straying from the point.

The next head which I mentioned as illustrating the process by which international intercourse worked in a direction favourable to literary progress, was the otherwise curious and interesting point, the number of Englishmen promoted in foreign churches; and, by interchange of good offices, the cases in which foreigners of note were promoted in the English Church. I say, in both cases, men of note, because no doubt many Frenchmen, and even Italians, of whom nothing else is known, were enriched with English preferment, and probably, the few names of Englishmen promoted abroad, which history has recorded, might be supplemented with large additions if the records of foreign churches had been kept as carefully as those of our own. And I am not careful to distinguish here between Norman and native Englishmen, because, from the very accession of Henry II, I regard the two elements as forming one people, and indeed, except in the very highest ranks of the baronage, it is impossible now to distinguish whether the English or the Norman strain was the strongest in any given Englishman. And for a similar reason, it is not necessary to include the Norman and Angevin provinces in our calculation. Many of the great families from which Norman bishops were taken, such as the Beaumonts and the Bohuns, were equally powerful on both sides of the channel, and, it may be added, in the Norman kingdom of Sicily also. Such men as Rotrou of Beaumont, Archbishop of Rouen, and Henry of Beaumont, Bishop of Bayeux, not only were members of a kinship which counted the English Earls of Warwick and Leicester, and the Norman Counts of Meulan as cousins, but were near relations of the Sicilian kings, and knew how to push in the southern regions the fortunes of their servants: the broken-up condition of France left potentates like the Counts of Champagne and Flanders able to treat on an equal footing with the royalties around them, and to govern their own churches quite as freely as the King of France or the Emperor could govern theirs. Hence there was a good deal of international promotion as a matter of course. I shall, however, name only the greatest names; and first take the Englishmen who were promoted abroad.

The two most eminent instances in France and the French-speaking countries are the two Johns, John of Poictiers and John of Salisbury; the latter a name that is so

intimately bound up with our literary history that it may be
adduced to illustrate almost every sort of distinction.   John
of Poictiers was a native of Kent, probably of Canterbury
itself; he was one of the fellow-scholars with Becket and
Roger of Pont l'Evêque in the household of Archbishop
Theobald, which, as I shall have to note presently, was
at that time a substitute in England for the as yet un-
developed Universities; he ran neck and neck with those
great candidates for promotion, and managed, by the adroit-
ness and moderation of his conduct, to steer clear of the
difficulties in which they were constantly embroiled with
either one another or some third party.   Promoted early in
the reign of Henry to the rich stall of treasurer at York, John
became in 1162 Bishop of Poictiers, and in 1181 Archbishop
of Lyons; that great and semi-independent see he held until
1193, when he resigned and fell back on his minor prefer-
ments and the company of the Cistercians of Clairvaux; but
to the day of his death he retained the living of Eynesford
in Kent, and kept up a close correspondence with the
Canterbury clergy and with the learned men of England,
especially Ralph de Diceto, Dean of St. Paul's, with whom
he had in his youth competed for the archdeaconry of
Middlesex.   The letters of John of Poictiers are among
the less important contributions to the Becket literature;
but they are worth reading as the composition of a man
of mark, of sound learning and prudent character, and an
eminent canonist.   The career of John of Salisbury I shall
recur to more particularly further on; he also was a son
of the Church of Canterbury, and retained the closest relations with his Alma Mater as long as he lived.

Another Canterbury man was Ralph de Serris, or Ralph
of Sarr in Thanet, who was Dean of Rheims from 1176 to
1194.   He was a most dutiful son of the Church to which
he owed his education, and no doubt a faithful agent of the

monastic interest, which found at Rheims such powerful protection in the Archbishop William of Champagne and the great family to which he belonged.   Of Ralph of Sarr as a literary man I only know that he wrote fairly good Latin. These three men, you will observe, although sons of the Convent of Canterbury, were not monks; they were pupils of the great school of the monastery and, as clerks of the primate, affiliated to that Church.   When they received foreign promotion they had to be released by a formal document from their allegiance to the mother Church.   John of Poictiers was one of the clerks whom Archbishop Baldwin, and Hubert after him, would have made canons of that college at Lambeth which they intended to set up as a centre of ecclesiastical learning and dignity, emancipated from monastic restrictions; a scheme which, if it had succeeded, might have possibly fixed the university life of England, and its ecclesiastical centre, in London itself.

Not to waste time upon minor names, we go on to Italy: there the greatest name of course is that of Nicolas Breakspere, the pupil of the Monastery of St. Alban's; the great legate of the north, the confidential friend of John of Salisbury, the one English pope, and the bestower of Ireland on Henry II.   His life and career lie only on the very edge of the period which we are considering; and I can say no more of him than that he is one of those figures of mediaeval history of which what little we know is suggestive of a great deal more that we should desire to know.   He was unquestionably a great pope; that is, a great constructive pope, not a controversial one, like those who preceded and followed; a man of organizing power and missionary zeal; a reformer, and, although he did not take a wise way of showing it, a true Englishman.   Next in dignity to him would come, if we were quite sure of anything respecting him, the great Robertus Pullus, who is said to have been made Chancellor of the Apostolic See under Lucius II and Eugenius III, and who likewise lies a little outside our limits. His history has yet to be worked out; but as he is, like John of Salisbury, a historical link of some importance, I must say a word or two about him. We know from a letter of St. Bernard addressed to Ascelin, Bishop of Rochester, between the years 1142 and 1148, that Robertus Pullus was at that time studying with great success in the University of Paris; he was then, it would appear from the Rochester Fasti, Archdeacon of Rochester; and St. Bernard's petition to the bishop, that he might be allowed to pursue his studies at Paris, is thus quite in character with the usual practice for an archdeacon to go and study for some time in a foreign university before he began the formal exercise of archidiaconal functions. In 1146, or thereabouts, Robert was still at Paris teaching theology, and there John of Salisbury attended his lectures during the last two of the twelve years, dating from 1136, that his education was in progress. If these dates are accurate, it is a little difficult to identify him with the person who appears as Chancellor of the Apostolic See in 1145 and 1146. It is not impossible that he was then for a short time transferred to Rome; this, however, will leave no time for his teaching divinity, as he is said to have done, at Exeter and Oxford. He is mentioned as Chancellor of the Apostolic See by the contemporary writer, John of Hexham, who dates him in 1146. Anyhow, he was a man of great mark; that we know from St. Bernard and John of Salisbury, and from his extant works, Sentences, and Sermons. But there was another Robert, also connected with Rochester, also an Italian Chancellor, and mentioned as a distinct person by the same historian of Hexham. He was a native of 'Salesby,' whether Selby or Salisbury I shall not decide, who tried his fortunes in Sicily and became chancellor to King Roger about the same year, 1146. Is it

possible or probable that he has somehow become confounded
with Robertus Pullus?   Certain it is that Paris, Archdeacon
of Rochester in Henry II's reign, was the nephew of
Robertus Pullus; certain it is also that Paris had relations in
Sicily, and was chosen as an envoy in 1176 to that court
because of his connexions there: it is needless to add that
archdeaconries went in those days very frequently from
uncle to nephew, and not uncommonly from father to son.
Whether, however, we have here two Roberts, or two
Roberti Pulli, for the sojourn in Apulia might entitle the
second Robert to the name of Pullanus, or only one, we
have the starting-point of the usage according to which
English ministers were domiciled at the Sicilian Court.
Robert may have been the first; he was not the last.

Master Thomas Brown, with whose name the readers of
Mr. Freeman's books must have become by this time
familiar, was another Englishman, a great financial authority,
who enjoyed the confidence of King Roger until the death
of that king in 1154.   Thomas Brown is the first modern
Englishman, if not the first Englishman of any sort, whose
name was written in Greek.   In that language, as Thomas
Brounos, it appears among the attestations of Greek charters
of King Roger.   After Roger's death, when a new king
arose, who, according to the Dialogus de Scaccario, knew
not Thomas, he returned to his native land, and was immediately summoned by Henry II to his restored exchequer;
he became the king's almoner, and kept at the exchequer a
separate roll of the king's doings.   He had a handsome
pension, too, £36 a year, if not more, and an allowance for
his nephew Ralph.   Madox goes so far as to conjecture
that the special duties which were assigned to him were the
basis of the later office of Chancellor of the Exchequer.

Another Englishman in Sicily was Herbert, a man of
Middlesex, who was Archbishop of Compsa between the

years 1169 and 1180; another, more famous, was Richard, surnamed Palmer, Bishop of Syracuse from 1165 to 1183, and Archbishop of Messina from 1183 onwards; a kindly man, who entertained the relations of Becket when they were driven into exile. He had the credit of first proposing a matrimonial alliance between the two royal houses, and seems to have been detached from Becket's interests by the hope of obtaining the Bishopric of Lincoln. Walter, Archbishop of Palermo 1169–1187, and Bartholomew his brother, Bishop of Agrigentum, who succeeded him at Palermo, are likewise called Englishmen. So close and continuous was the connexion maintained by these men with the kindred realm, that we can quite understand the influences which prevailed on William the Good to propose Henry II as his successor, and Richard I meditating the translation of the Archbishop of Monreale to Canterbury. More apposite, however, to our present subject is the fact that, owing to these men and their connexions at home, there was a constant flow of epistolary intercourse between England and Italy, independent of that which moved to and fro between Rome and the English Church. Henry II doubtless availed himself of both currents for his diplomatic intrigues. The King of Sicily and the Bishop of Syracuse, as well as the men of Milan and Bologna, were sub-agents in the great game which he was playing. And the Italians, Italian as they were, learned to feel some interest in England besides a pecuniary one. The books of later Italian heraldry recognize, I fear somewhat apocryphally, the exiled kinsfolk of Becket as the progenitors of the family of Becchetti of Fabriano. Now and then they repaid the loan of Robert Pullus and Thomas Brown with a scholar or clerk of half-English birth, as Robert and Thomas had in their turn repaid part of the debt incurred by England from Lanfranc of Pavia and Anselm of Aosta. But here I must stop; in the other lecture I shall hope to get into the more purely literary half of the subject, and trace some of the results that accrued from these multiplied relations of courts and councils. The subject, superficially as it must be treated in lectures like this, persistently grows upon our hands.

LEARNING AND LITERATURE AT THE COURT OF HENRY II

(June 13, 1878.)

IN following out the inquiry which I began in the last Lecture, in order to complete the outline of our subject and take into account all the influences that conduced to a full literary intercourse between England and the Continent during the period of Henry II, the next point that I should take would be the enumeration of those foreign scholars and literary ecclesiastics who were favoured or promoted in England. This point, however, need not detain us long, for there were very few. England itself had no love for foreigners; whether as captains of mercenaries, or as papal nominees to ecclesiastical preferment, they impartially detested them; and the detestation was very frequently justified by the view which the foreigners took of England and the English; a country out of which as much revenue as could be wrung should be wrung, and a people at whom, when they had plundered them, it was their delight to laugh. Nor were the Angevin kings much inclined to a policy which they knew to be most odious to their subjects; Henry II avoided either ruling or controlling England by foreign ministers, and did very little to encourage an influx of foreign ecclesiastics. Excepting such persons as, like Hugh de Puiset, Bishop of Durham, and two or three others, were closely connected by blood with the royal house, few foreigners were made bishops; and when Becket, according to his biographer, wished to restore learning at the court, he urged the king to recall home the English scholars who were studying abroad. Of the few, who would be all that could be named, the most prominent are Peter of Blois and Master Vacarius.

Peter of Blois seems to have made his home in England, after he had tried his chances in Sicily, where he had been tutor to William the Good. He settled here about the year 1173, after the Becket troubles were over, and made himself useful to both the king and the archbishops. Like John of Salisbury, he made his pen serviceable to his masters, and many of the letters of his composition which are preserved were written in their names. As chancellor or secretary to the Archbishop, as Archdeacon first of Bath and afterwards of London, and Dean of Wolverhampton, Peter seems to have led a scrambling sort of literary existence; being used by the kings and primates on services both diplomatic and ecclesiastical, for which his versatility and command of language qualified him, but not being much trusted or highly promoted. Master Vacarius, on the other hand, was a very obscure, or rather indistinct, person; indeed so little is known of him that it is almost hazardous to commit oneself to the theory that the earlier and later Vacarius were the same person. He is of course known to lawyers as the Lombard scholar, who, in 1149, attempted to introduce the study of the civil law into England and to teach it at Oxford. He is said to have been silenced by King Stephen, and as a teacher he disappears, but from two or three passages in the Becket letters it seems that he remained in England; in the list of the canons of Southwell his name occurs later on in the century, and as late even as 1198 Pope Innocent III commissioned Vacarius, with another ecclesiastic of the northern province, to carry into execution certain letters touching the crusade. If the name is indeed rightly read, and belongs to the Magister Vacarius of 1149, he must have been very old and of little use.   The history, however, both of Peter of Blois and of Vacarius, has been carefully worked out by independent writers of authority, and I use them here only as examples.   Mere ecclesiastics, such as Simon of Apulia, who was made Bishop of Exeter by King John after having been Dean of York for many years ; and ministers of state, such as Walter of Coutances, William of St. Mere l'Eglise, and perhaps William Longchamp, call for no notice in this connexion ; and I pass on to the much more important point—the literary intercourse and activity promoted by university life.

I have already mentioned the two or three foreign schools which were most frequented by English scholars.   Paris was the centre of theological learning and general culture, Bologna was the school for lawyers, especially the canon lawyers ; for the civil law, although equally well taught there, did not obtain much favour with Englishmen ; and besides these, the pupils who either could not afford to go to Paris, or could afford to exhaust all the teaching that the neighbour lands afforded, went to the school of Tours.   Tours had the advantage of being locally situated within the dominions of the king of England, and although it did not aspire to the character of a university, as later understood, it had a very ancient and very eminent succession of teachers.

John of Salisbury, in the second book of the Metalogicus, sketches the twelve years of his university career ; in 1136 he went to Paris and studied at St. Genevieve's under the *clarus doctor* identified with Abelard, who taught him dialectic, as did also Master Alberic, who succeeded, and Robert of Melun, the English doctor who, after the accession of Henry II, was invited home again and made Bishop of Hereford.   He then read for three years, with William of Conches, grammar ; then, with Richard l'Evêque, he attacked

the quadrivium, and, under Peter de Helie, rhetoric : after
that he took to Aristotle again under Adam of Petitpont, an
English scholar who was afterwards made Bishop of St. Asaph ;
his next teacher was William of Soissons, who was attempting
to upset the old logic. At this point of his career, after ten
years of study, he began to take pupils, his poverty com-
pelling. From William of Soissons he went on to Gilbert of
la Porrée and Robert Pullus. He had now reached the study
of divinity and wound up with Simon of Poissy, a faithful
lecturer but somewhat obtuse debater, 'fidus lector sed
obtusior disputator'; if he had gone through the discipline
that John had passed through, it was no wonder. After
these twelve years of study John went to Celles as chaplain
or secretary to the Abbot Peter ; and about 1150 returned to
England, where St. Bernard recommended him to Archbishop
Theobald. His career of usefulness in England thus began
just at the time when Vacarius was teaching law, and
Theobald was maintaining in his own palace the school of
literature from which so many conspicuous men afterwards
sprang. For thirty years John continued to live, the central
figure of English learning; suffering indeed many troubles
with Becket, whose companion he was in his exile, but
restored to his home in 1170; in 1176 he was made Bishop
of Chartres, and he died in 1180. His career is conspicuous,
and he had both ability and opportunity that were given
to few.

I can only mention now the names of the other students
at Paris who to some extent trod in his footsteps : Ralph de
Diceto the historian, Archdeacon of Middlesex and Dean
of St. Paul's, studied at St. Genevieve shortly after John of
Salisbury ; he lived to the end of the century ; Robert of
Melun and Robert Pullus had not only been pupils but
teachers at Paris, and Adam of Petitpont the same ; these
have been already mentioned. Walter Map, the poet and

satirist, afterwards Archdeacon of Oxford, was another
Parisian student; so was Giraldus Cambrensis; so probably
were Roger of Hoveden and most of those ecclesiastics of
the time to whom the title *magister* is given in formal documents, of whom it would be useless labour to give a catalogue.
The scholars of Tours were of the same class. Bologna was
the special university for young archdeacons; and, as most
archdeacons were appointed when very young and by family
interest, there was a tolerably rapid succession of them, and
I fear it must be added that they fell into a great many
temptations. We all know of the question discussed at this
period, 'An possit archidiaconus salvus esse'; whatever were
the peculiar temptations of his official career, he was lucky if
he passed without debt or difficulty through his university
course. In 1200 Henry de Jacea, Archdeacon of Liege, and
not only archdeacon but bishop-elect, was killed in a scuffle
with the townsmen of Paris. At Bologna debt seems to have
been the greater snare. Gilbert Foliot, when Bishop of
London, had sometimes two archdeacons at once studying
there; and at the same time there was resident there a
Canon of St. Paul's, Master David, whose letters have been
recently published in the Spicilegium Liberianum. David
was an Englishman who had studied at Clermont and at
Paris, and had gone on to Bologna in the idea of qualifying
himself for an archdeaconry, of which the bishop had
perhaps given him a half promise. At Bologna he had got
into debt, and set up as tutor to the young archdeacons; he
then went on to Rome, where, by the use of the names
of his great patrons, he nearly succeeded in getting a recommendation for the Deanery of St. Paul's. Very ungrateful
conduct this was, for the deanery was one of the best things
that could be got in London, and Master Ralph de Diceto,
who was to be the next dean, was actually being made to
allow Mr. David an exhibition of ten pounds a year from his

own archdeaconry towards his expenses. It is satisfactory
to know that David did not get the deanery, although we
know no more about him. The two young archdeacons
fulfilled their term of study, and one of them became a
bishop. All the three had, by the provisions of the cathedral
statutes, dispensation from residence whilst they were away
at the schools. The statute of St. Paul's, drawn by Ralph de
Diceto himself, allowed not only non-residence but a pension
of 40*s.* per annum from the communa or dividend of the
canons; the student must go for not less than a year; he
might go for two or three. This permission was freely
used: the great churches, which had thirty or forty canons,
at all stages of the ecclesiastical career, could well afford
to dispense with the services of the younger ones, and they,
notwithstanding the temptations of University life, could
scarcely fail to bring back with them at the end of the time
some experience, some culture and knowledge of the world,
that fitted them for the occupations of their later life, whether
their destiny was to serve the king in his court and
embassies, or to make themselves useful in the educational
work which was still carried on largely in all the cathedral
establishments.

And so by a natural transition we pass to another point
of interest, the attempts made by the bishops and clergy
to furnish to Englishmen in their own land some of the
appliances of learning which they found at the foreign
Universities. And this had a particular importance at this
particular time; for there is no doubt that the reign of
Henry II is a period which saw a great development of
University life, if not the very origin of University life itself,
at Oxford. Before this time we hear of Vacarius lecturing
in law, and, by somewhat questionable authority, of Robert
Pullus lecturing on theology here; but both, or either, may
have been mere teachers in the royal court, or private tutors

M

under the Canons of St. Frideswide. But before the end of
the reign there was a University with doctors and masters.
Yes, and public lectures; for did not Giraldus Cambrensis,
in 1187, come to Oxford and read his Expugnatio Hiberniae
in public lectures? and did he not secure himself an audience
by entertaining, on the first day, all the poor of the town at
his lodgings, and on the second all the doctors of the diverse
faculties and the more distinguished scholars; and on the
third day the rest of the scholars, the passmen as we should
put it, with the county people, the townsmen, and the citizens?
Ah! he tells us, it was a sumptuous and noble affair, a renewal
of the old and authentic days of the poets; 'nor has the
present age, or any antiquity, remembered in England any
such gaudy day.' It is a lesson for all time.

Beyond, however, the fact that thus comes full upon us,
that in 1187 there was at Oxford a great school with diverse
faculties of doctors, ergo, a constituted University, we know
little or nothing of University life here so early. Only we
know that those who in later times might have been able to
tell us something true about this, chose to tell us what was
false; and, by hunting up and forging evidences of greater
antiquity, lost their hold, and prevented us from ever obtaining a hold on the materials which might have furnished
authentic history. There can be no doubt that, when the
idea of the University had once impressed itself on the minds
of Englishmen, it would rapidly work a change. It centralized teaching and it promoted competition. Not that
the idea had to work itself out on English ground; our
English Universities, however far in the historic distance we
may throw back their origin, must have been framed on the
model of the Continental Universities. I do not mean that
they had not their rise in independent and special circumstances, or that they were not the successors of more ancient
schools of study, many of which continued to exist for some

time around the greater cathedrals; but that their University organization, their degrees and faculties, were borrowed from the established institutions on the Continent. They centralized however, and to a great extent superseded, the earlier schools; they afforded more room for speculation, gave greater scope for competition, and greater chances of independence.

But as this was the age of transition from the local to the centralized system, our business now is rather with the earlier than with the later form. I have already said that the household of Archbishop Theobald, in the reign of Stephen, to some extent satisfied the want which was afterwards met by the University system. He provided learned teachers, and his clerks, after learning what they could at Canterbury, went over to Paris and Bologna to take their degrees after sufficient and more advanced study. It was not however only in the palace of the Archbishop of Canterbury that such a school existed. Every great man had a great house and household, with his chapel or collegiate church at his capital house, and his school of clerks as well as pages. Many of these large establishments lasted, with diverse modifications, into comparatively modern times, and one of the traces of survival still subsists in the privilege of noblemen to qualify so many domestic chaplains, although the particular privileges of the chaplains are mostly things of the past. But, of course, as the castles of the Earls were rather schools of knightly than of clerkly accomplishments, the best illustrations of the scholarly life are found in the houses of the prelates.

The king's palace was not less a centre of learned talk and training, although, as the king was seldom at home more than two or three days together, it is not absolutely certain that he would take a strong interest in the matter; the fact of Oxford having been a convenient royal residence may account perhaps for one of the influences that fixed the University here, just as the school of St. Frideswide's priory may account for another. It is in the proof that there existed a general fashion of literary association and conversation that these clusters of scholars, settled in the great houses, are so interesting.

Peter of Blois gives a sketch of one such cluster in the house of the Archbishop. 'Good master,' he writes, 'you blame me for spending my days at court, when I might fructify in the scholastic camps. But this court in which I live is, I assure you, a camp of God, none other than the house of God and the gate of heaven. In the house of my lord the Archbishop are most scholarly men, with whom is found all the uprightness of justice, all the caution of providence, every form of learning. They, after prayers, and before meals (mark the connexion, and think of Giraldus's public lecture), in reading, in disputing, in the decision of causes, constantly exercise themselves. All the knotty questions of the realm are referred to us, and, when they are discussed in the common hearing, each of us, without strife or objectation, sharpens his wits to speak well upon them, and produces, from a more subtile vein, what he thinks the most prudent and sensible advice.' This is in contrast with the turbulent, and sometimes stormy, discussions in the rising Universities.

Herbert of Bosham, one of the biographers of St. Thomas and himself one of the Archbishop's clerks, affords us some glimpses into the working of this institution; and gives us long discussions between Becket and the learned staff that accompanied him in most of his tribulations. Some of these are very curious; they show that the Archbishop had amongst his chaplains a staff of professors on a small scale; this one skilled in canon law, that in historic precedent; one to whom they looked when an apposite quotation from the

poets was wanted, and another who had pretensions to be a
philosopher. In one of the supplementary chapters Herbert
gives a list of these, the *eruditi Sancti Thomae*; the catalogue
includes, of course, many of the names that I have already
mentioned, John of Salisbury, Archdeacon Robert Foliot,
and Ralph of Sarr; besides these there were, Lombardus
of Piacenza, afterwards Archbishop of Benevento, Reginald
the Lombard, son of Bishop Jocelin of Salisbury, afterwards
Bishop of Bath and Archbishop, Gerard la Pucelle, Hugh
of Nonant and Gilbert Glanville, afterwards bishops, and
several others; of whom the most famous was Uberto of
Milan, afterwards Pope Urban III, who had attached himself
to Becket in his exile.

I think that a generation further back, in the household
of Theobald or of Henry of Blois, we might perhaps find,
if record had remained, a more illustrious list; Theobald
certainly contributed the traditions of Bec Abbey, which had
gathered round Lanfranc and Anselm, whilst Henry concentrated about him all that remained of the enlightenment and
refinement of English and Norman society.

Whilst Theobald, however, collected learned men and
Henry collected statuary from Italy, whilst the great Bishop
Roger built his miracles of castles, England was a prey to
conflicting factions, and every great man was bound above
all things to be a politician. Hence the academic and
political elements were thus early found in closest union:
if Henry, Baldwin and Amalric, discussed deep questions of
theology with their councillors, the knotty questions of the
realm were laid before Peter of Blois and Giraldus Cambrensis; and the minds of the *curiales* were, notwithstanding
the sneers of the satirists, occupied on the same matters as
those of the *scholares*.

To this community of subject it is that we owe some of
the most significant anecdotes of the great men of the time:

the scraps of conversation of Ranulf Glanville, the great justiciar, who discussed, as he was riding out, the decay of valour among the French; the amusing exaggerations of Giraldus when he criticizes the colloquial Latin of Hubert Walter; the most interesting details of the friendship between St. Hugh of Lincoln and Henry II; and very much that enlivens such books as the Polycraticus of John of Salisbury, the de Nugis Curialium of Walter Map, the de Institutione Principum and other discursive productions of Giraldus, the Otia Imperialia of Gervase, and the Satires of Nigel of Canterbury. It is true indeed that men professedly literary would most naturally, I am afraid I cannot say necessarily or invariably, preserve such scraps as might be supposed to have a literary or historical interest; and therefore that such anecdotes may not be a fair specimen of the ordinary conversations of the educated classes of the time. Granting that, it is at least pleasant to find that amidst the great and varied mass of literary remains there is so very little, hardly anything, that would show the prevailing tone to have been coarse or base. There is some profanity, not a little hardness and narrowness, but very little indeed of the foolish and inconvenient jesting which later on becomes the mark of all courtly literature.

If now we were to imagine a foreign scholar visiting England at the period of which we are speaking, either, like Mabillon or Pertz, making an Iter Anglicum to collect materials for history, or like Solon simply, θεωρίης είνεκεν, to see what the world was like, or like the admirable Crichton to air his own erudition and try the mettle of English scholars in literary tournaments, or like John of Salisbury to gather all the knowledge that he could, how would he fare? He would land, we suppose, at Dover and be lodged in the Benedictine Priory there, where he would find that his visit was recorded among the visits of kings and ambassadors in a precious

chronicle that embodied the annals of all public events and
copies of public documents; then he would go on to Canterbury, where he would find himself at once in a great literary
centre, with teachers and libraries and all appliances that
stand to the population and society of the day in much the
same proportion as the literary life of Oxford or Cambridge
would at this moment. He would find Gervase, the sacrist,
busy over the chronicles of the kings and the history of his
own time; Nigel writing his verses, polishing the great
mediaeval satire Burnellus, or inditing the prose letter in
which he castigates the faults of the secular clergy; a monk
in a strictish convent, but corresponding with the ministers
of a powerful and politic court: there too he would find
Odo the prior, a great theologian, William the sub-prior and
Edward Grim, biographers of St. Thomas; if he came after
1186 he would find the whole convent busily writing Latin
letters, letters in very fair grammatical Latin, garnished with
quotations from Ovid and Lucan and the laws canon and
civil. If he went on to Rochester, there he would be entertained by Archdeacon Paris, the nephew of Robert Pullus,
possibly a near kinsman of the great chronicler of the next
age; there he might find Bishop Glanville, the preacher of the
Third Crusade, one of the learned pupils of St. Thomas, and
close kinsman of the great lawyer; or if he went on to
Chichester, he would fall in with the Dean Matthew, or
Jordan, or Gervase, all of them members of the same
company, and Herbert of Bosham in the close neighbourhood,
the squire parson of the time, also a careful and admiring
biographer. Going on to Winchester, he would be entertained either by the venerable Bishop Henry, whose memory
was a very storehouse of history; the grandson of the
Conqueror and depository of all the great traditions of the
generation, the king-maker of the twelfth century, who also
had his learned men around him; or by Richard of Ilchester,

the confidential minister of the king, himself no mean adept in the writing of historical dispatches; Richard of Devizes is there too writing the history of his time; further on, at Salisbury, another of the eminent ministers is the dean, John of Oxford, a traveller, and lawyer and divine, a man whose very name suggests that he might have been one of the first magistri of his own University: possibly John of Salisbury might be there too, or Reginald, the bishop's son, as archdeacon or bishop, a most intelligent and travelled diplomatist. At Exeter, early in the reign, he would find Bishop Bartholomew, the famous preacher and canonist, Baldwin, the archdeacon and scholasticus, afterwards archbishop and crusader, with his brother Joseph, the poet, who attempted in an Hexameter Epic to rival the glories of Virgil, and in his lost Antiocheis to build up a poetic memorial of the First Crusade; no mean poet, although ambitious, but considered worthy to rank with the classics edited, 'in usum serenissimi Delphini,' with Dictys of Crete and Dares of Phrygia.

But if our friend was bent northwards, we might take him at once to London and introduce him to the Dean and Chapter of St. Paul's or the great Bishop Foliot and the king's court. At St. Paul's he would meet, ten to one, not only the lord mayor, aldermen, and justices, whom the canon in residence was specially bound to entertain, but any distinguished strangers who happened to be in town: the venerable old dean, Ralph de Diceto, would show him the beautiful MS. of his *Ymagines*; from the canon Richard, the high treasurer, he might learn the history of the Exchequer, or even borrow the precious Tricolumnis before it was lost; Peter of Blois would be grumbling at the small profits of his archdeaconry, but wisely putting his pen to good interest; Roger Niger perhaps just flying from the wrath of the king, whom he has exasperated by savage invective; and

the great Foliot himself, the able statesman who pitted
all his skill, experience, and learning against the zeal of
Becket and lost the game, at least in the opinion of his
contemporaries.

At the court would be Ranulf Glanville, the father of the
study of English common law, and the astute band of justices
who shared with him the confidence of the most sagacious
and business-like of kings.   Our friend would find the
historical mind fairly well awake to the importance of the era
in which it found itself: the author of the Gesta Regis Henrici
may not yet have chosen to be anonymous, but have been
keeping a busy account from day to day of the king's doings;
Thomas Brown would be there with his roll, and Peter of
Blois moralizing ' de Praestigiis fortunae,' on the magic tricks
of Fortune exemplified in the career of his royal patron ;
and the author perhaps of the Draco Normannicus awaiting
a reward for panegyrizing the old Empress Maud ; not to
speak again of Ralph de Diceto and Gervase of Tilbury.   At
Westminster he would fall in with the Abbot Laurence, a
theologian of some note in those days when almost every
learned man was a theologian.   In London indeed, or at
Westminster, all the men whom I have mentioned might at
any stirring time be found together : William Fitz-Stephen,
the biographer of Becket, possibly becoming a judge after he
had tried his fortune as a scholar, but known to us by the
lively picture which he has drawn of London in his own days ;
Giraldus Cambrensis, the erratic Norman-Welshman, who, as
he would be looked for everywhere, might safely be caught
near the king ; even Roger of Hoveden, the learned Rector
of Howden and chronicler of the north, but a king's chaplain
and occasional justice of the forest.   Time would fail him to
learn even the names of all the subordinate scholars of London :
he goes on northwards by St. Alban's and Peterborough.

Nothing is more curious than the lively historic activity

going on in the monasteries: MSS. are copied, luxurious editions are recopied and illuminated; there is no lack of generosity in lending or of boldness in borrowing; there is brisk competition and liberal open rivalry. St. Alban's is especially rich in the collected materials that lie at the foundation of her great code of chronicles. At Peterborough Abbot Benedict is equally busy, directing transcription and compiling or editing his own recollections of St. Thomas; but every little monastery has its record: Crowland is thinking of hiring Peter of Blois, or some pretended Peter who borrows an illustrious name, to fabricate for her an apocryphal chronicle; at Ramsey there is an invaluable chronicle kept, going far back into the old English times, and there is the same at Ely conducted by a succession of learned and patriotic monks. But at Peterborough the pen has just dropped from the hand of the native annalists.

Coming to Lincoln, there is Walter Map with his poems and stories about the courtiers, acting as archdeacon or precentor; the wise St. Hugh himself, the bishop, has stories to tell at the high table in the hall, and admiring disciples anxious to gather up every word that falls from his lips.

So our friend goes on into Yorkshire; if he stays at Howden by the way he may be put under contribution by the rector and made to tell what marvellous tale he can tell about his own country; perhaps to compare notes about the news from Constantinople, or the story of the enchantment that guided the storms in the Gulf of Satalia, or the last enormity of Swerre Birkbain and the fellow kings of Norway. For Roger of Hoveden is quite Herodotean both in the faithfulness of his personal relations and in the wish to incorporate in his chronicle all that he can gather touching the geography and history of strange lands. Going on to York, the traveller finds himself in the midst of legal controversies; there had been good schools there once, but the

head master was lost in a storm at sea in 1177, and since then
the canons have taken to quarrelling.   There have always
been two parties there and some black sheep in the flock.
The archbishop too, since Becket's death, has been under a
cloud, so the chapter is at sixes and sevens.   Peter of Blois
looks in occasionally when in residence at Ripon, and Hubert
Walter, the dean, tries to keep matters fairly well together, but
there are quarrels even within the precincts of the church, and
in more than one case there are rival claimants for the same
stall : on one solemn occasion the precentor stops the music
to spite the treasurer, the treasurer puts out the lights to be
even with the precentor.   But, notwithstanding, there are
quiet pens taking notes ; and a good deal of York news
filters into the general history.   There is the biographer
of the archbishops, one or more than one ; not far off, at
Newburgh, in the Augustinian priory, is William, the little
inquisitive and intelligent canon, who is writing a history
of England, not in the mere receptive spirit of the annalist
like Hoveden, nor in the didactic style of William of Malmesbury, but like a thoughtful man who wishes to trace the
origins and tendencies of the events that he records, who
weighs his epithets and suspends his judgements, and, whilst
he admits the marvellous, argues only when and where he
has sufficient data.   If William of Newburgh ever comes
up to York, depend upon it he is well received by all the
thoughtful men.   The Prior of Hexham too is *ex officio* a
canon of York, and he also is, as his predecessor was, a
writer of history strikingly in advance of the mere annotator
of annals.

If the visitor can be prevailed on to go so far north as
Hexham, he may even reach Melrose, and there watch the
process of annal making, and come home by Durham.   There
he will find a magnificent court under Bishop Hugh, the
great prince prelate of the period, who lives in three-quarters

independence between the kings of Scots and English; and in his train poets, preachers and writers of histories, who are one after another continuing the work which had been begun by Bede, and continued after long breaks by Simeon and the Hexham writers. And so, having completely traversed the literary world of England, he may come south, through either the eastern or the western counties, sure to find at every monastery or cathedral he may visit some one employed in keeping up the record of public as well as local history, or otherwise attempting to keep alive the fire of literary zeal.

He would go away, I think, from such a view with the impression that, whatever drawbacks there might be to the full enjoyment of life, England was a paradise of clerks. True, the cruel legate, Hugeson, had betrayed them to the king, had actually yielded the point, that most important point, about the forest law, and allowed the king to prosecute clerical offenders against the peace of the king's venison, and have them hauled before the sheriffs in the county court;— but that was the only drawback to the free enjoyment of clerical society. So far as books were concerned, there was such a supply of writers and readers as would be found nowhere else in Europe, except in the University of Paris itself. Such an impression, I take it, would not be far from the truth: for the extant remains of the literary work of the period are so great, that, if we suppose them to bear the ordinary proportion to the lost works of the same age, they would prove it to be enormously prolific. I do not claim for it such a distinction, because I think that most of what was really worth preserving has been preserved; preserved because the men whose task it was to take care of it were sensible that it was the work of an age of transcendent importance in every region of English life; constitutional, moral and intellectual.

The greater works of the time survived not only because they were the most famous works of the time, but because

they were of really great value. Thus Glanville's work on
the Laws became the manual and textbook of the lawyers;
the Dialogus de Scaccario the standing order book of the
high Court of Exchequer; the annals of Roger Hoveden the
recognized book of authoritative chronicle record, to which,
whenever a question of foreign policy or even domestic
diplomacy arose, recourse might at once be had. That the
lawyers and statesmen of the day were not above the study
of history may be proved by the later use of these and the
like chronicles; especially when Stephen Langton produced
the Charter of Henry I before the barons at St. Paul's, or
when Edward I consulted all the cathedral and monastic
chronicles of England in order to ascertain the true nature
and extent of his claims over Scotland; or when Edward III
elaborated his claim to France; or when the Commission of
Doctors at Westminster searched all chronicles for information on the pedigree of the house of Lancaster; or when
Beaufort and Gloucester explored them to ascertain the
constitutional position of a regent; or when, to crown all,
poor Henry VI, who probably was the best historical scholar
in his divided realm, was requested by the lords of his
parliament to search, out of the chronicles which he had
loved so well, the materials by which they might come to the
conclusion that he was a traitor and a usurper.

There have been, as I said, losses; but it may well be
that the great value of the works that have survived may
lead us somewhat to exaggerate the worth of those which
have perished; the Antiocheis of Joseph of Exeter, the
Tricolumnis of Bishop Richard, the de Praestigiis Fortunae
of Peter of Blois, the Liber Facetiarum of Gervase of
Tilbury may not have been so permanently important as
we should suppose; but there is no question of the serious
importance of the lost leaves of the Gesta Stephani or the
Draco Normannicus.

I have, you may observe, given prominence in this lecture
to certain names and certain sorts of names.   I have given
them prominence because it was desireable, even at the risk
of repetition, to impress them on the memory, even if it
should prove impossible to form or fix any individual conception of them: they are the greatest names, and the names
of those who have left the most precious books behind them.
But they are very far from all; a reference to some such
book as Mr. Wright's Biographia Britannica Literaria would
furnish a long list cf names of men who have places in the
bibliographies; both historians, philosophers and naturalists,
according to the idea of those days.   If we turn, too, to
Leyser's Bibliotheca Poetica we find many names of English
poets, Englishmen, that is, who wrote Latin verses, but of
whom little else is really known, and whose verses are neither
in manner nor matter so good as the poorest prose of the
period.   Geoffrey Vinsauf, who no doubt was the best-known
Latin poet of the time, has left no personal history; his work,
framed on the Epistle to the Pisos, is by no means to be
despised as a guide to the mediaeval ideal of Latin poetry, nor
is it a mean work in itself.   But the average of the poetry,
with that exception and the Trojan War of Joseph of Exeter,
is low, whether we look at the classical forms followed by
these writers and some of the satirists or at the rhymed Latin
poems of which Walter Map was so fertile a producer.   A
great many of the good prose writers, however, attempted
versification.   We have, starting with Henry of Huntingdon,
a generation earlier, a fair list of good scholars who thought
verse the best medium of enthusiastic panegyric.   John of
Salisbury mingles encomium and sarcasm in his Entheticus, a
book in which he has described in enigmatic language most
of the courtiers of the time, with praise or dispraise.   William
Fitz-Stephen, the biographer of Becket, courted the ear of
Henry II with a poem which he presented to him at Brill,

and which seems to have been so far successful that the king pardoned him for his adherence to the archbishop ; Giraldus Cambrensis wrote epigrams, Walter Map hymns and poems of edification as well as satires ; the author of the Dialogus de Scaccario and the Latin biographer of Richard I both run into what would be doggerel if it were not Latin, apparently out of the very glee of their hearts and devotion to their subject-matter.

But as every one who could write prose thought that he could write verse, and as good Latin verse required a somewhat higher strain than passable Latin prose, it is not surprising that the verse has been mostly forgotten. The question then which this point seems to suggest, to what did it all come, what amount of real, critical, and literary culture does this great mass of Latin writing truly imply? must be answered thus : The Latin of the twelfth century is fairly good and grammatical Latin ; adjective agrees with substantive and verb with its nominative case; *ut* governs the subjunctive, and the dependent sentence follows the mood and tense prescribed by the principal sentence. There is a great fertility of vocabulary, there are frequent and consistent uses of words which in classical Latin are somewhat rare, as if the writer prided himself on knowing how to use *dumtaxat* and *quippe* and *utpote*, and brought them in at every turn : but even here there is nothing that is laboured; the Latin, if too free, is scarcely ever unnatural. It is Latin written as by men who on literary matters talked and thought in Latin ; it is not dead but a living language, senescent, perhaps, but in a green old age. The more pretentious writers, like Peter of Blois, wrote perhaps with fewer solecisms but with more pedantry, and certainly lost freedom by straining after elegance.

Just think now what this common familiarity with Latin implies. It implies almost as ready a hold on all the great works of antiquity as the power of reading English at the present day implies with respect to our own national classics.

To John of Salisbury, after his twelve years of study, all the writings of the Latin historians, poets and orators, the Christian fathers, the legists and the canonists, were not more ready of access than they were to the practical administrator, who could write freely and plainly an account of the details of his official board. This facility of learning was limited only by the scarcity of books; a very fatal limitation, but not half so fatal as the common fault of these days, when there are so many more books than there are readers with a will to read. All these writers of Latin were readers of Latin, and many of them read a great deal. John of Salisbury's reading certainly rivalled that of Burton, the author of the Anatomy of Melancholy, and his power of reference and quotation was assuredly not inferior. As he worked among the classics, Ralph de Diceto worked among the historians of the silver and later age; Aulus Gellius and Seneca, I will venture to say, were commoner books in the hands of ordinary readers then than now : as for the poets, I have spoken before. The great Roman historians were, I fear, less directly known. Some parts of Caesar's Commentaries, Suetonius, Florus, Eutropius, Justin, were, I think, directly known; I question whether Livy or Tacitus was; except so much as had filtered through the Historia Miscella, or the translations and additions to the Chronicon of Eusebius. Seneca certainly was read and utilized ; there is indeed a manuscript of Seneca which contains on a fly-leaf a trace of having been at the English court about this very time. But John of Salisbury's acquaintance with Roman literature can only be estimated by a careful reading of the Polycraticus ; and we must remember that what he could read was at least within the reach of his contemporaries.

I have not said much in these lectures about the vernacular writers of the reign, whether of the Norman or English race ; for indeed they can hardly as yet be said to be literary people. But I must not finish without a word about them, lest I should be thought to undervalue them. The poem of Jordan Fantosme, on the rebellion of the sons of Henry in 1173 and 1174; the poem on the Conquest of Ireland; the original French poem of Ambrose [1], on which the Gesta Ricardi are founded; the Life of St. Thomas of Canterbury, by Garnier of Pont St. Maxence; the valuable poetic chronicle of Benedict of St. Maur, are the beginnings of a new literature the value of which is prospective; predecessors of Villehardouin and Joinville and the Chronique d'Outremer, after the law, if there be such a law, that in the development of a vernacular literature poetry takes precedence of prose. I sometimes think that the growth of this school or schools of com-

---

[1] The poem of Ambrose here referred to has been, since the last edition of these lectures, edited by M. Gaston Paris, from the unique Vatican MS., and published at the Imprimerie Nationale, 1897. It is unquestionably the poem from which, in the Chronicon Terrae Sanctae (Martene and Durand, Amplissima Collectio, v. 577), the work known as Itinerarium Regis Ricardi is said to have been translated, from French into Latin, under the direction of the Prior of the Holy Trinity. The book in its Latin form is the work, according to Trivet, of Richard, Canon of the Holy Trinity; and as his original work was edited by me, under the direction of the Master of the Rolls, in 1864, it is perhaps a fair illustration of higher criticism, that having in the introduction to that volume proved $\pi\alpha\nu\tau\grave{\iota}$ $\dot{\epsilon}\xi\hat{\eta}s$ $\tau\epsilon\kappa\mu\eta\rho\acute{\iota}\wp$ that it could not have been translated from a poetical or French original, I am now glad to recognize that such a poetical French original is indeed forthcoming. I will add, however, as a mark of my contrition, that Ambrose was a historical person, and a clerk of the king's chapel, as shown by the document here quoted : " Rex etc. W. Thesaurario et camerariis de Scaccario &c. Liberate de thesauro nostro xxv solidos Eustacio capellano et Ambrosio clericis nostris, qui cantaverunt *Christus vicit* ad secundam coronationem nostram et ad unctionem et coronationem I. reginae uxoris nostrae. T. me ipso apud Westm. x° die Octobris." Rot. Contrabrev. Normanniae, 2 Joh. M. 2.; Madox, Exchequer, p. 119. The coronation was Oct. 8, 1200. See Itinerarium Regis Ricardi, pref. pp. lv–lxx. May I add that this book of mine was honoured in the *Times* with a full page of review, nine-tenths of which was an extract or series of extracts from the Introduction itself, printed as original matter. This is *ancient* history.

position was owing to the increased interest taken by women in the history of their country; certainly the spread and strengthening of it tend to show that the classes to whom the use of Latin, except in the Church services, was becoming less and less familiar, were beginning to care to have a literature of their own. It shows, moreover, taken in connexion with that deadly liveliness of the Latin poetry which I have adverted to, that, whilst Latin was still a ready enough medium for serious writing, it was necessary to find something better and freer than Latin verse to interest people. Mediaeval Latin prose never dies out; mediaeval Latin verse continues to live only as a pedantic and attenuated survival from the moment that either Norman French or mediaeval English poetry comes into fashion. Into these fields of investigation I do not now propose to intrude. I shall have done something to reconcile myself with the perfunctory and superficial way in which alone my irksome duty on these occasions can be discharged, if I have called your attention to the literary side of a period of our history which, although it may be the fashion to regard it as obscure and barbarous, still contains the germination and early growth of institutions which are vital portions of our national existence. An age so important as that of Henry II in constitutional growth could not be an age of barrenness and deadness in any department of culture, altogether; that it was not is amply proved not only by the remains of literary work which are still preserved to us, but by the glimpse they give us into circles of scholar-like activity, a highly stimulated growth of literature, and an extent of education which we ought to be the last to undervalue.

THE MEDIAEVAL KINGDOMS OF CYPRUS AND
ARMENIA

(Oct. 26 and 29, 1878.)

I HOPE that I need not apologize for my choice of a subject. The events of the last two years can scarcely be called to mind without much misgiving, both as to the way in which they have been construed by contemporary readers, and as to the way in which they will be judged by history. I am not one of those who hold that the maintenance of an opinion contrary to their own belief implies either moral delinquency or mental imbecility. I have been quite prepared to admit that two honest men, equally gifted and alike trying to be impartial, may come to diametrically opposite conclusions from the same evidence. But it is sickening to see the policy of a statesman, still more to see the question of a fact, debated, maintained or contradicted, by advocates whose arguments are not based upon attempts to find out the truth, but are simply weapons of attack and defence. ' This is to be believed because it suits the party ; this is to be discredited because it would damage the party : this is true because Pericles has said it ; this is false, or why should Alcibiades, or Cleon, or whoever it may be, have called heaven and earth to witness that it is true ? ' It will be a good thing if, after so much that is disheartening in the popular treatment of great questions, even one little benefit may be secured. Whatever may be thought of the Anglo-Turkish Convention, on whatever grounds, moral or political, we may determine that the salvation of Turkey is possible, or that Cyprus is an unhealthy island, a professor of History may draw some little comfort from the fact that the attention of people has been called to a portion of the history of Christendom of which little notice has been taken of late years, and which is closely connected with one of the greatest movements that ever affected the history of the world. Having said this, I will add that my object in this lecture is not to ventilate dogmas, to impress any principle, moral or political, or to justify any foregone conclusion. I plead guilty to the charge brought against me of choosing subjects which are of no importance to any human being ; I wish simply to talk about a subject on which a good deal of intelligent interest has arisen, and in the further discussion of which many fresh points of interest may be expected to present themselves.

It is right, however, that I should preface one word of caution against myself. The Crusades are not, in my mind, either the popular delusions that our cheap literature has determined them to be, nor papal conspiracies against kings and peoples, as they appear to the Protestant controversialist ; nor the savage outbreaks of expiring barbarism thirsting for blood and plunder, nor volcanic explosions of religious intolerance. I believe them to have been, in their deep sources, and in the minds of their best champions, and in the main tendency of their results, capable of ample justification. They were the first great effort of mediaeval life to go beyond the pursuit of selfish and isolated ambitions ; they were the trial-feat of the young world, essaying to use, to the glory of God and the benefit of man, the arms of its new knighthood. That they failed in their direct object is only what may be alleged against almost every great design which the great disposer of events has moulded to help the world's progress; for the world has grown wise by the experience of failure, rather than by the winning of high aims. That the good they did was largely leavened with evil may be said of every war that has ever been waged; that bad men rose by them while good men fell is, and must be, true wherever and whenever the race is to the swift and the battle to the strong. But that in the end they were a benefit to the world no one who reads can doubt; and that in their course they brought out a love for all that is heroic in human nature, the love of freedom, the honour of prowess, sympathy with sorrow, perseverance to the last, and patient endurance without hope, the chronicles of the age abundantly prove; proving, moreover, that it was by the experience of those times that the forms of those virtues were realized and presented to posterity. This much I say, by way of a caution, that you may not accuse me of an attempt to impose upon you. The history of the Crusades has always had for me an interest that quite rivals all the interest I could take in the history of the Greeks and Romans ; and very much of that interest is of the same sort ; a half archaeological interest in a life and growth from which we have ourselves received some great impulses, but almost all the minutiae of which are important only through their connexion with those great impulses. Such a half archaeological interest I hope you may feel in the history of mediaeval Cyprus, and what little is to be told of its sister kingdom.

The last decade of the twelfth century saw the establishment of two small Christian kingdoms in the Levant, which long outlived all other relics of the Crusades except the military orders ; and which, with very little help from the West, sustained a hazardous existence in complete contrast with almost everything around them. The kingdoms of Cyprus and Armenia have a history very closely intertwined, but their origin and most of their circumstances were very different.

By Armenia as a kingdom, is meant little more than the
ancient Cilicia, the land between Taurus and the sea, from
the frontier of the principality of Antioch, eastward, to Kelen-
deris or Palaeopolis, a little beyond Seleucia; this territory,
which was computed to contain sixteen days' journey in
length, measured from four miles of Antioch, by two in
breadth, was separated from the Greater Armenia, which
before the period on which we are employed had fallen under
the sway of the Seljuks, by the ridges of Taurus[1]. The
population was composed largely of the sweepings of Asia
Minor, Christian tribes which had taken refuge in the mountains. Their religion was partly Greek, partly Armenian, for
the Armenian Catholicos, after resting for a century and a
half in Mesopotamia, took refuge at Sis, and founded there
an independent or national Catholicate at the close of the
thirteenth[2] century. Their rulers were princes descended
from the house of the Bagratidae, who had governed the
Greater Armenia as kings from the year 885 to the reign
of Constantine Monomachus, and had then merged their
hazardous independence in the mass of the Greek empire[3].

[1] The boundaries of Armenia at its greatest extension are thus given
by Du Laurier, in the Armenian volume of the Recueil des Historiens
des Croisades, pp. xix. sq. :—Westward, Side or Eski-Adalieh; eastward,
the Pylae Ciliciae, or passes of the mountains close to the gulf of
Alexandretta. The custom-house, towards Iconium, was at Pilerga,
and the passes westward were at Germanicopolis and Claudiopolis.

[2] The Catholicate was without fixed residence from 1066–1114; it
was then settled at Hrom-Gla, on the Euphrates, in the principality
of Edessa, where it remained until 1292, when it settled at Sis.

[3] The Armenian historians describe the Greater Armenia after the
fall of the Arsacidae, under Arsaces IV, A.D. 387, as divided between
Persia and Byzantium; the Arsacide rulers governing as tributaries
until 428. From 428 to 625 it was governed by Persian governors,
'Marzbans,' frequently native Armenians of the house of the Bagratidae;
from 632 by a Curopalates or patrician named at Constantinople,
sometimes by the patriarch, sometimes by the Khalif. In 885 the
Bagratide, Aschod I, was recognized by the Khalif Motamed as king,

After the seizure of Asia Minor by the Seljuks, the few of the
Bagratidae who had retained possession of the mountain
fastnesses of Cilicia or the strongholds of Mesopotamia,
acted as independent lords, showing little respect for
Byzantium save where there was something to be gained.
Such was the lord Taphnuz of Edessa, on whose inheritance
Baldwin of Boulogne founded his principality; such were the
lords Leo, Thoros, Melier, and Rupin of the Mountains, who
ruled Cilicia during the twelfth century; trying to balance
their position between the Byzantine and Latin influences on
each side of them. Rupin of the Mountain was prince at
the time of the capture of Jerusalem by Saladin; he died in
1189, and his successor, Leo or Livon, after having successfully courted the favour of pope and emperor, was recognized
as king of Armenia by the emperor Henry VI, and crowned
by Conrad of Wittelsbach, Archbishop of Mainz, in 1198.
This act, which, although Livon forfeited his position by
obtaining recognition from Alexius Angelus, implied a
cessation of the old dependence on Byzantium and an
ecclesiastical reconciliation with Rome, was the typical act
of Armenian history; the whole of which, save and except
the defence against the Saracens and the Tartars of a later
date, was an attempt to secure independence by skilful
balancing of Greek and Roman influences; to obtain money

and was crowned. His successors were Sempad I, 890; Aschod II,
914; Apas, 928; Aschod III, the Merciful, 952; Sempad II, 977;
Kakig I, 989; John Sempad and Aschod IV, 1020; Interregnum, 1040;
Kakig II, 1042. Kakig gave up his kingdom to Constantine Monomachus in 1045, and was murdered in 1079. These kings reigned at
Ani. There was another principality at Kars, which surrendered to
Constantine Ducas in 1064. Senekerim John, King of Vasburagan,
had, in 1021, surrendered to Basil II, and received Sebaste in Cap-
padocia; and Abelgarib had Tarsus as a separate lordship from
Constantine Monomachus in 1042.—The Bagratidae claimed an Israelite
origin. St. Martin, Mémoires Historiques et Géographiques sur
l'Arménie.

from the West and arms from Constantinople, to obtain
alternate alliances by royal marriages, and ecclesiastical
freedom by regular variations between the two poles. For
this latter policy the position of the Armenian Church was
peculiarly fitted. It was so far schismatic as not to be
integrally a portion of either Roman or Byzantine obedience,
and so little heretical that its alliance was courted by both
communions. Hence its importance in the conciliar history
of the Middle Ages; an importance which has no sufficient
parallel in the secular history of Armenia.

The origin of the Latin kingdom of Cyprus is less obscure
and more romantic. Cyprus had been seized by the Arabs
in the early days of Islam (cir. 700–cir. 963), but recovered
for the empire by Nicephorus Phocas, and ruled by dukes
down to the reign of Manuel Comnenus. Its population was
a mixed one; there were Griffons or Greeks, Armenians,
Georgians, Maronites, native Cypriots, Greek paroeci, emancipated slaves, the descendants of Albanian soldiery of the
empire, and of Venetian emigrants of the first Crusade.
But the land was fertile, and they had dwelt together in
peace. In the reign of Manuel the happy days of Cyprus
ended and the period of calamity began. According to the
anchorite Neophytus, who wrote the tract 'de Calamitatibus
Cypri,' the native authority for the conquest by Richard
Cœur de Lion, Isaac Comnenus, a nephew of the emperor
Manuel, had been appointed by him to rule the Armenian
frontier; he had quarrelled with the Armenians, been taken
prisoner and sold to the Latins; that is, to Bohemond III
of Antioch, whose step-father, Reginald of Châtillon, had
many years before ravaged the isle of Cyprus in revenge for
the hostility of Manuel Comnenus. He was ransomed from
captivity by the emperor Andronicus, and, about the year
1184, came to Cyprus and set up an independent tyranny.
He called himself βασιλεύς, but ruled as a despot of the

worst order. All the better class of Greek inhabitants fled
to Constantinople; and the state of Cyprus under Isaac
Comnenus was only paralleled by that of Jerusalem under
Saladin. On the evidence of Neophytus, Richard of England
came not as a freebooter, but as a deliverer from utter misery.
In this point there is a fair consensus of Eastern and Western
testimony. Richard seized Cyprus not as a pirate, but as
an avenger and emancipator. The story is short, or may be
made so.

After wintering at Messina, Richard having with him, in
his fleet, not in his ship, his betrothed wife Berengaria and
his sister, Queen Johanna of Sicily, sailed for Acre on the
10th of April, 1191; the fleet was dispersed by a storm on
Good Friday, April 12; and Richard, after being obliged to
land at Rhodes, was driven by a second storm on the 1st of
May into the Gulf of Satalia. Before this day the queens
had appeared off Cyprus, and found anchorage off Limasol.
Isaac had attempted by courteous offers to get them into his
power, but his hospitality was presented in so military a
fashion, that the guardians of the royal ladies took fright,
and avoided landing. On the very day on which they were
obliged to promise that they would go on shore, Richard's
ship came in sight. His first act was to demand from Isaac
an account of the treatment of the wrecked vessels which
had been driven on the coast of the island and plundered
by the emperor. Isaac replied contumeliously, and Richard
landed in force. On the 6th of May Limasol was taken:
the emperor was unhorsed by Richard in single combat, and
fled to Nicosia. On the 12th of May Richard and Berengaria
were married at Limasol; and Berengaria was there crowned,
not queen of Cyprus, for the island was not yet taken or
claimed, but queen of the English. Negotiations for peace
and alliance were on foot, when Isaac suddenly broke off
the deliberations and fled to Famagosta. Richard, who had

now obtained the assistance of Guy of Lusignan and the prince of Antioch, and who was much pressed for time, left him no rest. Guy employed himself in capturing the chief strongholds; Richard, who was ill, after taking Buffevento, occupied Nicosia. There the emperor submitted to him on the 31st of May, and surrendered himself, his daughter and his treasures. Richard put him in silver chains, having promised that he would not put him in irons; placed the little girl under charge of the queen, and spent or distributed his treasure. Cyprus was conquered in a fortnight. Richard bestowed on the island the inestimable gift of his presence for five days after the emperor surrendered: Isaac he sent off under the charge of Ralph Fitz-Godfrey to Tripoli; he extorted from the Cypriots half their property, in return for a charter by which the laws of Manuel Comnenus were restored to them; constables were placed in the several castles, and Richard Camville and Robert of Turnham were left behind to govern Cyprus as justices and sheriffs on the English model [1]. What followed is not very clear. Before a month was over Camville was dead, and Turnham had been obliged to put down a revolt and hang a pretender. Richard found his new acquisition a burden; Neophytus briefly says that the 'Incliter' sold the island for 200,000 pounds of gold to the Latins. The Templars were the purchasers; they also found the burden a heavy one, especially at a moment when the war with Saladin demanded all their energies. The small garrison which they were able to keep in the island was shut up in Nicosia by the angry Griffons, and there was every chance that Cyprus would be lost as rapidly as it had been won. This was the state of affairs in May 1192, when Richard, by a piece of rough diplomacy, prevailed on Guy of Lusignan to surrender his claim to the shadowy crown of Jerusalem, and to accept the

[1] Ric. Divis. c. 61.

lordship of Cyprus instead. The Templars were glad enough
to sell their rights, and Guy, with Richard's advice, bought
them. A successful sally of the garrison of Nicosia saved
the Latins from massacre, the alarm of which they avenged
by an indiscriminate slaughter of the Greeks. Guy thus
obtained his first hold on the island; so much of the Greek
population as was still spared fled in panic; and way was
thus made for the institution, in this remote corner of the
Levant, of a dynasty and government of the straitest feudal
character; the introduction into a land, empty of all but
the cultivating classes and slaves, of the fully developed and
now crystallized block of feudal polity.

The house of Lusignan maintained itself in Cyprus for
nearly three centuries, during which, although fallen somewhat from the blessedness which had been broken up by
Isaac Comnenus, the island seems to have retained so much
fertility and prosperity internally as to make its later history
very dark by contrast. The flight of the Greek population,
which had begun under Isaac and been completed after the
massacre of Nicosia, left the island open to colonists from
the West. The peculiar privileges of the Cypriot Church,
which was autocephalous, made it easy for the remaining
prelates and people to accept the Western obedience, and
enabled the house of Lusignan to appeal confidently for the
support of European Christendom. The short period too
during which, under Guy and his successor, the administration of Cyprus was kept separate from that of the waning
kingdom of Palestine, gave those kings a moment's breathing
time, and this they improved with a success which the long
continuance of their dynasty against fearful odds may be
held to prove.

Guy, we are told, received Cyprus for life only, and did
homage for the island to Richard. As he already bore the
title of king, the question whether he should hold Cyprus as

a kingdom does not seem to have arisen. He appears in the
Lignages d'Outremer as 'seignor,' not as 'roi de Chypre;'
and no coins occur on which he is called king of Cyprus.
On his death, in April 1194, Richard putting in no claim for
the reversion, his brother, Amalric of Lusignan, constable of
Palestine, entered on the possession as his heir; he was not
as yet King of Jerusalem; it was a matter of importance to
him to be recognized as King of Cyprus; and he accordingly
did homage to the Emperor Henry VI. He was crowned
by the Bishop of Hildesheim, who was sent over from Sicily
to perform the ceremony; this was done in 1197. Immediately after this, Amalric succeeded to the crown of
Jerusalem. The crown of Jerusalem which, after the year
1269, became permanently united with that of Cyprus,
was an independent crown, and the king of Jerusalem an
anointed king: the union of the crowns therefore seems to
have precluded any question as to the tenure by which the
kingdom of Cyprus should be held. The crown of Cyprus
was conferred at Nicosia, that of Jerusalem at Tyre or at
Acre, and, after the capture of Acre, at Famagosta. The
homage then due to Richard, or to the crown of England,
ceased at the death of Guy; although the discontented barons
of Cyprus are said to have revived the idea of such a relation
when they wanted the aid of Edward I, in 1271. The
homage secured to the Emperor by Amalric was possibly
recognized until 1269, but was throughout complicated by
the claims of Frederick II and his sons on the kingdom
of Jerusalem. In 1459 the illegitimate pretender, James II,
did homage to the Sultan of Egypt as suzerain of Cyprus;
but that act was not the recognition of a right; it was only
a bid for support, and was one of the immediate causes of
the entire downfall of the house of Lusignan.

Guy, however, does not seem to have troubled himself about
his title. His reign lasted only two years, and his whole time

was given to the restoration of something like prosperity in
the desolate land [1].   According to the contemporary 'Chronique d'Outremer' he opened an asylum for the dispossessed
Franks of Armenia and Palestine.   These, to the amount of
300 knights and 200 men-at-arms, with a great number of
bourgeois, he enfeoffed with estates of land in Cyprus; so
liberal was he that he retained for himself only twenty
knights' fees.   Possibly the truth was that he was obliged
to sell the land of the island to find the money due to
the Templars ; but the mode in which it was done proves
that the feudal idea, on which a few years later the Latin
conquests in Romania were apportioned, was full grown.
The arrangement however made by Guy had to be altered
by Amalric when he reached the dignity of kingship.   He
threw himself on the mercy of his vassals ; they responded
liberally, and surrendered to him so many of his brother's
grants that at his death a royal revenue of 200,000 byzants
was forthcoming.   Guy had perhaps made as much as he
cared to make of his life interest, but he was, like his patron,
careless in the spending of money, whilst, unlike Richard's,
his opportunities of aquiring it were very limited.

Thus, however, the land system of Cyprus was restored ;
the 300 knights, 200 men-at-arms, and extensive bourgeoisie,
constituted one or two permanent estates of the kingdom.
The nobles, who were, no doubt, included in the number of
the knights, were the numerous lords who either had fled

---

[1] There were five classes of native cultivators in Guy's time :—

   (1) Parici—πάροικοι—slave cultivators.

   (3) Lefteri—ἐλεύθεροι—freed folk.

   (3) Albanesi—descendants of Albanian soldiery.

   (4) Veneziani bianchi—descended from the soldiers of Vital
       Michaele in the first Crusade.

   (5) Perperiarii, enfranchised Paroeci—paying a tax of 15 perperi ;
       (cited from Bustron by Beugnot, Assizes of Jerusalem,
       i. 207).

before Saladin, or were so little hopeful of the event of the Crusades, that they thought it wise to look to Cyprus as a prospective refuge. Hence throughout the Middle Ages the Cypriot lords retained the titles of their homes in Palestine; and the Palestine titles, when the families of their possessors were extinct, were conferred as a sort of life peerage at the will of the kings. Of the few Frank families that showed any vitality the house of Ibelin was far the most prominent and prolific; the lords of Ibelin and Mirabel, sprung from the house of Puiset, viscounts of Chartres, and closely connected with the counts of Champagne and Blois[1], had played a conspicuous part during the twelfth century in Palestine; they were still more prominent in Cyprus: from them the royal house received wives and guardians for the infant kings; two of the great recorders of the Assizes of Jerusalem were lords of Ibelin; one as regent or bailiff of Cyprus conducted the valiant resistance to the claims of Frederick II: and in fact, if any one had cared to write it, the fortunes of the house of Ibelin would have been as great part of the history of Cyprus as those of the house of Lusignan. Other great families were those of Gibeleth and Bethsan, named from Byblus and Bethshan or Scythopolis. The whole peerage of Cyprus however contained only a few names, which sound strangely enough, as they illustrate the geographical unity of history. There were princes of Antioch, Galilee, and Montreal, lords of Beyrout, Sidon, Toron,

---

[1] Balian le François, the first of the family, is described in the Lignages d'Outremer as brother of Count Guillin de Chartres; by which we are to understand that he was a relation of Hugh de Puiset, count of Joppa, son of Everard, and grandson of Geldewin, viscount of Chartres. His name Balian is probably a softened form of Waleran; see Du Cange on the Lignages, pp. 360, 361. One lady of this house married an English knight, Hamo l'Estrange, who died in Palestine about 1272; this was Isabella, daughter of the lord of Berytus and widow of the young king, Hugh III. See Assizes of Jerusalem, ii. 449.

Caesarea, Tyre, and Tiberias; counts of Jaffa, Tripoli, and
Carpasso; there were also, as grand serjeanties, the double
stewardships, constableships, and marshalships of Cyprus
and Jerusalem, and the chamberlainship of Cyprus; these
are all, or nearly all. They constituted a high court of
baronage or parliament, as they had done in Palestine, and
were the supreme council of the king, of which we have so
much information in the Assizes of Jerusalem.

As for the ecclesiastical estate, tradition assigns also to
King Guy some trenchant measures which help to complete
the parallel or the contrast between him and William the
Conqueror. The old Cypriot church had an archbishop
and fourteen suffragans; the archbishop was Archbishop of
Cyprus, and owed obedience to no patriarch. The flight or
submission of the Greeks left the field open to the Latin
clergy; and Guy placed a Latin archbishop at Nicosia, with
suffragans at Famagosta, Limasol and Baffo. This arrangement was sanctioned by Celestine III in 1196. As time
went on, the Greek clergy returned, and Jacobites and
Nestorians followed; very uneasy relations were produced
between the two chief hierarchies, one of which depended
on Rome, whilst the other, now seated at Famagosta,
claimed the ancient prerogative of the Cypriot church. The
schismatic clergy were, however, subjected by Honorius III
to the Latin bishops, whilst Alexander IV, in the year 1260,
went so far as to forbid the election of a Greek archbishop
after the death of the reigning prelate, and reduced the number
of Greek sees to four, Soli, Leucara, Arsinoe, and Carpasso;
the bishops were also subjected to the Latin metropolitan,
who was bound to administer justice among them. Probably
Guy has obtained credit for some of the measures which
properly belong to the popes and to a later date. The
clergy of the island were as numerous as the difference of
nationalities required. The Mendicant orders formed the

strength of the Latin portion, the secular priests that of the
Greek and Armenian. Monasteries abounded. In Nicosia
alone were 250 churches.

These then being the estates of the realm, the powerful
people wére all Franks; the returning Greeks and Armenians
would only creep into an equality of privilege, or return into
the enjoyment of their old customs, as the governing race
allowed; and, although they ultimately grew and prevailed
while the governing race dwindled and perished, all political
interest centres in the governing race. For them the existing polity of Palestine was transported across the sea; not
as yet reduced to writing, for the system of Godfrey of
Bouillon, 'the Letters of the Sepulchre,' if it were ever
codified, had perished, and the Assizes had not yet taken
their historic form. But the new kingdom was singularly
rich in lawyers, and this was early recognized; in 1214 we
find Lewis of France, son of Philip II, applying for a legal
opinion on a point of procedure to Hugh I of Cyprus; the
old lords of Palestine spent their leisure in Cyprus recording the customs of their lost inheritance, and the
extant Assizes of Jerusalem were the result of their studies.
The names of the great legists are Philip of Navarre, John
and James of Ibelin, and Guy le Tort. John of Ibelin,
who died in 1266, and bore the title of count of Jaffa,
Ramlah (Rames), and Ascalon, drew up the existing Assize
of the High Court. It is in exact symmetry with Western
usage, that this great compilation was not received as a
code until the year 1369: like the 'Siete Partidas' of
Alfonso the Wise, it was but a body of jurisprudence, the
use of which depended on its own reasonableness, or a
collection of customs which were recorded because they
were used, not merely used because they were recorded.
The Highest Law was still 'the custom' recorded in the
heart and mouth of the 'lawful man.'

The Assizes of Jerusalem, then, although no doubt they describe what we may call the common law of the Cypriot kingdom, so far as concerned the Franks, cannot be regarded during the greater part of the period as an authoritative code; the native population of Cyprus, like the native Syrians of Palestine, had laws and customs, such perhaps as the laws of Manuel Comnenus for which they obtained Richard's confirmation; and the city of Famagosta at a little later period, after having been for some years under the government of the Genoese, was allowed to retain the laws of Genoa. Within the feudal fabric itself, custom, or perhaps principle, was more dominant than law; the lords of the great fiefs did not accept the rules of the high court as binding unless they had themselves consented to them; the unity of feudal jurisprudence lay rather in ideas than in cogent uniformity. Add to this the fact that the Frank population of Cyprus showed no tendency to ordinary increase, but was either constantly diminishing or recruited by arrivals from the West, whilst the Greek population was at home, strong, numerous, and wealthy; that the Latin Church accordingly, although powerful in the protection of Rome and of the Cypriot crown, was surpassed in wealth and historical greatness by the Greek and Armenian communities; and we cannot but conclude that in this, which is regarded as the most flourishing period of Cypriot history, there was little chance of strong government or administrative development. The Assizes of Jerusalem lay like a crystal block, a model of usages, incapable of enforcement and incapable of growth. The kings lived for the most part the life of adventurers or knights-errant, playing their part in the defence of Christendom, but still, like the great military orders and fragmentary principalities of Palestine, only as an isolated garrison in the middle of a world out of which they were being gradually driven; no more, as

Richard had hoped, an advance post in the great campaign by which the East was to be humbled before the West.

Hence, no doubt, it is that, notwithstanding the example of the kingdom of Naples, which was the nearest Catholic neighbour of Cyprus, we find no traces of a Cypriot parliament. There were councils of nobles and councils of bishops; there were high courts and bourgeois courts; and there were, as elsewhere, three estates well defined, clergy, nobles, and burghers; but if there ever was any attempt to range these in an organized body either for legislation or for money grants, I have failed to discover it. The 'Bancs,' or ordinances, with which the customs of the Assizes were supplemented, were issued by the king's proclamation; in two or three cases the participation of the court or of the barons is expressed. In 1362 we have an ordinance issued by the king, Peter I, by the assent of the men of his court. A few years before, his father, King Hugh, issued his laws by proclamation: 'Hear the ban of God and of my Lord the King, Hugh of Lusignan of the Kingdom of Jerusalem and of Cyprus; know all men that on the 16th of May, 1355, the Lord King and his men ordained an assize.' Here it is possible there may be some reference to a general court or 'witenagemot,' but not, I think, to an assembly of estates. According to the Assizes of Jerusalem, every vassal who, whether immediately dependent on the king or on a mesne lord, had done homage to the king as chief lord, was a member of the royal court; a usage which in so small a state must have crushed out every tendency to representative government[1]. In default of further evidence we must, I think, assume that, as in France before the institution of the states-general, the only check on the king was his court of vassals; whereas, after the example had been set in the states-general, diets and

[1] Assizes, i. 254.

parliaments of the West, the national life of Cyprus was too much attenuated to allow it to reproduce such institutions on an unfriendly soil. The Basse Cour or Court of Bourgeois, organized under the viscounts or sheriffs of Cyprus, with jurats and other machinery of courts of law, was an organization of tribunals of justice and local government, not a legislative constitutional organization: its assizes are therefore a book of procedure rather than a code of laws, and, like the Assizes of the High Court, rather a record of customs than a body of statutes. These courts also, like the court of barons, may be regarded as developments towards constitutional growth, arrested and petrified at a certain stage.

But I have said more than enough upon a subject which, somewhat repulsive by itself, needs severe study before it will begin to be remunerative. The Assizes of Jerusalem will always remain a mine of feudal principles and a treasure to scientific jurists; they reflect infinite lustre on the Cypriot lawyers who, in an age of turmoil and exertion, continuous and overwhelming, found time and labour for recording them. We conceive that the lords of Ibelin must have been well acclimatized in more ways than one; it is certainly curious that they supplied the main historical support to the kings of Cyprus in marriage, war, and jurisprudence.

King Guy had a very short reign; and most of the acts that are ascribed to him I have already noted. After the collapse of the third crusade and the three years' truce between Richard and Saladin in 1192, he seems to have retired to Cyprus, and to have died in April 1194; the same year the old Emperor Isaac died in the custody of the Hospitallers at Merkeb. Isaac's daughter was still wandering up and down Christendom; by the agreement for Richard's release she was to have been handed over to Duke Leopold of Austria, her kinsman, but when Baldwin of Bethune brought her to Austria, she found Duke Leopold dead; she was accordingly brought back to Richard, and subsequently married to a Flemish knight, who came to the East in the fourth crusade in the retinue of John de Neesle, and, in her name, put in a claim for Cyprus, which King Amalric summarily rejected. The rights of Guy devolved upon his brother; or rather Cyprus, for the reversion of which no arrangements had been made, fell to the lot of the possessor.

Amalric of Lusignan had been, under his brother, constable of both kingdoms, and Prince of Tyre; he was thus in command of such military force as his brother had possessed, and succeeded quietly to his dominion: from Henry VI, as I said, he obtained recognition as king, and was crowned in 1197; in 1198 he obtained the crown of Jerusalem, marrying, as fourth husband, the lady Isabella of Anjou, who had carried the right of succession first to Henfrid of Toron, then to Conrad of Montferrat, and then to Henry of Champagne. The German chancellor, Bishop Conrad of Hildesheim, who had crowned the King of Cyprus, negotiated the marriage and succession, and Amalric, leaving Cyprus under the administration of the Hospitallers, transferred his court to Acre. We hear no more of Cyprus during Amalric's reign. He was an able warrior, and as successful as mere warlike ability, coupled with very indifferent morality towards the infidels, could make him. With the aid of the German crusaders of 1197 he recovered Berytus, where the ceremony of his coronation took place; he also took Byblus, and besieged Toron; but the difficulty of keeping terms between the Germans, the Franks, and the military orders, was too great for him. The siege was raised, the Germans retired, and Amalric had to make a truce with Saladin.

The Crusade of Villehardouin passed over without any

direct effect on either Cyprus or Palestine. Amalric died
at Acre in April, 1205, and was buried in the church of
St. Sophia at Nicosia. He left the crown of Cyprus to his
eldest son Hugh, the son of his first wife, Eschiva of Ibelin,
under the guardianship of Walter of Montbeliard, his
brother-in-law. The crown of Jerusalem, the right of which
depended on Queen Isabella, was left unclaimed; John of
Ibelin, half-brother of Isabella, and uncle of the jurist, was
lieutenant of that kingdom; and he, after some years'
searching, found a husband for Mary, the queen's eldest
daughter by Conrad of Montferrat; John of Brienne was
accepted as king of Jerusalem in 1210. The queen's second
daughter Alice, the child of Henry of Champagne, was given
to the young king, Hugh of Cyprus. The event of the
minority was a descent made by Walter of Montbeliard on
the coast of Asia Minor, the only result of which was booty.
Hugh came of age in 1211, and was in that year crowned at
Nicosia. His reign was short, and was devoted chiefly to the
restoration of order and prosperity in Cyprus. He encouraged
the study of law, and was so learned in it himself that Lewis
of France applied to him for an opinion on legal procedure,
which was held as authoritative by the feudal lawyers. From
Palestine he seems to have stood aloof, partly perhaps owing
to the fact that the death of Queen Mary, who, dying in
1212, left only an infant daughter, might seem to open the
succession to his wife, Queen Alice. In 1217 however he
joined the expedition against the fortress of Tabor, persuaded
by King Andrew of Hungary, who visited Cyprus on purpose
to engage his support. The attempt on Tabor was unsuccessful; and Hugh retired to Tripoli, where he died in
February, 1218. It thus happened that neither the great
Crusade of 1202 nor the expedition against Damietta in 1219
directly touched the fortunes of Cyprus; for the heir of King
Hugh was an infant of nine months old; and the Queen

Alice, who with the aid of the child's great-uncles, the lords
Philip and John of Ibelin, was guardian, seems to have
avoided too close alliance with the new troops of Crusaders.
Cyprus was, however, a regular station for the pilgrim fleets,
and as regularly an object of attack whenever the Sultans saw
an opportunity of unresisted devastation.

The little interest of the history runs rapidly on to the
Crusade of the Emperor Frederick II, which brought about
many other critical conjunctures in the history of Christendom.
This particular portion of the history is of no small legal as
well as historical interest. The kings of Jerusalem being men
of action, practising little self-restraint and never taking care
of themselves, generally died young, and left the fate of their
kingdom in suspense on the life of their young children.
Hence constant minorities, and the need of provisions for
guardianship, a need which, as yet, had scarcely begun to be
felt in the kingdoms of Europe. The practice therefore of
the kingdom of Jerusalem in the matter of regency became
a stock of legal cases, which, if not cited as occasion arose in
corresponding circumstances in the West, afford to us at least
a number of parallels. The earlier practice had been to give
the wardship of the person of the heir to the nearest relation
incapable of inheriting; that of the kingdom to the presumptive heir[1]. But the rule laid down in the Assizes, which
is really perhaps a generalization from the earlier cases rather
than a deliberate constitution, was that the mother of the heir
should be his guardian; in case of her death, the next relation
on the side on which the kingdom moved, that is, the heir-
presumptive; in case no such person could be found, it was

[1] Assizes, i. 261. If a vassal die the custody of the ward is not to
be in the heir, but in the nearest kinsman on the side on which the fief
cannot fall. Cf. Glanville, vii. c. 11 ; Establissemens, i. c. 117. If he
is a sovereign or suzerain, his men shall have care of his body and
fortresses, the heir to guard the heritage (i. 435). See Itinerar. R. R.
p. xcvii.

for the barons of the kingdom to meet and choose a regent or guardian. The practice seems to have been to leave the queen-mother as regent, with a bailiff or high-steward to do the work of government.

In the year 1228 the case in Cyprus was this: the King Henry, although old enough at seven to be crowned, was still a minor. His mother, Queen Alice, had married a second husband, Bohemond V, heir of Antioch, and had quarreled with the lords of Ibelin, who were not only her nearest relations, but the most powerful and cleverest of the acclimatized baronage. These lords were the sons of that Balian of Ibelin who was supposed, by going to mass instead of to battle, to have ruined the chances of Guy of Lusignan at Nazareth in May, 1187 : he had married the widow of King Amalric I, and his sons were thus half-brothers to the many-husbanded Queen Isabella, great-uncles to King Henry, and half-uncles to Queen Alice. So long then as the family party hung together, they formed a strong phalanx ; when they quarreled, all the internal strength of the kingdom was turned against itself. The second marriage of Queen Alice probably broke up the unity. Philip of Ibelin died in 1227 ; John of Ibelin, lord of Berytus, naturally expected to succeed him as bailiff ; the queen proposed a baron named Amalric Barlais. John succeeded in maintaining his position, and became bailiff or regent under the nominal guardianship of the queen. But the struggle was still proceeding when Frederick II, on his way to Palestine, arrived in the Levant. Frederick II, as I need not remind you, was already the 'Stupor mundi,' the man of unbounded ambition and almost ubiquitous versatility, who never did a great or truly kingly act, or followed any but a selfish aim. He was, as son of Henry VI, heir of imperial aspirations that coveted the whole world, and, as the husband of Yolanda of Brienne, father and guardian of the young heir of Palestine. Yolanda, who must have been a child when she

married him, died in this same year 1228, leaving an only
son, the luckless Conrad. When then Frederick reached the
Peloponnesus, he was met by five Cypriot barons of the
queen's party, who asked his aid against the lord of Berytus.
The emperor, whether desirous, as he might well be, to make
Cyprus available for military purposes, or simply wishing to
assert his right as overlord, undertook to deal with John of
Ibelin; the barons told him that the revenues of Cyprus were
large enough to secure the conquest of Palestine, and Frederick
thought them worth a trial. He arrived at Limasol, and
wrote to John as his dearest uncle, begging him to come to
him with all his family and concert measures for the crusade.
John called together his friends at Nicosia and consulted
them: they told him that to admit Frederick was to betray
the infant king, but advised him to return a courteous answer,
to meet craft with craft. But this John would not do; he
swore that he would rather die than let the Crusade fail by
his default; and therefore presented himself to the emperor
with all his force, and with the little king in his train.
Frederick received him ostentatiously, made him change his
black mourning robes for scarlet, and entertained him at
dinner: after dinner, the usual time apparently for quarreling,
he turned round upon him and insisted on the resignation
of the lordship of Berytus, which was a fief of the crown of
Jerusalem, and also of the office of bailiff of Cyprus. John
boldly told the emperor that this treatment was only what
his friends at Nicosia had bidden him expect. The emperor
changed colour at the reproach, which showed in what estimation his honour was held. But the friends of the Crusade
interfered, and an agreement was made that the question of
Berytus should be decided by the high court of Palestine, that
of the regency by the high court of Cyprus. This was not
carried into effect. John, dreading the emperor's treachery,
fled to Nicosia: there Frederick besieged him and forced

him to a compromise ; he did homage for Berytus, and the emperor was allowed to receive the revenues of Cyprus until King Henry reached the age of twenty-five, thus apparently exercising the rights, if not under the name, of an overlord ; but whether he claimed the right as emperor or as king of Jerusalem, or as representing the nearest kinsman, is not clear[1]. Frederick left Cyprus under charge of five barons of the island, and went on to Palestine. After his short stay in the Holy Land, and his politic but not very far-sighted treaty with the infidels, he left the East to take care of itself. For about three years the arrangement continued in force ; but in 1231 the emperor's marshal and deputy, Richard Filangier, tried to wrest Berytus from John of Ibelin, and threw him into open rebellion. John equipped a fleet, and, with the young king, landed in Cyprus. The marshal retired before him. John occupied Famagosta ; the marshal retreated to Nicosia ; there he was defeated and forced to disband his army, which passed over into the service of the king of Armenia. Cherin held out until Easter, 1233 ; and then the last remnant of Frederick's army left Cyprus.

John of Ibelin died in 1236 ; the imperial power was by that time broken up in Palestine as well as Cyprus ; and now Queen Alice attempted to turn the tables on Frederick himself. The relics of the whole Crusading history were imperilled ; Frederick would accept no invitations, nor would he send Conrad to assert the rights of Yolanda. Alice, therefore, as heir of Jerusalem, put in her claim for the regency of Palestine ; the poor barons clung to a straw ; they accepted her, and she named her third husband, Ralph of Soissons,

---

[1] That Hugh had to perform homage and swear fealty to Frederick II appears from the letter of Innocent IV, releasing him from the oath in 1247. See Mas-Latrie, Hist. de Chypre, vol. ii. p. 63. It is said that the barons recognized the emperor as suzerain, but refused liege homage.

bailiff of Jerusalem. No sooner was he appointed than he left his post and went back to France. Jerusalem had already fallen to the Sultan of Damascus in 1239; after a brief restoration in 1243, it fell to the Kharismians in 1244; to the Sultan of Egypt in the same year. The crown became a derelict; the title was borne after Conrad by his half-brother Henry, the son of Isabella of England; and subsequently by a number of ruling houses, who seem to have clung to the name far more faithfully than they had ever clung to the reality of the dominion. The remains of substantive power devolved with the title on Hugh the Great, King of Cyprus, in 1269.

The rest of the history of King Henry is soon told. He came of age in 1232, married a daughter of the house of Montferrat, and lost her the same year; a second wife, Stephanie of Armenia, died in 1250, and he then married Placentia of Antioch. Henry took a subordinate part in the Crusade of the middle of the century. His action is obscure, as are all the details of the period. In the expedition of 1240 he seems to have borne no part: Richard of Cornwall does not mention a visit to Cyprus either going or returning; but Henry seems to have, in 1246, asserted his right to Jerusalem on the death of his mother, and to have been recognized as king by Innocent IV, who included King Conrad in his father's doom. In the Crusade of St. Lewis, Henry is said by the Cypriot historians to have shared both perils and glories; he certainly received the French king, and entertained him at Nicosia during the winter of 1248, which was so fatal to many of the French nobles. We are not told that King Henry furnished any part of the supplies that St. Lewis collected in Cyprus, the mountains of corn or the towers of wine casks; all these were furnished by the emperor and the Venetians. The King of Cyprus entered Damietta with the French king in triumph in 1249; but he did not, as has been asserted, share his captivity. After this we read no more of him; he died early in 1253, having been the sport of fortune all his life, and leaving the inheritance of his history to a child of a few months old, Hugh II, who reigned from 1253 to 1267.

The only incident of the reign of Hugh II turns, like that in his father's reign, on the question of regency. Queen Placentia acted as regent, but in the second year of the reign went over to Palestine and married Balian of Ibelin, the reigning lord of Arsouf. As Hugh was the last of the Lusignans, the marriage seems to have been unpopular; and, either in consequence of it, or after the death of the queen herself, a new bailiff was appointed. This was Hugh of Antioch, son of Henry of Antioch, and grandson of Bohemond IV; his mother Isabella was daughter of King Hugh I. He was nearest in blood to King Hugh and his presumptive successor. One military exploit signalized the regency: in 1265 he led to the defence of Acre against the Sultan Bibars a fleet of Cypriot vessels. Then, says Sanuto, was the military force of Cyprus in great valour and of great prudence; there were in the company 130 knights and much cavalry besides. The contribution however helped the falling cause but little. All in Palestine was going to ruin; already the Venetians and the Genoese were at war; the Templars and the Hospitallers were irreconcileable; the Frank princes were selling their estates and returning westward. The lord of Sidon sold, in 1260, Sidon and Belfort to the Templars; Balian sold Arsouf to the Hospitallers. Henry of Antioch and his wife claimed the regency of Palestine as against the house of Brienne. In 1264 Bibars destroyed Caesarea; and the defenders of Acre were obliged, in self-defence, to lay waste their suburbs, and leave open to the Saracens the great poliandrum or cemetery of St. Nicolas, in which 124,000 men had been buried in one year during the third Crusade. In 1261, the year before Hugh's appointment to the regency, the Latin empire of Constantinople fell. All the older mediaeval things were passing away in both East and West, and the tide which had led on the Crusades was turning.

The child king, Hugh II, died in 1267; and the bailiff, Hugh III, succeeded as king. Hugh II was the last of the house of Lusignan who was left in the East; in the West there were still many members of the prolific family. Our memory recurs most naturally to that large family of the Aliens, the half-brothers of our king, Henry III, who nine years before had been banished in consequence of their opposition to the Provisions of Oxford; their father, Hugh X of Lusignan, Count of la Marche, was nephew to the Kings Guy and Amalric. Hugh of Antioch, too, the new king, represented the house of Poictiers, being sprung from Raymond of Poictiers, the uncle of Queen Eleanor, the wife of Henry II. The reigning house of Lusignan in la Marche came to an end in 1303. But although this was the case, the Cypriot dynasty continued to bear the name of Lusignan, to which by a female descent it was entitled; and there are many Lusignans, in England as elsewhere, flourishing at the present day.

Hugh III, the new king, had the advantage of acquiring the throne when he had age and experience to fill it: and he reigned fourteen years, long enough to establish his own authority, and to see the downfall of all the Frank states around him. I will mention three points only in his history; for although he bore the title of the Great, 'Hugh the Great,' it was a very forlorn hope that he was called on to lead. He seems to have been the king of Cyprus to whom St. Thomas Aquinas dedicated the famous treatise 'De Regimine Principum;' a book which, owing to the great reputation of its author and the definiteness of the principles which it enunciates, became a handbook of the relations of Church and

State in the Middle Ages. Of the work which we now possess
under this name, only a book and a half out of the four
books was the work of St. Thomas, the rest was added
probably by Ptolemy of Lucca ; but the book itself was
a model which later publicists chose to follow or to comment
upon.   Many of these commentaries are found in our
libraries ; and down to the age of Sir John Fortescue, the
book addressed to the King of Cyprus occupied a position
of authority inferior only to the Politics of Aristotle.   It is
not improbable that the book was originally written for the
education of the young King Hugh II ; but it is certainly
very curious that the composition both of the great Feudal
Code of the Assizes, and of the manual of mediaeval politics,
should have a direct relation to this remote little island.   The
second point to be noted is this :—

Hugh saw nearly all the Crusading conquests lost.   In
1268 Antioch was taken, and the prince, Bohemond VI,
retired to Tripoli.   In 1269 Hugh claimed the crown of
Jerusalem, and was crowned at Tyre on the 24th of
September.   But this empty honour was not obtained without competition.   The king's great-aunt, Mary of Antioch,
daughter of Bohemond IV, and grand-daughter of King
Amalric, contested the title ; she carried her cause to Rome
for the arbitration of the pope ; and unable to make good
any claim herself, she sold in 1277 her rights to Jerusalem
to Charles of Anjou, the King of Naples, the brother of
St. Lewis, and head of that Angevin house which transmitted
the crowns of Jerusalem and Sicily to René of Anjou, the
father-in-law of our King Henry VI.   Hugh III then was
King of Jerusalem when Edward I made his crusade.   In
May 1271, and for several months later, the two princes were
together at Acre ; and during their intimacy Hugh put before
Edward a question which bore a signally close relation to
that on which so much of the interest of Edward's own

reign was to turn. The documents concerning it are preserved among the Assizes of Jerusalem. Unfortunately we
have only the case, not the opinion which Edward gave.
The question was, what obligation lay on the knights of
Cyprus to feudal service within the kingdom of Jerusalem;
exactly parallel to the great question of 1297 in England,
upon which the Confirmation of Charters resulted.

It was not decided by Edward, but John of Ibelin had
laid down the rule: 'Three things are they bound to do outside the realm for the lord: 1. For the marriage of him or
any of his children; 2. To guard and defend his faith and
honour; 3. Por le besoing aparant de sa seignorie ou le
comun profit de sa terre.' When we find a jurist named
Accursi d'Arezzo practising at Acre in 1270, it becomes
even probable that Edward picked up his friend Francesco
there. It was possibly on this occasion that Edward laid
down the rule that, for the recovery of the East, Egypt
should be first occupied, then the Holy Land, and then
Constantinople. When that was done, and not till then,
would the Christian warriors, settled and established, be
able to dwell safely. So at least says Marino Sanuto, writing
in 1321.

But neither Edward's little army nor his legal skill could
save King Hugh from discomfiture; in 1272 he was forced
to submit to make a treaty with Bibars, which left him only
Acre and the right of pilgrimage to Nazareth, and for this
he had to thank, it was said, the diplomacy of Edward.
After Edward's departure, and an attempt to sustain the
Frank cause in Tripoli, Hugh seems to have devoted himself
to the care of his island kingdom, which was itself threatened
by the monstrous policy of Charles of Anjou. That wretched
tyrant, by way of inaugurating his purchased sovereignty,
wrested Acre from King Hugh in 1277. He did not live
to recover it. After a siege of four months the Cypriot

knights declared their term of service at an end, and the
siege was raised.   Hugh was a patron of learned men, and
a founder of monasteries.   Probably he saw that unless the
Christians were unanimous he must be content to sit still.
The Hospitallers supported him ; the Templars spited him ;
the Genoese helped him ; the Venetians thwarted him.   So
he stayed in Cyprus, where the people to a great extent
prospered under his care, and had sons and daughters.   His
wife was a lady of the house of Ibelin : he died at Tyre in
1284 ; he was buried in the abbey of Lapais.   His eldest
son, John I, who succeeded him, died in 1285 ; his brother
and successor, Henry II, reigned from 1285 to 1324 : witnessing a period of transitional history which affected the
East as well as the West, and which furnishes material of
more curious if not wider interest.

So long as Acre held out against the Infidels, that is
exactly a hundred years from the date when Richard restored
it to Christendom, almost all the living interest of the
Crusades centres in that curious stronghold ; for it must
have been a very strange encampment of fighting and
praying men of all nations.   There each of the great orders
had its strong tower, palace, and appointed share of the
wardship of the walls.   There the Hospitallers and the
Templars issued from their palaces the orders that governed
their brethren throughout Christendom ; the Genoese and
the Pisans had their quarters in close neighbourhood ; the
Venetians had their Tower far off, between the Tower of
the English and the ward of the Hospitallers; and the mendicant orders had each their house and church to themselves.
Immensely strong, and able to draw in supplies constantly
from the sea, Acre was a standing menace to the Eastern
world ; but without were fightings and within were fears.
The very closeness in which the conflicting powers were
encamped intensified the dangers of their disunion.   There

was still great appearance of strength; the King of Jerusalem and Cyprus was at least safe in the castle around which this fortified camp was spread; all along the coast northwards, of Syria and Armenia, were placed the strong munitions of the military orders; over the sea, a little way, was Cyprus the great granary of Palestine, and within the lines of Palestine itself were strongholds of both the knights and the 'pullani,' or acclimatized Franks, which were fortified with great skill, and need indeed succumb to nothing short of famine.   All this, however far short it fell of a well-administered state or a well-regulated camp, was still a strong power, when the fatal quarrels in the West, the downfall of the Hohenstaufen, the wicked policy of Charles of Anjou, the rivalry of the Venetians and the Genoese, combined to bring about the end.

Acre held out almost to the last; Antioch had fallen in 1268; all Palestine proper, save Acre and the road to Nazareth, had been surrendered in 1272; Tripoli was lost in 1286. Dependent on Acre were Tyre, Sidon, and Berytus, and a few straggling forts that must fall when Acre fell.   That was on the 18th of May, 1291.   The King of Jerusalem and Cyprus at the time was Henry II, the second son of Hugh III, who had succeeded his brother John in 1285, and had been duly crowned in 1286.   The recovery of Acre from the forces of the King of Naples, which was effected before he could duly receive the crown of Jerusalem, was the one brilliant exploit of a long and otherwise unhappy reign.   The assistance which the military orders afforded him on the occasion caused the regent of Naples to confiscate all the estates of those orders within the kingdom of Naples, which formed a precedent for the atrocious measures of Philip the Fair against the Templars.   Five years afterwards the Sultan Khalil Ashraf besieged Acre: King Henry brought his forces to the rescue, but, on the day of the

assault by the Mussulmans, lost heart and sailed away. For
three days the luckless defenders struggled and perished, and
on the fourth day the city was taken. I shall not dwell on
the valour of the knights or on the atrocities of the captors.
The same day at evening the Franks of Tyre embarked and
set sail for the West. The Templars left Sidon and went to
Cyprus; and the people of Berytus surrendered. The break-
up of the great camp was followed by the dispersion of the
forces of the Cross. The kingdom of Armenia began to
falter in its obedience to the Roman Church. The Armenian
Catholicos had to flee from Mesopotamia to Sis in 1292; and
about the same time the relics of Antiochene chivalry took
service under the Armenian king. The military orders were
only kept in Cyprus by the gift of Limasol, which King
Henry bestowed on them conjointly; but soon the Templars
sought their Western preceptories, within a very few years
to perish utterly; the Teutonic knights found work in the
conversion of the North; the Hospitallers, maintaining a
better heart, fitted out a new Crusade, and in 1308 seized
the island of Rhodes, whence for two hundred and fifteen
years they made the Mediterranean too hot to hold a Turkish
fleet. The rest of the unattached Franks found a home in
Cyprus.

Among these was one little known and obscure knightly
order, which Englishmen need not be ashamed to recognize;
the Order of the Knights of St. Thomas of Acre. This was
a little body of men who had formed themselves into a semi-
religious order on the model of the Hospitallers. In the
third Crusade, one William, an English priest, chaplain to
Ralph de Diceto, Dean of St. Paul's, had devoted himself to
the work of burying the dead at Acre, as the Hospitallers
had given themselves at first to the work of tending the sick.
He had built himself a little chapel there, and bought ground
for a cemetery; like a thorough Londoner of the period,

P

he had called it after St. Thomas the Martyr; and, somehow
or other, as his design was better known, the family of the
martyr seem to have approved of it; the brother-in-law and
sister of Becket became founders and benefactors, and a
Hospital of St. Thomas the Martyr of Canterbury, of Acre,
was built in London itself on the site of the house where
the martyr was born [1]. Little indeed is known of the early
days of the knights; they were not numerous, and probably
poor; but when Peter des Roches, the Bishop of Winchester
and ex-justiciar, was in Palestine in 1231, he placed them
in a new church and under the rule of the Templars, giving
them also in his will a legacy of 500 marks [2]. They had
their proper dress and cross: according to Favin their habit
was white, and the cross a full red cross charged with a white
scallop; but the existing cartulary of the order describes the
habit simply as a mantle with a cross of red and white [3].
They were building a new church when Edward was at Acre;
and in 1278 we find him writing to the king of Cyprus on
their behalf [4]. The Chronicle of the Teutonic knights, in

---

[1] In the ninth year of John, Oct. 13, 1207, messengers of the house
of St. Thomas at Acre, being canons, had a safe-conduct. They had
come to England to seek alms for the redemption of captives; Rot.
Pat., ed. Hardy, i. 76. The ' Terra Sancti Thomae ' abutted on the
land of the Temple at Casale Album, near Coquet; Paoli, Cod. Dipl.
S. Joh., i. 468. Richard, the English tanner, at Acre, in 1273 sold two
houses in the Street of the Tannery to the Hospitallers; ib. 195, 196.

[2] Matthew Paris, ed. Luard, iii. 489.

[3] MS. Cotton, Tiberius C. V.

[4] Mas-Latrie, Hist. de Chypre, ii. 81, 82, where two documents are
printed from the letters of Edward in the Public Record Office. In
one of these the king commends Ralph de Coumbe, master of the
Hospital of St. Thomas, to the good offices of Hugh of Lusignan, in
Cyprus; in another, dated Sept. 15, 1279, Ralph de Cardolio and the
brethren write to the king on the misfortunes of Palestine, and urge
that the master of the Order should be sent into Syria. See the 7th
Report of the Deputy Keeper of the Records, App. II. No. 2252; Royal
Letters, MS. (Chancery), No. 4260.

relating the capture of Acre, places the knights of St. Thomas at the head of the 5000 soldiers whom the king of England had sent to Palestine[1], and Herman Corner, who however wrote a century later, mentions them amongst the defenders of Acre. We know from their cartulary that they had lands in Yorkshire, Middlesex, Surrey, and Ireland[2]; their Master was called Master of the whole Order of the Knighthood of St. Thomas the Martyr, in the kingdom of Cyprus, Apulia, Sicily, Calabria, Brundusium, England, Flanders, Brabant, Scotland, Wales, Ireland, and Cornwall. Some few noble names of the masters have been preserved; Ralph of Coumbe was master in or about 1278[3], Henry de Bedford

[1] Matthaei, Vet. Aevi Analecta, x. 182; Eccard, Scriptores, i. 942.

[2] At Wapping, Plumstead, Coulsdon, and Doncaster. The estate at Wapping was the gift of Tierri of Alegate; MS. Cott. fo. 156: Coulsdon was confirmed to the master of the knights by a charter of Henry III, in 1261; fo. 236: the Hospital of St. James, at Doncaster, was given by Peter de Mauley; 'Deo et militiae beati Thomae martyris de Acon;' fo. 258: the benefactors in Ireland are enumerated by Edward I in a grant of confirmation, 5th June, A° 17—Fulk de Villars, John de la Zouche, Edmund Bret, Gilbert Marshall, Walter Marshall, and Philip Horsey. James Butler, Earl of Ormond, was another at a later date.

[3] Frater Radulfus preceptor fratrum Sancti Thomae de Acon in Anglia; A.D. 1249. William of Huntingfield 'magister militiae hospitalis B. Thomae Martyris de Acon Londini;' MS. Cotton, fo. 166. Richard of Southampton was master of the Hospital, 11 Edw. II; Thomas de Sallowe, 'magister domus,' 40 Edw. III.

Aug. 7, 1323, Henry de Bedford, master general of the order, creates John de Paris prior and custos of the chapel of St. Nicholas of Nicosia; sealing with his seal for Cyprus.

June 17, 1324, William de Glastingebury, preceptor of the house of St. Thomas of Acre, in the diocese of Nicosia, with consent of the chapter of the house, to wit, Nicolas Clifton, John of Paris, and William of St. Bartholomew, appoints Nicolas Clifton proctor against a brother Henry, who calls himself master; 'actum Nicosiae in capella Sancti Nicolai presentibus Henrico et Thoma presbyteris Anglicis et praedicto Johanne priore dictae capellae.'

Aug. 30, 1344, Robert Kendale, master of the whole order, appoints Henry of Colchester and William of Brunill to collect money for the

in 1323, and Robert de Kendale in 1344. In 1350 the
order was recognized as still existing by the German traveller
Ludolf of Suchen. In 1357 Hugh de Curteys, the preceptor
of Cyprus, invested one Richard of Tickhill with the habit
of the order, in the presence of Robert Swillington, canon,
Sir Richard Chatesby, an English priest, and William Gaston
of England, Turcopolier to the king of Cyprus. The
ceremony was performed in the church of St. Nicolas of the
English in the city of Nicosia; one of the many churches
which formerly, according to Father Stephen of Lusignan,
adorned that city, of which the Venetians destroyed 130 in
the process of fortification. [It is possible that it still exists,
and is indeed that church of St. Nicolas, which our dear
friend the bishop of Gibraltar tried to recover in 1879.]
The hospital in London became, probably at the fall of the
Templars, a mere Augustinian hospital. Its church, or
one built on the site of it, is now the chapel of the Mercers'
Company [1].

England had not, with all her business under Henry III
and Edward I, forgotten Palestine: some of her sons fell
at Acre, and the remnant of the little order found a home
at Nicosia. But the great king himself never forgot his
first love; in fact all the nobler Plantagenets, Richard of
Cornwall, Edward I, Henry of Lancaster, Henry of Boling-

order; 'dat. Nicosiae' in the house of Guddefrid, archdeacon of the
church of Famagosta, vicar of Philip, archbishop of Nicosia.

Feb. 2, 1357, Hugh Curteys invests Richard of Tickhill; 'actum
in regno Cypri in Nicosia intra ecclesiam Beati Nicolai Anglicorum,
praesentibus Francisco de Gave burgensi Nicosiae, domino Rob. de
Swillington canonico, domino Ricardo de Chatesby presbytero Anglico;
Guillelmo Gaston de Anglia Turcopolo regis et pluribus aliis.'

[1] The history of the London house may be read in Newcourt, Re-
pertorium, i. 553; and Mon. Angl. vi. 645, and in the account of the
Hospital of St. Thomas of Acon, by John Watney, F.S.A., printed in
1892: it must be carefully distinguished from the Hospital of St. Thomas
the Martyr in Southwark, the germ of the present St. Thomas's Hospital.

broke, Henry V, and Cardinal Beaufort, all either made
the pilgrimage or looked forward to a great crusade.   To
Edward I, in or about 1303, was addressed the very amusing 'Libellus de recuperatione Terrae Sanctae[1],' the work
of Peter de Bosco, an ecclesiastical judge in Aquitaine,
but who speculates like a special correspondent of the
period; a book which shows a just sense of the evils which
had rendered the united action of Christendom impossible;
points out ways in which all political dangers in Europe can
be avoided; stigmatizes the crime of war between Christian
princes, the ruinous discord between Venice, Pisa, and
Genoa, and proposes to settle the military orders chiefly
in Cyprus, and employ them in the recovery of the holy
places.   Curiously enough, one of the remedial measures
proposed by the writer, who is especially strong on the
subject of natural science, is that girls should be taught
to practise medicine and surgery; they are to learn grammar,
and logic also, natural principles, and mathematics, but
it is that they may qualify as wives for the Oriental princes.

But to return to Cyprus: Edward, as I said, was not the
only one of his family who remembered it: Henry III had
proposed to the bishop of Bethlehem a marriage between his
son Edmund and the queen-mother Placentia in 1256; the
young king was also to marry one of his daughters[2].   The
records however, of both that reign and the next, contain
more references to Armenia than to Cyprus; thus in 1260
Alexander IV exhorts Edward to defend Armenia against
the Tartars; in 1280 the bishop of Hebron, vicegerent of
the patriarch, sends the thanks of the Franks, and adds that
Armenia and Cyprus have been laid waste by a plague of
locusts[3]; the same intelligence is sent by the master of

---

[1] Printed at the end of the second volume of Bongars' *Gesta Dei per
Francos*, and edited in 1891 at Paris by C. V. Langlois.

[2] Foed. i. 341.   [3] Ib. 402, 586.

St. Thomas from Acre; the wars of Charles of Anjou cut off
all hope of succour, and the king of the Tartars had demanded provisions from Acre.   Boniface VIII was unwearied
in impressing on England the importance of these regions;
in 1298 he urges the sending of a subsidy to Sembat, King
of Armenia[1]; in 1300 he is negotiating a general confederacy
which will include the princes of Armenia and Georgia.
Edward cannot do much, but if he cannot send knights he
will send missionaries.   The king of the Tartars sends envoys
to him, and one of them is baptized.   The last measures of
Edward I and the first of Edward II are to the same purpose.
Edward I issues safe-conduct to the bishop of Lydda and
other Dominicans who are going to convert the heathen;
Edward II sends a warning to the king of the Tartars
against Mahometanism.   The kings of Armenia, who have
apparently little else to do, send constant appeals for money.
Faithful Armenia, says Sanuto, writing in 1321, lies among
the wild beasts; on one side the lion, the Tartar; on another
the leopard, the Sultan; on a third the wolf, the Turks;
on the fourth the serpent, the Corsairs.   But these I must
notice by and by.

Henry II of Cyprus reigned nominally from 1285 to
1324; but during great part of the time he was superseded
by one or other of his brothers: his quarrels with them
form the whole history of his reign; at one time he was
a prisoner in Armenia, whither his brother, Amalric, the
prince of Tyre, had sent him; another brother, Guy, the
constable of Cyprus, was put to death by his orders for a
conspiracy against him.   The Popes were much exercised
by this fraternal strife; but it was not until after the death
of Guy that Henry had peace.   As so often happens after
an unquiet reign, he outlived all his enemies, and died rather
regretted than not.   This was in 1324: he was buried in

[1] Foed. i. 900, 742, 749, 902, 919.

the church of the Franciscans at Nicosia. When he had been able to exercise independent authority he had used it well; he had welcomed the refugees from Acre and fortified Famagosta; he contributed largely to the judicial decisions which form the supplement to the Assizes, and he established a strong judicature in Cyprus. But he was an epileptic, which perhaps accounts for his incapacity to retain the rule; and he left no children.

With the accession of his nephew, Hugh IV, begins a more stirring, and, perhaps, the most interesting, period of the Cypriot history. Before however entering on the outline of this portion of our subject, we may just look back to Armenia, where the native kingdom and the native dynasty were nearly coming to an end. Leo I, the first king, who was regarded by the Armenian writers as a really great and patriotic ruler, died in 1219, leaving an infant daughter, who carried the crown to her husbands in succession; Philip of Antioch first, who, failing to make himself agreeable on the Church question to the native lords, especially a great lord called Constantius, or Constantine, was put to death with his partisans. The second husband was Hayton, the son of Constantius, who reigned for nearly fifty years, at first under his father's directions, and after the year 1237 independently. Hayton was thus king during the whole of the crusading period of the thirteenth century, and had dealings with Lewis IX in his first Crusade, and with Edward of England during his stay in Palestine. He was moreover the king of Armenia in whose time Marco Polo set out on his travels in Asia; and it was through his means that the Western kings became acquainted with the Tartar dynasty at Samarcand and its tendencies to favour Christianity. For the Tartar rulers during this period were far from being committed to Islam; they received and favoured missions and protected Christian doctrines in a liberal fashion, without understanding them or finally committing themselves[1]. Hayton may possibly have the credit of having stirred up the Mongols against the Khalifate of Bagdad, which Hulaku brought to an end in 1259. The alliance with the Tartars brought down the Sultan of Egypt on Armenia; and, after the capture of Antioch, Hayton resigned his throne and retired to a monastery, where he took the name of Macarius, and died soon after. His brother, the constable of Armenia, Sempad, Sembat, or Sinibald, was the author of an Armenian chronological history of authority. A better-known person, also of the royal house, was the monk Hayton, who about the year 1305 wrote a history called the Flower of the Histories of the East. Hayton's career is curious. He had been lord of Gorigos, or Corycus, on the Mediterranean coast, and had both fought in Palestine and negotiated among the Tartars, where the Armenian princes were constantly tantalized with the hope of converting the khans. About 1290 he went to Cyprus and became a Praemonstratensian canon, as Brother Antony. From Cyprus he turned westward and came to France, where the Pope was. It was at Poictiers that he dictated his history, which accordingly was written in Latin. It has been printed both in Latin and in a French translation of the same century, but contains more about the Tartars than about the Franks.[2] It is not improbable that to Hayton's influence we may trace some of the interest shown in Armenia by Edward I and Edward II.

King Hayton, however, who died in 1271, was succeeded

---

[1] Mosheim in his ' Historia Tartarorum ' has collected all the notices accessible in his time of the attempts to convert the Tartars, which for a long time had a show of success. After dallying with Christianity, the Khans seem to have become finally Mahometan and hostile at the beginning of the 14th century. But the subject, since the publication of the Armenian authorities, has become susceptible of much more elucidation.

[2] Ed. Rigaut, 1585; cf. Hist. Litt. xxv. 479-507.

on the Armenian throne by his son Leo II, who seems to
have clung to the Tartar alliance as against Egypt, and to
have come to an open rupture with the Pope on the other
side. He was likewise in close alliance with Byzantium, and,
although his history is obscure, he seems to have asserted an
independent position for which his successors toiled in vain.
He reigned eighteen years, and was followed by four of his
sons in succession. Of these Hayton II purchased the support
of the West by reconciling himself and his people to Rome ;
he was a poet and historian also, and ended in becoming a
Franciscan as Friar John. With his brother, Thoros, who
on his withdrawal became king, he went to Constantinople
to obtain help from Andronicus Paleologus. On their return
they found themselves unseated by a third brother, Sembat ;
fled to Cyprus first and then to Tartary, but were taken ;
Hayton was blinded and Thoros strangled. Sembat had
thrown over the Roman alliance and been crowned by the
Armenian Catholicos ; but, finding the Saracens still gaining
ground, he changed his tactics, and obtained from Boniface VIII a bull for a subsidy, which was circulated in
England in 1298[1]. He was supplanted in his turn by his
brother Constantius. He, after a short reign, was succeeded
by Leo III, son of Thoros, who reigned under the guardianship of his uncle, the blind brother John, who had been king
as Hayton II. Both Leo and his uncle were put to death by
a Tartar general, at the suggestion, according to the Roman
writers, of the discontented Armenians, who had been again
too summarily reconciled to the papacy in a council at Sis,
in 1307. Oissim, who succeeded in 1308, was another son
of Leo II. He was connected with the Cypriot history,
taking part with the brothers of King Henry against him ;
and he also obtained a confirmation of the union with the
Roman Church in 1316. Leo IV, who was the last of the

---

[1] Foed. i. 900.

native dynasty, succeeded his father Oissim in 1320. His whole reign was a continued struggle against the Moslems, who were encroaching on every side, and his name became very well known in the West. It was in his defence that John XXII proclaimed a Crusade in 1333; and, among other helps, Edward III, in 1335, allowed his ambassadors £40 from the London subsidy. Leo found himself before his death reduced to the few mountain fortresses from which his ancestors had emerged two centuries before. He failed to gain the support of the Armenians, and was thus thrown on that of the Latins, who could really give him no aid. He was assassinated about 1342, and his dynasty ended with him. The five remaining kings of Armenia sprang from a branch of the Cypriot house of Lusignan, and were little more than Latin exiles in the midst of several strange populations all alike hostile.

We have now to return to Hugh IV, King of Cyprus, a prince who is known in literary history as the king to whom Boccaccio dedicated his Genealogy of the Gods. He reigned twenty-five years, and has the merit of setting on foot the great alliance between the Venetians, the Pope, and the knights of Rhodes, to which the chief successes of his reign and that of his son were due. It is true that these successes wear to modern eyes the look of mere piratical exploits: but we have two points to remember in this connexion. All naval war, not only during the Middle Ages, but down to the seventeenth century, was more or less piratical; and the war between the Christians and the Saracens, although interrupted now and then by truces, which both parties felt ashamed to make and took the first opportunity of breaking, was really continuous and internecine. The coasts of Asia Minor had been gradually lost to the Christians; the coasts of Egypt were to some extent open to reprisals. The fact that the coast of Syria and Palestine afforded so few harbours had, when once the fortified harbour of Acre had fallen into the hands of the Saracens, the effect of removing the seat of war to the Asiatic and Egyptian coasts. That was the deliberate opinion of King Edward I, who had ruled that Egypt must be the first point of attack, then Palestine, and then Constantinople. Hence the two attacks on Damietta in 1219 and 1249. Now, after a long period of defence, the Christians took the initiative. The leaders and fighters in all this from 1308 to 1523 were the knights of Rhodes, but Cyprus was very frequently the head-quarters and source of supplies, and the Western pilgrims were not chary of labour, blood, or treasure. In all the great achievements of the time too some English pilgrims were associated. The single exploit however of King Hugh's reign was a descent on Smyrna in 1344. John of Biandra, Grand Prior of Lombardy, the head of the expedition, made himself master of the citadel; and Smyrna remained in the hands of the knights until the close of the century. The king of Cyprus had contributed a contingent towards the fleet, but, except by weakening the Saracen power a little, he obtained no immediate benefit for his state[1].

The great plague of 1349 fell with especial fatality on Cyprus; only one castle, that of Dieudamour, was safe for the king to dwell in; and the island got such a reputation for unwholesome air that the trade almost ceased. The Frank population especially diminished. In 1349 the traveller, Ludolf of Suchen, described the barons of Cyprus as the richest in the world: after the plague Hugh had to recruit the ranks of the nobles by conferring titles on the merchant class. The succours sought in Europe were only scantily afforded. The king of Armenia cried louder and got more

---

[1] Paoli, Cod. Dipl. Ord. S. Joh. ii. 93, gives a commission from the Pope to the archbishop of Candia to recover from the king of Cyprus, the Grand-Master of Rhodes, and the Doge of Venice, the money covenanted for the defence of Smyrna.

sympathy than the king of Cyprus. Still some brave men
went out to the East. It is at least to this period that we
have to refer the pilgrimage and warlike exploits of Henry
of Lancaster, the great duke-palatine and father-in-law of
John of Gaunt. He, according to his biographer Capgrave,
about the year 1351 made his grand tour, and fought not
only in Prussia, where he went first, but also in Rhodes,
Cyprus, and the East, ending his military education with a
campaign in Granada. William Lord Roos of Hamlake
died in 1352, either in Palestine or in Cyprus, on a more
distinctly religious pilgrimage: to 1357 we have referred
our last glimpse of the English order and their church at
Nicosia. In 1352 Henry Lord Percy left by will 1000 marks
sterling in florins of Florence for his son Henry to make
the pilgrimage. But the French war in the West, and the
struggles of the Venetians with the Genoese, prevented
anything like national or united expeditions. In the midst
of turmoil King Hugh died in 1359, and was buried in the
Blackfriars' church at Nicosia. His eldest son, Guy, prince
of Galilee and constable of Cyprus, had died before him,
leaving a son, Hugh of Lusignan. He, on his grandfather's
death, went into the West to obtain some support in his
claim on the crown, which, owing to the fact that representation was not allowed by the laws of Cyprus, failed to
obtain recognition. This is that Hugh of Cyprus whom the
Pope in 1360 made senator of Rome, and who really
ruled there from January to August 1361. He has been
confounded by some of the Cypriot historians with his
grandfather, who accordingly is made to abdicate and die at
Rome. Hugh, having failed to find employment for his
military genius at Rome, resigned the senatorship, and we
hear no more of him [1].

[1] Gregorovius, Gesch. d. St. Rom., vi. 393 ; Theiner, Diplom.
S. Sedis, ii. 391.

The crown of Cyprus had been secured by Hugh IV to his second son Peter, whom he had had crowned, before his death, at Nicosia.

Peter, with apparently some characteristics of genius, had several more or less allied to insanity. He had made a vow of slaughter against all Mussulmans generally, and, for the purpose of keeping it, wore his naked sword hung round his neck. Our acquaintance with him is largely due to Froissart, who follows his exploits with some minuteness; but we have a more valuable record in the work written by Philip de Mazzeriis, chancellor of Cyprus, on the life of the legate Peter Thomasius, whose period of activity nearly coincides with the reign of King Peter, 1361–1369[1]. Peter Thomasius was a native of Guienne, a born subject of Edward III, and was probably instrumental personally in creating the interest felt in England and Guienne in the plans of the king of Cyprus. He crowned Peter at Famagosta, and made an attempt to bring over the Greek population of Cyprus to the Roman obedience. The first exploit of King Peter was the voyage across the enchanted gulf to Satalia, and the capture of the place, where, as Froissart tells us, he slew without exception all the inhabitants of both sexes whom he found there. In this expedition he was assisted not only by the Catalans and the fleet of Rhodes, but by an English force, or a force under an English knight, whom the Italian historians name Robert of Toulouse[2], and describe as sent into Armenia to demand tribute from the princes. If Robert of Toulouse was engaged in the sack of Satalia, we must hope, for our national credit's sake, that he was only an Englishman by courtesy, a knight of Rhodes of the langue of England, which would contain knights drawn from the continental estates of the Planta-

---

[1] Acta Sanctorum, Boll. Jan. ii. 995–1023.
[2] The name is variously given: Dulaurier reads it Lusugnan; it also appears as Julassan, which looks like a corruption of an English name.

genets. Having fleshed his maiden sword at Satalia, King
Peter set out on a mission westward, a general canvass of
Christendom. Having gone by way of Rhodes to Venice, the
legate, making known the approach of the king, applied for
succour to the 'communitates, dominos et tyrannos' of Lombardy, and then passed on to Avignon. In March 1363,
King Peter himself reached Avignon, where the Pope gladly
received him, and determined to preach a new Crusade, of
which King John of France, who had just emerged from
his prison in England, should be the leader. After settling
this, the king went to Prague, where he saw the Emperor
Charles IV, and so to Juliers, Brussels, and Bruges. Everywhere he was received with suppers and tournaments, in both
of which he seems to have played his part. Whilst he was
enjoying himself, the legate was negotiating, and it was
determined that the Crusade under King John should start
from Marseilles in the following March. Froissart follows
the movements of King Peter through Picardy to Calais,
and on to London. At London he was well entertained;
Queen Philippa made him handsome presents; King Edward
gave him a ship named the Catharine. The mayor, Henry
Picard, gave him a dinner, and allowed him to win fifty marks
at play: but when the mayor won his money back, and fifty
marks more, as the poor king did not lose with a good grace,
he gave him his money back again. Of substantial aid he got
little; and Edward was not liberal even with promises; he
himself was too old to go, but his sons and nobles might.
Peter went back therefore to France. Before he went he was
robbed by some English highwaymen; as however Edward
paid all his expenses, he was probably no great loser.

King John had during this time returned to England,
where he took part in the festivities, but died soon after, in
April 1364, thus putting an end to one part of the great
design; and one of Peter's first acts after returning through

Guienne to Paris, was to attend King John's funeral, May 7, 1364, and the coronation of his successor. He seems then to have revisited the emperor and the kings of Hungary and Poland, a route which hindered him from reaching Venice until the legate had left. The legate had been called away to Cyprus to settle a quarrel between the Genoese and King Peter's officers. Peter appeared at Venice rather forlorn; but he had obtained the support of some English lords, one of whom, the Earl of Warwick, must, if the traditions of the Beauchamps are to be trusted, have gone on before him; for in the great battle in Turkey, fought Nov. 1, 1364, he took prisoner a son of the king of Lithuania, whom he brought back to England and made a Christian. Two other Englishmen of distinction are known to have followed Peter; John Lord Grey of Codnor, and a knight of the house of Stapylton, who had been especially impressed by the virtues of the legate.

Having got together as many volunteers as he could, and a considerable fleet, King Peter sailed from Venice and joined the fleet of the Hospitallers. The great stroke to be made was the capture of Alexandria. This was effected with no small bloodshed and very rich spoils. Alexandria taken, the next object was to strengthen the fortifications and make it the head-quarters of a Crusade. But here the English auxiliaries objected. There can be no doubt that the story is true, for it is from the pen of the legate himself: they refused even to stay all night in Alexandria, and having conspired with a certain prince, whose name the legate feels bound to keep secret, set sail for Cyprus. They sent word home too that the city was only half taken[1]. It was a great disappointment to the ardent crusaders; but no doubt the English lords who had had experience in foreign warfare

---

[1] 'Recesserunt Anglici qui videbantur fortiores, facta conspiratione cum principe cujus ex parentela et dolosa sequela nomen tacere debeo;' P. de Mazz. AA. SS. l. c. p. 1016.

saw that Alexandria was untenable, and the season, for it
was now the 10th of October, 1365, was too far advanced.
The failure of the Crusade was bitterly commented on by
Petrarch, who in a letter to Boccaccio writes, at the time,
in the severest way of the greediness and irresolution of the
Transalpines [1], and many years after laments, in an epistle to
Philip de Mazzeriis, the loss to Christendom, and the wretched
effect produced, by the failure, on the character and fate
of the king [2]. The English lords seem to have stayed
sometime longer in Cyprus: the legate died at Famagosta
in January, 1366, and they brought back to England the
biography by Philip the Chancellor, which has furnished the
most certain details of the story. After the Alexandrian
expedition the Venetians, whose commerce was suffering,
prevailed on Peter to treat for a peace with Egypt, which
was to establish Cypriot consulates and reduce the customs
in the ports of the Levant; but the attempt failed. The
next year, with the Genoese and the Hospitallers, he ravaged
the Syrian coast, but again had to make peace. He then
visited Rome in search of succour, and returned finally to
Cyprus in September 1368. The rest of King Peter's life
was very wretched: he had left his queen during his long
visit to the West, and she had proved faithless: he retaliated
on the nobles who had been her favourites, and gave rein
to his cruelty and lasciviousness. If he were not mad, as

---

[1] 'Siquidem Petrus Cypri rex Alexandriam cepit in Egypto, magnum
opus et memorabile nostraeque religionis in immensum amplificandae
fundamentum ingens, si quantum ad capiendam tantum ad servandam
urbem animi fuisset; qui certe non defuit, ut fama, nisi comitatus ejus ex
transalpinis maxime gentibus collectus, melioribus semper ad principia
rerum quam ad exitus, illum in medio praestantissimi operis deserentes,
ut qui pium regem non pietate sed cupiditate sequentes, collectis spoliis
abiere piique voti impotem avari voti compotes fecere;' Petrarch,
Opp. p. 843 ; Ep. Senil. lib. 8. ep. 8.

[2] Ib. lib. 13. ep. 2 : 'Petrus rex Cypri, indigni vir exitus sed sacrae
memoriae nisi,' etc.

seems most probable, he was desperate; and his family took the lead in getting rid of him. He was assassinated by a body of nobles, who acted with the concurrence of his brother John, the prince of Antioch, on the 16th of January, 1369. His wife was Eleanor of Aragon; and it was this connexion, no doubt, that gave him a higher place than his predecessors had enjoyed in the estimation of the Western kings.

Peter II, who succeeded him, was a boy of thirteen; his uncle John acted as regent. Peter reigned till 1382. He avenged his father's death by murdering his uncle in 1375. His reign witnessed a fatal rupture between the Venetians and Genoese, which accelerated the fate of Cyprus. The representatives of the two republics quarrelled about precedence at the coronation: the court decided in favour of Venice. This was complicated by a quarrel between the queen-mother and the prince of Antioch. The Genoese took up arms and overran the whole island. The boy king was taken prisoner, and to secure his ransom had to pledge Famagosta to the Genoese. This great city and the port, which Sir John Mandeville thought the finest in the world, was permanently lost to the kings, for it was subsequently made over to the Genoese altogether in order to obtain the release of James, the king's uncle and successor, who had been detained as a hostage by the admiral Fregoso.

The particular interest which attaches to the struggle of Venice and Genoa,—a struggle which only ended when the Levant was left to the Turks, and was one great cause of the abridgement of Christendom at the close of the Middle Ages,—and the glorious exploits of the knights of Rhodes, however close to our subject, are far too wide and engrossing topics to be discussed incidentally. But the fate of Armenia, where the very succession of the kings is very obscure, demands a word. The first Latin king, according to the native historians, was John of Lusignan, also called Constantine, who reigned only a year; his brother, Guy of Lusignan, who succeeded in 1343, was connected by marriage with the Cantacuzenes, and even addressed Edward III as cousin[1]. Both the brothers were little else than adventurers. Guy reigned for only three years. In 1347 his successor Constantius, or Constantine, was, through an envoy of the same name, collecting money in England by virtue of a brief issued by Clement VI[2]. He seems to be identical with Constantine, who, in 1351, was on the throne; in his favour also alms were collected in England. He died in 1361. After an interval of three years, during which the crown was offered to Peter of Cyprus, and an unknown fourth king may possibly have reigned, Leo V appears on the throne in 1365. He had a hard fight for it; from 1371 to 1373 he was lost to his people, concealed in a mountain fortress where he had been obliged to take refuge. A new king was sought for, a husband for the supposed widow, and Gregory XI offered the crown to Otto of Brunswick. He, however, preferred to marry Johanna of Naples, and Leo emerged from seclusion. But with little better prospects; taken prisoner by the Egyptian sultan in 1375, he was released in 1382, to be thenceforth a wanderer and a pensioner on the Western princes. After his release he made the pilgrimage to Jerusalem, and went thence to Avignon and so to Spain. In Spain he obtained a provision. King John of Castile gave him three lordships, one of them Madrid; and as lord of Madrid King Leo granted a charter to the burghers of the town. But he did not stay in Spain. In 1384 he was in France offering his services as a mediator between Charles VI and Richard II. His offers were not welcome to the English lords, who then held the king in tutelage. They refused him in the first instance his passport

---

[1] Foed. ii. 1220.   [2] Ib. 1234; iii. 103.

—said that though he proffered peace he only wanted
money; he was an illusor, and they would have nothing to
do with him. Notwithstanding this he obtained not only
a safe-conduct but a permit for a cargo of French wine to
be brought to England for him; he made an eloquent speech
before the king and council at the palace of Westminster; and
received a pension of £1000 a year; the first instalment of
which was paid into his own hands in gold nobles. He had a
passport again in 1392, a few months before his death. His
pension was still paid in 1391, in the fifteenth year of the
unlucky king: at that time Leo, it was said, had been driven
from his dominions; the pension was to be continued until
he regained them. Fortunately for the English exchequer,
it was not required, for according to the epitaph of King Leo
in the Church of the Celestines at Paris, the very noble and
very excellent Prince Lyon of Lusignan, fifth Latin king
of Armenia, rendered his soul to God Nov. 29, 1393.
He left no legitimate issue, and his claims devolved on his
cousin of Cyprus. The name of the kingdom of Armenia
was thus familiar in English ears at this time. English
sympathy had not flagged during these years. In 1383
another Lord de Roos, Thomas, son of the lord who died
in 1352, had set out for the East, but died before he left
England; his son John fulfilled the vow, and having reached
Cyprus, died at Paphos in 1393. A large party of English
visitors had appeared there in that year.

James I, the uncle and successor of Peter II, reigned from
1382 to 1398, and was on excellent terms with England.
There is a letter addressed by him to Richard II, in July,
1393[1], in which he acknowledges the receipt of the epistle of
commendation brought by Lord de Roos, and tells him that
it was needless, because all the King of England's friends
were welcome. He thanks him too for the message which

[1] Raine, Extracts from Northern Registers, p. 425.

he had received by his most noble cousin, Sir Henry Percy.
We learn from this that Hotspur had made Cyprus a part
of his great tour. The same year witnessed the pilgrimage
of the Earl of Derby, afterwards King Henry IV. Henry of
Bolingbroke, having sailed in July 1392 from the Norfolk
coast, went by way of Prussia, Poland, Hungary, and Venice
to Jerusalem; on his return he visited Cyprus in February,
and so back by Italy and Bohemia [1]. King James was a
kindly old man, but much tied up between the Venetians and
the Genoese. He had accumulated three crowns; he had
received that of Jerusalem at Nicosia, as Famagosta was now
lost; in 1393 he received that of Armenia, which he handed
on to his successors. James had been a hostage or prisoner
at Genoa when the crown of Cyprus fell to him; he had been
sent thither when the perfidious Admiral Fregoso had seized
the island; and at Genoa his son, King Janus or John II,
was born.

The reign of Janus, thirty-four years long, was one sad
struggle, with the Genoese on the one hand and the Turks
on the other. The main features of the story are these.
King Janus, with a very natural ambition, stimulated moreover by hereditary and personal enmity, made it his first
object to recover Famagosta from Genoa, and for this end,
in the year 1402, prepared a force and fleet to besiege the
Genoese there. The days of Genoese greatness were over.
In 1396 the Doge Adorno had submitted to Charles VI of
France, and Genoa had become a French dependency.
Famagosta had been won by the Fregosi, the opposite
faction to that of Adorno, but the French were, as usual,
ready to maintain their claim to conquests under whatever
régime they were acquired. On the alarm of war in Cyprus,

---

[1] Capgrave, Illustrious Henries, p. 100. The accounts of the expedition were published in 1894 by the Camden Society.

they sent Marshal Boucicault with a small fleet into the
Levant. King Janus prepared for resistance, but the Grand-
Master of Rhodes, Philibert of Naillac, interposed as mediator,
and a collision was avoided; the poor king had to pay
150,000 ducats for the expenses of the expedition. Peace
was however made, and both parties turned their arms
against the Mahometan neighbours. The Genoese ravaged
the Syrian coast; King Janus plundered the shore of Egypt.
Booty was abundant, but the inexorable vengeance of the
Sultans was aroused; the ravaging of Syria ended in the
loss of the last fragments of Armenian sovereignty; and the
plundering of Egypt drew down the Mameluke Sultan on
Cyprus. Truces and treaties were made, but were kept on
neither side. In the midst of war Cyprus was again, for the
third time since the year 1349, devastated by the plague;
and the Sultan saw his opportunity; in 1417 he took and
wrecked Limasol. In 1420 he swore the entire destruction
of the Cypriots, and prepared for a final conquest. Four
years after, during which King Janus, although he continued
his policy of piratic expeditions, had made scarcely any preparation for defence, he attacked the island, including
Cypriots and Genoese in a common purpose of extirpation.
Famagosta was taken and pillaged. Two years later the
king was defeated and taken prisoner, and Nicosia was
sacked. The king's imprisonment lasted fifteen months;
during which an attempt was made by an Italian, Sforza
Pallavicino, to seize the government. In this he was defeated by the Queen Charlotte of Bourbon, who sent against
him Carion of Ibelin, one of the last, if not the last of that
great house, of whom anything historical is recorded. Ransomed at an enormous cost, Janus returned in 1427, but
thoroughly broken in spirit and despairing of the fortunes of
his house. One of his last acts was to marry his daughter
Anne to Lewis of Savoy, a connexion which in the next

generation helped to place the nominal crowns of Cyprus, Armenia and Jerusalem among the honours of that aspiring house. He died in 1432, and with him the last sunset gleams of Cypriot glory vanished.

The native historians trace the beginning of the downfall to the murder of King Peter in 1369; and if that date be taken we must allow that Petrarch, who thought that that event determined the loss of the East, was gifted with somewhat of prophetic spirit. But I think that, unfortunate as that event was for the Lusignan house, the doom of the Levantine principalities was already sealed. The great plague had swept off the old acclimatized Franks, especially those nobles who, like the lords of Ibelin, had increased and multiplied in the land. With all their faults these nobles were *bona fide* Crusaders; men who, like the first champions, were ready to cast in their lot in a Promised Land, and not, like the later adventurers, anxious merely to get all they could out of it, to make their fortunes. They were swept away. Then there was the antagonism of Genoa and Venice, a piece of history which, so long as history is read in books written in direct hostility to Venice, will be read two ways. Genoa had from the very early Crusades been the ally of France, as Pisa had been the ally of England. Venice had succeeded to the political connexions of Pisa; the tower of the English at Acre abutted on the ward of the Venetians and the Hospitallers; not that during these ages the English national power was of any weight in the Mediterranean, but a good deal of national piety and knight-errantry found expression in pilgrimages which were now conducted by way of Venice, in alliance with the Teutonic knights and the Hospitallers. The final acquisition of Cyprus by Venice, and the extremely unfair way in which it was acquired, seem to have afforded the grounds for supposing that the republic had long coveted the island, and that her policy had been

for several generations directed to that end.   This crooked
policy is contrasted by the hostile writers with the open
violence of the Genoese, exemplified in the war of 1374 and
the seizure of Famagosta.   But I confess that I see little to
choose between the two, and that what little there is seems
in favour of Venice.   Neither republic looked at the defence
of Christendom as the great thing to be sought.   The trading
interest, or territorial ambition complicated with trading
interest, was the main thing.   If Venice profited most by
the common policy, it is not so much a proof of previous
diplomacy as a result of her longer tenure of power.   That
the Venetians however had an equal share with the Genoese
in weakening the Frank kingdom it is impossible to prove :
the Genoese hold on Famagosta was a fatal if not a mortal
wound.

But still more powerful agencies were at work.   The hands
of Christendom were paralyzed, and the barbarians were
gaining strength and unity.   The close of the fourteenth
century, an exceptional but a very critical era, seems to show
us all nations, all royalties, churches, religions, civilized and
barbarous, in a cauldron or a whirlpool from which there
was very small chance of emerging whole.   A madman on
the throne of France, an impotent drunkard claiming the
crown of the Caesars, a frantic absolutist overthrowing the
constitution of England ; the see of St. Peter divided between
two, three, four Popes ; the Emperor of Constantinople
begging money openly in the courts of the West ; the three
barbarian powers pitted against each other—providentially,
we may say, for who could have resisted their united force ?—
the Ottoman sultan the prisoner of Tamerlane ; the Mameluke
sultan only sustained in independence by the contest between
the Turks and the Tartars.   Yet Europe does emerge ; the
battle of Nicopolis puts an end to the Crusades ; the retreat
of the Tartars enables the Ottomans to recover their ground ;

Byzantium has a respite of half a century, and Egypt of more than a hundred years of Mameluke tyranny. It takes a century more to constitute the great national factors of modern history. But out of the whirlpool little states like Cyprus do not emerge; and after the death of King Janus, the causes that were at work worked quickly and steadily.

The immediate cause of the break-up was connected with the same sort of religious disputes which, after occupying half the century in councils and debates, left the Byzantine empire defenceless before the Ottomans. King John III, who succeeded in 1432, took for his second wife, in 1435, Helena, the daughter of the despot of the Peloponnese, Theodore Paleologus. The house of Lusignan had been hitherto, as a matter of necessity, devotedly Catholic; the house of Paleologus was devotedly orthodox; Cyprus was a Catholic kingdom with an orthodox population; a Latin king with a Greek people; the Latin Church was rich, and the Greek Church was not poor, but the political power was engrossed by the former. Helena would not see this. She determined, if she could, to make Cyprus orthodox; she, through her husband, who was a weak and vicious man, refused the papal nominee to the archbishopric of Nicosia, imprisoned him, and was accused of poisoning him. The grand-master of Rhodes came in, as usual, in the part of a peace-maker, and prevailed on the king to receive the prelate; and soon after, in 1458, both Helena and her husband died. But the quarrel had shaken the tottering kingdom; the Grand Caraman, the Turcoman ruler of Caramania, took the opportunity of these quarrels to seize Corycus, the last Frank stronghold of Armenia. The Cilician and Syrian begs, with the Egyptian sultan, formed a league for the conquest of Cyprus, which was foiled by the Rhodian galleys, or the Latin kingdom would have succumbed before the capture of Constantinople. The end was clearly coming, and it was

not now a question between Venetians and Genoese, but
between Christian and Moslem, which should take the
island as a derelict. The royal house was nearly extinct.
Charlotte of Lusignan, the only legitimate child of John III,
succeeded him in 1458. She was the widow of John of
Portugal, prince of Antioch, who had been poisoned by the
creatures of Helena in 1457. She married, in 1459, her
cousin Lewis count of Geneva, of the house of Savoy, who
was crowned the same year. Her bastard brother, James,
archbishop-elect of Nicosia, the son of a Greek lady, whose
nose Queen Helena had bitten off, was disappointed of the
succession, and turned traitor. He aspired to the vainglory
of sovereignty, and, having done homage to the sultan of
Egypt, invaded Cyprus. For four years Queen Charlotte
was besieged at Cherin; in 1464 she fled to Rhodes, and
thence to Italy, where, in 1485, her rights and the three
crowns she wore she made over to the house of Savoy.
James II, a prince of some power, governed or commanded
in Cyprus from 1464 to 1473, and to some extent justified
his usurpation by taking Famagosta from the Genoese, but
his reign was one long series of conspiracies. He was
assassinated two years after his marriage with Caterina
Cornaro (in 1471), who bore a son after her husband's
death. This was King James III, who died when he was
two years old. The Venetians held that the rights of the
infant king devolved on his mother, and in her name
governed Cyprus.

On the details of the Venetian title I cannot now enter;
the whole history has been accepted on the evidence of the
enemies of the republic, whose story is briefly this. In order
to qualify Caterina for a foreign marriage she was declared
the adopted daughter of St. Mark, and her husband the
son-in-law of the republic. The republic, anxious for the
succession, poisoned the son-in-law, who in his will entailed

the crown on his children, posthumous and illegitimate, with remainder to the house of Lusignan. But this was set aside by the connivance of Caterina with the Venetians, who, after they had ruled Cyprus for fifteen years in her name, obtained from her a renunciation of her rights in favour of the republic ; this was done in 1489; and then, formally as well as actually, Cyprus became a Venetian dependency, tributary to the Sultan of Egypt. Caterina herself retired to the Venetian territory, where she lived at the villa Paradiso in the Trevisan mountains, painted by Titian, and patronizing the scholars of the renaissance, until the year of her death, 1510. After eighty-one years spent under Venice, Cyprus was conquered by the Turks in 1570. From the date then of Caterina's surrender, and indeed from the death of King James, the history of the island falls into the mass of that wonderful Venetian history of which we read so little, but which must contain so many lessons, and so many warnings for a nation like our own.

The titles of the several royalties which thus came to an end were claimed, as titles easily may be claimed, by other competitors : the Dukes of Savoy called themselves Kings of Cyprus and Jerusalem from the date of Queen Charlotte's settlement; the Kings of Naples had called themselves Kings of Jerusalem since the transfer of the rights of Mary of Antioch, in 1277, to Charles of Anjou; and the title has run on to the present day in the houses of Spain and Austria, the Dukes of Lorraine, and the successive dynasties of Naples. The kingdom of Armenia must, I think, have been dropped ; but the Savoyard claim to Cyprus was held as an offence to the Venetian republic, a point of ceremonial which, in the seventeenth century, put a stop for thirty years to any diplomatic intercourse between Venice and Savoy. The successors of Richard I never put in a claim to the reversion ; the quartering of the arms of Cyprus, which is said to appear on the tomb of Queen Elizabeth, being no doubt a part of the bearings derived from her great-grandmother, Jacquetta of Luxemburg, whose daughter, Elizabeth Wydville, carried the blood of the house of Brienne and the Dukes of Athens into the line of York [1]. The Kings of Sardinia continued to strike money as Kings of Cyprus and Jerusalem, until they became Kings of Italy. There is no recognized King of Cyprus now, but there are two or three Kings of Jerusalem; and the Cypriot title is claimed, I believe, by some obscure branch of the house of Lusignan, under the will of King James II.

So much for the archaeology of the question. The interest of England in the affairs of the Levant did not come to an end with the surrender of Cyprus to Venice; for the Knights of Rhodes maintained the defence of Christendom for half a century longer, and England was a close friend of the order until Henry VIII confiscated its estates. The Turcopolier of the Knights Hospitallers was always an Englishman; he was the commander of the light infantry of the order. I have found no list of the Turcopoliers; but in the fifteenth century we have the names of Peter Holt, Thomas Launcleve, or Langcliffe, Hugh Middleton, and John Kendall; all of them

[1] The descent is a long one, and there is a question whether the arms are those of Cyprus at all. But certain claims to represent the elder house of Lusignan had come into the family of Luxemburg. Jacquetta was daughter of the Count Peter of S. Pol, whose mother, Marguerite of Enghien, carried the representation of the Counts of Brienne to the Luxemburgs. Mary, daughter of Hugh I of Cyprus and his queen, married Walter IV of Brienne, father of Hugh, and grandfather of Walter V, duke of Athens; Walter V had a daughter Isabel, who married Walter IV of Enghien, father of Lewis, Count of Brienne and Conversano, and grandfather of Margaret, who was the heiress of Enghien. She married John of Luxemburg, and was mother of Peter, Count of S. Pol. As a claim to the throne of Cyprus, this descent was worthless; but it was a royal descent, and, after the extinction of the Lusignans and the house of Antioch-Lusignan, might be thought to have a value of its own. Queen Elizabeth, however, was in no sense the heiress of S. Pol, much less of Lusignan.

would seem North-countrymen.   In the last century a medal
of John Kendall was found in Knaresborough Forest, and it
would appear that he was a member of the family which was
particularly marked by its devotion to St. Wilfrid of Ripon.
The last known brother of the Order of St. Thomas of Acre,
Richard of Tickhill, must also have been a Yorkshire man.
The Cypriot king too had a Turcopolier, who, in 1357, was
an Englishman.   But these are trifles.

I said in beginning my lecture that I should draw no moral
or political lesson from the history of Cyprus and Armenia.
No lesson can safely be drawn from it, if by lesson we mean
absolute instruction or warning that it would be foolish to
despise.   But it does suggest some generalizations and
prompt some questions.   We can see that the loss of the
Levantine states in the Middle Ages, that is, the cessation of
the defence of Christendom against Mahometanism, was
mainly caused by the jealousies of the Christian powers
themselves :   the determination of the Venetians and the
Genoese to set their respective commercial profits above all
other considerations.   Whilst the Teutonic knights were fighting in the North and the Hospitallers in the South, Cyprus,
the storehouse of Palestine, was left a prey to the evils out of
which the Genoese and Venetians could make their market.
It was so in the age that followed: the alliance between
Francis I and Solyman paralyzed all action by which
Charles V and Ferdinand I would have defended the
provinces on the Danube and Transylvania, and suffered
the Turkish dominion to grow almost unimpeded, until the
world began to think that the Turks had a vested interest
in the lands they devastated.   But the questions which arise
are not easily stated, and not easily answered.   How can
the East be redeemed by the acclimatization of Northern
races ? are the Northern races the only races that can redeem
the East, and if so, how are they to be saved from the evils,

moral, intellectual, and political, which acclimatization seems invariably to bring with it? Are the Eastern races to be redeemed at all, or is that part of the aspiration of the Christian Church and of social philanthropists to be a vain dream? Is the task of empires to conquer or to colonize; the task of colonies to extirpate or to develop? Is a commercial or a military policy the surest agent of civilization? Can a worn-out nation be revived and refreshed and recruited by a bracing treatment? can it be revived at all? Does the difference between European and Asiatic history consist in the vitality of the historic nations in Europe and the inexhaustibleness of the hive in Asia? If not, how is Europe to treat Asia, so that the march of civilization may affect the lands in which the stream of history seems to have long been stayed? if it is so, how shall the East be rescued from the successive waves of barbarism which may be now impending, and how kept alive when those successive impulses are exhausted? Small as our subject was, it was a part of that which touches all, the world's government and the long patience of Providence. 'And I said, It is mine own infirmity, but I will remember the years of the right hand of the Most Highest.'

ON THE CHARACTERISTIC DIFFERENCES BETWEEN
MEDIAEVAL AND MODERN HISTORY

(April 15, 1880.)

IF I were asked for what reason I have, in my teaching in this place, preferred mediaeval to later modern history, I should answer, because I think that for the training of the judgement, the former furnishes material more readily applicable to educational purposes than the latter. It is further removed from the arena of political controversy, and, whilst it possesses interest quite sufficient to awaken every sentiment that may lawfully affect the judgement, it stirs no emotion that could reasonably be expected to pervert or overbalance it. We find in it heroes and heroines quite heroic enough to justify hero-worship; we find in it questions of controversy quite sufficiently exciting to divide parties; and points of sufficiently continuing and permanent importance to kindle our zeal in a moderate degree in connexion with the questions and interests of to-day. The rights and wrongs of the political life of modern Europe are rooted in the mediaeval history of Europe, and we can trace sufficient connexion between the extreme past and the present to give interest to the earliest investigations. So we try to train the judgement by investigating causes, effects, ideas and results, rights and wrongs, in a subject-matter sufficiently akin to modern life to engage lively feeling, and yet sufficiently apart from it to prevent party views from being predominant. I have said this so often on these occasions that I am almost ashamed to say it again; I must however go on until I can find some one to believe me. The use to which the trained student may put his judgement when he has educated it is a quite different thing: only I believe that whatever side he may take, or, even if he turn his back altogether on the line of study along which I have tried to lead him, he will approach questions of the day with a more balanced judgement; he will be less disposed to see all good on one side of the great questions, and all evil on the other; he will come to the strife of politics with his weapons more carefully chosen, better handled and better sharpened than if he had never passed through the training.

Mediaeval History is a history of rights and wrongs; modern History as contrasted with mediaeval divides itself into two portions; the first a history of powers, forces, and dynasties; the second, a history in which ideas take the place of both rights and forces. The point of time at which we should mark the separation in the latter is the first French revolution. There is a continuity of life through the three; the fundamental principle, which still holds its ground in the struggle of ideas, is distinctly traceable in the primitive struggle of rights and wrongs; and far more and more distinctly in the more modern struggle of the balance of power; but in the first and second period, ideas have little weight compared with rights and forces; in the first rights are more potent than forces, in the second forces are more potent than rights; and now rights, forces, and ideas are matched in the arena of modern politics in such a way as to make right and force themselves ideas. At this moment—I use an illustration which ought properly to grow out of something that must show further on—Austria may be regarded as representing the more ancient form of right, Russia as representing the

form of force, and Germany, Italy, and France different forms
of leading idea. I do not mean that Austria is justified on
appeal to right, or that Russia relies solely on force, or that
the other three states have not ample grounds, both in right
and force, for their present position, but that historically those
are distinctions essentially characteristic.

You may wonder at my temerity in the use of such very
abstract terms, and you have a right to bid me define more
clearly the historical periods of which I am speaking; I will
then define mediaeval history for our present purpose as
beginning with the eleventh century, and proceed to state
next what sorts of rights, forces, and ideas, I consider, mark
differentially the three periods at which I have been looking.
It may almost provoke a smile that I should use words so,
that I should speak of rights and wrongs in ages in which all
was done with the strong hand, or of forces where intrigue
and policy conspicuously take the place of violence and
bloodshed, or of ideas in connexion with the present age at
all.   I do not care now to justify my use of these particular
words, but I can tell you what I mean, and then, if you can
supply me with better formulae, I will use them.

Our first position then is, that the idea of right or rights
was the leading idea of the Middle Ages. I say now right or
rights, because, whilst in the greatest men of the period there
was a conscious attempt to exalt law and a willingness to
abide by it, there was in the inferior actors, in the worse
men, a disposition to maintain their own rights within recognized limits, and, when they attacked the possessions or
infringed the apparently equal rights of their opponents, to do
it on the ground of legal pleas.   We all know how enormous
is the debt which English law owes to the great legislators
of the twelfth, thirteenth, and fourteenth centuries; Henry II
and Edward I are, both of them, conspicuous examples of
both the tendencies which I have coupled under the term ; in

their better actions defenders of the law, in their worse actions captious defenders of their right. The same is approximately true in other countries; Lewis IX is not only the great legislator of France, but almost the single example of the period, in which the more powerful sovereign grants to his competitor, even in the hour of his utmost weakness, the full extent of his legal right; the treatment of Henry III by St. Lewis is a very striking example of the respect for rights that do not happen to be your own. As to generalities, I need only remark that the names of Frederick II and Alfonso the Wise stand by those of Edward and Lewis as the founders of the non-Roman jurisprudence of Europe, and that in Germany in the fourteenth century the two great legislators are the two champions of the rival houses, Lewis of Bavaria on the one side, and Charles the IVth on the other ; the codification of Bavarian law and the issue of the Golden Bull were at all events attempts in the direction of civilization in accordance with the highest existing ideal.

The foundation of legal studies in the Universities, the attempts by legal means to control the customs of private war—private war being itself an example of the strength of the idea of rights—the proclamation of the public peace from time to time in Germany by emperors who had the will but not the power to enforce it, and the multiplication of central tribunals in the place of local ones, are examples of the same. No doubt they are developments, evolutions of the unconscious progress of civilization ; that I am not enough of a philosopher to dogmatize about, but if they were, that is the line which the development or evolution took. The Middle Ages proper, the centuries from the year 1000 to the year 1500, from the Emperor Henry II to the Emperor Maximilian, were ages of legal growth, ages in which the idea of right, as embodied in law, was the leading idea of statesmen, and the idea of rights justified or justifiable by the letter of law,

R

was a profound influence with politicians. It may seem fanciful, but I cannot help adding a parallel illustration. The scholastic philosophy was an attempt to codify all existing knowledge under laws or formulae analogous to the general principles of justice. It was no attempt, as is sometimes said, to bind all knowledge with chains to the rock of St. Peter, or even to the rock of Aristotle; just as right is one and indivisible, and all rights are referable to it (if we only knew where to find it) as the ultimate touchstone and arbiter, so Truth is one and indivisible, and the mediaeval philosophy found its work in reconciling all existing knowledge logically with the One Truth which it believed itself to possess. What logic was to the philosopher legislation was to the statesman and moralist, a practical, as the other was a theoretical, casuistry; an attempt to justify all its conclusions by direct reference to first principles.

You may tell me, if this is true, the age of which you are speaking ought to have been a scientific age, or at least a mathematical age, and it was not. I reply that it was a scientific age in many respects, only it had misunderstood to some extent the character of its subject-matter; it applied scientific method to matters which were not capable of being scientifically treated, an error which it had in common with a good deal of the scientific philosophy of other ages, the present age not least signally. It used principles and applied demonstration in matter to which neither the principles nor the method were properly applicable; it argued too rashly from the known to the unknown, and relied too implicitly on its own implements. But that is by the way: our present parallel is simply, that in both philosophy and law the Middle Ages exemplified a like tendency to generalize and to syllogize; the names of Thomas Aquinas and Duns Scotus stand over against the names of Edward I and Lewis IX as leaders of thought, emancipators for the time, imprisoners for the future, in a far wider realm than that of practical legislation.

But this has taken me rather off the point. The great men, I have said, were law abiding; so also were the small men: and the same standing ground furnished the strength of both. Perhaps the easiest example to take is from the end of the period, the Emperor Frederick III; a man whose history, if it did not fall in a period of worn-out influences, in which the old order was vanishing in the twilight that ushered in the new, would be worthy of the deepest study. Here was a man, nominally the master of the world; a man capable of the highest aspirations for the future of his house, able to lay his plans and to compass designs which, read by the light of his existing means, look like the merest dreams of the merest visionary; a man of capacity and a man of ambition, but possessing with the crown of the Caesars hardly a rood of land in his own undivided possession ;—within his reach, with but an infant's life between, a great inheritance to which he might assert a colourable claim, and which ultimately fell to his descendants, yet silently, patiently waiting, and holding back his hand from all unrighteous aggression : his designs, dreams as they seem, come to fruition in the third generation, and his impoverished house becomes mistress of half, or more than half, the world. He contented himself with his right and his rights, and the idea was still so potent as to lay the basis for the powers of the next age. Unfortunately no one can be enthusiastic about Frederick III, but he has his place in the moral history of kings.

But to proceed; the continued existence of small states throughout the Middle Ages is a very important illustration of the subject before us; another is the extreme dislike, apparent in both continental and English history, to the forcible extinction of historical claims to territory. I do not mean to say that there were not some very remarkable instances of departure from this rule; indeed, as I shall show, two at least of the most important changes in the map of Europe, the most potential and far-reaching changes, were produced by the breach of it; but the rule as a rule was observed. In England we know how the long-suffering of the Plantagenet kings allowed the continuance of such houses as the Mowbrays, the Ferrers, the Mortimers, the Despensers; how, when generation after generation had proved that disaffection was a part of the hereditary constitution of the offending races, the heirs of the traitors were restored or rehabilitated, until, in the Wars of the Roses, the opposing houses perished in one another's downfall. There was no fear of shedding blood, but there was great fear of destroying right. So, too, with small states abroad. The little principalities of the Low Countries subsisted side by side with their powerful neighbours; the small kingdoms of Spain united and separated according to the special law of inheritance that was recognized by each; and where an attempt at infringement was made, the aggressor found himself matched against a wide and powerful union of powers instinctively actuated by the intention of right. In France we see this exemplified, not merely by the long continuance of the Plantagenet inheritance in the South, but by the existence of Provence, by the toleration of the accumulations of the Burgundian inheritance, by the independence of Flanders and Lorraine. In all these cases there were conducing causes, but in each case there was also the plea of right. Proprietary right, we say; the recognition by kings that, if they do not recognize the proprietary rights of the weaker, then the stronger will not consider theirs; proprietary rights, the leading idea that the tenant belongs to the land and the land to the landlord, and if the principle be broken down in one case, it cannot be maintained in another: proprietary right, I grant, but still right, still something that may be justified by law, not merely by the logic of the strong hand.

The whole history of Germany is, during this period, full of the same idea: small states continuing to exist side by side with larger ones; each of them in one aspect a centre of light and political culture, in another a centre of intrigue and petty tyranny: I am not concerned to defend them, but to adduce them as facts. Italy can show parallels, but her history is, to a great extent, here, as elsewhere, exceptional, and may more instructively be made to furnish counter illustrations; but the long struggle of the Hohenstaufen in the South, and of the Lombard cities in the North, is capable of being read in the same light: they would have perished before they did, if not as they did, if it had not been for the idea of right, inspiriting the weak, dismaying the strong, and affording a rallying point for the wronged from generation to generation.

But two great influences in the mediaeval world, the mediaeval empire and the mediaeval papacy, how are we to class them? Is the permanent toleration of their existence to be accounted for by the fact of their legal claims, or by that sort of prestige which might seem to throw them into the class of ideas; the inherited dignity of Caesar and of Peter? The imperial dignity, during a great part of the period before us, was shadowy in the extreme ; nay, during the whole period its substantive existence depended on the strength which the families who passed it on amongst themselves derived from their patrimonial estates. After the extinction of the Hohenstaufen, the imperial dignity became in itself an almost honorary distinction; either shunned for its costliness or coveted for the chances which it gave to a second-rate house of increasing its power by such little windfalls as might come to it. Yet it continued to subsist when any one of the great vassals might with impunity not only have declared his own independence but have extinguished the dignity which had ceased to symbolize, not only universal empire, but even national unity.

From time to time the phantom empire clothes itself in power and strength; the house of Bavaria fails to hold the dignity, but, on legal pleas which, if their legality were contested, it could not vindicate by arms, possesses itself of two or three electorates, and founds a distinct family policy of most important consequence. The house of Luxemburg, a little county under Henry VII, gains in the third generation the superiority of the two non-Teutonic kingdoms, and under Sigismund, knight-errant and political pedant, sways the destinies, for the moment, of Christendom itself. The house of Austria, in the same way, lays thus the foundation of that empire which is to be one of the great forces of the next age; not by fraud, not by violence, but here by a politic marriage, here by a well advocated inheritance, here by a claim on an imperial fief forfeited or escheated : honestly where the letter of the law is in her favour, by chicanery it may be here and there, but that a chicanery that wears a specious garb of right. The imperial idea was but a small influence compared with the superstructure of right, inheritance, and suzerainty, that legal instincts and a general acquiescence in legal forms had raised upon it. In the counter influence, that of the Roman see, there is perhaps more of the idea and less of the substantive right. I am speaking, of course, politically, and not theologically. The idea of the Petrine succession was a developing idea, that of the Caesarean succession was a waning and diminishing one : the latter was the declining from a great fact, the ancient dignity and power of imperial Rome; the former was the growth into a great fiction, the temporal supremacy of papal Rome.

The empire astonishes us with the vitality which the

universal acquiescence in its rights, however attenuated, conserves to it: the papacy appals us by the arrogance and grandeur of assumption which it raises on a foundation that seems to be itself a hypothesis, to say the least. Yet, as the languishing empire lives by law, the aspiring papacy must live by law, and rights and proprietary rights too. So the forged donations of Italian territory, the baseless claims to feudal supremacy within the Sicilian kingdom; the spiritual position based on the false decretals; all of them attempts to supply to the rising power the sort of strength that sustained the falling power. When the point of substantive independence is reached, how are the wider claims made to rest on the firmer basis of spiritual and religious obedience? the law of papal Rome becomes the living voice of the Catholic Church, the voice of the pope *in cathedra* an infallible utterance; the jurisprudence of the decretals a universal jurisprudence; the sovereignty of Innocent III and Boniface VIII a sovereignty which it is blasphemous to deny, criminal to gainsay. But when the idea has gained recognition, far be it from us to say that the power so won was used unlawfully. No, the spiritual claims of the papacy, however unjustifiable in their early history, were to a large extent justified by the beneficial use to which they were put by the better pontiffs. The Court of Rome was a tribunal for international arbitrament, the efficiency of which was one great proof of the law-abiding character of the ages which it influenced. I do not forget the wars of the mediaeval papacy, wars, some of them, which were encouraged and even prompted by those who were *ex officio* the peacemakers of the world: but when we consider how, with all those exceptions, the influence of the Church, during these ages worked from the Roman centre, was as a rule employed for the prevention of war, for the shortening of inevitable struggles, and for the healing of wounds that could not otherwise have been healed, we cannot deny to it such justification as belongs to men who believe themselves to be the ministers of a higher than human righteousness.

But I have no wish to touch more on controversial points: let papal Rome, as the law-giver of the mediaeval Church, have all the credit of her great achievements: however based, on law or on idea, her position was a standing protest against brutal force, a standing offer of peace and goodwill to those who could pay for it; a great office of incipient diplomacy, a great treasury of legal chicanery, but still a refuge against overbearing violence. The position of both empire and papacy is historically maintained by a public sense of law and right.

But perhaps the field in which the most abundant illustrations of the thesis will be found is that in which *a priori* we should be least inclined to look for it; in the region of war; in the drum and trumpet territory in which, according to the new reading of history, so little can be found to indicate the growth of human thought or the development of national character and life. Mediaeval wars are, as a rule, wars of rights: they are seldom wars of unprovoked, never wars of absolutely unjustifiable, aggression; they are not wars of idea, of liberation, or of glory, or of nationality, or of propagandism. Ah, you will say to me, you are wrong there; how about the Crusades, how about the Norman Conquest, how about Scottish independence, how about Lewis of Bavaria and John XXII, how about the Hundred Years' War? Not one of these was simply a war of aggression which those who waged it felt to be without justification, except perhaps the Norman Conquest; and we all know what an amount of special pleading was thought necessary to justify that. Do not mistake me: if I had meant to say that law and right were the ruling ideas of mediaeval

politicians, I should have said so at first; but I could only
have proved my thesis by showing that there was no war at all.
There was war in abundance, public war and private war :
the Temple of Janus could not have been shut for all those
centuries, if it had been still standing and put to its mythical
purpose. What was meant was not that men loved law,
but that they did so far respect it as to wish to seem to
have it always on their side. They did not attack their
neighbours because they wanted glory; or because they
could not bear rivalry, or because their neighbours' armies
were too strong for their safety, or because their neighbours'
armies were so ill equipped that they might be an easy conquest; but they alleged a legal claim or a legal grievance;
and in the majority of cases really legal claims and really
legal grievances. Of course, if law had been supreme, the
wrongdoer would have yielded at once, the false claimant
would have hid his diminished head at the first expression of
the opinion of a competent counsel or an authorized judge;
we know how often that is done in these days in quarrels
great and small. But I make no such claim for those ages;
I only say that, when a man coveted his neighbour's vine-
yard, he went as it were to law for it, and did not simply
take it by force. The Norman Conquest of England, I need
hardly say, is scarcely a fair illustration. It is at least as
much a viking invasion as a war waged according to the
international law of the age; yet the pleas of bequest, the
legacy of Edward the Confessor, the papal sanction, the
oath of Harold, the legal election by the witenagemot of
the humbled race, alike the inventions and the ceremonial of
the succession, were a concession to a public sense of right.
Take the other great wars; of England first: we cannot
doubt that in all the quarrels arising from the Norman,
Angevin, and Poictevin inheritances, the right of proprietary
succession was on both sides distinctly recognized: the wars

arose not on account of the mere wish of France to re-
vindicate her alienated provinces, but on account of the
disputed right to a feudal superiority, or the possession of
a debateable frontier, or the division between two co-heiresses,
or the existence of a custom of representation. When, as
under Philip Augustus, the design of aggression was strong
enough to take a more decided line, still it was on no false
pretext that war was waged, and on no merely imaginary
process that forfeiture was decreed; the barons of Poictou
legally impleaded John for his treatment of the Count
of la Marche, the barons of Brittany legally arraigned him
for the destruction of Arthur: as his feudal lord, Philip
summoned him, and John, as a contumacious vassal, suffered
judgement by default. In the execution of the sentence Philip
had on his side, not only the popular hatred of his competitor, but the conscious recognition that legally John had
lost his cause. Normandy and Anjou were practically un-
defended; Philip's victories were justified by the recognition
of the countries which renounced their old rulers for sound
and lawful reasons. There were no nonjuring bishops in
Normandy and Anjou. It would not be difficult to show
how the legal aspect of the Poictevin succession affected
the different fate of Guienne and Gascony; but I pass on,
for I have mentioned that already in reference to Henry III
and St. Lewis; I may just add that when Lewis, in 1259,
obtained from his brother-in-law a final surrender of Normandy and homage and fealty for Guienne, Henry formally
acknowledged the justice of the sentence under which his
father had forfeited the former, and Lewis practically
acknowledged the justice of the claim by which Henry
retained his hold upon the latter. A piece of legal formalism this, we say; yet it was so powerful a piece of
formalism that it unquestionably made the breach between
Simon de Montfort and the royal party an irreparable

breach, and led directly to the catastrophes of Lewes and Evesham.

We come next to the French and Scottish wars of Edward I. The claim of the Scottish overlordship was made with every pretence to legality, and, there can be little doubt, was believed by the king himself and accepted by the lords of Scotland as long as they remained hopeless of their national independence or blind to their chances of escape. John Balliol's forfeiture, his renunciation of homage, his cession of the crown to Edward, were all legal acts : the attempt of Philip the Fair to exert over Edward the same sort of jurisdiction that Philip Augustus had successfully exercised over John, was foiled by Edward, but was in itself an almost exact parallel to his treatment of Balliol. The Scottish war was again, in his eyes, an attempt not to choke national independence, but to enforce legal right. As the age advances, we find Philip of Valois and Edward III comparing pedigrees before they go to war ; for more than a century two rival kings, Philip and Charles, kings of the French, and Edward, Richard and the Henries, kings of France, dispute the sovereignty of a great nation which is not consulted under which lord it will live, but has to abide by the conflicting judgements of varying courts appellate on the field of battle.

After that come the Wars of the Roses ; wars which were at once fought out in battle, camp and court, pamphlet, book and parliament. In the wars of York and Lancaster, just as in the war of Stephen and Matilda, the legal recognition of the rightful king, the existence of the king *de facto* as a bar to the recognition of the king *de jure* ; the solemn character of the ties that unite the baronage to the head, which they are determined to disown, but will not disown without a formal legal sentence ; the parallels furnished by the cession of Edward II and Richard II, the curious pedantic circumstantiality of processes which, before they reached the stage of reality, had cost the lives of thousands; all these mark not merely the legal character and instinct of Englishmen, but the characteristic of the long mediaeval centuries, the conscience that war is justifiable only by law.

If we turn to Germany, the great struggle of the Investitures is in its outer aspect a struggle about legal forms : there were deeper causes at work, the national schism between Saxony and Swabia, caused by the legal wrongs which the Saxons believed themselves to have endured from Henry III, and the religious schism which arose from the rival ambitions, personal and ideal, of Henry IV and the popes; but the bone of contention was a legal claim. The struggle of the Welf and the Hohenstaufen was a legal struggle ; although the weaker went to the wall, his cause was capable of very definite defence; the sentence under which he fell, although unrighteous, was formally legal. Other illustrations are furnished by the dealings of the Hohenstaufen with the popes; the great house falls by manœuvres and expedients of much the same sort as those by which it had destroyed the Welfs: the papacy expands the principles on which it had claimed the inheritance of the countess Matilda, and at the same time formulates the claims by which in the fourteenth century it was to cripple the central power of Europe and reduce, itself an exile, the rival influence to the shadow of a shade.

Let these, however, suffice for the pattern wars ; the same characteristics belong in varying intensity to all the minor quarrels, down to the lowest grades of recognized private wars ; war for the right of a bridge-toll, a mill or a pigeon-cote. War was, in one aspect, a sublime ordeal, but, like the ordeal, it was attended with all the forms and ceremonies of law: public war was an ordeal resorted to when all inferior tribunals had failed to satisfy the litigants; and private war was little else, except that there the coercive power of the tribunals which should have been appealed to was greater, and the waging of war in contempt or despite of them a bolder defiance of the laws of human society. Public war was not, like private war, branded as a social crime, because the one tribunal which might have decided the questions at issue without bloodshed was both dishonest and weak. Private war was not only a contempt of competent jurisdiction but a sin against social order. Yet down to the close of the period, the habit of private war was in a great part of Europe unbroken and unrepressed: in the empire the successive proclamations of the peace were inoperative; in the other states the custom was extinguished only with the independence of the powers that practised it: wherever there was disorganization, wherever the feudal spirit broke the bonds in which constitutional rule had limited its powers, there private war was regarded as the ultimate appeal: men went to law to avenge their wrongs and to vindicate rights, and, when they could not get law that was strong enough to enforce itself, they went to war.

Lastly, look at the Crusades. The Crusades were the great exception to the rule as I have stated it; they were not wars waged for proprietary rights; they scarcely even pretended to be so. The Holy Land, the patrimony of the Crucified, as the Crusaders called it, was not theirs by any title of law; historically the only power which had a legal claim to Palestine was the Byzantine empire, but the territorial claims of the Comneni were, throughout the crusading period, defied where they were not ignored; the Crusaders believed the Greek emperors to be either in league with the Moslems, ready to betray Christendom for a price, or else, as schismatics, one shade more or less culpable than

the Mahometans. The Crusades were, moreover, at least
in the commencement, originated not by the national authority, king or emperor, of a Christian state, but by
adventurers, who might for the purpose be called private
adventurers, acting under the exhortations of the popes.
In one aspect they were wars of speculation, in another
wars of religion, in another wars of defence. The first
Crusade was perhaps more than the others a war of speculation, the second a war of religion, the third a war of
defence; in the fourth, again, speculation under Venetian
influence threw both religion and defence into the shade:
and all the later Crusades were wars of defence. Yet,
although to say this is a partial condemnation, I cannot
go further. The conquest of Palestine was to Robert of
Normandy, Raymond of Toulouse, Bohemond of Tarentum,
a sanctified experiment of vikingism; but to Godfrey of
Bouillon, to the great mass of the Crusading armies, to
the popes even, it was something far different. It was a
war of idea; a going forth to recover the heritage of Christ,
the land, as they termed it, on which His feet had stood: it
was a going out of the petty range of proprietary rights and
wrongs, out of the petty interests of armed litigation. As I
have said before in this place, the Crusades, with all their
drawbacks, were the trial feat of a new world, a reconstituted
Christendom, striving after a better ideal than that of piracy
and fraternal bloodshed. In the character of wars of defence
they need not be defended: they stemmed the tide that but
for them must have covered Europe, as it had covered Asia,
with desolation.

Perhaps I need go no further; but there is one class of
wars which I have not yet noticed, and which yet are, in their
history, very characteristic of the principle for which I have
been contending. The civil wars which were waged for
national liberties were not in any great measure wars for

ideas, but wars for rights. I do not mean to say that this was quite the case in Italy: in Italy the question of rights had become so complicated that nothing but the infusion of an element of idea could have produced even a semblance of order out of the chaos. The old sway of Rome, the successive deluges of Goth, Lombard, Greek and German, had thrown rights and wrongs into an inextricable hotchpot. The restoration of order was the initiation of liberty; with liberty, or the idea of it, came new forms of organization, democracies, aristocracies, municipalities, tyrannies, monarchies ; each formulating rights and laws as they arose, but less bound by laws of rights and obligations because for the most part they lacked historic basis. What the faction of to-day might set up, the faction of to-morrow might pull down : the exiles of to-day were the governors of to-morrow, the forfeitures of to-day only the reprisals for the forfeitures of yesterday. In England it is very different. Here the rights struggled for are historical rights, and the liberties secured are historical liberties. Step by step, from precedent to precedent, the national growth asserts itself, and the kings, yielding their consent, recognize the justice of the claim, or, exchanging resistance for sympathy, throw new but still historical energies into the common growth. We have in the mediaeval growth of our constitution little to be ashamed of; little of conspiracy, little of fanaticism, little—as little as there can be in the essential character of a politician—of self-seeking. There is enough of the idea of liberty and sound government to lift the struggle out of the region of mere legal resistance to mere legal oppression: there is a growth towards liberty in all the vindication of even class rights and special privileges : a growth towards liberty so spontaneous, I had almost said so little self-conscious, as to show that it is a natural, not a factitious growth : it is not taught by philosophers, it is not extorted by agitators, it is the outgrowth of law and a law-abiding spirit, tending by its very nature to freedom and order conjointly. The transition from mediaeval to modern history is in this department of national life not an abrupt transition, but a growth befitting a land of settled government;

> ' A land of just and old renown,
> Where Freedom broadens slowly down
>   From precedent to precedent;
> Where faction seldom gathers head,
> But, by degrees to fulness wrought,
> The strength of some diffusive thought
> Hath time and space to work and spread.'

X.

ON THE CHARACTERISTIC DIFFERENCES BETWEEN MEDIAEVAL AND MODERN HISTORY.

(April 17, 1880.)

IN the lecture which I gave the other day, and of which the present is a continuation, I made an attempt to show what I meant by a distinction which I had drawn between mediaeval history and modern history, in the two divisions into which it is separated by the gulf of the French revolution. I had begun by a little self-justification in the preference of mediaeval to modern history as an instrument of education, and, while treating the subject from a higher point of view than that of mere utility, had run off into a disquisition on the distinguishing characteristics of the divisions in question. On the remark which I have made elsewhere that the leading influence of early mediaeval history was the strong insistence on law and right, I had founded a somewhat rambling examination of the main points of the history of the Middle Ages, the characters of their great men, the permanence of their institutions, and the peculiar character of their wars. I had marked the characteristics of the second division as power or force, and that of the third as the influence of ideas. I now proceed to explain what I meant by this and to illustrate it, leaving my hearers to infer, as I proceed, what my reasons have been for preferring the earlier portion as the subject of my own teaching. When I have said what will no doubt appear to you to be more than enough about that, I shall venture to make some remarks on the influence of the ideas by which at the present day politics and politicians seem or profess to be guided. In that division of the subject I may seem to become somewhat political myself; if I do, I shall not ask your pardon. I have never been ashamed to express my convictions where they happened to differ from those of my friends with whom on most other subjects I should be willing to agree. I shall not, therefore, I think, rightly be thought rash or disputatious if I venture to express difference from those modern political schools with which I feel that I cannot sympathize at all.

So now to the subject. Almost any student who has read the usual books, if he were asked to mark what was the foremost idea of the three centuries that intervene between the year 1500 and the year 1800, would reply that it was the idea of the balance of power. The balance of power, however it be defined, i.e. whatever the powers were between which it was necessary to maintain such equilibrium, that the weaker should not be crushed by the union of the stronger, is the principle which gives unity to the political plot of modern European history. Whether the balance is to be maintained against the preponderance of the house of Hapsburg, or the preponderance of France, or the preponderance of Catholic powers as opposed to Protestant ones; this is the key to the plot.

But it is not the existence of the key or the character of the plot, but the existence of the drama of modern European politics, that is the first feature of our sketch: the existence of the powers by whom the drama is played and between whom the balance is maintained. Mediaeval history may, it is true, be read as a drama, but it is not one in which the plot is obvious; it is rather more a series of dramas which may be combined, like Greek trilogies, but have unities and plots

of their own. The history of each great nation is a drama by
itself; the blending of the several dramas may be so read as
to show how the nations were severally being educated for
work on a stage in which they should appear together: in the
modern life of Europe they do appear together, and take each
the part for which it has been educated in the earlier stage.
But that early preparation had been carried on, to a great
extent, separately. England and France had been no doubt
training one another for centuries, but the balance of power
between England and France never came into the great plot
of later days; the discipline of Spain had been worked out
within the walls of the peninsula; between France and
Germany there had never been a great war; between
Germany and Italy, as nationalities, no struggle had as yet
been possible; and the border warfare of the border states
had been carried on without any great amount of interest or
interference from the greater or growing agglomerations of
territory which under the name of nations, states or dynasties,
now come to the front. The Crusades had been a common
field of work and a common stage of action, but the
nationalities which in the Crusades had fought side by side
in union or in rivalry had long retired from the uncongenial
work, and all the zeal of the best popes and the most heroic
kings had been unequal to the task of uniting Christendom
again for the common emancipation.

There was, however, no great crash at the passing away
of the old things and the coming in of the new. The new
influences, many and various in character, quickly combine
to produce the new actors and to clear the common stage.
The concentration of power in the royal hands in France,
under Charles VII and Lewis XI; the creation of a compact
and solid kingdom out of a number of rival and hostile feudal
provinces or dynastic appanages, a concentration for which,
during the whole of the mediaeval period from Lewis VI

onwards, the kings had been working, but which only became possible when the long struggle with England had made it necessary; a concentration of power which signified not only territorial union, but administrative autocracy; which reduced all powers except that of the crown, states general, parliament, clergy, feudatories, all to a shadow; a concentration in which, in the language of the time, France emerged from tutelage and attained to such maturity of manhood as might be expressed in the later formula 'The state, it is I myself;'—this compactness, this concentration, equipped France for her part.

Just at the same moment England emerged from the terrible dynastic struggle in which, with the competing houses, the very bone and sinew of liberty seemed to have perished. The baronage, attenuated to a shadow of its former bulk, and with its power as attenuated as its numbers; the Commons wearied, exhausted with political struggles, turning their back on politics altogether to seek new and more profitable interests in new channels, and to leave the battle of rights and wrongs to settle itself; the clergy, on the one side left alone among the estates to continue the tradition of liberty, but on the other declining rapidly from their function of the national conscience and memory, to be mere officials, servants of the great monarchical administrative unity that towered so high over the prostrate estates; all three alike, in isolation or in pitiful sympathy, left the national action at the disposal of a king, a king like Henry VII, who would be a tyrant only in self-defence, to be succeeded by a son who would be a tyrant in very self-will. England, growing rich in the peace which its politic king and its busy people alike left all else to cultivate, growing stronger in wealth and union and abeyance of liberty, was likewise ready to act as a force at the will of one man.

Spain had finished the seven centuries of her crusade, and

the two rival kingdoms, rid at last of the enemy, met and were united in the Catholic couple. In Germany Maximilian had at last concentrated in his own hands the territorial acquisitions of his house, had united Austria and her outlying states, had obtained for his son the accumulation of Burgundian fiefs, and for his grandsons the crowns of Spain and Sicily, the reversion of Hungary and Bohemia besides. The Hapsburg power is a union of many unions, ill compacted, heterogeneous, uncongenial, but of extremely great might, a power consolidated by legal titles, happy and unhappy marriages, legal windfalls, traditional pretensions, but yet the most important factor for many years to come in the welfare of Europe. The strength of France is in her compactness and concentration, that of Charles V, for in him the Austrian force is first impersonated, in its extent and universality. To that extent and universality the discovery and the rapid pouring in of the wealth of America gave still new weapons and greater opportunities. France and Austria were both equipped for their struggle.

The minor actors had somehow girt up their loins also: the popes, giving up their place as the overseers of a too wide dominion, had begun to accumulate the territorial aggregate of provinces in which they also could call themselves the state. Gustavus Vasa was reconstructing Sweden ; although the attempt to unite the Scandinavian kingdoms had failed, the same influence that was knotting up the south into bundles was knotting up the north.

And so the struggle of powers begins. First comes the rivalry of Francis I and Charles V ; with Henry VIII and the popes hovering round the combatants, aspiring to hold the balance between them, and made alternately their tools and scapegoats. The struggle is a curious one : the older idea of rights to be fought for has not altogether disappeared, but now the interest is not in the right, but in the battle. So it has been since Charles VIII, marching into Italy, had opened the new drama. Rights were sought out and put forward as the pretexts of the struggle, but the struggle was for superiority and the hold on power. The action of the house of Austria was in itself defensive action; on every side its spreading dominions were at the mercy of the strong enemy whom they seemed to hem in; the action of Francis and Henry II was necessarily aggressive; wherever they turned, except seawards, there were the forces of Austria watching them; over the Pyrenees, over the Alps, over the Rhone, over the Rhine, within the historic limits of France, northwards and eastwards, there was the rival power, and even on the seaboard there were the hostile fleets.

Next comes the Reformation, a struggle it may be said of ideas, as the Hapsburg struggle with France is a struggle of rights, but primarily a struggle of powers; the rights in the one case, the ideas in the other, being the occasion rather than the essential ingredients of the rivalry.

But setting the idea side of the Reformation for the moment in the background, follow the rivalry of the foremost powers. In this aspect the Reformation cuts curiously across the earlier dividing lines: it breaks up such unity of German action as has yet existed, and gives France its first great advantage: the strange alliance of Henry II with the Protestant powers, an alliance most distinctly of force, not of idea, strikes the first hard blow at the preponderance of Austria, and the irrecoverable loss of the three bishoprics is one of the mortal wounds of the empire. The next act is the rebellion of the Netherlands and the contemporary wars of the league in France; the Austrian heritage is broken in two, but the family interest and alliance for a time supplies the place of personal union. For a generation, however, Austria proper stands outside the struggle of the balance; she has to repress the movements towards religious reformation, and to ward off the attacks of the Turks on the side of Hungary. Where her weight is at all operative it is thrown on the side of Spain. Spain is the overshadowing, all-threatening force; France doing her best to produce the disruption of the Netherlands, Spain doing her best to produce the disruption of France; again the reformed party, acting as a force rather than a sentiment; for although on Philip's side the interests of Spain and religion are at one, France is persecuting at home the very ideas for which she intrigues abroad.

After a while the balance wavers: the strong hand of Philip II is taken off, the unworthy hand of the Valois lets fall the sceptre which it had held with so weak and vacillating grasp. Henry IV becomes the dominating influence. Henry IV is a man of ideas, a man of sentiment, a man of force; not of much sense of law and right. To his mind a reconstituted Europe was the ideal; not of course to accept as his the minute remodelling of the map which was once ascribed to him and his advisers, we can yet see enough of his design to know that he planned a forcible partition of the Hapsburg inheritances, the erection of a counterpoise to the empire in Germany itself, and the re-arrangement of the minor states in a way which would have left France the civil and religious arbiter of Christendom. His day is but a short one, and the ideas which he or his counsellors conceived came to a bearing in the struggle of forces which occupied the long reign of his grandson.

But the scene of the drama changes at the same time. The United Provinces have gained recognition; the action of Spain is becoming languid, and its energy bears no proportion to its still subsisting power and mass. The great act is now in Germany, the Thirty Years' War: a war of two forces, two rights, two ideas: Austria against the princes, Catholic against Protestant, ancient territorial right as against new territorial force. Here too the religious influence produces cross division; the Lutheran and the Calvinist will not fight side by side; the Bavarian sets Catholicism before imperialism; Austria sets the family interest before either; yet Austria is as Catholic as the Jesuits and as imperial as the jurists can make her. But notwithstanding this cross influence of rights and ideas, the Thirty Years' War is mainly a war of force, a war for determining the balance, not between ideas or rights, not between competing religions or competing liberties, but between armed sovereignties and territorial aggregations. Make the utmost of the idealism of Gustavus Adolphus, the legal pretexts of his interference are even worse founded than those under which Denmark in the earlier stage of the war had thrown in her lot as against the empire; and the idealism of Gustavus, his high and noble purpose of coming down as the saviour of religion, ends in the artificial aggrandisement of Sweden, as the luckless intriguing policy of Christian ends in the complete humiliation of Denmark. The interference of France, without sympathy of idea, without pretext of legality, is a simple intrusion of force. But I pass on.

The Thirty Years' War exhausted Germany; even the victorious powers were worn out, much more the defeated ones: the stage is left clear for the glories of Lewis XIV. 'The state is myself.' 'The right is the glory of France.' Perhaps the lurid glare of the glories of this act, the act of the Great Monarch, throws a shade on minor actors and less prominent motives, but it can scarcely be misread; it is the triumph of force over both old rights and new ideas; a *régime* in which might is construed as right. The dominance of the idea of force in the aggression produces a corresponding influence in the resisting powers. They are bound not by sympathy but by necessity; the alliances that resist the great monarch are alliances of expediency, not of principle, and when the resistance is past they are ever ready for new combinations.

The struggle of the Spanish succession followed, a struggle in which ancestral right was matched against the doctrine of the balance, and the force of the stronger determined the verdict. The struggle of the Imperial succession next led on to the triumphant career of Frederick II, and that unmistakeably to the new forms of political combination and antagonism which emerged from the French Revolution. Lewis XIV and Frederick the Great impersonate the two principles, or aspects of the one principle, that might gives right; Frederick was far the greater man, of course; Frederick had rights; he had claims old and legal on Silesia, and the old question of the Cleves Juliers inheritance had been a burning question for a century before he began to fight; and he had ideas—who so many? Lewis XIV had scarcely any plea of right for his aggressions, and his sole idea, as his sole policy, was himself, his interest and glory and that of France in him. But it all came to the same thing. Frederick knew that he was strong, and revived old pleas that his father had let slumber. Lewis knew that he was strong: the rival powers at both conjunctures were exhausted; war, policy, money, philosophy, intrigue, rights and ideas, all gave way or led on to the triumph of force. The right, the idea, the balance of power, was on the side of the strongest battalions.

But now I must turn back to the Reformation, for there can be no question that, in the changes that brought about and resulted from that crisis, both rights and ideas were very strong within certain circles of their own, and to make the balance of power, the struggle of material forces, the sole lesson of this portion of history, would be a serious mistake. Yet I think even here we shall see that the principle of the idea was less operative than the principle of force, the policy

of force more effective than the policy of idea. The crisis
of the Reformation is not less remarkable for its results than
for its causes. The throwing off of the Roman supremacy,
in doctrine and ecclesiastical government, was, in those
countries in which it was permanently effected, a most complex proceeding. No doubt there was throughout Europe
much religious disaffection at the opening of the sixteenth
century; but for a century before there had been even more
prominent doctrinal disaffection, and only just a century
before the Church had passed through a most dangerous
schism, which threatened its substantial organization as well
as its doctrine. The desired reformation in head and
members had been familiar all this time. But it did not
come till now: till the stage had, as we have seen, been
cleared for the new actors. We might conjecture that whilst
the concentration of the new powers gave them in themselves greater vitality and more manageable force, it would
exhaust the vitality of the older organization, which had kept
them together whilst the divisions were smaller and the
common action less vivid. Whilst all the powers of Christendom were busy with their own internal rights and border
quarrels, a languid acquiescence in the undivided supremacy
of Rome was more a powerful influence than it could be
when two or three new and well girt combatants were ready
to assert their own αὐτάρκεια; still more, when the new combatants saw the truth that they must be lords in their own
houses. As we saw, the concentration of power in Spain,
France, and Germany meant more than the absorption of
weaker states; it meant the absorption of inferior powers in
the state. The strong actors in the new drama must be
strong governors at home as well as strong combatants
abroad. Great designs, great rivalries, demanded concentrated energies, determined wills. Strong government came
in with the sixteenth century, and strong government was a

very strong element in reformation history, for it weakened the solidarity of the Catholic Church and prepared the way for the formula 'cujus regio ejus religio,' the disruption of national churches as well.

But neither these causes, religious disaffection and the dis-integration of the weak church organization by the growing strength of absolutism, nor the ideas of the new learning, nor the rivalries of political rulers fostering abroad forms of discontent which they persecuted at home, nor the lust of enlarged territory, nor the coveting of ecclesiastical wealth, nor the envy of unprivileged classes, nor the new power of the press, would alone have sufficed to do the work that was done. Who could have reckoned on the coincidence of the Indulgence agitation in Germany, the divorce agitation in England, the growth of Huguenotism in France, the rising up of men like Luther, Zwingli, Calvin and Knox in such rapid succession, and with such marked differences, and such diverse contributions to such a complex result? There was unquestionably, in conjunction with the yearnings for spiritual change, a deep and strong impulse for breaking with the past; breaking with national traditions and with religious traditions; a tendency which would, if it had been unchecked, unobstructed, or not diverted into other channels, almost of necessity have amounted to revolution. Strong government had not come too soon; but for that, with all its oppressions, its repressions, and its persecutions, there would have been a period of anarchy in the breaking up of the deeps of old society.

Well, however it was to be met, reformation came; the absorption of a great part of the lands of the churches followed or accompanied reformation; either, as in England, by the seizure and surrender of monastic estates, or as in Germany by the adoption of transparent fictions which enabled Protestant princes to lay on ecclesiastical positions a hold which was never to be relaxed; or, as in Scotland, by sweeping away the old fabric altogether. The ancient right of territorial ownership was weakened, and the process of secularization, which was in Germany completed at the peace of Westphalia, set the seal of legality on the status quo.

Protestantism had done its utmost to shift the balance of power. Yet, as I said before, it had really done little more than produce a cross division in the conflicting parties. Where Protestantism was an idea only, as in Spain and Italy, it was crushed out by the Inquisition; where, in conjunction with political power and sustained by ecclesiastical confiscation, it became a physical force, there it was lasting. It is not a pleasant view to take of the doctrinal change, to see that, where the movement towards it was pure and unworldly, it failed; where it was seconded by territorial greed and political animosity, it succeeded. But so it has been with many of the changes by which in the long run both Church and world have been benefited. In the case of the English reformation, it is certain that without the redistribution of monastic estates the change must have been long delayed, and might have been suddenly and permanently reversed. Anarchy and confusion were imminent under the puritan rule of Edward VI, as well as under the papal reaction of Mary. If Elizabeth and her advisers had leaned to either, the flood must have poured in; unsympathetic as is the Elizabethan Church rule, little as we can find to love among the men whom she set up as Fathers to the Church, it was their strong rule that saved England from revolution far more dangerous, far more calamitous, than all the mistakes, the terrors, the persecutions, the reactions, of the so-called rebellion and revolution periods of the seventeenth century. But again the subject is one that tempts to too wide digression: only, after what I have said, whether you agree with me or no, you will see why I have thought it better to treat the Reformation under the aspect of force rather than idea.

We must not, however, imagine that in any but the extremest cases of change, political, territorial, or religious, the old landmarks were so entirely swept away that none of the earlier ideas of rights remained. No: it was the conflict between the old influence of right and the new influence of force, between old legality and new strong government that forced into existence the diplomacy of the sixteenth and following centuries,—diplomacy, in its beginning a sort of kriegspiel, in which threats and bribes on paper took the place of mobilisations and marches, sieges and invasions. Most curious are the beginnings of the diplomatic policy of Wolsey and his master; the restless attempts to make the political force felt without the cost of exerting it; how as soon as they have concluded an alliance, do they begin to work for a counter alliance; how they seem to conclude treaties with one high conflicting party that overlap the treaties they have just made with the other; what secrecy, what mystery, what bribery, what intimidation; and amid all, a little sour grain of conscience, that the old law-abiding, treaty-keeping faith and loyalty would have been better. A plea must be sought for every aggression ; no compact must be broken without hesitation unless a flaw can be found. Whether it be true that Charles V justified the imprisonment of Philip the Magnanimous by the misreading of a single letter in the word which had induced him to surrender, I do not know; the story may be false, but the moral is true : men were loth to own themselves actuated by simple greed. And as diplomacy was in its beginnings, so it lasted for a long time ; the ambassador was the man who was sent to lie abroad for the good of his country. Rights, pleas, grudges, were registered against the time when strength would accrue to make them real weapons of argument and instruments of aggression.

But as the old influence of right lingered on, the new influence of idea was from time to time giving distinct warnings of a further change. There was an idea of religion, there was an idea of liberty, struggles for the vindication of historical nationalities, although, as ideas, they were overborne or absorbed by the mightier forces which played around them. It could scarcely be but that strong government should force up premature longings for liberty, or that religious repression should compel a desire for tolerance. Yet we must not make too much of the first glimmerings of the changes that were coming. The revolt of the Netherlands was perhaps the most resolute attempt at liberty that had been seen since the Middle Ages opened; the idea of nationality was strong in the Spanish provinces of the Hapsburg inheritance and in the Bohemia of the Thirty Years' War. But they never became ruling principles; nor were they likely to do so until they were emancipated from the mere selfish and localized interests with which they were bound up. Class liberties, isolated nationalities, local privileges, may keep up the memory, the tradition, of liberty, nationality, and privilege, but they do not become leading ideas until they have been accepted as universally just and desireable, until they can command assent and inspire sympathy. The religions that demanded toleration but meant tyranny were no true exponents of religious liberty: the classes that would limit royal prerogative to lay their hand heavier on their own vassals were no true exponents of constitutional government. The hand that cherishes nationality in Italy, and represses it in Greece, is no true defender of nationality.

But the clock and the limit of my paper warn me to proceed at once, imperfectly as I must have indicated or suggested my view, to the third portion of the subject. Later modern history, the history of the last hundred years, seems

to me to differ from that of the two preceding divisions, by
the prominence and real importance of ideas, as compared
with the earlier reigns of right and force. I need not repeat
that the prominence and real importance, the theoretical and
practical weight, of political ideas being admitted, we need
not suppose either of the preceding principles to be extinguished; nor, on the other hand, need we suppose that the
ideas which latterly come to the forefront were either unknown
or unappreciated in the earlier periods. I have just said
that liberty, nationality, and the like were strong agents
before they became the strongest; we may freely admit that
both force and right still exercise a strong influence, though
not the strongest, in modern politics. Keeping this in mind,
you will not expect me to discuss the origin and growth of
the ideas in question; rather it will be enough to indicate the
point at which they seem to take such hold on the political
mind as to presage their future importance.

It seems to me that the partition of Poland, in the last
century, was the event that forced the idea of nationality
upon the world, and the revolt of the American provinces of
the British empire that which forced the idea of self-government, not as a local British invention, but as a sort of political
gospel, upon general belief. You will not suspect me of being
a believer in the ' rights of man,' or in the legal position of the
American revolutionists ; you will not, I trust, suspect me of
believing that territorial right can ever be made a justification
of moral iniquity or of abandoned misgovernment and
tyranny: and yet I may insist more strongly on territorial
right and believe more strongly in the universality of true
principles than others who talk politics more fluently than I
can deliver public statutory lectures.

But to stick to facts: as the suppression of Poland, on
the one side, forced on the world the conscience that
nationality is more than a geographical formula, on the

other hand, it showed how easily force and fraud could remove the ancient landmarks of territorial right. It was, therefore, a two-edged experiment, and no doubt it cut the hands of all the intermeddling powers. As the vindication of American liberties made a precedent for the ideas of the French Revolution, the partition of Poland pointed to the reconstruction of the map of Europe; the destruction of that kingdom was a precedent for the destruction of any kingdom; the extinction of that nationality aroused a sympathy, awakened an idea of the importance of nationality as a re-constituting idea in reformed society.

Well, the French Revolution set at liberty all the disruptive influences that existed in the weakly governed states of the continent, and roused to a somewhat rash, hurried, and incautious hostility the instincts of the strongly governed but ill-prepared powers like Prussia, Austria, Russia, and England. And the first attempts at a propaganda of liberty, and the first attempts at a propaganda of nationality, were marked by great excesses and great mistakes: excesses and mistakes so potential that the propaganda of the two influences together determined, in the Napoleonic empire, the tyranny and glory of France and the privilege of all nations to acknowledge and toil under the shadow of her supremacy. Liberties were enunciated in fulsome language, nationalities were carved out with amusing caprice; but glory and victory were the real aim; force exerted itself as strongly under Napoleon as under Peter the Great and Frederick the Great and Lewis the Great. By-and-by came the recoil. Napoleon was humbled; the map of Europe was reformed on a plan which showed a respect for territorial rights, and a just recognition both of the earnings of force and of the growth of ideas. But the end was not yet; liberty, though recognized, was distrusted; nationality, though allowed some weight, was everywhere set beneath territorial right and material power : and self-government made very little way in the world for at least fifteen years after the battle of Waterloo.

When the world had rested, when politics began to move again, both these ideas came to the front: the nationality of Greece; the independence of Belgium, a distinct nationality as regarded the state with which it had been bound up: these were the first notes of the triumph of one idea : the second French Revolution cannot be said to have opened the campaign of self-government, for the revolt of the Spanish and Portuguese colonies had done that; but it was an important contribution to the cause among the old countries of Europe : the German principalities had to hasten the gift of constitutional governments which had been long deferred, and were, even when granted, to a great extent illusory.

An uneasy time of peace and repression were the seventeen years that followed : since 1848 the action of the drama has been exciting and unintermitting. France, dissatisfied with her government, threw Europe again into turmoil ; again there was a cry of liberty and nationality, again force and legality were equal to the occasion, and society was saved. France sank under a military despotism which subsisted by keeping the world in arms. But the ideas were stronger at each revolution and each struggle. France went to war for the idea when she had nothing else to go to war for ; and, having bound liberty hand and foot at home, proclaimed herself again the apostle of liberty. It was liberty for your friends, humiliation for your enemies, as usual : but the result far outran the intention.

After the Crimean War, of which I will not trust myself to speak further than to say that I believe it to have been a profound misunderstanding of the current of the world's progress, a mistake of legality, a miscalculation of force, a

T

misconception of idea, but which had the sole merit of teaching the generation of soldiers to fight and of diplomatists to conjure; after the Crimean War we get, first, the reconstruction of Italy on the principles of nationality and with a free constitution; then the reconstruction of Germany, then the reconstruction of Austria; of Germany on a principle of nationality and self-government which has yet to find a balance for the preponderance of force, and in Austria on a principle of nationality and self-government that has yet to determine its relations to the older rules of legality on which historically the unity of Austria depends. And within the last two years the world has been kept alive by the struggle for nationality and freedom, between Russian force and Turkish tyranny.

Out of the crucible, out of the fiery furnace, against the will of the potent actors, as if by a law that may not be broken, the victory of the idea is rapidly being realized. There are, of course, other ideas, counter ideas, ideas which are only the old legality and the old material force disguised under new names. Such ideas may be Pansclavism, or Internationalism, or Nihilism, if it be anything but a negation of ideas. Such ideas may be that of Russia at Constantinople, of a restored Poland, of a free church in a free state, of universal voluntaryism, of scientific frontiers. I am not here to justify or to condemn, much less to prophesy; and whatever it is that is coming, I am sure we are only at the beginning of it. At present Russia stands before the world, really as representing force, in pretension,—pretension which I am far from believing to be insincere,—as the liberator of the Christian races of the East. Austria is far the most conspicuous defender of historic territorial right; and all those who are not afraid of the nickname of reactionists will be slow to condemn her for the maintenance of a principle on which she has grown into power, and which she is doing her best to reconcile with more potent ideas and influences more likely to be permanent. France to some extent represents democracy ; to a far greater extent she still, as ever, represents the old claim to arbitrate in Europe. Prussia or Germany, in the same way, represents the force which, relying on the strength of nationality, has for the moment made her the leading power in Christendom. For the perishing remnants of Turkey a faint plea of territorial possession has gone forth, but the conscience of friends and the determination of foes have alike repudiated it as an excuse for misgovernment and palliation of tyranny. There is no idea, no such justification for that curse of Christendom. Turkey means nothing, represents nothing but butchery, barbarism, and the vilest slavery. What does England represent? What is she to represent in the future? What would we wish for her but clear-sighted justice and living sympathy with what is good and sound in the progress of the world?

Having achieved that sentiment, I must now slip into bathos. I have preferred mediaeval history to modern in my own teaching, partly because I believe the study of rights is more wholesome as an educational study than that of the balance of forces, partly because I think it a safer study altogether than the theoretical study of political ideas. Political ideas are apt to lay hold on the fancy and on the affections, and to make men partisans before they are at all competent to weigh the merits of parties, to adjust the balance between order and progress, between historical right and historical growth : and there is in the study of them very little training. Educationally, I prefer the first division. I may also be turned towards it by certain legal tendencies and documentary tastes of my own. I am only justifying myself, not laying down a law for others. There are other sorts of studies here besides law and history. I can conceive the man who has spent his terms here on philosophy taking more naturally to the examination and analysis of ideas, and the mathematician being more charmed by the thought of reading national complications as illustrations of the parallelogram of forces: the student of physical science will no doubt soon be able to infer the national idiosyncrasy of races from the shape of their skulls. With all this I am so far from finding fault that I rejoice and delight in the thought of so many minds and so many studies working towards my truth. But I plead for a toleration which I have done my best to justify.

THE REIGN OF HENRY VIII.

(June 7, 1881.)

I SHALL not trouble you with any detailed reasons for my choice of a subject for this Term's statutory lectures; it is enough to observe that I have been busily employed upon the reign of Henry VIII for some months of ordinary lecturing, and that there is every probability that I may have to work upon him for some months to come. You will at once admit that Henry VIII is too big a subject to admit any rival on the same canvas, or under the same hand; whoever undertakes him at all must be content to devote himself for the time entirely to him. This being said, you must further concede to me that, although the subject is interesting enough, two lectures, in which anything like a bird's-eye view can be afforded, must be very dry ; I will not say dull, but so concentrated as not to allow much extraneous illustration. That granted, I propose to put before you, in as concise a form as possible, the main points of importance in the reign, in some degree adopting the method which I have followed in the analytical chapters of my Constitutional History. If, in doing this, I succeed only in drawing out a plan on which the long history of the reign may be arranged for subsequent reading, I feel that I shall have done something. I intend to try to do more, but I may not, in the further aim, satisfy you, and I certainly shall not satisfy myself.

My plan will be to offer you, at the beginning and end of the lectures, some general remarks on the position and character of England and her king at the beginning and end of the reign ; but to devote the main part of our discussion to the definite arrangement of the particular acts and measures of the period, saying as little as possible about external matters, but fixing as accurately as we can the framework of internal history ; its principal changes and their tendency. I will not now anticipate any general conclusions, but simply propose an arrangement under the ordinary heads of taxation, legislation, administrative action, ecclesiastical reform, and parliamentary history.

The position of England at the opening of Modern History, the position which she had assumed under Henry VII and in which Henry VIII found her at his accession, was that of a young, well-concentrated and well-equipped, but untrained, actor for the great drama of European politics.   England had had more than twenty years of such peace as amounted to a disuse of warfare; that is, her yeomanry had only maintained the use of arms as a part of their education, they had no practical acquaintance with military tactics or with blood and iron.   But in other respects she was well furnished ; she had money, and good intelligence, and astute ministers, men of wide mind like Wolsey, and of minute experience, and of no small ambitions.   I am not going to say that England came upon the stage with more real wisdom or with more honesty of purpose than the other powers : her diplomacy seems to have partaken quite as much of the character of chicanery as did that of Spain, France, or Austria : but her interests in the struggle of European forces, which is now commencing, were not so direct as theirs ; her sympathies were not definitely with either the one side or the other; and, if her hereditary antipathy to France might seem likely to throw her too unreservedly on the side of France's enemies, the cool way in which, on all occasions except when money was wanted, her attentions were received by the Imperial administration in Spain and the Netherlands, was quite enough to repel any approach to sympathy.

So, as a rule, throughout the reign of Henry VIII, the cool heads among English politicians dreamed of nothing more for their country than the position of an arbitrator, an umpire between great rival parties on the Continent, from whose humiliation nothing was to be gained, and from whose over-exaltation something was to be feared. Henry VIII might sometimes dream of the Empire, or of the recovery of Normandy and Aquitaine, as Wolsey might dream of the Papacy; but the wiser heads contemplated no such shadows; nor, I think, had those aims more than a slight and momentary influence on the king and cardinal; the people were not unwilling, up to a certain point, to fight and, up to a certain point, to pay: but they did not care to sacrifice their blood and money, and win neither spoils nor glory. So, although there was much talk of war, and much money spent on armaments, money well spent perhaps in part, for the armed power of England was a not unimportant qualification for her position as arbitrator, there was very little real war; there were countless treaties, leagues, unions, truces, armistices, sufferances, neutralities and abstentions, but the expeditions of Dorset and Howard to Spain and France in 1512, the king's expedition to Tournay in 1513, the invasion of France by the Duke of Suffolk in 1523, and the expedition of Henry to Boulogne in 1543, are the sum and substance of his military doings outside of Great Britain.

A momentary effort, a little advantage gained, time taken to secure it, and the utmost terms exacted for the surrender of it, is the whole story. In spite of many leagues with France, the sword is never really drawn against Charles; and, in spite of many leagues with Charles, war of England against France has no other direct object than the acquisition of a stronghold on or near the coast. Money is spent in loans, or dangled in the shape of promises, there are threats of diversion and plans of united campaigns which come to nothing more. England claiming to be an arbitrator is really a make-weight.

I cannot therefore agree with those who would extol the foreign policy of England in the beginning and end of the reign as a masterpiece of diplomacy. Honesty would have been the simpler, the wiser, and the cheaper policy; and so I think the nation itself felt. Far more would really have been gained by letting the competitors fight out their quarrel and exhaust themselves; and the position of England could have been made safe at a tenth of the cost. But it was a new game, a new drama, and England as represented by Henry must have a leading part.

Within the borders of the island, the old struggle of Scotland, allied with and prompted by France, is a matter of secondary interest; and the two great crises, the battle of Flodden in 1513 and the death of James V in 1542, great as they are in picturesque and personal interest, scarcely trouble the current of peace at home; the border warfare, seldom intermitted, the party struggles of the Scots themselves, whether the time is one of truce or of hostility, furnish opportunity for military and administrative occupation, and for the energies of uneasy men. I pass then rapidly and generally over these external points in which so much of contemporary history is expended, and prefer to look more closely at home.

And let us first look at the king. I am not one of those critics who incline to a very disparaging estimate of Henry VIII. He was not, as a man, more vicious than many kings who have maintained a very fair reputation in history. In force of character there are few indeed that come near him;

if he seems to act upon pure self-will, he is able to give a reason for his acts, and that such a reason as we cannot on mere prejudice determine to be unreasonable; he makes his way with good men and bad men alike, and, with a few notable exceptions, he is able to overrule all protest. On mature consideration, I am inclined to regard Henry himself as the main originator of the greatest and most critical changes of his reign; and I am sure that, after the fall of Wolsey, there is no minister, great or small, who can claim anything like an original share in determining the royal policy. He could keep More as his chancellor, and Warham as his archbishop, whilst he was pushing measures which they abhorred; he could send Cromwell to the block the moment he discovered that he was pursuing designs of a colour which did not recommend itself to him; and to Audley and Wriothesley no one would dream of giving the name of an independent or original minister. Cranmer and Gardiner he tolerated alike and in turn, but Cranmer kept his place by abstention from politics and by the facility with which Henry could use him when he wanted; whilst Gardiner, on the other hand, sank the ecclesiastic in the politician, until his time came.

So, for all the critical years of the reign, Henry's strong will threw the advice or agency of any subordinate politician into the shade. Henry was every inch a king; the king, the whole king, and nothing but the king. Another of our kings, George IV, I think, who also had matrimonial troubles, in writing to his ministers used to employ an expressive phrase to describe a contingency which it was useless to contemplate. 'If I were an individual,' he writes, 'I might, should, or would do so and so.' Now Henry VIII in that sense was never an individual: he was always a king, looking on himself as a thing apart from mankind, on kingship as an end in itself, on kingly volition as the only and ample reason for anything whatever; on his dignity as such a complete vice-Deity that, under his fiat, municipal law rose, without any further sanction, to the level of divine revelation. His marriages are royal marriages, his murders royal murders, his diseases royal diseases. There is nothing to hide, nothing to be ashamed of. Bessie Blount is as much a fact as Anne Boleyn, and Anne Boleyn as Katharine of Aragon. If they are to his taste they are honoured and worshipped with him; if he is tired of them the country is tired of them too; they are abominable; they confess themselves guilty of impossible sins; send them by parliamentary petition to the block.

What is strange in all this is not the idea itself, which George IV may have had as strongly as Henry VIII: it is the force of character that makes the idea tolerable to other men; that makes More, Warham, Cranmer, Gardiner, Cromwell, faithful administrators of the idea; and that forces, against their will evidently, but still effectively forces, Parliament and Convocation, Lords, Clergy and Commons, to register simply the peremptory orders of the king as their own wishes. There were cliques and parties at Henry's court during the whole of his reign, there was a strong party against Wolsey, there was a Protestant and a Catholic party, and a Norfolk and a Suffolk party; but I am sure that it is a mistake to regard Henry as pulled by one or other of these alternately; or to think that the changes of his policy, and I am not at all sure that the changes were at all so great as they are commonly regarded, were dictated by any other than his own despotic will: he used, I think, the parties, not they him; what influence he allowed them was allowed for his ends, and the moment he saw them pursuing their own ends he stopped them.

Of course such a theory about him, if true, necessitates the belief of great development of design and new purpose in the king himself: but that I think is the most natural solution

of most of the critical questions of the reign.   The words
which More addressed to Cromwell, soon after he resigned
the chancellorship, seem to be a key, almost prophetic in
simplicity, to the after-history.   'Master Cromwell,' he says,
'you are now entered into the service of a most noble, wise,
and liberal prince: if you will follow my poor advice, you
shall in your counsel-giving to his Grace, ever tell him what he
ought to do, but never what he is able to do.'   'For if a lion
knew his own strength, hard were it for any man to rule him [1].'

From the very beginning of his reign, he is finding out
what he can do; from the fall of Wolsey, and especially
after the sacrifice of More, he is coming to regard what he
can do as the only measure of what he ought to do: he is
becoming the king for whom the kingdom is, the tyrant
whose every caprice is wise and sacred: he turns the theory
of kingship into action; the king can do no wrong; therefore men shall call right all that he does: he is the king, not
an individual; what in an individual would be theft, is no
theft in him; all property is the king's, he can take it, and he
takes it; all that proceeds from his mouth is law; the king's
heart is in the hand of the Lord, therefore all that comes out
of the king's heart is the Lord's doing.

Yet with all his grotesque and inhuman self-absorption,
the miserable and growing result of the long tenure of
irresponsible power, we cannot wisely deny the king some
great qualities besides mere force.   Contemporary foreigners,
the justice of whose general judgement is amply proved by
later history, and whose opinion, according to Lord Bacon's
dictum, is generally that which future ages will be found to
confirm, are unanimous in their glorification of Henry's
personal and mental gifts.   His beauty was of that sort that
commended itself to the taste of those times.   And more

---

[1] Rooper, *Life and Death of Sir Thomas Moore* (ed. 1729), p. 69.

than that: for the painters of his portrait have succeeded in giving him an individuality and a humanity which shows either that he possessed a remarkable physique, or that they took more pains with him than they did with his wives—the deadly-lively sort of ladies whose portraits are, if not a justification, at least a colourable occasion for understanding the readiness with which he put them away. Henry's portrait, I said, would fill any canvas; and, allowing for what must be allowed for, dress, expression, and attitude, it must be allowed to be the portrait of a personable king.

His mental abilities I rank very high: he had been carefully educated by good scholars, and had made remarkable progress; not so great, Lord Bacon tells us, as his brother Arthur; but still remarkable at a remarkable time: he did not let his knowledge acquired in boyhood fade out of his mind: after his accession he must have continued his reading; his book against Luther, which, whatever assistance he may have received, was in conception and execution entirely his own, was an extraordinary work for a young king; and the intelligent interest which, down to the last, he showed in religious and other ecclesiastical questions, even when he was most capricious and peremptory, evinces both memory and a real appreciation of subjects on which contemporary kings thought it sinful to think at all. If it were not for the miserable self-will and self-worship which runs through these, there might be something to admire.

Well, it is not for us to judge. The king is apart from other men in his opportunities, in his excuses, in his temptations; even in his responsibility for the direct results of his acts; and he must stand alone in the judgement. But I will leave the remaining sentiments or reflexions which suggest themselves, to be justified after the review of the reign which I propose to take now.

The first question, who were Henry's responsible advisers,

is capable of a very short answer considering the length of his reign : he succeeded a king who had been his own first minister, and who had under him two sorts of secondary ministers ; one set, like Warham and Fox, trustworthy men to whom he gave official confidence, that confidence which a self-confident autocrat can afford to give to men whose interests are the same as his own ; and another set, like Empson and Dudley, whom he used as tools, responsible tools, to be used as long as they were useful, but to be held responsible the moment their use was over or the outcry they provoked became more noxious than the ends they served were advantageous. Henry VIII, doing everything on a larger scale than his father, had the same ideas of ministerial usefulness : during a reign of thirty-eight years he had only five chancellors, Warham, Wolsey, More, Audley, and Wriothesley ; and the office of lord high treasurer was held by two Dukes of Norfolk in succcession during the whole reign. Of the chancellors, Wolsey alone was displaced against his will ; Warham had been long anxious to retire ; More resigned in disgust ; Audley retained the seals to his death, and Wriothesley was chancellor when the king died.

Of these seven ministers we may summarily conclude thus : the two Norfolks and Warham were in position ministers of the old type, official and confidential, but not leaders of political parties, until, after the fall of Wolsey and, in the later years of the reign, after the fall of Cromwell, the second duke undertook the more onerous and critical position which in the end was so nearly fatal to him. Wolsey was too great a man, and More too good a man, to be tools of Henry, especially after the inclination towards tyrannic caprice became more pronounced ; Audley and Wriothesley were tools, either altogether selfish and un-principled, or, like Cromwell, able to combine self-aggrandise-ment and servility with some quantum of ulterior political design, which raises them above that common herd into which Empson and Dudley fall.

Besides these ostensible ministers, Henry had a council, in which perhaps more influential advisers might be looked for : such as were his brother-in-law, friend, and boon companion Suffolk, who, worthless enough himself, still was no man's enemy ; Cromwell, the greatest and most famous, whose character and career are even more mysterious than his master's ; and the men who made their position and reputation by their share in the business of the divorce, such as Cranmer, of whom, in this aspect, the less said the better, and Gardiner, the rough and ready, faithful, skilful, imperious yet adroit minister, on whose back history has laid so great burdens. It is no doubt within the walls of the council chamber that we have to look for the suggestions of such parts of the royal policy as were not due to Henry himself : we can hardly, except in the cases of Wolsey and Cromwell, very distinctly lay our hand on the authorship of a particular scheme : and it is quite certain that, when a particular scheme that pleased the king was started, he adopted it as his own with an ardour and pertinacity fully in keeping with his own idea of his infallibility. So, although for a time Wolsey, and after him Norfolk, and after him Cromwell, and after him Norfolk again, seem to be the prime ministers of a country in which for at least two centuries such prime ministers had been constitutional facts, and although there was in the council a fertile seminary of politicians creeping into power, yet on the whole Henry was his own chief counsellor ; in spite of his inconsistencies the most consistent, and in spite of his changes and caprices the most persistent, of all the men who changed, at this great critical juncture, the whole face and attitude of England. What more need be noted, in such a brief outline as I am now drawing of these things, of the vast industry and broad views of Wolsey, of the wisdom and virtue of More, of the mysterious unconscientiousness of Cromwell, and the like, may be taken as we proceed.

The first region of constitutional action that lies before us is the finance of the reign; a subject on which we have abundant, though not very conclusive data, in the acts of the Parliaments which now begin to put on record the amounts expected from the several grants; in the subsidy rolls, which show how the sums granted were assessed and collected; in the correspondence of the period, which sets before us what the estimated expenditure was from time to time; and in the incidental references of the annalists, which tell us how the imposts were from time to time felt by the people. Of the thirty-eight years of the reign, twenty-one passed away without a Parliament, and therefore without a budget; and long prorogations had now become so much the rule, that only nine new Parliaments, nine general elections, were held during the whole time; the country therefore had not much opportunity of showing a change of feeling in this respect.

It is thus comparatively simple to state the parliamentary grants: tunnage and poundage, and the subsidy on wool, woolfells and leather, were, in the first Parliament of the reign, granted to the king for his life: the ancient vote of tenths and fifteenths was made on eleven occasions, sometimes as a sufficient grant and sometimes as a supplementary grant when a more grasping exaction had disappointed the officers of the Exchequer; and nine several subsidies of a new kind, a graduated income and property tax, were levied at more critical periods, as for the expeditions of 1512 and 1513, for the payment of expenses in 1515, and for the warlike preparations made in 1523, 1539, and 1543. These later taxes were exactions on lands and goods according to fixed scale, minutely drawn out in each of the acts that

sanctioned them: but, as the impost invariably fell short
of the amount expected from it, we must conclude that,
like the old tenths and fifteenths, it was assessed on fancy
valuations and produced no very pressing hardships; judging
from the existing returns, it pressed very lightly upon
individual payers, from the highest class to the lowest.

Besides these legal taxes from the laity, the king had votes
from Convocation following those of Parliament in due proportion, the clergy paying a tenth whenever the Parliament
voted a tenth and fifteenth, adding a subsidy when the
Parliament granted a subsidy; and, after the Parliament of
1534, paying to the king a whole tenth annually, which had
been previously paid, almost if not quite regularly, as a contribution to the funds of the Papacy. These were the regular
and constitutional sources of income.

Besides these, we have to include in the list of the king's
resources, first the heavy loans which were exacted by a
regular process, not very far removed from compulsion, in
the years 1522–8 and 1542, and which were so fully remitted
by the Parliaments of 1529 and 1543, that even those unlucky
creditors whom the king had paid were obliged to refund the
money; secondly, the exactions from the clergy under the threat
of praemunire in 1531, amounting to about £120,000; thirdly,
the very large payments of tribute from France under the
treaties of Edward IV and Henry VII; and, fourthly, the
enormous revenue, enormous at the lowest estimate, which
accrued during the last years of the reign from the spoils of
the shrines and the plunder of the monasteries. Besides these,
there was an occasional devotion money, like that collected
in 1544 nominally for war against the Turks; a benevolence,
or amicable contribution, such as in 1525 produced considerable disaffection in the country; and lastly, enormous
sums raised under occasional forfeitures. I shall not attempt
a summary of these taxes, but may mention a few data that

may be relied upon : the value of a tenth and fifteenth was
£30,000 ; of a clerical tenth, £10,000 ; the estimated
amount of the subsidy of 1513 was £160,000 ; the estimate
for the royal expedition made in 1522, £372,404 18s. 4d. ;
the estimated sum of the loans of 1523 was £260,000 ; the
income from the monasteries cannot be stated in reasonable
figures ; but of this a considerable part was during the few
years that it accrued expended in pensions. Of estimated
outlays we have but a few illustrations ; the expenses of the
household were a little over £20,000 a year, but these
of course represent only the fixed charges, not the king's
lavish personal expenditure ; Wolsey's estimate for the war
of 1513 was £640,000 ; and when we find Giustiniani
estimating the outlay at half of the ten millions of ducats
which was the treasure supposed to be left by Henry VII,
we are inclined to conclude that the estimate was not
below the mark ; anyhow the cost of the expedition to
Tournay was such as to recommend a peace policy for
several years.

The time may come when these accounts may be subjected
to a formal historical audit, that is when the researches at
the Record Office furnish us with a complete view of extant
material ; but it would be very rash now to define with any
exactness either income or outlay for a reign of such abnormal
character.   The only general conclusion that I can come to is
that, in despite of Wolsey's financial ability and the cleverness
of the agents who were trained under him, the policy of the
whole reign in this respect was a hand-to-mouth policy,
assisted by occasional godsends in the shape of forfeitures
and benevolences. In this department the Parliaments
showed some spirit, as we shall see ; the result of that was
the grant of subsidies to reach over several years ; under
these subsidy-acts the king collected as much as he could,
and then collected money in other ways until, the patience

of the lenders being exhausted, a new Parliament was got
together to wipe off the old debt or promise a new subsidy.
There can be little doubt that some of the most important
legislative acts were carried, at least through the Commons,
by the inducement that the king would be able to dispense
with direct taxation; and, although that undertaking was a
fallacious one, men could be found to overawe opposition
or make a show of self-sacrifice which was sure of subsequent reward. I may note some of the parliamentary
methods when I reach that part of our subject: for this is
the only point on which Henry in his Parliaments had any
real difficulty.

A hand-to-mouth policy has this drawback; that, on
critical occasions, it involves critical demands, and critical
demands produce special irritation. That rule is exemplified
very clearly in the reign of Henry VII, whose financial policy
was much safer than his son's; it was not a hand-to-mouth
policy, but a severely economical one; and both policies
coincide in having nothing to spare for emergencies;
accordingly we find, on every imposition of a subsidy in
the reign of Henry VII, an outbreak of popular disaffection,
taking hold of some political quarrel. There was under
Henry VIII something of the same sort; but it was, as a
rule, more easily localized, and put down at once; the
restoration of law and order by his father had borne this
good fruit. In 1497 a rising in Devonshire caused by an
income tax, utilized by a faction and facilitated by the weakness of local organization, could affect all Southern England,
and force the king into the field. In 1536, even a great
religious movement like the Pilgrimage of Grace sinks into a
local and provincial rising, an abortive tumult. It is not
necessary, however, at this point to formulate a general conclusion as to the oppressive character of Henry's financial
administration: the legal taxes were not excessively heavy,

and the illegal exactions were condoned by subservient Parliaments. The question of the high-handed confiscations leads on to further questions.

I do not wish in these lectures to give more than its proper prominence to the great question of the divorce ; even to give it its proper prominence would involve discussions far more lengthy than I have time for now ; I shall therefore hope that you will take as read all the details of the negotiations concerning it, and simply look upon it as a force, or the application of an impact, which had much greater consequences, and originated a larger developing series of measures, than could have possibly been calculated on. In a word, to use Sir Thomas More's expressive formula, it opened the eyes of the lion as to what he could do ; not all at once, but by a very gradual process, which may indeed be traced most distinctly with reference to the Reformation history, but is also apparent in the other departments of administration.

It is clear, from the beginning of his reign, that Henry was a prince who had only to learn the extent of his powers, in order to attempt to exercise them. If we may believe the law reporters, as early as 1515 he had declared himself determined not to allow any superiority of external spiritual courts in a country of which he was sovereign ; and there are signs, in Wolsey's history, that the imminent danger of the king's taking advantage of the Statute of Praemunire was in his mind long before he was actually sacrificed. But the earlier years of the reign were remarkably free from occasions on which any great constitutional crisis could arise. Henry's ambition, like Wolsey's, was mainly set upon an influential place in the councils of Europe, and among the people at large there was contentment. Henry had been brought up very strictly, and married, very young, to a wife, to whom he gave his full affection ; the good impressions of his training were, at least for several years, strong enough to keep him out of the domestic scandals that divide courts; and although Bessie Blount and the Duke of Richmond became prominent about ten years after the reign begins, it is not until 1524 or 1525 that the divorce question even looms in the distance. Up to that time the want of constitutional principle in the king and his minister has been chiefly apparent in the matter of money-getting. Soon after this Henry seems to have fallen in love with Anne Boleyn, and to have begun to contemplate the divorce. The mere formalities of obtaining such a divorce were not formidable; but the parties interested in preventing it were very formidable indeed. The emperor was the queen's nephew. The pope's power was being rudely shaken both in Germany and in Italy. To be brief; the pope was prevailed on to commission Wolsey and Campegio to determine the validity of the king's marriage; when the trial had begun, the cause was called back to Rome; Henry felt that his only chance of getting the divorce was to have it tried in England; the pope felt that the only chance of avoiding a crisis, in which between Henry and Charles he must certainly either temporally or spiritually be ruined, was to keep the discussion languidly dragging on at Rome until the parties were tired, or something else turned up. This, thus early, Henry had the sense to see; he therefore destroyed Wolsey, and that by the very Statute of Praemunire at the evasion of which he had so long connived: his eyes were opened to the powers of the Praemunire, and in his confiscation of Wolsey's estates he had his first taste of spoil. He saw that the Praemunire made him absolutely master of the clergy, and, as absolute master, the primary owner of all Church property. Hence the great chain of ecclesiastical statutes follows in an order that we might almost dignify by the name of Evolution. As lord and master of the Church, he could utilize Church machinery to obtain the divorce and the marriage on which he had set his king's heart; and, when he was tired of the second wife, he could obtain, from the archbishop he had made, an annulling of that marriage as easily as he could obtain a Bill of Attainder from the Parliament; and, when in time he married another woman whom he did not like, he could by a commission to the national synod obtain another judgement of nullity of marriage, and by negotiating with Parliament another petition for another marriage. This wonderful Praemunire, of which the foreign residents at the English court speak with horror as a mystery of which the king alone possessed the key, might be a lash brandished over laity and clergy alike so long as the papal supremacy was admitted by either.

Thus the desire of spoil, the ambition of uncontrolled sovereignty, and the facilities of gaining his own immediate ends in marriage, urged on the king in the line of doing, not what he ought, but what he could. In 1531, by the threat of Praemunire he compelled the clergy to recognize him as the supreme head on earth of the Church of England, and to pay him £118,840 by votes of Convocation: he tried the same policy with the Commons; endeavouring to compel them to purchase their exemption from the same sentence, if not by votes of money, at least by modifications of the land laws in the direction of wills and uses. In this he was for the moment defeated by the vigilance of the Commons, but he kept this line of legislation before his eyes, and with singular pertinacity; the Statute of Uses was delayed until 1536 and the Statute of Wills until 1540, but both statutes were promulgated in 1532, and formed part of a policy which we may compare, not favourably, with that of Edward I; but which has a special legal side of such importance, that only the superior importance of the ecclesiastical questions of the time can account for its being overlooked. It is true that, in their later results, the two statutes of which I have spoken seem small and beneficial as compared with the mischievous results of the Church policy, but they were, like it, distinct puttings out of the claws of the awakened lion, which would have gone much further and held much tighter if they could.

But I proceed with the ecclesiastical evolution. The recognition of the king in 1531 as supreme head on earth of the Church of England was closely connected with the appropriation of the £118,840 by the supreme head. But the facility with which the Church parted with its money opened the supreme eyes a little wider. If they will pay money they will surrender power : a form of three articles is sent to Convocation in 1532 by which the clergy are to renounce their right of spiritual legislation without royal licence, and consent to a reform of the canon law under the king's authority. After some discussion, with the fear of another Praemunire, the clergy consent to that also. By crafty dealing with the House of Commons, the Court, in which Cromwell is now becoming a leading man, obtains an address complaining of the ecclesiastical courts, their use of canon law on the one side and their practical abuses on the other ; if the Commons will help the king against the pope, the king will help the Commons against the spiritual courts ; he will not press the Statutes of Uses and Wills if they will agree that he shall forbid the payment of annates. The Commons resist, but their strong men have gone over to the king. The Annates Bill is passed ; the Submission of the clergy is exacted ; and More, the good and wise chancellor, resigns the seals. He and the foreign ambassadors saw which way the Lion was looking better than the Lion himself. If the clergy accept the Submission, says the Imperial resident, they will for the future have less power than the shoemakers, who at least can make regulations for their own craft. That was done however.

In the autumn Archbishop Warham died; it became clear to the king that, if he appointed Cranmer, who was already committed to him in the question of the marriage, that long-standing difficulty could be got over. As yet there was no formal breach with Rome, his hand had lain heavy only on his own Church; the Annates Bill even had not been confirmed yet. Cranmer should be regularly consecrated, commissioned, and made legate, and then called on to act up to his expressed convictions. So certain was the king of his power, that, in anticipation of the sentence, he married Anne Boleyn; appointed Cranmer archbishop, obtained from him a sentence of the nullity of his previous marriage and of the validity of his new marriage, and got opinions from the divines and canonists in Convocation which had a similar effect. Then, and not before, he confirmed the act about Annates, and defied the papal power.

But, having gone so far, why not go a little further? In the Parliament of 1533 he obtained the passing of the Statute of Appeals, founded on what seems to be the true theory of Church and State; forbidding the carrying of appeals to Rome at all, and providing sufficient machinery for appeals at home: the Annates Bill had provided for the confirmation and consecration of bishops, and the two together proclaimed with one breath the emancipation of the Church from Roman supremacy, and its competence for complete internal administration under the supremacy of the king. But from this moment the ecclesiastical reforms became involved more and more with the king's marriage policy. Anne Boleyn, her father, and Cranmer, who seems to have been their family counsellor, were bent on further measures of hostility to Rome; and Cromwell, who was the king's minister rather than the queen's, was likewise politically a Protestant. The year 1534 saw the clergy, both secular and regular, compelled to make a new submission, to recognize the validity of the marriage and the succession, and to admit a new and comprehensive oath for the maintenance of the two. A new Statute of Appeals, founded on the Submission of 1532, modified the appellate jurisdiction, and furnished a recourse to the king in chancery, as the final reference, which in the former statute had been left to the archbishop and, in causes touching the king, to the Upper House of Convocation; a new statute on Annates reformed the regulations for the appointment of bishops; the synodical declaration which denied the authority of Rome, and a statute which forbade all payments to Rome, swept away all signs of the old subjection.

But there is no step, in Parliament at least, towards doctrinal change: the law of heresy is reformed but not made less stringent, and it is no longer heretical to speak against the pope. Even in the Articles of 1536 the progress towards change is defined by the simple elimination of distinctive papal doctrine; the Convocation urges an authorized translation of Holy Scripture as the best antidote to heresy. But events were proceeding more rapidly than ideas: the oath of succession necessitated the imprisonment of More and Fisher; a second session in the autumn of 1534 gave the secular recognition to the king's style as supreme head on earth of the Church of England; that title was publicly promulgated by letters patent in January, 1535; and the accusation of attempting to deprive the king of this designation brought the two worthiest men in England to the block during the summer of that year. The death of Fisher, the confidential friend of his father and grandmother, and that of More, who represented all that was good in his own early experience, whether they were wrung from him by the importunities of his wife, or coldly acquiesced in as cases in which all human feeling must be sunk before the self-idolatry of the theoretic kingship, seem to prove and to have proved to the king himself that no scruples should ever hereafter touch him.

The next step of change was the dissolution of the smaller monasteries : Wolsey, in his great scheme for Church reforms, had led the way to this. He had seen the increasing importance of the great towns of England, and the increasing mischief caused by the incurable uselessness of the monastic foundations; and he had obtained bulls of legation from Rome enabling him to suppress convents and establish bishoprics. That had opened the king's eyes to a new possibility, and, although he waited several years before he executed his scheme, all that was good in the scheme was Wolsey's, all that was bad in it wears an unfortunate air of having been done by Cromwell. But it was almost a point of honour with Henry to show that without the pope he could do all that Wolsey had been empowered to do. So in the autumn of 1535 Cromwell and his agents effected a visitation of the monasteries, the report of which insured their condemnation ; and, in the last session of the Long Parliament in 1536, the dissolution of the smaller houses was decreed. A new court, the Court of Augmentations, was founded to manage the property which by the same act was vested in the king and his heirs. The greater monasteries survived a little longer, and in their case the process of surrender took the place of a general and compulsory dissolution. In the session of 1539, however, a similar act vested in the king the property of the surrendered houses, and in that year the abbots disappeared from Parliament. At the same time the king was empowered to establish new bishoprics ; suffragan bishops had been the subject of legislation in 1534, when the act was passed which supplied to the more aged and busy prelates the assistance that had been hitherto furnished by titular bishops *in partibus* commissioned at Rome.

These acts very nearly complete the series by which

Henry evolved the idea of a regal papacy out of the royal supremacy. For some subordinate purposes, as for dispensations and faculties, he allowed the Archbishop of Canterbury to exercise a quasi-legatine authority under himself, and with a check in Chancery on his proceedings; but in all such matters he was himself the fountain of power. The climax was reached when, by the appointment of Cromwell as Vicar-General, with an authority and precedence above all prelates and nobles, he emulated the papal assumption of exercising direct powers through a legate *a latere*. Unluckily for himself, and for Henry also, the royal legate *a latere* proved too great a power to manage; meddled with too many things, provoked too much hostility, got his feet entangled in the marriage net he had provided for the old lion, and perished more sadly, because more ignominiously, than his predecessors in power and ruin.

I have spoken thus far mainly of Henry's ecclesiastical measures as they affected endowments and jurisdictions; but there is a side, the side of doctrine, which is not less important. He never forgot that he was the defender of the faith; nor, whatever were his eccentricities and aberrations in minor particulars, does he seem ever to have gone in this region further in the direction of change than the more enlightened popes and cardinals of his own age would have gone. Wolsey would have agreed with him in the dissolution of the monasteries; the Convocation had petitioned for a translation of the Bible; the worship of the saints and the excessive devotions at their shrines had long been a burden to the souls of men, not merely men like Erasmus, but of far more unimpeachable orthodoxy. The supremacy of the chair of St. Peter was by no means as yet an article of unquestioning faith; even the marriage of the clergy was a point not beyond discussion. But there were things which, quite irrespective of the pope and his claims, could not be touched without the taint of heresy. And of these Henry, with all his inconsistencies, was a constant defender. He might tolerate a certain evangelical obliquity in Boleyn's eyes; he might choose to be blind to Cromwell's sympathies with foreign Protestantism; he might tolerate Mrs. Cranmer, as he had not looked too curiously into the semi-matrimonial connexions of the great cardinal; he might even go the length of marrying a lady like Anne of Cleves, in whom, through the phlegmatic impenetrability of the Flanders mare, some instincts of unorthodox skittishness might be detected. But Henry was royally orthodox. If, for any purpose of the moment, he relaxed the stringency of the courts, he kept the law very strong against heresy. This acted in a curious way. The king's idea that he was supreme in Church and State, whilst in some regions it led him to maintain the administrative machinery of the two severely separate, in others led him to some mixture of his functions. In his first act of heresy he repealed the statute of Henry IV 'de hereticis comburendis' which seemed to give too much power to the bishops, but re-enacted those of Richard II and Henry V which tended to make heresy an offence at common law. A similar intention is clear in the Act of Six Articles of 1539, and, with this light upon it, in the several modifications of the Six Articles which were proposed in the later Parliaments. I shall not speculate on the possibility that, if he had lived longer, he might have developed more in the direction of Protestant doctrine; I think however that it is unlikely; doctrinally, although quite able to maintain his own line, he clearly symbolized consistently with Gardiner and not with Cranmer. The extinction of the Norfolk interest might have led him to further negotiations with Protestantism abroad, but of any sympathy with domestic Puritanism, such as that by which Somerset palliated his greed for confiscation, there is no trace

in Henry.　For spoil however the old lion went on yearning
to the last; the dissolution of chantries and colleges, to follow
that of the monasteries, was one of the measures of his last
Parliament.

It may strike some of us that the process of change had
now gone far enough; the English Church was freed from
the yoke of Rome, but she retained all her proper framework and at least half of her old endowments; I say at
least half, I should not like to commit myself to a statement
that there was much more.　She had obtained the Bible
in English and the use of the chief forms of prayer in the
vernacular, and was preparing for a revision in form of
the Sacramental Services; she had rid herself of a mass
of superstitious usages.　It is true that the king remained
a believer in Roman Catholic forms of doctrine; but it
must always be remembered that those forms had not yet,
by the Tridentine decrees, been hardened into their later
inflexibility; and, when we consider the terrible risks which,
in the next reign, the Church of England ran, of losing all
sense or desire of continuity, identity, or communion with
the historic Catholic Christendom, we may feel thankful
that such risk was run under a weak king and feeble
ministers, not under the influence of a strong will and
strong hand like Henry's.

You will see thus that I believe him to have been a man
of purpose; not the mere capricious tyrant who found it
a pleasant exercise of despotic power to burn Catholics
and Protestants on the same day, or found a malicious
gratification in making Cranmer support the Catholic doctrine of the Eucharist and Gardiner the doctrine of unlimited obedience: further than this I do not go.　I believe
him to have been a man of unbounded selfishness; a man
to whom the acquisition of power was precious mainly as
a step towards the acquisition of greater power; a man

of whom we may say, as I said at first, that he was the king, the whole king, and nothing but the king; that he wished to be, with regard to the Church of England, the pope, the whole pope, and something more than the pope. You remember how in his early days Maximilian had tempted him with the offer of the Empire, he himself to retire on the popedom with an inchoate claim to canonization. Henry was determined to have in England at least both Empire and Papacy, to make the best, or rather the most, of both worlds.

I have said more than in proper proportion I ought to have said with reference to Henry's ecclesiastical policy, and left but little time for the analogous features that may be traced in his temporal policy : one reason for that is the greater interest we all feel in the religious question of the Reformation ; another is in the fact that his ecclesiastical measures had a much more lasting consequence than his temporal ones.   We have long rid ourselves of all the secular burdens imposed by what we call the Tudor dictatorship, but we are still living under religious or ecclesiastical conditions that owe very much, even of their present form, to the hand of Henry.   You will, I hope, know me too well to misinterpret me in these expressions ; you will not suspect me of making Henry VIII the founder of the Church of England; but I do not conceal from myself that, under the Divine power which brings good out of evil and overrules the wrath of man to the praise of God, we have received good as well as evil through the means of this ' majestic lord who broke the bonds of Rome.'

If now we attempt to find in Henry's treatment of the temporalty a reflexion of the principles on which he dealt thus summarily with the spiritualty, what do we find?   The answer to one important part of that question I propose to

take in the next lecture, in which I shall make, with rather
more detail than is possible in so wide a *résumé* as I have
attempted in this, an examination of his dealings with the
administrative machinery of the Parliaments.   But in a
general way I will attempt to state the answer now.   As
for taxation, we have seen how, by his early as well
as his later policy, the real hold on the purse-strings
was wrested from the hand of the nation.   A king who
had over his Parliaments the strong hold that Henry had,
who could dictate to them the measures he wished to pass,
even down to the smallest details, and even make them
petition for acts when he was the only man in the kingdom that desired them, might, we think, have contented
himself with taking money through the overawed or subservient Commons.   But he did not; he chose to exact
money by loan and then to come to the nation that lent
the money for exoneration ;   the very fact that he went
about the loan by exactly the same process of assessment
and collection that he used in assessing and collecting a
legal tax, shows that he saw what he was doing : he saw
that he had the power, and he used it.   Wolsey might dislike
the idea of meeting a Parliament that might speak unreservedly about himself; Henry had no such dislike; he
could browbeat, or bribe, or bully, or divide, or balance
parties, but he never could have doubted for a moment
that in the end he should get his own way.

Next to taxation, perhaps even more important than
taxation, was the right of legislation ;   legislation of the
temporalty could at no time be carried through without the
king's enacting words ;   and the submission of the clergy
in 1532, embodied in the Statute of Appeals in 1534,
had established the same rule for the spiritualty.   But this
did not content the Lion.   In the Proclamation Act of 1539
the Parliament is made to surrender to the king the power

of legislation; as the head on earth of the Church he might already issue, and had issued, proclamations touching Christian faith; and by the natural power of king he had issued proclamations for the public peace : but, O strange wilfulness of human nature! men had not much minded: these proclamations alike were set at nought by those who would not consider the divinity of royalty; therefore, lest the king should be tempted to become a tyrant, lest the king should be compelled by the wilfulness of his subjects to extend beyond their natural limits the liberty and supremacy of his royal power and dignity, what was to be done? Was he to renounce the power of proclaiming, and bind the Parliament to codify the temporal law, as he had promised to the spiritualty to codify and reform the canon law? Quite the reverse; in order that he might not be tempted to usurp the functions of legislator, the Parliament was to invest him with those functions, and, provided his proclamations did not contravene the existing laws, to give to them the full force and virtue of acts of the whole body of the realm. Here was a 'lex regia' indeed; a dictatorship which, with all conceivable limitations, left the 'king master and only master' in his own house.

The security of life and property was of course worth little when such things were possible : but Henry had a strong executive force at his disposal, and the actual working of this despotism did not affect the body of the people so much as might be expected. The clergy were of course in constant terror of the shadow of a Praemunire; the reformers, alternately flattered and banished, had no easy time of it; and the position of even a bishop's lady must have been, to say the least, peculiar. But on the great men, the taller poppies, the actual pressure occasionally fell. The nation had fought hard for justice in the tribunals and for the limitation of the doctrine of treasons. Bills of attainder, trials in Star Chamber, and multiplication of treasons, form the dark side of the policy of Henry VII; they come to full development under Henry VIII.

Edmund de la Pole, Buckingham, Wolsey, Fisher, More, Anne Boleyn, Cromwell, the Marquess of Exeter, the Countess of Salisbury, Montacute, and last of all Surrey and his father, were victims of a system, of various contrivances but of one purport, for destroying without law, or without trial, or without defence, those whom the king determined, from whatever motive of policy or of caprice, of jealousy or of satiety, to sacrifice. Add to these the religious or ecclesiastical holocausts, and the number of inferior victims who were involved in the fall of the great ones, and for whom there was no need to violate laws that could so easily be manipulated. The liberty of the subject to act or speak, or even to think, was reduced to a minimum under an executive familiar with constructive treasons.

But it is time to close this part of our discussion; and I must leave some, especially of the legal measures of the reign which would most naturally have fallen in with the line of this lecture, for the more formal treatment, which I propose to take in the next lecture, of Henry's dealings with Parliament. Perhaps when we have looked at these, we may find time to inquire to what extent he really fulfilled the office of dictator, anticipated the line of history, or carried with him the wishes of the nation.

PARLIAMENT UNDER HENRY VIII

(June 9, 1881.)

THE great question of the reign of Henry VIII is, no doubt, this: to what extent did he, in the remarkable career of destruction and reconstruction, of public and private self-will, of commingled revolutionism and conservatism, carry with him the assent and goodwill of his people? then, when we have determined to what extent the national participation in his measures is to be admitted, would be the time to ask by what means he obtained that assent and goodwill. I do not flatter myself that I am going to answer the question or to solve the problem, either to your satisfaction or to my own. Far too many considerations are concerned in both, far too many facts of doubtful interpretation, and certainly too many historical theories. All that I can undertake to do is to prepare the clearing of the way for some later and more fully equipped investigator; more fully equipped, I say, because, as you will see, there is every reason to hope that in a few years, owing to the labours of the scholars employed in calendaring the State papers, many of the facts which are now capable of contradictory interpretations will be set forth in their true light and relation to one another.

In the former lecture I confined myself to such illustrations of the subject as belong to the royal character of Henry VIII himself; and you will not have mistaken my provisional conclusion that the great factor in the whole

complication is the strong, intelligent, self-willed force of
the king; that that alone seems to give purpose and consistency to the eventful policy of the period; that Henry VIII
is neither the puppet of parties, nor the victim of circumstances, nor the shifty politician, nor the capricious tyrant,
but a man of light and leading, of power, force and foresight, a man of opportunities, stratagems, and surprises, but
not the less of iron will and determined purpose; purpose not
at once realized or systematized, but widening, deepening,
and strengthening as the way opens before it; a man accordingly who might have been very great, and could under no
circumstances be accounted less than great, but who would
have been infinitely greater, and better, and more fortunate,
if he would have lived for his people, and not for himself.

But the subject of the present lecture is the parliamentary
history of the reign; and I will keep back any general or
personal remarks until that has been treated as it can be
treated in a public lecture. It helps to answer the question
and problem which I have stated, for it is through the
Parliament that Henry inquires of the goodwill and support
of the nation, as it is through the Convocation he inquires
of the goodwill and support of the clergy. If we believe
the Acts of Parliament, we shall find the nation not merely
acquiescing in but petitioning for measures, some of which
had no importance except as fulfilling the wishes of the
king, others of which were in strong opposition to all that
is known of national feeling both in and out of Parliament;
if we look at the early ecclesiastical measures we find the
same acquiescence in great constitutional changes, abdi-
cations of power which could not be spontaneous, and
acknowledgements of the truth of statements and principles
which, if true at all, were far too novel to have been accepted
without discussion. We may, if we please, admit the conclusion that the nation accepted the king's action as that

of a divinely constituted dictator; a theory which involves the assumption, which is altogether groundless, that the nation saw, or thought they saw, the existing circumstances to be such as demanded a dictatorship. I do not think they did, and I am persuaded that the theory is based on that process of reading history backward, which it has been my fate, in this Chair, to have constantly to struggle against.

There was nothing in the circumstances of Europe during the whole life of Henry VIII, such as there was under Queen Elizabeth, which might persuade people then living of the need of such an extraordinary officer. We, looking back on the time, may see how dangerous a time it was, how full of pitfalls and snares, and how, in the result, a great advantage was gained by England having had such a hand as even the blood-stained hand of Henry to guide her through: but the critical character of the time was not apparent to the time, or to the leading men of England during it; and the later reading of it cannot be made to account for the condition of feeling and action that we are now contemplating.

The opposite view, that Henry and his advisers concocted the parliamentary acts and manifestoes in such a way as to make them embody a national adhesion, sympathy, and even enthusiasm, by the simple process of falsification, is, on the other hand, too arbitrary, too shameful, for us to contemplate with equanimity : history may be, and ought to be, tested at every turn ; Acts of Parliament, when they are tested, may, and often do, turn out very unsound and unsatisfactory in their statements of fact, and disputable and inconsistent in their statements of law; but, if we could believe in such a wholesale perversion of evidences as this theory involves, we must resign all theories of history at once, and relegate the inquiring world to a combination of natural laws with historical novels. The fact of the

matter, I take it, we may accept : that the nation and the
Church accepted, acquiesced in, and petitioned for, in Parliament and in Convocation, the things which the Acts of
Parliament and Convocation declare that they accepted,
acquiesced in, and petitioned for ; but the question remains
how we are to interpret that co-operation, and by what
means the conceivable measure of co-operation was obtained.
With so much preface, more than I intended, let us approach this branch of the subject, the history, modifications,
and alterations of the government by Parliament and Convocation, as it appears to be modified and altered or
maintained during the great changes of the reign.

I have already mentioned that Henry VIII held nine
Parliaments in his thirty-eight years, and that of those one
was extended over the best part of seven years, that is the
great organic Parliament, which began in 1529 and ran
on to the spring of 1536 : a Parliament which, both on
account of its length and for the importance of its Acts,
may deserve the title of the Long Parliament of Henry VIII.
Of the other eight Parliaments, two, that summoned in 1512
and that summoned in 1542, ran over three years with
short sessions ; the others are all shorter, of one or two
sessions. All these Parliaments were held in London, either
at Westminster or, in one instance and possibly an ac-
casional sitting, at Blackfriars, and in the old places of
assembly ; the Convocation of Canterbury met at St. Paul's,
and so continued to meet, as it still does on the first day
of the session. In 1523 Wolsey summoned it to Westminster ; and, after the Submission in 1532, it was frequently
adjourned from St. Paul's to Westminster for the convenience
of the bishops, whose hands were full of business in both
chambers. The House of Lords continued to meet in the
Parliament Chamber, and the Commons sat in the chapter-
house or refectory of the Abbey until the end of the reign ;

Edward VI, in his first Parliament, took the Commons to
St. Stephen's Chapel. The Parliament Chamber, or the
Chamber of the Holy Cross, the situation of which is un-
known to me unless it was the Painted Chamber under
a new name, was the place of opening the session under
Henry VII and Henry VIII.

Our first question, however, is concerned with the personal composition of the assembly. The House of Lords
is the chamber that undergoes the greatest modifications
during the period. We take the lords spiritual first; the
Parliaments of Henry VII had contained two archbishops,
nineteen bishops, and twenty-eight abbots; Henry VIII
added three abbots, the Abbot of Tewkesbury in 1521,
the Abbot of Tavistock in 1514, and the Abbot of Burton
in 1534; and after the foundation of the new bishoprics,
he added the six new Bishops of Oxford, Peterborough,
Gloucester, Bristol, Chester, and Westminster: but before
that was done the abbots had disappeared from Parliament;
so at the beginning of the reign the number of spiritual
peers was 49; at the maximum in 1534 it was 52, and
after the dissolution of the monasteries, it fell to 26. The
number of lay peers varied little, for there were few new
creations except where an old peerage had been extinguished.
The minimum number was called in 1523, being only 28,
several of the peers being that year employed in military
affairs abroad; the maximum was in 1536, in the Parliament called to approve of the destruction of Anne Boleyn,
and the number was 51. In the other Parliaments it varied
between 36 and 46. It will be thus observed that, until
the dissolution of the monasteries, the spiritual lords were
always in a numerical majority, but that the tendency
was decided towards an equalization; a tendency which
is ocularly perceptible in the journals where, in the list of
attendances, which from 1515 onwards are marked daily,

the two bodies are arranged in parallel columns. It would, however, be wrong to infer from this that there was an equality of voting bodies, for of the clerical members the attendance was throughout the reign very irregular; and the proportion, on most critical occasions, seems to have been about 20 bishops and abbots to 30 lay lords. It is true they both had the power of giving proxies, but the irregularity of attendance does not seem to be compensated by the proxies: the prelate who is attendant one day is absent the next, doubtless without proxy; and some are absent for whole sessions.

Convocation during the whole reign sits at the same time with the Parliament; and generally the Friday in each week, sometimes the Tuesday also, is marked by adjournment that the prelates may attend Convocation, the Wednesday in some cases being likewise surrendered for the session of the Star Chamber. No doubt the business of the Upper House of Convocation engrossed the time of most of the absent bishops and abbots, for that assembly was, before the dissolution, a very large body, nearly as large as the House of Commons; it included, as is seen in the great divisions on the divorce, between two and three hundred abbots and priors; and much of the business undertaken in it was of a far more critical character than that which was gone through in the Parliament.

The House of Commons was a little, only a little, so far as concerns England proper, modified by Henry VIII: Preston, Lancaster, Thetford, Orford, Berwick, and possibly one or two more towns, gained the privilege of representation; but by bestowing representation on the towns and counties of Wales, Calais, and Chester, Henry added in 1543 thirty-two members, knights and burgesses, to the old number.

The suffrage, as we know from the case of Leicester, was in the corporate towns being altogether appropriated by the

councillors and other officers who constituted the corporation. This loss of distinctly representative importance is
accompanied by a certain rise in the position of the borough
members. Up to this time the office of Speaker has been
engrossed by the knights of the shire, and the only names
of men who have taken a prominent part in the debates of
the Commons have been those of county members. In this
reign, however, Humfrey Wingfield, member for Yarmouth,
was chosen Speaker in succession to Audley; and the only
persons who are found taking a leading part in the discussions of the Long Parliament of 1529–1536 are Thomas
Cromwell, member for Taunton, who before he placed
himself in the king's service had succeeded in throwing
out the bill of attainder against Wolsey, and Mr. Temys,
the member for Westbury, who had proposed that the king
should be asked to give up his plan for divorce.

Still we do not possess journals of the proceedings of the
Commons before the year 1547. Those of the Lords begin
in 1509, and furnish us with much of the information that
we have looked for in vain in the older Rolls of Parliament.
From them we learn to how large an extent the use of
proxies prevailed in the House of Lords, notwithstanding
the careful way in which it was limited and tested; a usage
which shows how it was so easy for the king, by dealing
with one or two of the more prominent prelates, generally
to secure an ecclesiastical majority in Parliament, and even
in Convocation. In the Lower House the Speaker of the
Tudor reigns is in very much the same position as the
Chancellor in the Upper House : he is the manager of
business on the part of the crown, and probably the nominee
either of the king himself or of the chancellor. Although
the forms of election, apology and protest, of address to
the king and royal admission, were maintained and developed, we know both from Sir Thomas Smith and from

Coke that the king appointed the Speaker: even in the House of Lords the sovereign exercised the same right when the chancellor was not a peer; in 1529, as we learn from Chapuys' dispatches, Archbishop Warham was elected but set aside as too old. The result was that the Speaker, instead of being the defender of the liberties of the house, had often to reduce it to an order that meant obsequious reticence or sullen submission. Happily it was not every Speaker that was like Rich, whose extant addresses to the king are nauseous compliments on his majesty's gifts of nature, fortune, and grace, the beauty of his person, the felicity of his enterprises, the perfect virtue of his character; compliments which the king deprecates with a modest reference to the Giver of all good gifts, but with a conscious acquiescence as ridiculous as the mock humility of the Speaker. But where even More himself had the greatest difficulty in behaving with decent independence, so poor a creature as Rich may stand excused.

The early Speakers of the reign were Sir Thomas Englefield, M.P. for Berks; Sir Thomas Sheffield, for Lincolnshire; Sir Thomas Nevill, possibly for Kent; all men of dignity and simplicity. The Speaker of 1523 was Sir Thomas More; he was succeeded in the Parliament of 1529 by Audley, who succeeded him also as Chancellor in 1532. Humfrey Wingfield, whom I have mentioned, succeeded Audley; Rich was Speaker in 1536, Sir Nicolas Hare in 1539, and Sir Thomas Moyle in 1542. Moyle's speeches were formed on the model of Rich's; Hare's speech in 1540, although scarcely less complimentary, was better put together: he congratulated the realm on the felicity of having such a king as Henry, who had won, a boon which had fallen to the lot of no other Christian commonwealth, the distinction that under him, without any single calamity, the land had not only flourished but had been restored to her perfect freedom. These words had a meaning; no doubt the absence of external calamity was a feature of Henry's reign, and was one cause of his influence with the people : on the other hand, the recovery of what seemed to the age to be spiritual liberty from Rome was a real thing in Hare's mind, not the mere compliment that was designed in the comparison by which Rich equalled Henry with Solomon, Samson and Absalom ; or with the sun itself, as drying up noxious vapours and cherishing the growth of all good seeds. Hare, however, had a difficult part to play, for, just before he made this speech, he had been sent to the Tower for offending against the king's prerogative ; he had regained his liberty and his appointment as Speaker by a complete submission. There is no evidence, so far as I know, that the Commons had treated this imprisonment as a matter of privilege.

It would be easy to parallel from the speeches of the chancellor the fulsome compliments of the Speakers, but I must hasten on to the more important questions of the direct dealings of the king or his prime ministers with the two houses; and, as it would be impossible to go into any thorough details on this, I must content myself with occasional illustrations. Henry was generally present at the opening and closing of the sessions, but he did not, in his later years, scruple to interpose from time to time in the deliberations of either house, and influence the voting. The first sensational event of the kind is Wolsey's adventure in the Parliament of 1523, when More was Speaker. The great chancellor had in the usual way come down to the Commons and told them that the king's needs amounted to a sum of £800,000, and to raise that amount a subsidy of a fifth would be required, payable in five years. After the cardinal's departure a discussion arose on particulars, which is amusingly described by Cromwell as a communing on war, peace, strife, contention, debate, murmur, grudge, riches, poverty, penury, truth, falsehood, justice, equity, deceit, oppression, magnanimity, force, activity, temperance, treason, murder, felony, and how a commonwealth might be edified and continued in our realm. But the economical discussions were pulled up by the announcement of another visit from the chancellor. Then arose the question, how is he to come; is he to come as chancellor, or as cardinal in state; let him come as cardinal, for then, if there should be a riot, the blame can be laid on his attendants. So he comes in state, and asks an answer about the subsidy. He is met with sullen silence; not even Mr. Marney, who is just going to be made a baron, and whom Wolsey applies to directly, will utter a word. Then poor More, on his knees, has to represent to the cardinal, who had made him Speaker, that this manner of coming, on which, you observe, he and the House had already calculated, was not expedient or in conformity with ancient liberties. So the cardinal had to go away in a rage; the Commons were willing to listen to him, but would not debate in his presence. Still the visit was not in vain; the deliberation was resumed, and a very heavy impost was agreed to, when Sir John Hussey, the member for Lincolnshire, who also was made a peer soon after, proposed a substantial addition on the tax from land; only eleven or twelve members voted for it, but, notwithstanding the abstention of the majority, it was allowed to be added; then the session was prorogued. After the vacation it was proposed by the knights of the shire to extend to goods the tax which Hussey had fixed on the land; a division took place with the curious result that all the county members voted one way and all the burgesses the other; yet, notwithstanding the enormous majority against the tax, More, in his capacity of the king's agent, prevailed on the House to pass the bill.

Here you have a very illustrative case of the way in which

even a most unpopular measure could be forced through Parliament; well might Cromwell conclude the letter in which he describes the session, 'after seventeen weeks of discussion we have done as our predecessors have been wont to do, that is to say as well as we might, and have left off where we began[1].' I do not think that any of the fourteenth-century Parliaments would have stood this; Wolsey can have been no believer in Parliaments, for this is the only one that was held whilst he was chancellor.

I pass on to the Long Parliament of 1529–1536, of the early doings of which, thanks to the chronicle of Hall and the reports of the Imperial ambassador, we know more minute detail than we do of any preceding session. Cromwell's defence of Wolsey in the first session, which prevented the passing of the bill of attainder in the House of Commons, is a fact which rests on historical testimony too good to be rejected; but the circumstances in which it took place are obscure; there can be little doubt that Henry acquiesced in, perhaps prompted the rejection; and it is quite certain that to have forced it through Parliament would have made a serious addition to his already awkward complications.

There were two other pieces of debateable policy in the short session of 1529: the remittal of the loans of 1523–8, and the opening of the attack on the minor privileges of the clergy. The Convocation passed the bill of remittal, and it was likewise read three times by the Lords; the Commons however were sorely perplexed by it; hitherto the royal receipt and promise to repay had been regarded as good security; new debts had been incurred on the strength of it and men had left it to their children as an adequate and safe provision. Now

---

[1] Letters and Papers of Henry VIII, ed. Brewer, Vol. III, Part ii, p. 1350. In lack of references to this portion of the lecture, I may refer to Appendix IV to the Report of the Ecclesiastical Courts Commission, 1883.

it was proposed to deprive pay, receipts and bonds, of all validity; the Commons refused to pass the bill without conditions, and the only condition to be got was a general pardon, out of which the penalties for praemunire, which had been so fatal to Wolsey, were omitted: the nominal victory was with the Commons, the substantial fruits were with the king, who saw his way to the great exaction from the clergy obtained in the next session.

The other contest involves more interest and more questions. Already Henry was beginning to feel his way against the clergy; the clergy themselves were discussing points of reform, and these points were even hinted at in the opening speech of the Chancellor More. The points raised seem to us, in the light of the later history, only small points; the expenses of probate and mortuaries, non-residence and pluralities, and the interference of the clergy as farmers and tanners with the trade of the laity. But unfortunately they were points that divided the ecclesiastical interest: the bishops were willing to enforce discipline on the lower clergy; the lower clergy were willing to reduce the profits of probate which went to the officials of the bishops; but the lower clergy would defend their trade and their benefices, and the bishops could not allow the profits of their courts to be touched. Both would have agreed in strong measures against heresy; and both agreed in regarding the discussion of these things in Parliament as an attack, as indeed they were, on the Church itself. Bishop Fisher, in his apprehension, proclaimed that lack of faith ruins the country in which it prevails, as it was ruining Bohemia. This imputation roused the spirit of the faithful Commons; the Speaker Audley and thirty other members were sent to complain to the king, and the bishop had to explain that he meant only to refer to Bohemia. Archbishop Warham and six other bishops attesting this apology, the king accepted the excuse and reported it to the Commons. Fanning the flame of dissension, he then suggested that the Commons should pass the two most obnoxious bills, strike a blow at the bishops by the bill on probate, and at the parochial clergy by the bill against mortuaries. This was done. The other points, non-residence, pluralities, and trading, were decided likewise: the lords spiritual by their majority in the upper house rejected the bills; the Commons insisted on pressing them; the king suggested a conference, in Star Chamber, of eight members from each house; the lay lords on the committee voted with the Commons, and by this contrivance the bills were passed. This little trick shows that it was not by force alone that the Parliament was manipulated to pass the king's bills. More as chancellor must, in this business, as in 1523, when he was Speaker, have acted as the king's agent, but the burden was already too heavy for his back.

If I were now tracing the progress of the Reformation, I might say more on the antagonism thus established between the Clergy and the Commons; it is enough however to observe that Henry had clearly got a Parliament on which he could depend; and that every point he now gained became a fresh vantage-ground from which he could grasp at more.

In 1530 there was no parliamentary session; the king and his agents were busily collecting opinions about the divorce; and the constitutional struggle begins again in 1531. Not even now did the king think matters ripe for discussion of the divorce in Parliament; and, in the council which was held preparatory to the session, it was determined that the queen's business should not be brought forward; the chief thing proposed was the exaction of money from the clergy under the threat of praemunire. The Duke of Norfolk, who was to all intents and purposes the prime minister, was negotiating with the emperor, and is said to have sworn that nothing in that Parliament should be done against

Katharine; Anne Boleyn and her father were drawing to the Protestants, but their time was not yet come. All the important business was done in Convocation. Parliament, as the imperial envoy remarked, was employed on nothing more serious than cross-bows and hand-guns. But in the Convocation matters were important indeed; the king was the only person who had the skill to understand, or the will to define, the doctrine of praemunire, and it was not by praemunire alone that he could manipulate the clergy; he tried to tamper with Warham, threatened intrigue with the German Protestants, or the restraint of mortmain, or the appointment of a council of heresy which would take that question out of the hands of Convocation, and other things which, vague threats at first, became realities of oppression as soon as they were familiarized to his mind. By threats and blandishments he obtained the Recognition of his headship of the Church, and the payment of £100,000. It was not done all at once; the clergy kicked against the pricks very hard: they offered 160,000 ducats, the king insisted on 400,000; the papal nuncio was pressed into the service, and even forced his way into the Lower House of Convocation: but the Clergy, following the example of the Commons of 1523, stopped their ears, and bade him negotiate in the right way through the archbishop: as yet there was no breach with Clement VII, and in the delay of the divorce both parties were for the moment at peace. At last the clergy granted the king's terms; but they did not like the form of Recognition, and in the end it was passed by an evasion for which Warham must answer. He proposed the form suggested by Lord Rochford, and, in putting it to the vote, added, 'qui tacet consentire videtur.' The clergy by an anticipation of Jesuitic subterfuge, and by a practical Irish Bull, cried out, 'Itaque tacemus omnes[1].' By this levity the great act was

[1] Feb. 11, 1531. Wilkins, Concilia, iii. 725.

consummated, which was to be the fulcrum for the whole
ecclesiastical policy of the future ; the Recognition was understood to be passed unanimously.

But not even here were matters completely arranged ; the
king now haggled about the praemunire ; the clergy threatened
to withdraw their promise to pay unless this mysterious monster were defined as well as remitted.   It ended however as I
have said ; the clergy voted the money and the king promised
the pardon.   But the pardon must be secured by the confirmation of Parliament ; and, when the bill came before the
Commons, they soon saw that it did not comprise the laity,
and refused to pass it.   The king's agents urged that this
opposition would damage the clergy and not benefit the
Commons ; that the king could not be compelled to pardon,
and that, without their consent, he could pass the pardon under
the great seal.   The Speaker and a committee attended
the king, and getting no other answer, went away sorrowing
and declaring that Cromwell had betrayed their proceedings
to Henry.   Then there was some bitter talking about the
exactions and the remittal of the loan ; but at last the king
issued the pardon, and the Commons, knowing that something would be taken for the boon, sulkily accepted it.

The next day the chancellor laid before them the documents touching the divorce, and the Commons were enlightened by speeches on the subject from the Bishops of
London and Bath.   But they remained sulky ; whether it
was that the king was not prepared to go further, or that
the attitude of Parliament, still faithful to the queen and in-
disposed to quarrel with the pope, dismayed him, there the
matter stayed, and the Commons were ordered to carry down
to their constituencies the information laid before them.   So
the session ended, and the Convocation, which had engaged
on the reform of grammar schools and the publishing of a
uniform Latin grammar, in addition to the restoration of

discipline and the translation of the Scriptures, was prorogued at the same time. The same measures which passed
the Canterbury Convocation were likewise adopted at York;
that is the clergy remitted the loans, paid £18,840 for the
pardon, and acknowledged the supremacy. Bishop Tunstall
however made a protest against the form of Recognition,
and proposed that for fear of misinterpretation by heretics,
the words *in temporalibus post Christum* should be inserted;
but this had only the effect of offending the king, who
directed that the bishop's house at Auckland should be
searched for heretical books; and also, according to Chapuys,
omitted to summon him to the next session of Parliament.

I go on now to that third session of the Long Parliament;
it opened on the 22nd of January 1532. Its events are extremely important, and fortunately are illustrated fairly well
by contemporary evidence. It was understood, says the imperial resident, to have been called for two purposes, money
and the divorce. The king wanted 2,000,000 ducats;
Rochford and Anne Boleyn were apparently given *carte
blanche* as to their dealing with the clergy for the divorce;
Henry, however, keeping watch, and ready to make the most
of an opportunity. The clergy were now having their eyes
opened; a bold attempt made by the Boleyns to 'suborn,'
that is, I suppose, to bribe Archbishop Warham, at last
shook the old man's faith in the stability of things. Norfolk
and Rochford, who were now acting together, proposed that
matrimonial causes should be declared a matter of temporal
jurisdiction. Warham, as an old lawyer, protested in a formal
document against all legislation which might be enacted
against ecclesiastical or papal power. This protest seems
to have had the effect of deterring any further procedure on
the divorce itself during the archbishop's life, but to have
provoked the king to more trenchant action against the

constitutional arrangements which Warham and his party now saw to be assailed.

The history of the session falls into two sections, divided by a short recess at Easter for about a fortnight. The first portion was devoted to the question of supplies, the second to that of Church reform: Convocation sat during the whole time. The measures proposed by the king with a view to increase the royal revenue were fair enough, and were, as it seems to me, in strict analogy with the policy of his greatest ancestor, Edward I. The first was the bill for the withdrawal of Annates from the pope; a measure intended to secure for the king the profits and firstfruits on all appointments to bishoprics; the act allowed the king to compound with the pope for all reasonable payments, and also provided for the confirmation and consecration of bishops without recourse to Rome. As a companion to this measure the king introduced bills of the same purport affecting the laity; just as on the transmission of ecclesiastical property the firstfruits went to Rome, so, on the transmission of lay property in land, by the operation of the doctrine of wills and uses, the king lost his reliefs and primer seisins; accordingly he proposed two measures, or one measure with double purpose,—a statute of wills, allowing a man to devise half his land by will, provided the other half, left to the heir, secured the king in his feudal rights; and a statute of uses, intended to take the force out of the old practice of feoffment to uses. Both these statutes ultimately passed in a modified form, the Statute of Uses in 1536 and the Statute of Wills in 1540. By that time it would seem it was discovered that they might be accepted as boons, now they were vehemently objected to, and the opposition they excited threw the Commons for the moment on the side of the pope, and into opposition to the Annates Bill. The latter bill was presented to the Commons as a measure of their own: the king protested and pretended, sending Norfolk to assure the imperial ambassador that the Commons had called for it; that he himself was borne on and overpowered by their zeal for reform; the prelates had refused their consent, but the people willed to have it; at last by the 19th of March, after two personal visitations, the king forced it through the Lords; all the bishops and two abbots voted against it; of the lay peers only one lord, Arundel, had the courage to support them; thirty lay lords formed a majority for the bill and it went down to the Commons. There also the king's presence was required; in the house the noes had it. Then Henry insisted on a division; a taking of single votes which, from some other illustrations which it would be tedious now to refer to, we infer to have been as yet an exceptional method of ascertaining the sense of the house. Partly by promising that there should be no more acts against the pope, partly by the terror of his majestic eyes, he obtained a majority; men could not comfortably vote in the presence of the definer of all praemunires[1]. This much was accomplished before the Easter adjournment; the Statutes of Wills and Uses passed the Lords but were rejected by the Commons, and the king did not press them at the time.

The question of the Annates had opened his eyes to his power of obtaining further concessions. In the beginning of March, by the contrivance of Rochford, the Parliament was discussing the possibility of transferring to the king all the power and authority of the archbishops and bishops: the divorce question was simmering in both houses; and Warham had plucked up spirit to speak up for the queen. This was not to be endured. Accordingly the old antagonism of the Commons to the spiritual courts was utilized, and an address drawn up by the king's secretaries was put in their hands to be delivered to the king as the prayer of the Commons. Audley, as Speaker, and a number of his

[1] Letters and Papers, v. 413, 422.

own servile party presented it; it contained a bitter attack on the canon law and ecclesiastical jurisdictions generally, and, in twelve clauses, some of greater and some of less importance, singled out points for reform. The king received it on the 18th of March, and, as soon as Easter was over, it was laid before Convocation for an answer. Both Houses of Convocation discussed it in detail; the Upper House prepared an answer on the points that touched the bishops; the Lower on those touching the parochial clergy: both agreed in demanding a specific statement instead of general charges. The answer was sent to the king about the 27th of April; and the king was of course prepared to find it unsatisfactory.

On the 30th his Majesty sent for the Speaker and showed him the answer, referring it, as a very slender production, to the consideration of that 'grete sorte of wise men to be found in the House of Commons[1].' There were indeed both wise men and foolish in that assembly; and both had the divorce business in their minds. They were again busy on the supplies: Henry wanted money to fortify the border and the coast: they offered a tenth and fifteenth, £28,000; that was not enough; the Statutes of Wills and Uses were again broached and rejected. Independent members went further. Mr. Thomas Temys, M.P. for Westbury, proposed, and found a seconder, that the king should be asked to take back his wife; 'if he would, there would be no danger from the emperor; if he would not, fortification would be useless.' The king could not stand that: he sent for Audley, and through him explained to the Commons what a horrible conscience a man had who married his brother's wife. The question of the divorce was not before them: if they would mind their own business he would help them against the clergy; if not, not.

Whilst this was going on in Parliament, Convocation was

[1] Hall's Chronicle, p. 788.

asked for a grant: the clergy discussed the subject, and determined to send to the king a supplication for help. They were in a strait; the Commons were insisting on severer measures against heresy, and still were impugning the laws and courts, by which only heresy could be extirpated. Rochford and Cromwell were intriguing with the heretics; Henry himself, pretending to stand aloof, was watching every point of vantage. But they got little comfort: in answer to their supplication, the king sent down to them in a bill the three points of submission, the abdication of the right to legislate in Convocation, the consent to the reform of ecclesiastical law, and the sufferance of existing canons only under the king's approval. The day after this bill was sent to the clergy, Henry, still intent on exciting the Commons against them, summoned Audley and his friends, and put before him the oath taken by the prelates to the pope on appointment; an oath which he declared incompatible with their allegiance to himself. That was something for the Commons to consider: the Lords were consulted on the points which had been laid before Convocation. The imperial ambassador was on the watch for results: the king was proposing, he heard, to abolish synods and synodal legislation, and to take into his own hands all coercive jurisdiction on heresy; the bishops might have the souls of the sinners, he would have their bodies; it was a strange thing; priests would be of less account than shoemakers, who at least might regulate their own trade. The Venetian ambassador foresaw a new praemunire, and fixed the amount of money that the king would take, 400,000 crowns from the clergy, a vote of a fifteenth, and a year's income as succession duty. Evidently a storm was rising. The royal propositions were, however, on the 15th of May, accepted by Convocation, after brisk discussion and several significant divisions. In the House of Lords the chancellor and the bishops opposed them, and prevented them from becoming law as yet. The great Lion was nearer a defeat than he had ever been before: and, when More resigned the great seal, which he did on the day that the Submission was presented, the king became very sulky. On the day of prorogation he would not show himself: as for the grant of money, the fifteenth, he did not care about it; he would neither accept nor refuse, and the clergy would not now grant more; as a matter of fact no subsidy was granted. But the clergy were brought to their knees, and the king lost his wisest and most faithful adviser. The session ended on the 14th of May: Convocation was prorogued on the 15th, and on the 16th More resigned. His successor was the Speaker Audley; a change indeed.

After losing More, Henry seems to have acted more and more on the counsels of the Boleyns; and circumstances rapidly accelerated the course of events. Gardiner, who was probably his near kinsman and who certainly had helped him in every way until now, left the court, and was in disgrace for refusing to preach in favour of the divorce. Warham's death, in the following August, removed the last of the old party whose advice had any chance of being listened to. A visit to Francis I in the next month seems to have determined the king to cut the knot by peremptory action. Immediately on his return he is said to have married Anne Boleyn. As each old friend dropped off Cromwell rose a step, and the royal determination increased. Cranmer was designated for the primacy; Audley from being Lord Keeper was raised to the Chancellorship; the Parliament, which had been prorogued to November, was adjourned to January, and in January both Houses and Convocation met.

For the parliamentary session of 1533 we have no journals, and the reports of the Venetian ambassador do not supply the gap caused by the imperfect continuation of the Austrian dispatches. Two subjects, however, alone occupied both the secular and the ecclesiastical assemblies : the divorce and the abolition of appeals to Rome. In Parliament the divorce business proceeded slowly; the king visited it more than once with a view to expediting that, and the provision of an army against the Scots; but the month of February passed over without any real business being done. At last Henry resumed the plan by which he had succeeded in 1532, putting the initiation of his own measures in the mouth of a private member of the Commons; on the 15th of March a London member was found to propose that the judges of the divorce should be appointed in England. Immediately after this Cranmer was consecrated, and he undertook to deal with Convocation. In Convocation the two questions on which the divorce turned were debated in the manner of University disputations; the theologians disputed as to the dispensability of a marriage with a brother's widow, the canonists on the facts of Arthur's marriage with Katharine : there were formal divisions, but the conclusion was foregone, the Bishop of Rochester was the only steady opponent. In the same way the York Convocation was dealt with by Archbishop Lee.

Notwithstanding the acquiescence of Convocation, the Commons as late as April 10 were still reluctant. We are told that one of the members for London offered to raise £200,000 if the king would refer the question of the divorce to a general council. But in vain. The servility of Cranmer and Lee had provided a short and easy method; on the 23rd of May, at Dunstable, Cranmer, on the strength of the opinions thus obtained, pronounced in favour of the divorce and the Boleyn marriage; and on the 1st of June Anne Boleyn was crowned; Parliament having adjourned from April 12 to June 7.

The other great act of the year was the Statute of Appeals, of the discussion of which we have few data. On the 14th of

March, according to Chapuys, it was proposed in Parliament to make a statute declaring that the pope has no authority in this kingdom ; the king was set upon it and was arranging all his policy to that end.   On the 30th it is mentioned in the Venetian dispatches as being then pushed in Convocation. The next day the imperial envoy announces that the Convocation has passed the Divorce Bill, but the House of Commons has refused to pass the Statute of Appeals, mainly on the ground that, if the pope were offended, he might injure the wool trade.   But before the 10th of April he has to record that the opposition has given way before the king's threat to enforce the penalties of praemunire against the laity. A week later he reports that he has remonstrated with Henry and put him in a rage.   Yet raging, still he was not without hope ; he had sent to tell the pope that if, even now, he would send a dispensation for the second marriage, he would undo all that, in his wish to please his people, he had done against Rome.   It is no doubt an exaggeration of Chapuys when he says that the nation would have welcomed the emperor as a deliverer, but there can be no reason to question his statements as to the sincerity of the opposition. The work of the year ended there ; no business session was again attempted ; the question of supplies, which had been brought forward in February, dropped and no grant was made.

The next session, that of January 1534, was a heavy one : we have the Lords' Journals, but very scanty details about Convocation, which is unfortunate as the most important business was ecclesiastical.   We know, however, from the Lords' Journals, that the clerical assembly sat on regular days, every Friday and sometimes on Tuesdays, the lords adjourning on those days for the convenience of the prelates, and on the Wednesdays for the session of Star Chamber. The attendance of prelates in the House of Lords was very scanty, and they were generally outnumbered two to one by the lay lords: there were discussions and differences of opinion between the Lords and Commons; a Bill on the consecration of bishops sent up from the Commons was rejected by the Lords, and a new Bill drawn by the Lords was passed by the Commons. The Submission Bill or second Statute of Appeals was presented by the Commons in a body on the 27th of March, and passed on the 30th. In Convocation, on the 31st, the question that the pope has no more power than any other bishop was determined; this being probably regarded as their formal judgement on more than one of the statutes which had passed the Commons. We look in vain for any more determined or resolute action on either side. And again the session passes without a money grant. A second session was held in November mainly for this purpose; and a second meeting of Convocation, in which the king was petitioned to expedite the authoritative translation of the Bible. I enumerated I think in the last lecture the important acts of these sessions.

There was no session in 1535. The Long Parliament came to an end in 1536. Of its last session we have no definite details, simply the Acts which it passed: the Journals of Convocation deal only with the question of the subsidy. Henry had, we may presume, quelled all opposition in Parliament; and, if contemporary annotators had been minded to preserve particulars, they were lost in the grand and tragic interest of public events[1]. The dissolution of the monasteries,

---

[1] Here is a trace of Henry's management: 'On Saterdaye in the ymbre weke the Kyngis Grace came in amonge the burgesis of the parliament, and delyvered to them a bylle, and bade theym loke upon it, and waye it in conscience, for he wold nott, he saide, have them passe over it, nor over any other thynge because his Grace gevith in the bill, but they to see yf it be for a comyn wele to his subjectis and have an eye thederwarde, and on Wedynsday next he will be there agaiyne to here their mynde.' Excerpta Historica, p. 292.

the death of Queen Katharine, the awful tragedy that closed
the career of the Boleyns, the Pilgrimage of Grace, and
mutterings of rebellion in north and south, fill the pages
of the annalists.

For the second Parliament of 1536, that newly elected
after the fall of Anne Boleyn, we have much material: it sat
for six weeks, and has left full journals, as has Convocation
also. There is no reaction traceable in either. If the
Seymours inherited the influence of the Boleyns, they were
even more zealous for change and plunder than their predecessors: but the real hero of the hour is Cromwell, doing
his master's work with zeal. Cromwell, as the king's vicegerent, claims for himself or his deputy the presidency
of Convocation, and by his presence there invests the
proceedings of that body with an importance that Cranmer
could not have given. All that he proposes in the way of
change is passed without show of division; and, even in the
direction of doctrinal reform, he carries things as far as
the king allowed. The legislation in Parliament likewise
is mainly ecclesiastical; and the journals record nothing but
assents.

I must pass on very rapidly now. The session of 1539,
in which the dissolution of the greater monasteries was
accomplished and the Bill of Six Articles passed, was
likewise held under the predominating power of Cromwell,
who had, however, learned to sink his Protestant tendencies
before his master's stern orthodoxy. Convocation again
worked with the Parliament, and there are traces also that
the clergy attended under the praemunientes clause; but the
new prelates of Henry's nomination now outnumbered the
old, and in both assemblies the abbots and priors knew that
they appeared for the last time.

Yet abject as was the condition of a Parliament which
could pass the Proclamation Act, there were still two parties

at work in it. The secret history of the Six Articles, when it is known, will show that Cromwell's influence was already shaken. The king proposes to abolish the diversities of religion; Cromwell, the two archbishops, and six bishops, are named as a committee on the 5th of May. On the 16th the Duke of Norfolk announces that the committee cannot agree, and proposes that the Six Articles be discussed in Parliament. After some delay two committees are, on the 30th, appointed to draw up alternative schemes for the king's approval on the following Sunday; the king approves apparently that which is subsequently chosen. It goes down in Cromwell's hand to the Convocation on June 2, and is accepted there. Between June 7 and June 16 it passes the Lords, and the Commons also adopt it before the 28th, on which day the session ends. Of the other important acts of the session that which empowered the king to create new sees was passed through the whole of its stages in both Houses in one day: the Proclamation Act, and another for the rehabilitation of the religious, were, on the other hand, rejected by the Commons, redrawn, and passed after several days' discussion.

I must now pass very briefly over the incidents of the remaining Parliaments. In that of 1540 the king's matrimonial relations with Anne of Cleves were, by petition of Parliament, referred to and discussed in the Convocations: the abbots finally disappeared from Parliament; the House of Lords agreed that Mondays, Wednesdays, and Fridays should be devoted, by the Royal Commissioners appointed for the purpose, to the preparation of measures of religious reform. Bishop Tunstall is bold enough to draw up a protest against the subsidy, but this is the only trace of opposition. Cromwell's fall was sudden and without sympathy; the Bill of Attainder for treason passed the House of Lords without an opposing vote; the Commons added attaint for heresy as well as for treason; not a voice seems to have been raised for him. Nay, in the House of Lords not a single measure of the king's was opposed at all, and it is left on record in the most unsentimental of all registers, the Journals of the Lords, that not a single division occurred during the whole session[1]. In 1542, in the same way, no protest is made against the sacrifice of Catharine Howard. But the king is not satisfied with silent acquiescence; he does not hesitate to urge both houses to work harder at that and other public business; again we find Tunstall protesting alone against some minor measure: the most remarkable event, from our point of view, is the withdrawal from the House of Lords, at the request of Convocation, of a bill allowing married men to act as ecclesiastical judges[2]; a measure which, though withdrawn now, became law in 1545. The Convocation itself was very busy in the matter of the translation of the Bible and Scriptural formulae of prayer and belief. The same work occupied the session of 1543, in which we find Lord Mountjoy voting by himself against the amplification of the Proclamation Act; and four bishops opposing the Bill for Collectors and Receivers. Clearly the independent spirit has nearly evaporated. The ecclesiastical bills pass without a protest, but the Lords are not reduced so low as they were in 1540. The remaining sessions, those of 1544, 1545, and 1546, furnish nothing that illustrates our subject: the journals record no opposition or protest; the king has his own way in everything.

Time would fail me if I were to attempt to go into the minor parliamentary cases of privilege, or to clothe or colour the dry facts that I have been retailing to you; or I might describe how, when the Duke of Suffolk opened Parliament, all the members, every time the king's name occurred, bowed

---

[1] Journals, July 24.　　　　[2] Wilkins, Concilia, iii. 862.

until their heads all but touched the ground; or how Henry himself closed the session of 1545 with a sermon on charity; how in 1515 Parliament and Convocation were so comfortably at one that Taylor, the clerk of the Parliament, was prolocutor of the Lower House of Canterbury: or how ecstatically Hare and Moyle praised the beauty of their royal master; or how, when he brought the news of the king's death, the rough old Wriothesley could not speak for tears: or how weary the clerk of the Parliament was of Audley's speeches, which took such a long time to deliver, and so much more to write out and read.

All our authorities, even the dry journals themselves, furnish matters of amusement to inquiring minds. But time has failed me already, and I must wind up with a few words of sentiment.

I think, that after what I have said, you will allow me to say that I have grounds for believing that Henry VIII was the master, and in no sense the minister, of his people: that, where he carried their goodwill with him, it was by forcing not by anticipating or even educating it. I am obliged altogether to reject the notion that he was the interpreter in any sense of the wishes of his people: the utmost that he did in this direction was to manipulate and utilize their prejudices to his own purposes. I allow fully the truth of the theory that one great principle of his policy was to obtain for his measures, for all his measures, the acquiescence of his people, and thus to invest them with a safe, irrefragable authority; but I must add that he knew how to turn opposition into acquiescence, or to take acquiescence for granted. Further, I am convinced, as I said in the last lecture, that he was his own chief, I might say sole, counsellor, not one of his other advisers, after the fall of Wolsey, succeeding in becoming anything more than the instrument of a grand, imperious, ever-encroaching will.

And now let me confess that I do not think so badly of Henry VIII as the received views of either his advocates or his enemies would suggest. The unhappy, most unhappy history of his wives, has brought upon him an amount of moral hatred which is excessive. Nine kings out of any ten whom you may pick out of the list would have saved their character for humanity by simple self-indulgence. No absolutely profligate king could have got into the miserable abyss in which we find Henry VIII struggling during the latter half of his reign. I do not believe that he was abnormally profligate: in this region of morality he was not better perhaps than Charles V, but he was much better than Francis I, and Philip II, and Henry IV. But he was cruelly, royally vindictive; there was in him an ever-increasing, ever-encroaching self-will, ever grasping and grasping more and more of power: a self-will guided by a high intellect, and that sort of sincerity which arises from a thorough belief in himself. I am not prepared to deny that deep, cunning, unscrupulous men, like Cromwell, traded on their knowledge of his character; but not one of those who tried to work their own ends through Henry escaped the doom to which false friends and open foes alike found their way.

Well, you say, you would not wish to see him worse cursed. I do not condemn him. God forbid, in whose hand are the hearts of kings. I do not believe him to have been a monster of lust and blood, as so many of the Roman Catholic writers regard him. I cannot accept at all the picture which Mr. Froude has drawn. I think that even Lord Herbert's estimate of him is deficient in the perception of his surpassing self-wilfulness. I do not attempt to pourtray him after my own idea; but I seem to see in him a grand gross figure, very far removed from ordinary human sympathies, self-engrossed, self-confident, self-willed; unscrupulous in act, violent and crafty, but justifying to himself, by his belief in himself, both unscrupulousness, violence, and craft. A man who regarded himself as the highest justice, and who looked on mercy as a mere human weakness. And with all this, as needs must have been, a very unhappy man, wretched in his family, wretched in his friends, wretched in his servants, most wretched in his loneliness: that awful loneliness in which a king lives, and which the worst as well as the best of despots realizes. Have I drawn the outline of a monster? Well, perhaps; but not the popular notion of this particular portent. A strong, high-spirited, ruthless, disappointed, solitary creature; a thing to hate, or to pity, or to smile at, or to shudder at, or to wonder at, but not to judge.

NOTE ON

LECTURES XIII AND XIV

THE following two lectures, with the exception of two or three passages where I am conscious that I overstated my own views, are printed as they were delivered and as they appeared in the earlier editions of this volume. They contain what at the time I wrote them seemed to me to be a true and somewhat elementary treatment of the subject with which they are concerned. But they are obviously susceptible of a good deal of criticism and correction. I would refer my readers for this purpose to Professor Maitland's recent work on the *Canon Law*. I have so great respect for his knowledge, critical insight, and fairness, that I would gladly submit to any amount of adjustment of facts and authorities that he might prescribe to me.

There is however a discrepancy between his general conclusions on the authority which the Canon Law of Rome had in England before the Reformation and the theory which is more than once stated by me in these lectures and elsewhere. The one view concludes that the Canon Law of Rome as held in England was regarded not only with respect but as absolutely binding. The other, which is more or less the opinion that has been held by English jurists, is that the authority given to the Corpus Juris Canonici in practice was rather of the nature of scientific jurisprudence than of recognized, accepted and enacted law. The difference is no doubt real, although the immediate result of the divergence of view is not of so great importance as it might in the light of later controversy be made to appear.

I have thought and intended to maintain my belief that the Corpus Juris Canonici in its various expansions affected the law and process of the English courts, which had been framed before the Decretum was published, not as statute law, but rather as case law, or precedents, or as in a sense modifying or expounding the common law of the Church; determining the mind of the judge rather than pronouncing indisputable or immediately applicable conclusions. In this I may have been quite wrong: if so I would have these lectures read with that amount and measure of reserve. On the other hand I never doubted that within its own area of applicability the Roman Canon Law did practically govern the ecclesiastical courts wherever it was not contrariant to the common law, nor overruled by the use of prohibitions, or thrown out of use by the protests of parliaments or such statutes as those of Praemunire and Provisors. That a code liable to be overruled in such ways should be regarded as having a vitality and force analogous to that of the national law in temporal matters—that is, that the Corpus Juris stood, in the strict ecclesiastical courts, on the same level as the Statute Book in the temporal courts, I could not see; and knowing that what authority it had it owed rather to tacit assumption than to formal and constitutional acceptance by Church or State, I offered my explanation as sufficient. The question does not affect the fact, but the nature of the authority.

For as to the practical working and influence of the Corpus Juris, and as to its authority, as utilized in the work of John of Athon and Lyndwood, I had no doubt, nor as to the importance of the Reformation policy which forbade the study of it, which it intended to supersede and replace by something better.

It would however be impossible by annotation ever so careful to eliminate this view from these lectures, and I leave them accordingly to the corrections of competent authority, gladly submitting to be set right. As to the further issues from this divergence of view, which have been in opposite quarters regarded as bearing for the moment on some of the ritual and judicial questions of the controversies of the day, and even on the essential identity of a National Church, I can only add that, even more obviously, it would be out of place to consider them here. If the Corpus Juris is the Universal Law of the Universal Church, *cadit quaestio*—and a good deal besides.

XIII

THE HISTORY OF THE CANON LAW IN ENGLAND

(April 19, 1882.)

IT requires no small amount of moral courage to approach a subject of legal history without being either a lawyer or a philosopher. A lawyer, no doubt, would make short work of it, and pronounce a definitive judgement, without misgiving, on any subject, historical or other, human or divine, on which he had evidence before him; and a philosopher would systematize to his own satisfaction any accumulation of details that could possibly be referred to the categories of cause and effect. The student of history has not, *ex officio*, any such privilege of infallibility; the highest point to which he can rise is the entire conviction of his own ignorance and incapacity before the vast material of his investigation; the highest approach to infallibility is the willingness to learn and correct his own mistakes. If he wishes to learn something of a subject, his best policy is to write a book upon it, or to deliver two public statutory lectures. Here then you have my motive; wanting to know something of the history of Canonical Jurisprudence, I undertake to lecture upon it. I shall be wiser, that is, more convinced of my own ignorance, before I have done.

If I were a philosopher I should begin thus: The legal history of a nation or institution must be the history of the successive stages by which it develops or adopts laws, according to the stages of its social, or moral, or political, or religious development; or thus: As a nation develops in civilization, or foreign policy, or in specialized ambitions, or in consciousness of nationality, or in peculiar constitutional identity, it has to develop new branches or systems of law, or to borrow them ready-made from nations whose polity is in advance of its own, who have made themselves representative nations in the particular branch of sociology in which it desires to regulate itself. Hence, in England, on the original superstructure of ancient popular law is superinduced, in the age of the Conquest, the *jus honorarium* of the royal courts; and, when the royal courts have become the courts of common law, on their rigour is superinduced the moderating influence of Equity and Appeal: on the conversion of the nation to Christianity a religious discipline is a necessity, and on that religious discipline, as the framework of the Church is built up, there is based a canonical jurisprudence; if the nation is in close communication with foreign churches or a great Catholic religion, it naturally adopts, from them or it, its religious legislation; if not in such close intercourse, it develops a system of its own, and, when the intercourse becomes closer, modifies its own until it is more or less in harmony with that of the nations round it, always retaining more or less of its own home growth. Or again, still as the philosopher, I might say: Religion, Law and Morality cover the area of human action with rules and sanctions, and, with different origins, motives, and machinery, regulate regions of common energy, a number of acts that fall within reach of each or all. The fact that they spring from different sources necessitates the formation of distinct systems; the fact that they cover the same ground accounts for the possibility of conflicting operation; the fact that, whilst they overlap one another, their proper areas nowhere coincide, necessitates some sort of definition and limitation of the scope and system of each, which definition and limitation must be supplied either by a concordat between them or by the subordination of one to the other. And once more : within the region of religious activity itself there are provinces which demand varying degrees of distinctness in definition and graduation of discipline ; there are matters of doctrine, of discipline proper, of property and of judicature ; there are legislation, jurisdiction, administration ; there are functions for the theologian, the casuist, the canonist, and the civilian ; questions of doctrine for the theologian, of morals for the casuist, of discipline for the canonist, of procedure for the civil lawyer.

Well, philosophical or not, these considerations seem to give us a clue to the method of our investigation, and suggest a division into two heads : first, the tracing of the growth of the ecclesiastical law, including both the material and the scientific study ; and secondly, the history of its working in competition with and in general relations to the other systems of law. In such a cursory attempt to examine these heads as is possible in such a lecture as this, it is necessary to limit the field of survey as much as possible. I shall therefore restrict myself chiefly to the history of ecclesiastical jurisprudence in England, taking liberty, where it is necessary, to go beyond, but not attempting any general treatment. I have, you will observe, coupled together four topics under two heads ; I propose to take the two heads separately, but to discuss the two topics that fall under each conjointly.

The first head is the growth of ecclesiastical law, and its two branches are the materials and the study. The materials arrange themselves thus : the New Testament contains not only all doctrine necessary to salvation, but all necessary moral teaching, and as much social teaching as was needed for the age in which it was propounded, and for the society which in the first instance was embodied under apostolic government. But in the very nature of things, and you must here recollect that I am trying to look at the subject rather as a philosopher than as a divine, Christianity, as a growing religion, was certain to require an expansion, in expanding circumstances, of the principles which were clearly enough stated in the Gospel, but the application of which had to be regulated by some other process than the will of the individual. The moral teaching had to be expanded authoritatively, the dogmatic teaching had to be fenced by definitions, the administrative machinery had to be framed with some attempt at uniformity, so that, whilst the Christian society remained a simple voluntary society with no power of enforcing its own precepts by material sanctions, it should have a common jurisprudence recognized by the conscience of its members and by their general consent. Hence from the days of the apostles there were councils, and canons, and constitutions, and books of discipline ; at first the canons, councils, and books of discipline covered all the ground of which I have spoken—doctrine, discipline, and administration, although some councils may be more famous for their decisions on one point than on another. Not perhaps to speak of the Apostolic Constitutions, take the council of Nicaea for an example, and remember that we owe to it not only a formulated creed, but directions about consecration of bishops and ordination of priests, and likewise rules for the treatment of the lapsed and apostates, and the prohibition of usury. The legislation of Constantine added a new element which worked itself into all these three ; giving a coercive and material force to rules which had been hitherto matters of conscience and consensus ; the Church was empowered to enforce her doctrinal decisions, her rules of discipline, and her frame of administration ; and that so completely that from this date the ecclesiastical administration in Christian countries under the empire became so wedded to the secular administration as to be at times almost indistinguishable from it except on close investigation. From this date then

our materials begin to sort themselves : the doctrinal definitions are embodied in the Creeds, and need not be pursued
further than the fourth, or, at the outside, the sixth general
council : but the canons of discipline and administration are
worked into great detail for a long period and in many
countries.   And here I must take a new point : the coercive
authority given to the Churches in matters of morals becomes
henceforth a branch of jurisdiction, but there still remain
branches of moral discipline which depend on voluntary
obedience, in which a powerful offender, or a man who does
not choose to confess, may defy law and order.   For the
latter were invented what may be called manuals of casuistry,
the Penitentials ; for the jurisdiction proper there remained
the canons of the councils, now possessing cogent authority,
and the laws of the empire, now framed on a strict conformity
between Church and State.

Here then we reach the historical materials on which is
based the later canon law ; and almost at the same time the
date at which the conversion of England began.   In the
middle of the sixth century Dionysius Exiguus, a Roman
abbot, compiled the collection of canons which was the germ
and model of all later collections.   Nearly at the same time,
both in the Eastern Church under John the Faster, and in
the extreme West under the Irish and other Celtic missionaries, began the compilation of Penitentials ; and in the
same century the emperor Justinian completed the great body
of the civil law.   Thus you get the three conjoint systems
of jurisprudence : not distinct in fact from each other ; overlapping everywhere, and even containing much common
matter, but distinct in basis.   Take the Penitential first :
that was in reality a list of sins and their penances ; sins so
ticketed and valued as to please even the most abstract
philosopher ; permutated and combined to mathematical pre-
cision.   This sort of literature, belonging especially to ages

and nations brought into close contact with heathen abomina-
tions, was very important in the last converted countries
of East and West; Archbishop Theodore of Canterbury,
the Venerable Bede, Egbert of York, and among the Celts
Columbanus, Cummian, Vinniaus, and Adamnan, founded
the penitential system here: from them the Frank and
German Churches adopted their rules, and by and by, when
Anglo-Saxon literature was borrowing from the Continent,
our scholars translated back with interest the developed
systems which their predecessors had sent abroad. These
rules of penance continue to be elaborated in England to
the time of the Conquest; and bear some analogy to the
early laws of the Anglo-Saxon kings, which consist so largely
of definitions of crimes and penalties. It is to be remembered, however, that the Penitentials were private compilations, the authority of which depended on the estimation or
dignity of their authors, and not on any legislative sanction;
but, notwithstanding that, there is sufficient harmony amongst
them to show that they incorporate the rules on which the
episcopal jurisdiction pure and simple generally proceeded;
they were a sort of customary church law for their own
province. But over and above these there were the canons,
or authorized church law; and of these also there was a
series of important collections. I am unable to say how far
the collection of Dionysius Exiguus was received in England
and Ireland at first: but from the beginning of the Church
History of United England, a series of new canons began
to be added to the early collections: Theodore himself added
the decisions of Roman and Byzantine councils to the re-
solutions of his own national synods: a great and important
succession of Anglo-Saxon councils issued canons which were
received with great respect in all the Western Churches, as
we know from St. Boniface's letters and the remains of the
canons themselves. From Ireland likewise proceeded a great

collection of canons—the famous Collatio Hibernica, which,
beginning with the edicts of St. Patrick, went on to embody
the results of ecclesiastical legislation in West and East, and,
by the time of Dunstan, whose copy of it we possess in the
Bodleian, had added by successive accretions all that was
thought worth preserving even in the capitularies of the
Frank kings. The Anglo-Saxon Church possessed no such
comprehensive collection of its own; but abroad the codification of church law proceeded rapidly. I have seen in
the National Library at Paris some invaluable MS. collections
earlier than the date of the forged decretals; and the forged
decretals themselves were probably not the work of one man
or one generation. Not however to tread again this well-
trodden path, pass on to the collectors of genuine or less
suspected canons: of whom the most important is Burchard
of Worms[1]. He, at the beginning of the eleventh century,
got together and arranged systematically all the materials
he could find: borrowing authoritative determinations from
the penitentials, the canons of councils, articles of the civil
law as known to him by the Theodosian code, and the
capitularies of the emperors. A century later, Bishop Ivo of
Chartres produced the Pannormia, a similar collection, improved on that of Burchard by the use of the Digest and
Code of Justinian. Ivo was a contemporary of Henry I of
England, and his date carries us past the Norman Conquest
and the Hildebrandine period.

We must revert to the third element of church law, the
religious laws of the kings. Of these the history in England
is straightforward enough. The Anglo-Saxon sovereigns,
acting in the closest union with their bishops, made eccle-

---

[1] Wasserschleben in the introduction to Regino of Prum (A.D. 915)
de Synodalibus causis, gives references to several of the older compilations; the Vatican collection (ed. Dachery, Spic. i. 510) and that of
Halitgar of Cambrai; but the subject is too large for a note.

siastical laws which clothed the spiritual enactments with
coercive authority, and sometimes seemed to ignore the lines
which separate the two legislatures; such sacred laws of
Alfred, Canute, and Ethelred only affect our subject so far as
they operated on the common law of the country in such
matters as tithes, observance of holy days, and the like; they
do not become by themselves a part of the later church law.
On the Continent there is this difference:—the Theodosian
code had to a great extent won its way over Western Europe;
it enters into the codes of the barbarians, into the law of the
Pays du droit écrit, and into the canon law of France; the
capitularies of Charles the Great and his successors, even to
a greater extent than the Anglo-Saxon laws, combine ecclesiastical with secular dooms; and such of them as are
accepted find their way into the church law. But, over
and above this infiltration, comes the necessary requirement
of developing jurisprudence. The New Testament, the
canons of the General Councils, the Penitentials, the Decretals, did not invent new systems of procedure. Where
the Roman courts existed they became the model of the
Church courts, and where they did not the ecclesiastical
procedure followed the lines of the national and customary
tribunals. Hence, wherever the Theodosian code spread,
it carried the Roman procedure as a part of church administration; where, as in England, only faint scintillae of
the civil law were to be found, the Church courts must
have proceeded on much the same rules as the popular
courts. And this is a matter to be seriously noted as we
reach the critical point of the Norman Conquest. It is
true we know very little about ecclesiastical procedure before
this date, and what we do know is not very clear; we
may however affirm pretty confidently that there was, over
and above the strictly private discipline of the Confessional,
a system of Church judicature with properly designated

judges, and a recognized though not well-defined area of subject-matter in persons and things. To put it very briefly, sacred persons and sacred things, men in orders, monks and nuns, sacred places, churches and churchyards, sacred property, lands, books and the furniture of churches, were under the special protection, and, as protection implied jurisdiction, under the jurisdiction of the bishops, who likewise had authority in matrimonial and like causes. There was a territorial episcopate, and the bishops exercised their judicial powers with the help of archdeacons and deans. But, it would appear, these judicial matters were transacted in the ordinary gemots of the hundred and the shire. Just as the court baron, court leet, and court customary of a manor are held together, so the court spiritual and the hundred or county court were held together; and the proceedings were probably in strict analogy. Just as suretyship was the rule in the hundred court, it was in the bishop's court; so also compurgation and ordeal, the law of witness, and the claim of the mundborh over the person of the litigant. I am not prepared to say that through intercourse with the French Church some portions of the Roman procedure may not already have crept in, but, so far as I can see, I am inclined to the belief that, whilst there was a customary canonical law and a substantially canonical judicature, the character of the procedure was customary and primitive and differed in nothing materially from the lay procedure. The bishop declared the ecclesiastical law as the ealdorman did the secular, the assessors determined the point on which evidence or oaths were to be taken, and the suitors were technically the judges. Of course all this is stated subject to correction: but this I suppose to be the case at the Conquest, and more or less the case until the close of the reign of Henry I, for the changes introduced by the Conqueror were not instantaneous in their effects.

And we come now to the consideration of the effects of the Conquest on this branch of our constitutional system. Here we have to remember two things : first, that the Norman Conquest coincided in time with the Hildebrandine revival; and secondly, that the Conqueror carried through his most important measures of change by the work of Norman ecclesiastics, many of them lawyers rather than theologians; of whom Lanfranc, the representative of a family of Lombard lawyers, was the chief. These two points enable us at once to estimate the importance of the act by which William separated the work of the bishops' courts from the work of the sheriffs' courts, and promised the assistance of the royal or secular justice in carrying into effect the sentences of the episcopal laws.   In the first place he had substituted for the native bishops, used to national law and customary procedure, foreign bishops learned in the Hildebrandine jurisprudence and the Roman procedure; and in the second he had liberated the Church judicature from its association with the popular judicature. But, you will observe, much still remained to be done; for not yet had either Ivo or Gratian collected the Decretum, nor had Irnerius and the Bolognese lawyers begun to lecture on the Pandects; there was not as yet a recognized canon law or a complete civil law procedure.

One immediate result more I will notice, the breaking up of the dioceses into archdeaconries; for up to this time the bishops had done most of their own work.   Dunstan had sat at the south door of Canterbury Cathedral and had administered supreme justice; and one archdeacon, generally in deacon's orders, had been a sufficient eye for the bishop where he could not be personally present.   The Norman bishops wanted more than one eye, and, almost immediately after the Conqueror's legislative separation of the courts, we find that the archidiaconal service is formed on the

plan of that of the sheriffs; the larger dioceses, such as
Lincoln and London, being broken up into many archdeaconries; and the smaller ones, such as Norwich, following
the example. There was a vast increase in ecclesiastical
litigation, great profits and fees to be made out of it; a
craving for canonical jurisprudence and reformed judicature
analogous to the development of constitutional machinery;
and with it the accompanying evils of ill-trained judges and
an ill-understood system of law. This continued to be the
case throughout the twelfth century, and very conspicuously
so in the earlier part of it. The archdeacons were worldly,
mercenary, and unjust; the law was uncertain and unauthori-
tative; the procedure was hurried and irregular. The
evils were not confined to England, although they were here
intensified by the fact of the novelty of the system.

On this condition of things a new light arose in the
middle of the century; the resuscitation of the jurisprudence
of Justinian and the codification of the canons by Gratian.
The one supplied the necessary procedure, the other the
necessary law. I place them together, because their operation
reaches England nearly at the same time; more minutely,
the civil law revival precedes the canon law revival by about
forty years. I must say also that, when I speak of the civil
law as remodelling procedure, I do not mean that it introduced any sudden changes, but that it supplied principles
and precedents for the due development of the older Roman
procedure, which had become as much a matter of custom
as that of the popular jurisprudence was. The real founder
of the mediaeval canon law jurisprudence in England was
Theobald, Archbishop of Canterbury, who was consecrated
in 1139 and ruled the Church until 1161; he is best known
popularly as the rival of Henry of Blois, Bishop of Winchester, and as the patron of Thomas Becket; but his real
importance is irrespective of personal matters. He saw the

mischief which the maladministration of the archdeacons was doing, and instituted a nearer official of greater authority and more direct responsibility.   John of Salisbury, the philosopher and historian, was, as secretary to Archbishop Theobald, the ancestor of the diocesan chancellors, officials and vicar-generals, who begin to execute with more regularity and intelligence the law of the Church.   Henry of Blois when legate had, as we are told, greatly encouraged the practice of appeals; and an immense proportion of John of Salisbury's letters, written in the name of Theobald, are concerned with questions of appeal, on the rights of advowsons, and other branches of clerical discipline.   But that was not all.   In the year 1149 Theobald brought from Lombardy and settled at Oxford as a teacher Master Vacarius, who had given himself to the study of the Code and Digest, and drawn up handbooks of procedure sufficient to settle all the quarrels of the law schools.   Stephen, the reigning king, set himself steadfastly against this new teaching and expelled Vacarius; he had on his side the unintelligent dislike of foreign manners, the prudent conservatism of the elder prelates, and the personal jealousies of his brother Henry, whose opponent in political matters Theobald was. Accordingly the civil law was for the time banished.   In the year 1151 Gratian completed the Decretum, the concordance of the canon laws; and they shortly found their way to England, where however they were scarcely more warmly received than the civil laws had been, but were not directly banished.   It is curious that both Prynne and Selden, not to mention Coke, have confounded the teaching of Vacarius with the attempt to introduce canon law.   It is certain that what Vacarius taught was the Corpus Juris of Justinian; but the two systems are thus closely joined together both in time and in essential character.   And from this time dates in England that extremely close connexion

between the two systems which is recognized in the
'Utriusque juris doctoratus' and in the fact that every
great canonist throughout the Middle Ages in England was
also a great civilian.

The first result perhaps of these novelties, so far as
English law is concerned, was the improvement in legal
education. Although Bologna and Pavia could not be
suffered to come to England, England might go to Bologna ;
and a stream of young archdeacons, at the age at which
in England a boy is articled to an attorney, poured forth
to the Italian law schools. Many and varied were their
experiences ; but invariably they get into debt and write
home for money ; some of them fall in love and become
the quasi-husbands of Italian ladies ; some get a bad character for learning the Italian art of poisoning ;. some are
killed in frays with the natives ; some remain abroad and
become professors ; all more or less illustrate the scholastic
question which John of Salisbury propounds, Is it possible
for an archdeacon to be saved? There are some few
exceptions, but they seem to be generally of the men who
stuck to theology and went for their education no further
than Paris. The scrapes of the archdeacons however I have
spoken of before ; they are a really amusing feature of the
epistolary correspondence of the time. I pass on to something more important.

Great as the advantages might be of an improved code of
laws and system of procedure, neither the canon law nor
the civil law was welcomed here ; they were repulsive not
only to the stubborn obscurantism of Stephen, but to the
bright and sagacious intellect of Henry II. Now, considering the close political connexion between Theobald
and the Plantagenet party, it is not at all impossible that
Henry II may have been among the pupils of Vacarius :
certainly he was more of a lawyer than mere empirical

education could make him, and, as certainly, he was awake
to the difficulties to which too ready acceptance of the
reformed jurisprudence would expose him. How great a
lawyer he was I need not tell you; how directly his difficulties were owing to the new doctrines of the canon lawyers
we know from the history of Becket. I will only mention
two points that illustrate his permanent relation to the subject: first, his Assize of Darrein Presentment removed all
questions of advowsons and presentations from the ecclesiastical courts where they were the source of constant
appeals to Rome; and secondly, by the Constitutions of
Clarendon he did his best to limit the powers of the ecclesiastical lawyers in criminal matters and in all points
touching secular interests. Against this must be set the
fact that to his days must be fixed the final sliding of
testamentary jurisdiction into the hands of the bishops, which
was by the legislation of the next century permanently left
there, in a way which, however accordant with the policy
of the papacy, was an exception to the rule of the rest of
Christendom. Henry, although not by any known assize
or constitution, must have restrained the ecclesiastical judicature from interfering in secular matters, except in the
two points of matrimony, which was closely connected with
a sacramental theory, and of testamentary business. These
two, however, furnished matter sufficiently remunerative for
a school of church lawyers; and the more distinctly ecclesiastical jurisdiction over spiritual things and persons provided much more. A thoroughly learned class of civil and
canon lawyers is required over and above the thoroughly
learned class of common law and (to anticipate a little)
chancery lawyers of the royal courts.

Here then we begin to mark signs of increasing divergence. The common lawyers of England, the men who
tread in the steps of Glanville, who are closely allied with

the baronage and with the customary theories of prerogative, are opposed to the introduction of either branch of the Roman law. Glanville, anticipating the decision of the Statute of Merton on the question of legitimisation of children by the subsequent marriage of their parents, speaks of the 'canones legesque Romanas[1]' with the same tone of aversion. The ecclesiastics who followed the common law were as adverse to the Roman law as were the knights and barons who learned secular jurisprudence in the discharge of executive office: and very rarely do we find a great judge of the courts of Westminster taken from the ranks of canonists or civilians. Yet the educational influence of these two great systems was making itself felt very early indeed. Not only does Glanville, in the preface to his manual, cite from the Institutes the language in which he addresses his master, but large importations from the civil law procedure must have come in as the jurisprudence developed; and Bracton, who wrote a century after Glanville, makes direct citations from the compilations of Justinian. If I were not afraid of the lawyers, I should venture to say that the whole theory of Appeals and the whole subject of Equity are strange to the national growth of the common law, and, although widely differing in details, far more akin to the civil law, the practice of which in ecclesiastical causes was steadily before men's eyes whilst they were developing the new systems. But I dare not venture to say this without more authority.

As we proceed, however, we are struck more and more with the prominence of the scientific element in legal education. The great compilations are not formally and explicitly received as having authority[2] in England, but they

---

[1] Glanville, *Tractatus*, &c. vii. 15.

[2] I have altered my words here; it is too much to say that they are 'not received as having any authority.' The reception may have been a matter of course.

are the sole legal teaching which is to be obtained in the schools where Englishmen go to learn law. The common law judges may not be canonists or civilians, but the statesmen, in many cases at least, are; certainly Archbishops Langton and Boniface and Peckham and Winchelsey. And even of the common lawyers it must be affirmed that their teaching, such as they had, was not merely empirical, not the mere knowledge of customs and the few statutes that were as yet incorporated in the common law code; but scientific, that is, learned from the writings of jurists who treated not merely of the letter or the case, but of the spirit and reason of legislation. Glanville's is indeed but a book of procedure, but Bracton, Fleta, and Britton are jurists, and whilst they illustrate and explain the common law, bring to the interpretation an intelligence and authority that look to something far higher than precedent. We see how long the old doctrine of the authority that is in the mouth of the judge stands out against the new doctrine that is in the letter of the law. Like the 'decretum,' like the 'responsa prudentum' of the Pandects, the work of Bracton is a scientific rather than an authoritative text-book. But I am anticipating what I ought to put in proper order somewhat later.

Whilst the study of these foreign systems was becoming increasingly important and increasingly common, the popular dislike of foreign law was not in the least diminished. I must here couple the two Roman systems together, for to all purposes of domestic litigation they were inseparable : the 'canones legesque Romanorum' were classed together and worked together, mainly because it was only on ecclesiastical questions that the civil law touched Englishmen at all, but also because without the machinery of the civil law the canon law could not be worked; if you take any well-drawn case of litigation in the Middle Ages, such as that of the monks of Canterbury against the archbishops, you will find that its citations from the Code and Digest are at least as numerous as from the Decretum. Moreover the accretions of the Decretum, the Extravagants as they were called, that is the authoritative sentences of the Popes which were not yet codified, were many of them conveyed in answers to English bishops, or brought at once to England by the clergy with the same avidity that lawyers now read the terminal reports in the Law Journal. The famous decision which Glanville quotes about legitimation is embodied in what then was an Extravagant of Alexander III, delivered to the Bishop of Exeter in 1172, founded no doubt on a Novel of Justinian but not till now distinctly made a part of Church law. And this point further illustrates what I was saying: for it is the point on which the great dictum of the Council of Merton turns in 1236. The English hatred of the foreigners was in that year fanned to white heat by the importation of the king's half-brothers and the new queen's uncles: it was an unlucky moment for Grosseteste and the bishops to press that the English law of bastardy should be altered to suit the canon and civil law of Rome. The murmurs were already rising that William of Valence was going to change the constitution. Notwithstanding the influence of Grosseteste, the king and the barons declared 'Nolumus leges Angliae mutari.' That is a well-known story; but it is perhaps not equally well known that the king had just a year before issued an order which stands in close parallelism with the banishment of Vacarius. By a letter to the Lord Mayor of London, dated Dec. 11, 1234, he had directed that no one should be allowed to hold law schools in the city of London or teach the Laws. What laws were these? Coke thought that the king referred to Magna Carta and the Carta de Forestis; but Selden, and Prynne after him,

pointed out that this was inconceivable ; and that doubtless
the LAWS were the civil and canon laws[1].   I think that under
the term Leges both civil and canon law were intended, but
certainly at the moment the danger from the canon law was
greater.   In the year 1230 Gregory IX had approved of the
five books of Decretals codified by Raymund of Pennafort
from the Extravagants of the recent popes and added to the
Decretum of Gratian.   In 1235 Matthew Paris tells us the
pope was urging the adoption of them throughout Christendom.   But we hear of no formal acceptance[2], although they
continued to be the code by which English causes were
decided at Rome, and began to be an integral part of the
education of English canonists.   And here again we have
to distinguish between the scientific or implicit and the
explicit authority of these books.   Great as the influence
of Justinian's code has been, there are very few countries in
Europe where it has been received as more than a treasury
of jurisprudence ; the ' Siete partidas ' of Alfonso the Wise
was a book of jurisprudence, not a code of law ; the
independence of the Gallican Church turns, as a historical
question, on the non-reception of Roman decrees, the
acceptance of the Council of Basel, and the non-reception
of portions of the Tridentine canons, the incidental working
of which must, notwithstanding, have been irresistible and
undeniable.   So in England neither the civil law nor the
canon law was ever received as authoritative[3], but rather as
peremptorily furnishing scientific confirmation for professional

[1] Prynne, Records, iii. 86 ; Selden on Fleta, ed. 1685, p. 525.

[2] As a part of the canon law they had practical acceptance: and may be
held to have passed into use as a matter of course.   But see note, p. 336.

[3] I said ' as authoritative, except educationally,' but if I were writing
this now, I should use different words; or rather should put the distinction more guardedly : cf. the note at the beginning of the lecture.
No doubt the canon law was regarded as an authoritative interpretation and application of Ecclesiastical Justice.

or empiric argument; or, in other words, where expressly or accidentally it agrees with the law of the land. Nay, the scientific treatment itself serves to confuse men's minds as to the real value of the text; and in both laws the opinion of the glossers are often cited as of equal authority with the letter of the law or canon.

But this same date 1236 brings me to another point; the beginning of the Codex receptus of Canon Law in England; in spite of the Council of Merton and the closing of the law schools of London. Since the Conquest most of the archbishops had held provincial synods and issued provincial canons; but many of these were acts of a temporary character only, and, even when they received support and confirmation from the kings, seldom amounted to more than the enforcement of discipline which had previously been authorized by papal or conciliar decrees. These canons are extant in the pages of the annalists, but remain rather among the Responsa Prudentum than as materials for a code. Just, however, as the statute law of England begins with the reign of Henry III, so does the codification of the national canon law. Archbishop Langton's Constitutions may be set first, but next in order, and even of greater authority, come the Constitutions of the legate Otho, which were passed in a national council of 1237. After these come Constitutions of the successive archbishops, especially Boniface of Savoy and Peckham, which were drawn up in a very aggressive spirit; Boniface taking advantage of Henry III's weakness to urge every claim that the English law had not yet cut down, and Peckham going beyond him in asserting the right of the Church against even the statutable enactments of the State. Between Boniface and Peckham in the year 1268 come the Constitutions of Othobon, which were confirmed by Peckham at Lambeth in 1281, and which, with those of Otho, were the first codified and glossed portions of the national Church law. In the reign of Edward III, John of Ayton, Canon of Lincoln, an Oxford jurist it is said, collected the canons adopted since Langton's time and largely annotated the Constitutions of Otho and Othobon. Contemporaneously with this accumulation of national materials, the Corpus Juris of the Church of Rome was increasing; Boniface VIII added the sixth book to the five of Gregory IX, and John XXII added the Clementines in 1318; and his own decisions, with those of the succeeding popes, were from time to time added as Extravagants unsystematized. The seventh book of the Decretals was drawn up under Sixtus V as late as 1588; so that practically it lies outside our comparative view. Of course very much of the spirit of both the sixth book and the Clementines found its way into England, but the statute law was increasing in vigour, the kings were increasing in vigilance, and after the pontificate of Clement V the hold of the Papacy on the nation was relaxing. Occasionally we find an archbishop like Stratford using the papal authority and asserting high ecclesiastical claims against the king, but the age of the Statutes of Praemunire and Provisors was come, and no wholesale importation of foreign law was possible. Not to multiply details, I will summarily state that in the reign of Henry V William Lyndwood, the Dean of the Arches, collected, arranged, and annotated the accepted Constitutions of the Church of England in his Provinciale, which, with the collections of John of Ayton generally found in the same volume, became the authoritative canon law of the realm [1]. It of course was proper in the first instance to the Province of Canterbury, but in 1462 the Convocation of York accepted the Constitutions of the southern province

---

[1] That is, for the sections of law which they comprised : they did not supersede the action of the canon law proper, from which they were largely derived and more largely illustrated. See note, p. 336.

as authoritative wherever they did not differ from those of York, and from the earlier date the compilation was received as the treasury of law and practice. Nor were any very material additions made to it before the Reformation; for although the Church of England was deeply involved in the transactions of the Council of Basel, and might, if the matter had been broached as distinctly as it was in France, have formally accepted its canons, no such incorporation of those canons ever took place here as was accomplished in the Pragmatic Sanction of Bourges in 1438.

Still, authoritative as Lyndwood's code undoubtedly was, it was rather as the work of an expert than as a body of statutes that it had its chief force. The study of the canon law was a scientific and professional, not merely mechanical study; and just as much was the study of the civil law also. I think that I am right in repeating that it was mainly as a branch of Church law that the civil law was studied at all; but I do not mean that it was so exclusively. In the infancy of international law and the administration of both admiralty and martial law, the English jurists had to go beyond their insular practice, and to no other source could they apply themselves; hence the association which to the present day has subsisted between the curiously unconnected departments of maritime and matrimonial jurisdiction. It is really owing to the distinction between scientifically and empirically trained lawyers. Of the indirect influence of scientific jurisprudence on the common law and chancery I have spoken already.

England has then for at least two centuries before the Reformation a body of law and a body of judges, for ecclesiastical and allied questions, quite apart from the law and judicial staff of the secular courts; and, with the growth of the Universities, she begins to have educational machinery for training her lawyers. In this department of work, however, the scientific study has a long start and advantage over

the empirical. The common law has to be learned by
practising in the courts, or by attending on their sessions.
The apprentices and serjeants of the Inns of Court learn
their work in London; their study is in the year books and
the statute book, a valuable and even curiously interesting
accumulation of material, but thoroughly insular, or less
than that, simply English. The canonists and civilians have
also their house in London, the ‘ Hospitium dominorum
advocatorum de arcubus,’ but they are scarcely less at home
at Rome and Avignon. The canonist and civilian learn the
legal language of entire Christendom; the London lawyer
sticks to his Norman-French. The Norman-French of
Westminster is unintelligible beyond the Channel and beyond
the border. Scotland, the sister kingdom, is toiling without
a common law system at all until, in the sixteenth century,
James V introduces the law of Justinian as her treasury of
common law, and thus gains University training and foreign
experience for her lawyers: but England has an ancient
system and is content with her own superiority ; her common
law is of native growth, strengthening with the strength of
her people ; she sees the nations that have accepted the
civil law sinking under absolutism ; as distinctly as ever ‘ non
vult leges Angliae mutari.’ But she has ceased to banish the
skilled jurist. Oxford and Cambridge have their schools of
both the faculties. The civil law at Oxford had its schools
from the fourteenth century in Cat Street, on the north of
St. Mary’s, in Schidyard Street, and in the great civil law
school in St. Edward’s parish where Archbishop Warham
learned law. The canon law school was in the neighbourhood of St. Edward’s Church also, and was rebuilt in 1489 by
subscription of the canonists. Wood enumerates no less
than seven distinct sets of Scholae Legum, the majority being
for civil law. In the colleges legal study has its proper
endowments. At Merton the study of the canon law is by

the founder's statutes permitted to four or five of his scholars, that of the civil law is allowed to the canonists as subsidiary to their proper study, *pro utilitate ecclesiastici regiminis*.   At Oriel five or six fellows, with consent of the seniors, might read the canon law, and by dispensation of the provost, the civil law also.   At Exeter, one of Stapledon's fellows was to study Scripture or the canon law.   We learn from Mr. Mullinger's invaluable book on Cambridge, that at Gonville Hall, founded about seventy years after Merton, each fellow was allowed to study canon law for two years.   It might be possible to trace in the successive foundations vestiges of the old subsisting and often revived jealousy of the studies; for Merton was founded at a time when, as Roger Bacon tells us, the civil law was looked on with jealousy as a mere professional or money-making study, whilst before the foundation of Gonville Hall the conflict between John XXII and Lewis of Bavaria had made the political tendencies of these studies more important and obvious.   At Trinity Hall, which was nearly of the same date as Gonville, ten civilians and seven canonists were seventeen out of the twenty statutory fellows.   At New College, out of seventy there were to be ten civilians and ten canonists, but these were reduced by Waynflete to two civilians and four canonists. At All Souls, sixteen out of forty were to be lawyers; at King's College, Cambridge, out of seventy, two civilians and four canonists; while at Catharine Hall both the canon and civil law were excluded.   These variations depend no doubt on the special intentions of the founders to promote scientific study, or to insure the worldly advancement of their pupils, and, to some extent, on the varying relations between theology and law of which I must speak in the next lecture. It is however clear, at the lowest estimate, that abundant encouragement and opportunities for the study could be found in both the seats of learning.   Closely allied as the canon and civil laws were, they composed two faculties; with regular schemes of lectures, fees, and exercises; the doctor of the civil law had to prove his knowledge of the Digest and the Institutes; the doctor of the canon law must have worked three years at the Digest and three at the Decretals, and studied theology also for two years. It is, you observe, not the national Church law, but the universal or scientific material, on which he is employed. In a great number of cases the degrees were taken at the same time; but as the era of the Reformation approaches, the canonists become more numerous than the civilians at Cambridge, and probably at Oxford also. But these points belong to a view of the subject on which I cannot pretend to enter now; and indeed it is in the conflict of laws rather than the conflict of studies that the present interest of the subject lies. In the next lecture I shall have to recur for some points to the ground which I have attempted to cover in this, for the struggles and jealousies of the rival and allied systems of jurisprudence do not date from the Reformation only. Here, however, I stop now, having in a cursory way traced the history of the materials of the canonical jurisprudence so far down. We shall have to begin by looking at the later history from the theological as well as from the legal side, and to follow it through the Reformation period, steering clear, as much as possible, of questions of modern controversy.

THE HISTORY OF THE CANON LAW IN ENGLAND

(April 20, 1882.)

IN the first of these two public lectures I attempted to give a sketch of the growth of the canon law; its origin and materials, its introduction into England and the limits of authority which it attained here, its relation to the civil law of Rome, and the distinction between the scientific study of the Decretals in the Universities and the professional use of the Provinciale in the Ecclesiastical Courts. The second branch of the subject, as I proposed to treat it in opening the lecture, is the history of its working in competition with and in general relations to other systems of law: a branch of the discussion which compels us at once to go back to the very root of the subject. Canon law as a code, and the civil law of Rome as a treasury of procedure, working together in the hands of ecclesiastical lawyers, may be for the moment looked at together; and the first aspect which our subject then takes is the attitude of the system towards theology on the one side and to the national, or, as lawyers would perhaps call it, municipal law on the other. From the Conquest to the Reformation canon law, proceeding by civilian method and being able to call on the principal executive to put its sentences in force, is a strong link between theology and national discipline; but a link with so much intricate workmanship employed upon it as to be offensive in many ways both to theology and to the common law. The theologian saw the great commandments of God, and the statutes of the Church, and the voice of conscience, lowered by being made dependent for their cogency on an elaborate system of human

invention which fettered freedom of action, and in some
respects freedom of thought also; which reduced moral
obligations to a system of penances, pecuniary commuta-
tions, monitions, and excommunications, and which made
use of the Sacraments of the Church as the mere means and
appliances of a coercion to external good behaviour, which
ought to be a free-will offering and the instinctive product
of a sincere heart.   Do not think that I am exaggerating the
attitude of repulsion in which the pure theologian and the
pure moralist stood to the ecclesiastical lawyer who was
making money out of the practice of the Courts Christian.
You remember how John of Salisbury had doubted whether
an archdeacon could be saved : Roger Bacon declares that
the study of the civil law, attracting the clever men among
the clergy, threw the study of theology into a second place,
and secularized the clerical character, making the priest as
much a layman as the common lawyer; while Richard of
Bury, the author of the Philobiblion, and Holcot the great
scholastic, declared, the one that the civilian, although he
gained the friendship of the world, was an enemy of God ;
the other, that under existing relations the handmaid Hagar,
despising the true wife, was in apt analogy to the contempt
under which neglected theology sank in the estimation of the
world as compared with the law.   It is true that these
remarks have a primary reference to the civil law, but, as I
showed, the civil law was learned chiefly as the executive
of the canon law, and it was by its relations to the canon law
that it became practical and remunerative.   I need not go
into much detail about this, but, if I am speaking to any
who attended my lectures on Ockham and Marsilius, they
will remember how not only those great writers, but a crowd
of minor ones, attack the canon law and its professors as
the great enemies, not only of civil government but of vital
religion : an exaggeration no doubt, but founded on a true

principle. 'Who,' says John of Salisbury, himself a canonist, 'ever rises pricked at heart from the reading of the laws, or even of the canons[1]?' The practice of these studies stood to theology, stood to religion itself, in the relation in which the casuistry of the confessional stood to true moral teaching.

When however we turn, as we must do, to consider the attitude of the national law and the national lawyers, we see more distinctly how incompatible were the systems which, for four hundred years, from the Conquest to the Reformation, stood side by side, with rival bodies of administrators and rival or conflicting processes. Look first at the area of matters with which the canon law assumed to deal: it claimed jurisdiction over everything that had to do with the souls of men, and I think there is scarcely a region of social obligation into which, so defined, it would not claim to enter. It claimed authority over the clergy, in matters civil and criminal, in doctrine and practice, in morals and in manners, education and dress, in church and out. It claimed authority over all suits in which clergymen were parties, or in which ecclesiastical property was involved; I say, mark you, claimed, rather than exercised, for some of these are the points in which the struggle with the national law arises. It claimed authority over the belief and morals of the laity, in the most comprehensive way. The whole of the matrimonial jurisdiction, the whole of the testamentary jurisdiction was, we know, specially regarded as a branch of canon law; but by its jurisdiction for correction of life, 'pro salute animae,' it entered into every man's house; attempted to regulate his servants, to secure his attendance at church, to make him pay his debts, to make him observe his oaths, to make him by spiritual censures, which by the alliance with the State had coercive force, by the dread of a writ of *capias excommunicatum*,

[1] Joh. Salisb. i. 196, epist. 138.

to keep all the weightier matters of the law, not only judgement, mercy, and truth, but faith, hope, and charity also.   Now the common law of the land was quite competent to deal first with ecclesiastical property, temporalities, advowsons, and the right to tithes; the canon law dealt with the qualifications of presentees and the exaction of tithes: the common law was competent to deal with matters of debt or theft; the canon law claimed to deal with matters of credit or dishonesty in legal and moral as in spiritual obligations: the common law dealt with dower, the canon law with matrimony; the common law with succession to property, the canon law with legitimacy.   So over great regions of property law, and over the whole domain of moral delinquency, the mediaeval world had two sets of courts at which they might sue, and two sets of lawyers to keep alive with fees and retainers.   The canonists affirm that a suit may be brought in the ecclesiastical court for every matter which is not cognizable in the courts of secular law, and for a great many matters which are so cognizable. There is surely an ample claim.   I do not want to go into detail, but I will just point out one particular; the commissary of the Bishop of London entertained suits exactly analogous to those of the trades unions of the present day, turning on the question how far it is a breach of oath for the sworn member of a guild to impart the arts and mysteries of his guild to outsiders.

Here then you see the elements of a pretty conflict; between the jurists as a matter of scientific or empiric lore, between the practising lawyers a conflict for practice and for profits; and you can see how degrading the practical part of the profession was to the theological student, or to the parish priest.   Over and above this, there was the natural jealousy of the Crown and the Parliament.   If the canon law had restricted itself to really spiritual questions, matters of belief or of morals for which the national code had no provision, it is not likely that the kings would have been jealous of papal or archiepiscopal enactments, or would have stood on their rights when the exact line was occasionally overstepped. But the extravagance of ecclesiastical claims provoked them to opposition and justified it. When the archbishops of Henry III's reign claimed exclusive jurisdiction in suits of advowsons, the right to exact personal tithes, and to try all questions of credit granted ' fide interposita,' even so gentle a worm as the king turned again ; and we find among his letters, and still more among those of his son, constant cautions to the primates and their convocations not to attempt anything to the prejudice of the crown and customs of the land, as well as innumerable prohibitions to ecclesiastical judges against their trying other civil suits than those which touch testamentary or matrimonial matters. Edward II had to prohibit the employment of imperial notaries. In the spiritual matters proper, the kings seldom interfered; only where a political motive was suspected, or where a servant of the crown was attacked, or where the spiritual judge had clearly gone beyond his discretion. The Church history of the thirteenth and fourteenth centuries is full of cautions and prohibitions, and of struggles between the officers who had thus to interfere with one another; and the definitions of the ' Articuli Cleri ' under Edward II which prescribed the points on which prohibitions were to be granted, and the Statute of Praemunire under Edward III, which forbade the multiplication of appeals to Rome, did little to ameliorate relations. When however heresy became a matter of litigation, the two systems deliberately worked together ; and, although there were many hitches, during the whole of the Lancastrian period there was more definite co-operation and less conflict. The common law was really becoming more a matter of scientific treatment, and the greatest judges were men who had had scientific education on both sides. Sometimes there was, as was natural, a little inconsistency and awkwardness; the bowsprit got mixed up with the rudder; as when Morton, at once archbishop and chancellor, allowed his judgement on a fraudulent executor to be modified by the reflexion that he would be 'damnée in hell.' But this may have been exceptional.

It must not however be supposed that the fault in this rivalry was altogether to be ascribed to the canonists. The English-trained lawyer was as infallible in that age as in this; and when we find him, and his brethren in the Parliament, constantly hampering the legitimate work of the Church, we see that there were two sides to the question; when in the fourteenth century the Commons petition that the clergy may not make in their Convocation canons to bind the laity, it is rather a relief to find that the canons in question relate to tithe of underwood: but when in 1446 we find the clergy remonstrating that the professional lawyers 'pretended privilege, by what right,' they say, 'we know not, to interpret Acts of Parliament and explain the mind of the legislature, and by thus practising upon the statutes sometimes ground their opinion on mysterious and unintelligible reasons, and so wrest the laws contrary to the meaning and intention of Parliament;' or petitioning that the judges who showed such strong bias should no longer issue prohibitions, but, when questions arose concerning the limits and jurisdiction of the rival courts, indifferent persons should be pitched upon to judge them; or the lawyers, on the other hand, striking at the root of all ecclesiastical jurisdiction as if it were a transgression of the Statute of Praemunire[1],—well, when we look at these things, we shall see that there were questions unsettled even before the Council of Trent, and hear opinions and

[1] Wilkins, iii. 555 (1447); Parker's Antiquitates, 429.

complaints that sound like echoes beforehand of voices with which in these days our ears are too familiar.

I must, however, now proceed to the Reformation, and endeavour to determine, as strongly and as clearly as I can, the bearing of that most critical era on our subject. Henry VIII had, as early as 1515, seen a struggle between the secular and ecclesiastical jurisdictions in Standish's case, in the course of which he is said to have expressed himself as determined to endure no division of sovereignty in his own realm. Whether that was really said or merely put into his mouth afterwards, I cannot say; but certainly no scheme of change in the relation between Church and State was set on foot for nearly seventeen years. Then the business of the divorce at Rome, and the discontent of the king with the half-hearted support of the clergy at home, completed his disgust, and he set out in the course of radical change. Having in 1531 compelled the clergy by the threat of prae-munire to recognize him as supreme head 'quantum per Christi legem licet,' he induced the Commons in 1532 to present a petition or remonstrance against the whole theory and practice of the canon law. They attacked the power of the clergy to make canons in Convocation, they protested against the exaction of fees and mortuaries, and deliberately impugned the honesty and purity of the episcopal courts in all their branches and with reference both to jurisdiction and to procedure. This petition had two results; the Parliament passed bills to limit the benefit of clergy and forbid feoffments to the use of churches. An earlier session in 1529 had attempted to deal with probate and mortuaries; this, by the Statute of Citations, cut down the power of the Archbishop of Canterbury to entertain suits from other dioceses except by appeal or on request, and so struck at the root of the universal jurisdiction enjoyed by the Court of Arches and its advocates. The same term—the second result of the king's policy—the Convocation was compelled to surrender its right of meeting and legislating, and to consent to a revision of the canon law to be carried into execution by a mixed body of clergy and laity whom the king should appoint. This last concession sealed the fate of the old scientific study of the canon law, which, as we have seen, was a distinctly popish study; and, if it had not been accompanied by a limiting clause, allowing the old canons, so far as they were not opposed to the law of the land, to stand until the revision was published, there would have been an entire abolition of ecclesiastical jurisdiction of any kind. In 1535 Cromwell, as the king's vicegerent, visited the two Universities, and in both issued injunctions, that both the old scholastic teaching of the Sentences should cease, and that the teaching in the Decretals and the conferring of degrees in canon law should be abolished. What the exact legal force of Cromwell's injunctions was has never been determined; but in these points they were obeyed: the Universities ceased to teach the systematic theology of the Schools and the systematic jurisprudence of the Decretals; and the ancient degrees of bachelor and doctor of the canon law are known, except during the reign of Mary, no more. How did this affect the civil law? you ask: well, just as it might be expected; the scientific study was abolished, the old canons were in abeyance, but the courts continued to practise, the civil law procedure was as lively as ever; and students who intended to practise as advocates took degrees in civil law instead of in both. Oxford dropped the canon law degree altogether; Cambridge, by adopting a more general form, retained a shadowy presentment of the double honour.

And now we come again to an Act which shows the continuity of the inherent rivalry between two systems which, for the sake of mutual profit, had so long worked together.

In 1541 a bill was introduced into Parliament which enabled married D.C.L.'s to exercise ecclesiastical jurisdiction as chancellors and commissaries ; it did not pass in that year, being withdrawn on the request of Convocation, but was re-introduced and passed in 1545. So long as the two degrees were granted together the D.C.L.'s were, as doctors of decrees, bound by the canon which forbade a married man to act as an ecclesiastical judge ; but now the right of the D.C.L. simple, both to marry and to act as a judge, was secured : as the civil doctors of Bologna had done in the thirteenth century, their successors in England now married ; before this they were probably, as a rule, in minor orders.

I must pass over the more important of Henry VIII's other Acts, especially the Statutes of Appeals and Submission, except just to recall the fact that in the preamble to the former of those Acts passed in 1533 he had expressed himself confident that the realm of England would, as it always had done, provide a sufficient number of spiritual men to decide spiritual questions, and of secular men to decide secular questions, under his own supreme authority and to the exclusion of any foreign jurisdiction. The other matters in which those statutes affected ecclesiastical jurisdiction lie somewhat deeper than our present speculations.

We are not however to suppose that, when the king practically abolished the canon law, he intended to hand the clergy over to the common lawyers. The procedure was, as we have seen, still kept in the hands of the civilians ; but the theologians were a body of men whose functions had been to some extent usurped by the canonists, and who now for some years, under Tudor and Puritan and Laudian influences, were to come to the front. The theologians or divines divided with the canonico-civilians the authority of the ecclesiastical jurisdiction : the character of a bishop in itself was that of a divine, not of a lawyer, and we might almost say that whilst questions of application of law and procedure belonged to the lawyer, the interpretation was claimed for the divine. In cases of heresy, for instance, the theologians formulated the definition, whilst the canonists and civilians examined the teaching of the accused and determined how far he had contravened the definition. So in the question of Henry's divorce, the divines had been called on to define 'Can the pope dispense with a marriage with a deceased brother's wife?' the canonists had to determine whether the marriage between Arthur and Katharine was such a marriage as precluded the dispensation. This rule of combining theologians with canonists or civilians for commissions on ecclesiastical suits continued long after the Reformation, and ought never to have been disused.

These measures of change, sufficiently drastic one would think, had in this department satisfied Henry VIII; the scheme for revising the canon law hung fire; the powers granted to the king in 1534 were renewed for three years in 1536, and again for his life in 1544, but nothing was done in the matter during the remainder of the reign. But what had sufficed Henry VIII did not suffice Somerset or Northumberland, or the poor boy-king who succeeded him. The second statute of the first year of Edward VI went as near as possible to extinguish the episcopate; there were still to be bishops, but they were to be nominated by the king without any form of election; they were as a matter of fact appointed during good behaviour; and their jurisdiction was henceforth to be exercised in the king's name. In him all ecclesiastical authority was vested, they were to be his ministers, their writs were to be issued in his name, their seals were to bear the royal arms; and it was only to such of them as he pleased that even such authority was to be intrusted. It was proposed, though not passed, that a Court of Chancery should be erected for ecclesiastical causes. The revision of the canon law was to be urged on, and the Universities were to be further purged from the old leaven. All this was done: in vain the Protestant bishops pleaded in the House of Lords that their position was intolerable and their dignity a mere mockery, that the moral discipline of clergy and people was entirely broken down; no act for rehabilitating them was got through Parliament; the dominant interests were opposed to it. The injunctions sent to the Universities prescribed some renewal of studies; the poor canonists of course were left out in the cold, although not treated as if they were illegal or irregular: the civilians were authorized to read the Institutes, and the D.C.L., when he had reached that dignity, was exhorted to devote himself more zealously to the study of the king's laws, both temporal and ecclesiastical. And work was to be found for him: bills were introduced to lodge ecclesiastical jurisdiction in the hands of students of the Universities, who were admitted by the archbishop. By these, however, all special privileges of the advocates were endangered and the bills dropped after passing most stages: four bills on this point were before the Parliament of 1550. But again the revision of the canons was dragging behind. The king's power of nominating revisers was asserted by an act of 1550 to last for three years, and an abortive attempt was made in the session of 1552 to renew or enlarge it; but whether it was that Cranmer found it impossible to obtain skilled assistants, or that the division of parties prevented a joint effort, it was not until near the end of the reign that the project was carried on: in 1551 and 1552 Edward issued two commissions of thirty-two, composed of equal numbers of bishops, divines, civilians, and common lawyers; the number thirty-two was reduced to eight; practically the work was done by Peter Martyr, the Oxford Professor of Divinity, under Cranmer's eye, and the result was the compilation known as the *Reformatio Legum ;* a curious congeries of old and new material which really pleased no party; showing too much respect for antiquity and divine ordinance to please the Puritan, and too little to satisfy the men who had guided the Reformation under Henry VIII and those who were to do so under Elizabeth.

The legislation and policy of Mary were directed to uproot everything that Edward VI had originated; his bishops appointed ' quamdiu se bene gesserint,' were dispossessed without a struggle ; his laws were repealed, many of them never to be revived; his advisers, where they would not comply, were exiled or burned : but the efforts to reinstate the old system were not successful; the monastic property could not be restored ; the ranks of the lower clergy, reduced to a fraction by the abolition of chantries and private masses, could not be recruited ; and all the restored fabric hung on the life of a woman and a few worn-out old men. For the moment the canon lawyers lifted up their heads, and a few civilians took the doctorate of decrees at Oxford and Cambridge ; but the complete extinction of reactionary forces, on Mary's death, showed that the papal system, with all that was dangerous to national life contained in it, was, so far as England was concerned, practically extinct : six years of blood and fire, of tears and prayers, of cruel jealousies and heartbreaking divisions, wrought this ; and Elizabeth for some years after her accession had before her a task, not certainly easy, but not encumbered with insuperable difficulties.

The subject which we are treating now contracts its limits ; for to attempt anything like circumstantial discussion of the legal history of a period into which ecclesiastical quarrels so largely enter, would be to lose oneself at once in a wilderness of controversy. I must content myself with a few generalizations

and a few significant facts. The Elizabethan settlement
in Church and State was a compromise, satisfactory to no
party, and very unsatisfactory indeed to the constitutional
lawyer or historian; but, possibly, the best arrangement com-
patible with circumstances. She began her reign, of course,
by a reversal of her sister's legislation; but she did not
restore the Edwardian system; she did not revive the Act of
Henry VIII which had asserted the king's headship of the
Church, or the Act of Edward which deprived the bishops
of all original jurisdiction: the doctrine of the headship was
opposed both by the Puritans and by the Catholic party; the
abolition of all the high functions of the episcopate which
was aimed at by Edward's advisers was a measure which
contemporary history was showing to be dangerous. But,
whilst she minimized the definition of authority, she retained
the virtual exercise of it: her explanation of her supreme
governorship might have satisfied every one but the most
Tridentine papist, but she re-enacted the most stringent part
of her father's Act of Supremacy; and, whilst she allowed
the continuance of the Church jurisdiction, she kept all control over the religious discipline of clergy and laity under
the hands of the Court of High Commission. The Court of
High Commission, consisting of a large number of lawyers
and laymen and a small number of bishops and divines,
stands to the Church in much the same relation as the Court
of Star Chamber stands to the Courts of Common Law, and
the Court of Requests to Chancery, a legal but most unconstitutional relation, and one which, however long it might
be tolerated, was sure in the long run to endanger the whole
fabric. As for legislation, Elizabeth acted, as we know, on
a high principle of supremacy; such measures of Church
discipline as required coercive authority she allowed the
Parliaments to pass, but she forbade any interference whatever where that authority was not necessary. As for the

ecclesiastical legislation in Convocation, she exercised her
veto, i. e. she granted or withheld the consent which would
make it valid, according to her own views of high policy.
The rulers of the Church, who were not free from the same
humiliating bondage of adulation that influenced all around
the great queen, tolerated a system which gave them the substance of power, although in an unpopular and unhistorical
shape.   Their legislative authority was paralyzed, but they
could exercise a real authority as the queen's advisers; and
the jurisdiction, which they had difficulties in enforcing
through their own courts, they could enforce as members of
the High Commission Court.   But the ecclesiastical law—
how did it fare under the circumstances?   In the first place
the forms of the courts were maintained, and were enough
to sustain the civilians who worked in them; the Prerogative
Court and the consistory courts lived on the testamentary
and matrimonial jurisdiction; and before the spiritual courts
were tried the smaller cases of discipline which were not
important enough for the High Commission Court.   Doctors'
Commons, which had dwelt before in Paternoster Row or at
the Queen's Head, under the auspices of Dr. Henry Harvey,
built itself a new home, with hall and library and plate and
privileges for importing wine.   Knowledge of canon and civil
law was in Parliament, as in 1585, regarded as a special qualification for service in the House of Commons on committees.
In the Parliaments of 1559 and 1563 were introduced bills to
make a University degree necessary for ecclesiastical judges.
And the canon law, as drawn up by Lyndwood, and the
civilian procedure, subsisted, for the revision which had been
completed by Edward's commissioners did not approve itself
to Elizabeth or her advisers, and after an abortive attempt to
carry it through the Parliament of 1559, took its place on
the shelf of broken projects.   Even the Court of High Commission, novel as its functions were and unfettered as it was

in the exercise of them, condescended to borrow from the canonical jurisprudence some of its most offensive details, its *ex officio* oath and the censures by which it would enforce its sentences.

It was a strange composite system, perhaps the only one possible consistently with the retention of historic continuity, but obviously and most certainly tolerable only for a time. What was the attitude of theologians, of common lawyers, and of canonists towards this critically-balanced structure ? To the true theologians, whether Catholic or Puritan, the whole was repulsive : we see this in the half-hearted, almost despairing adhesion of Archbishop Parker, and in the strong and justifiable protests of the Puritans; and I mention them with respect here, because this opposition to unconstitutional tyranny is the only point in which I have any sympathy with them; their tenets I hold to be untenable, and their methods of promoting them by calumny, detraction, and coarse ribaldry I think entirely detestable; but I do think they were right in denouncing the Court of High Commission and all its works. Even conservative churchmen like Hooker, in their defence of the ecclesiastical system, are hampered by the consciousness that much of what existed was indefensible. The bishops saw their position as bishops ignored, and the Puritans saw the power which they thought should be exercised by their own ministers exercised through a royal commission : the bishops however had the power and endured the ignominy, the Puritans suffered and waited for their turn to persecute.

The lawyers were not all of one mind; Coke the great lawyer was himself of two minds ; he liked the crown better than the episcopate, but he loved the common law better than the crown ; and his inconsistency produces some curious results on his teaching. This leads us to two or three facts. From 1587 to 1591 the famous Cawdrey's case drew its grievous length along.   The High Commission had deprived Cawdrey for nonconformity; the question arose, had the Commission under the terms of the Act of the queen's first year exceeded its authority?   The resolution finally adopted by all the judges, and recorded and approved by Coke, affirmed that the ecclesiastical prerogative of the crown was such that the powers of a commission issued by it were not limited by that statute, but covered the whole range of ecclesiastical jurisdiction; and therefore the sentence was good.   The judgement in Cawdrey's case, full of bad law and worse history, is often referred to even now by lawyers with a respect which it does not merit; here it is useful as showing to what lengths the common lawyers under Elizabeth would go in support of the authority of the crown over things ecclesiastical.   It stimulated the Puritans in and out of the Church to bitterer action, and disabled the hands of the bishops who, like Andrewes, would rather have taken the responsibility of their own acts.   Twenty years later Coke himself declared against the constitutional character of the Court of High Commission, and, by refusing to act upon it, paved the way for its downfall.   But Coke was then in opposition to the king's advisers, and made it his account to be an independent judge.   But I am anticipating.

The change of Elizabeth for James I was a critical event in English Church history.   James's dealings with the Church are not among the strongest, but are perhaps among the least reprehensible parts of his administration.   He willingly confirmed the canons of 1604, which make a substantive addition to the canonical lore of the clergy.   He failed to secure co-operation between the House of Commons and the Convocation, or between the bishops and the Puritan divines. But this is no wonder.   A House of Commons which could listen to Sir Herbert Crofts declaring that the Church had declined ever since doctors began to wear boots; or could

expel Mr. Sheppard, M.P. for Shaftesbury, for explaining
that 'dies Sabbati' meant not the Sabaoth as they called it,
but Saturday, and suggesting that, as David danced before
the ark, the legality of dancing was a question on which
the bishops might decide before it was altogether forbidden,
—such a House of Commons was not likely to impress men
like Hooker or Andrewes with respect, or King James either.
It is clear I think that, if the Puritan party had been well
represented at the Hampton Court Conference, James would
have seen justice done to them ; but he saw their intolerance
and their frivolity, and the balance remained unredressed.
One of their minor complaints, against the issuing of ecclesiastical sentences by lay chancellors, touches directly on our
subject: their idea was to give all the disciplinary power to
the clergy, but to their own clergy: the prelates of the time
chose to maintain the *status quo* which left the power where
it was. On this point the civilians were peremptory. Some
of the prelates, either wishful to promote their sons or willing
to lodge Church discipline in clerical hands, appointed clergymen to be chancellors. The doctors took umbrage at this,
petitioned King Charles I in 1625, and obtained from him
an order to remove the intruding officials and to substitute
qualified civilians.

Another interesting point arises at James's accession. In
the hurry of his first Parliament the Act of Mary which repealed the 1 Edw. VI. c. 2, by which the *congé d'eslire* and
the independent jurisdiction of the bishops were abolished,
was itself repealed; and the lawyers, or some of them,
held that the Edwardian law was revived, that the whole
episcopate was intrusive, and the whole of the Church courts
illegal. This was long in controversy, and it was only in
1637 that the judges finally resolved that the law of Edward,
as contravening a law of Henry VIII which had been
formally re-enacted, was not revived by the repeal of the

Marian statute. If that resolution had not been accepted, the whole existing fabric of the Church must, so far as secular interests were concerned, have fallen to the ground.

But the opening of James I's reign is important for a third critical question. In 1605 Archbishop Bancroft presented from Convocation a series of articles against the proceedings of the common law judges in issuing prohibitions and claiming the exclusive right to interpret Acts of Parliament touching the Church. The long argument on this subject, which is to Coke's Second Institute what Cawdrey's case is to the Reports, is of considerably greater weight; no doubt there was much to be said on both sides, and the voice of the Convocation of 1605 was in harmony with that of 1559 and 1446, where the claims of the theologians to interpret acts that touched theology were fairly stated; but Coke embellishes the report with words that have an amusing cogency even in the present day; 'for judges expounding of statutes that concern the ecclesiastical government or proceedings, it belongeth unto the temporal judges, and we think they have been expounded as much to the clergy's advantage as either the letter or intention of laws would or could allow of: and when they have been expounded to their liking then they could approve of it, but if the exposition be not for their purpose then they will say as now they do that it appertaineth not unto us to determine of them.' Anyhow the judges agreed that they were the proper interpreters of the Acts of Parliament; and as the whole liturgy, and indeed the Bible also, might be brought under those terms, there was practically no limit to their assumption of infallibility; for the common law judges could not, like theologians, afford to leave any question unsolved.

Well, Coke was right as to the bishops, as was proved in 1612, when the common lawyers allowed Bishops King and Neill to burn two heretics under a common law writ, for which Coke's authority might be pleaded, although all the earlier legislation against heretical pravity had been abrogated. The invulnerability of the common law which had maintained the High Commission in Cawdrey's case, now treated the issue of the writ ' de haeretico comburendo ' as a matter of its own, and brought equal shame on theology and jurisprudence. The heretics who were burned were men whom the Puritans did not care to defend ; they would have burned them as willingly as they would have done the bishops.

And here let me say by the way, great as the horrors of religious persecution are, they cannot be properly estimated without some consideration of the value set upon human life both at the period in which they occur and at other times : I am told that it could be shown that all the executions for religious causes in England, by all sides and during all time, are not so many as were the sentences of death passed in one year of the reign of George III for one single sort of crime, the forging of bank-notes.

But I must pass on, leaving the Laudian period altogether out of sight : and indeed it is not, for our purpose, so important as the earlier portion : Laud and Charles were, neither of them, men who were satisfied with such things as the High Commission Court, and the sinking of ecclesiastical discipline in the state administration ; but they did not make their way to any better system, and supported that which was to them for the time the only possible system. With the opening of the struggle in 1641 the Court of High Commission fell to the ground, and at the Restoration its abolition was confirmed by the first Parliament of Charles II.

During the Elizabethan and Jacobean period the study of Church law had not been neglected ; for it had shared the benefit of the great historical and antiquarian revival of which Parker was the first leader, to which Spelman belonged, and which reached its climax in Selden and Prynne. Both of these eminent writers studied canon law from antagonistic grounds: Selden regarded it as a philosopher ardent for liberty; Prynne as an enthusiast, who had his own persecution to avenge and the thesis of royal prerogative to defend with all the zeal and learning of a convert. Selden was a real jurist; Prynne an indefatigable searcher of records. But, when at the Restoration the removal of the incubus of the High Commission, and the political education which the Caroline divines had gone through, enabled them to restore the old ecclesiastical jurisdiction with some hope of honest and successful issue, the canonists and civilians showed that life was still in them. The old black-letter Lyndwood was taken down from the shelf, rebound, and annotated. Dr. Sharrock in 1664 abridged the Provinciale for the use of students, and in 1679 the Oxford edition, which rapidly displaced the black-letter, was published with all Lyndwood's commentaries and Ayton's work on the Constitutions. The study of the civil law needed no revival; it had been kept up by the antiquaries and admiralty in the worst times; and, in the Universities, the faculty fellowships secured at least a languid succession of law degrees. The D.C.L. of Oxford too had achieved the dignity which now belongs to the honorary degrees at Commemoration; and in 1649, at what Antony Wood calls the Fairfaxian Creation, both Fairfax and Cromwell were made doctors of the civil law. According to Wood, in 1659 Nicolas Staughton, of Exeter College, was admitted doctor both of civil and canon law; and it is not impossible that there were other attempts to revive the canon law doctorate as an adjunct to the degree in civil law. Cambridge had always retained the shadow of the double degree, for the Leges or LL. to which she admits her doctors are a possible survival of the 'Utrumque Jus' of the old University system; and in 1669, Richard Pearson, brother of Bishop Pearson the commentator on the Creed, claimed to be admitted in distinct terms to both faculties. The Archbishop of Canterbury also, under the Dispensation Act, has the unquestioned right to make a doctor of canon law, although I am not sure that it has ever been exercised. But at Oxford the designation of the degree had latterly come to be restricted to civil law; and when in 1715, or thereabouts, Mr. Charles Browne of Balliol College applied to the Vice-Chancellor, Dr. Gardiner, for leave to proceed as bachelor and doctor of the canon law, he was told that he could not be prevented from doing so if he wished it, but that it would give the University a great deal of trouble; and the poor man died before he achieved the object of his ambition.

These notes are, however, of little importance, except as illustrating the revival of the ancient study, and the attention which the ecclesiastical questions of the day were calling to ancient practice. In point of fact, the whole of the second and last act of the Stewart dynasty was full of ecclesiastical questionings and excitements, which, though they did not directly touch our subject, stimulated the studies most closely connected with it. The struggle under James II, the position of the Nonjurors, the relation of Convocation to Parliament, the Whistonian and Bangorian controversies, all drew in lively partisans to the investigation of legal and ecclesiastical problems. The names of Hody, Kennet, Atterbury, Wake, and Gibson, all leading Oxford men, and men of deep research and minute if not accurate reading, are conspicuous in this regard; and, as for constitutional purposes it may be said that the very dust of their writings is gold, it would be ungrateful indeed to speak of their earnestness in the main object as misplaced. Gibson stands out more distinctly than any of the others as a great canonist, and his Codex or Collection of English Church Statutes is still the standard work and treasury of all sorts of such lore. There were too Johnson, Wilkins, and many other honest and subordinate workers on the theological as well as on the legal side. But the history of this department of law draws quickly to an end. The Hanoverian policy with regard to the Church and Convocation fell on all politico-ecclesiastical life as a blight. The Nonjurors were left out of the pale of the recognized laity, the common lawyers edged the theologians out of the court of delegates, the Convocations were silenced, and the bishops, almost as much as in Elizabeth's time, made their position in the House of Lords the fulcrum of all the force they ventured to exercise. Except for testamentary causes, and rare occasions of matrimonial and slanderous causes, the Church jurisdiction ceased to exist, and so continued dormant until in our times, in 1849 and in 1850, the Gorham case roused the attention of both lawyers and clergymen to the fact that without knowing they had let the centre of ecclesiastical gravity become seriously misplaced. Into this region of discussion, for many reasons, I must not attempt now to make my way.

A few years after the Gorham controversy, a change or series of changes set in from another quarter: the matrimonial jurisdiction was remodelled when the facilities for divorce were increased, and the whole testamentary jurisdiction was withdrawn from the nominal superintendence of the archbishops. The Courts, the profits and privileges of which had so long maintained the close corporation of Doctors' Commons, and had caused the study of canon law in some at least of its branches to be languidly pursued, were radically and fundamentally changed; and, although it was difficult at once to improvise new forms and rules of procedure to take the place of the ancient forms and those which had grown out of them, these forms also were doomed. In the still more recent remodelling of the whole judicial system further changes have forced themselves in; and where the lawyers could find it their policy to acquiesce in the consolidation of the common law and chancery, they could without the slightest reluctance throw the ecclesiastical and admiralty law into the same cauldron. Out of that cauldron arises a new supreme judicature, which requires, every two or three years, to be amended and strengthened. It is supposed that thereby justice is quickened and law made so cheap, that any man, poor or rich, may ruin himself with a light heart. It yet remains to be seen whether this amended system, easier and less intricate than the old, supplies as good material for training or provides as sound schools of lawyers. It is no doubt philosophically more capable of perfection. The lore of Coke and Selden, like the lore of Eldon and Stowell, is for the present at a discount. Of course looking on all this with an historical eye, one is apt to be a little disconsolate; but time will avenge them, and the neo-legal jurisprudence will soon have an array of reports and decisions that will outweigh, physically at least, the Year-books and Institutes. As for the ecclesiastical law, which by its very nature, if it loses continuity, loses identity, in the present changing aspect of the world's politics, I for my part do not intend to prophesy. No one can investigate the letter and working of the canon law without being struck by the marvellous mixture of lofty and eternal principles of right, with arbitrary and disingenuous evasions of obligation: it reads as if the jurists, finding that the Church could not be ruled by the true principles, were determined to rule by special pleadings and artful circumventions. For the future the theologians must look to the true principles, and let the canonists and civilians pass with their evasions and circumventions into the twilight of archaeology. Whether that will be so or not, or how soon, we may some of us live to see.

THE REIGN OF HENRY VII

(April 24, 1883.)

MY kindest friends will hardly be able this year to charge me with having chosen the subject of my public statutory lectures with a view of attracting an audience. I never, in the course of a long historical experience, met with any one who wished to attend a second course of lectures on Henry VII, or indeed with any one who expressed any interest in him at all. It is just possible that I may be suspected of a design to attract the admirers of the Lady Margaret, by advertising a discourse upon her son; but, although the idea did occur to me, I set it aside as feeling it my duty to guard against any over-sanguine expectations. No; I chose the subject because I have to lecture, and, after sixteen successive ceremonies of humiliation, I thought that I had a right to throw some part of the imputation of dulness off myself upon my subject. If the men will not come, let it be as much Henry VII's fault as mine.

Yet to begin with, it is a curious thing that the subject should be so dull; and perhaps my first point should be to account for that. I do not question the fact. It is so; but why? The period is full of interest: it is the beginning of modern as distinguished from mediaeval history; it exhibits to us, in their first definite and specialized forms, the forces which constitute the dramatic elements of the state of society in which we are living; the great powers in their newly consolidated condition, the balance of which makes up European history ever since. It is the age of the discovery of the New World, the age of the birth of modern commerce and colonization; it is the eve of the Reformation, and of that wonderful renaissance which I believe exists at the present day, in prize essays and schools examinations, much more vividly, and alas in much greater solid bulk than it ever had in the most flourishing days *in rerum natura*. And it is a period too in which we begin to have, more distinctly and more numerously than before, representative men as they are called; that is, men whose greatness and prominence consists not in their being exceptions to or protests against, or glories or shames to the age in which they lived, but in concentrating in themselves and giving force to the ideas, the accomplishments, the hopes and aspirations, the greatnesses and littlenesses of their own times. In the play of character also there should be something interesting in a period which embraces Ferdinand and Isabella the Catholic, the delightful old Frederick III, and the still more charming Maximilian; the age of Charles VIII, and Philip the Handsome, not to speak of the Borgias, the Medici, and the Farnesi.

Yet the reign of Henry VII is dull. Look at it in relation to English history; there also it should be important; there also it comes between the ancient and the modern; bridges over the strait between the Wars of the Roses and the Reformation, between England isolated and England taking a first place in the counsels of Europe, between England weak and England strong. The reign itself may be almost exactly divided between fifteenth century influences and sixteenth century influences; the one series winding up in final bloodshed, the other opening with initial intrigue. We are really able to trace the last links of the chain of political murders which had begun when Warwick and Lancaster slew Piers Gaveston, and which ends or almost ends with the sacrifice of Edward of Warwick and the De la Poles; and we trace the first links of the policy which grew and strengthened in intensity to the days of Waterloo.

But still it is dull: we do not much care about the effete struggles of the dynastic parties, and we cannot get up a lively interest in the negotiations for the Scottish or Spanish marriage. It is our own fault perhaps that we want more sensationalism. But there is a lack of it notwithstanding.

One reason I will shortly dismiss. I verily believe that one reason why this period is dull is that it was the period of the discovery and development of printing, and of the use of paper instead of parchment. Men began to write freely and to destroy freely; instead of writing for private purposes of record, they wrote for other men to read; they wrote not what was worth writing, but what would catch readers; they wrote what it was safe to write when every one could read; they wrote because they could write, not because there was a necessity for them to write; that is, anybody wrote, and few wrote what was worth preserving. One popular book destroyed a thousand chances of having invaluable records of timid private annals. And, when destruction began, it found paper more easy to dispose of than parchment: the age that could make tailors' measures out of Magna Carta, lighted its fires with State papers. Growing criticism, careful public administration, even before the age of destruction began, had not learned to be careful as to what should be preserved and what should be destroyed. And when the age of destruction did come, it was divided between the Roman Catholic force that destroyed everything new, and the Puritan force that destroyed everything old. So it is not so much a wonder that we have so little documentary remains of Henry VII's reign, as that we have anything at all. The only strictly contemporary account of the king's life and character is to be found in a few half-rotten, half-legible paper sheets in the Cottonian Library. All the more circumstantial parts of the history have to be worked out of the annalists of the next generation.

But there must have been a deeper cause. Why should a king with a good character and a romantic career subside into a historical fogey? Look closely at Frederick III, the splendid old gipsy, in name governor of the world, ever august, and increaser of the empire, yet owning no more territory than an English alderman; sitting in his study elaborating a horoscope with destiny of universal dominion for his grandchildren unborn, inventing the motto of empire for an Austria that was yet in embryo: honourable, perhaps, and careless about selfish gains, but a dreamer, about whom the strange thing is that so many of his dreams came true. Look at Maximilian, the most delightfully unprincipled hero of the age of transition; always in every feast and every fray, always wanting money and selling himself for promises, and never getting the money and never keeping his engagements; a good deal of the rake and a good deal of the knight-errant; to himself a portentous politician, a reformer of Church and empire, yet willing to set Church and empire to sale, and himself to retire from the Caesarship, to accept the chair of St. Peter, and provide before his death for his own canonization; yet with all that the founder of one of the great powers of modern history, grandfather of Charles V, and contriver of the scheme which placed half Christendom under his grandson's sceptre. I have often thought of Maximilian in contrast with Henry VII; all the balance of real goodness, what measure there is of politic honesty, purity of life, reality of character, straightforwardness in religion, intelligent appreciation of his people's needs, every moral consideration is in favour of Henry Tudor: yet we like Maximilian better. With all his undeniable faults, his absurd dishonesty which did more harm to himself than to any one else, his grotesque pretensions, the astounding inconsistency between his undertakings and his fulfilments; there is an attractiveness about him which there is not

about Henry VII. We will not stay to compare him with
Charles VIII or Ferdinand the Catholic; I do not know
that we can care much for either, but we do care very little
for Henry VII.

Yet, again, here is the uniter of the Roses, the founder of
the Tudor dictatorship which steered England through the
age of the Reformation, which projected and secured the
union with Scotland, which started England in the race of
commercial enterprise; here is the hero of romance, in whom
the prophetic eye of the saintly Henry of Lancaster had seen
the Joash of the British Zion; the child of exile, hunted, like
David, as a partridge on the mountains; the knight-errant
coming to rescue the distressed lady, as Perseus to Andro-
meda; the avenger of blood at Bosworth field; the Hercules
of the twelve labours; who overcame the Nemean lion in
Edward IV; the Erymanthian boar in Richard III; the
Arcadian stag in John of Lincoln; the Cretan bull in James
of Scotland; the mares of Diomedes in Martin Swart; whose
hydra had been the civil wars; who had put down the
Stymphalian birds by the agency of the Star Chamber; had
thwarted in Margaret of York the host of the Amazons;
and found the three heads of Geryon in Maximilian, the
Archduke Philip, and the dowager of Burgundy; who had
beaten Cacus in Perkin Warbeck, and Cerberus in three
still more insignificant enemies, and by overcoming Max's
opposition to the French alliance had lulled the dragon
and made his way into the garden of the Hesperides. It
is not every Hercules who answers so precisely to the
archetype.

And then think of him as the eligible *parti* of Europe;
the young pretender of fifty looking out for a wife; thinking of the Queen of Naples as very practicable, and at all
events worth very minute inquiries as to teeth and stay-
laces; or perhaps Margaret of Austria, who could make him

arbiter of the Netherlands, and possibly of Spain; or Johanna of Castile, if she could have been consoled for the death of the archduke; or that delightful Countess of Angoulême, Louise of Savoy, the mother of Francis I, and destroyer of the Constable of Bourbon; or last, but not least, Katharine of Aragon, his own daughter-in-law, if the pope, whose conscience was elastic enough to dispense a marriage with a brother's wife, could so far stretch a point of infallibility as to connive at such a politic enormity. Well, the Lady Margaret, poor thing, had four husbands, and Henry VIII had six wives; matrimony was clearly a feature in the germinating policy of the Magians of the renaissance. And then, did ever English king receive, like Henry VII, three caps and swords from three successive popes,—from Innocent VIII, Alexander VI, and Julius II? And last, but not least, Francis Bacon for a biographer! And yet we want something more!

But it is time to be serious. If it is fair to estimate the importance of a reign by the contrast which may be drawn between the two that precede and follow it, the reign of Henry VII should be regarded as one of the most important, and in some respects the most important reign in English History. But to argue thus would really be a mistake; really much of the importance that does attach to it is not its own, but arises from the general character of the age in which it fell, the critical, transitional age, which would have been very much what it was whatever sort of king was on the throne of England.

If the points which English History has thus in common with general European History during this period be left out of consideration, both the interest and the real significance of the actual events of the history of England fall into the background. Such interest as it has becomes a dreary and commonplace interest; its dramatic action, if it can be said to have any, is extremely slow; there is little that calls for sympathy in men or institutions, and the pages of the annalist are dry and jejune to an exceptional degree. And what interest it has in the nature of personal incident is apart from the life of the nation. With the single exception of that part of the incident which concerns the conspiracies and pretensions of the Yorkist faction, which again derives its interest from the tragedy of the preceding reign, the pages of the annalist, where there are any, are so dull that we scarcely complain of their jejuneness. We have no temptation to follow the humdrum movements of the court as we trace the military itinerary of Edward I or the judicial itinerary of Henry II; and it is by an effort that we have to remind ourselves what great things, irrespective of political events, were going on in England during these years; how it was the period of the great activity of Caxton and his early followers, the period of the foundation or development of colleges in Oxford and Cambridge, of the renewal of old studies, of the friendship of Erasmus and More; of discovery of a new world, and of unexampled development of commercial enterprise.

It is curious how little notice is taken of these things in the contemporary annals; they lie, for the most part, outside of the limited area that we are wont to take for constitutional history. But we do not doubt that an immense part of the life of the next age was wrapped up in these things. Certainly the invention of printing, not less than the agglomeration of the new factors of the European balance, was a starting-point of a new stage of History; and the freedoms and jealousies of commerce and conquest in the New World were factors in the new drama second only in importance to the accumulations of power and territory in Europe. But they are both of them events of a class which finds for contemporaries too much work to allow of much talk or many contemplative jottings. Few very busy men keep minute or accurate diaries; few very busy ages possess very picturesque or very circumstantial chronicles. The early printers and the early discoverers left material enough for the next generation to dispute about, but did little in record of their own exploits. Many navigators lived and died and perished from memory before Columbus, and even the continent which he discovered is not called by his name. The inventor of printing is still unknown, and we cannot tell when, or very distinctly where, even Caxton set up the first English press; they were too busy.

And yet more might be expected in the way of history. Caxton himself was a compiler of history; the old monasteries, like Crowland, still contained men capable of writing annals, and of combining annals into chronicles, and of drawing out of chronicles the lessons of History. There is no *a priori* reason why the English history of the age should be sought in Bernard Andreas of Toulouse, or in Polydore Vergil of Urbino, or from the relations of foreign ambassadors. We conclude that the really important things, in which the critical change was, were things that did not come easily into historical contemporaneous exposition. Perhaps too it was hardly safe to write history when the printing-press might diffuse it to distances that would be dangerous; kings and courts would read, and woe to those who wrote what would not please them; or perhaps the revival of ancient literature engrossed the minds of those who, without such employment, might have continued the roll of ancient scholars.

It was not history alone, but theology and science also, that languished under the sudden revival of classical learning; men lost themselves in the history of early Rome who might have told us something worth knowing about their own England; or satisfied themselves with simple attempts to write fine Latin, not troubling themselves much as to whether they had anything to say; or with pronouncing eulogistic orations fit for kings and chancellors to read. But you will be thinking that is just what I am doing now; it is too obvious that a public statutory lecture is not a labour of love.

It is clear, then, not from the distinct enunciations of the time, but from the lessons of preceding and following reigns, what England wanted, and what it got in Henry VII. England did not want to become territorially one, as France, Spain, and Germany did before the new drama of politics began. England had long been territorially one; but it required constitutional and governmental consistency. It required an equability of the execution of law, the abolition of local partisanships, the abeyance of political questionings and controversies, thorough concentration in the hands of strong kings and able ministers. Such a king Henry VII was; such a king Henry VIII was during the better part of his reign, and to some extent Elizabeth was a successor of the same kind; strong in will, strong in wealth, strong in definite personal aims, but even stronger in the way in which their absolute power could be manipulated. It wanted too such things as, first, the vindication of a dynastic title to the throne by the victory of the king over the Yorkist party, by the union of family titles in his marriage, by the securing of every possible lawful guarantee to the succession, so that there might be no more Wars of the Roses; and consequent upon this, the enriching of the crown to such an extent as to make the king almost, if not entirely, independent of taxation for purposes of ordinary expenditure : or, secondly, the humiliation of the baronage by exhaustion, impoverishment, and reduction of numbers, leaving scarcely a trace of the divisions of party between the adherents of the two Roses, extinguishing the hereditary politics of the great houses and almost extinguishing the constitutional powers of the House

of Lords. The concentration of power in the hands of a
royal council of nominees was another result of the abject
condition of the smaller and southern nobles. Even the
greatest magnates were content to serve in the council as
ministers and advisers, rather than to act up to their position
constitutionally as members of a great estate in Parliament.

Or, thirdly, the humiliation of proper ecclesiastical independence, which resulted from the isolation of Church power
in the face of the throne. The Papacy, which might have
lent strength to the clerical estate, was itself weak, and
changing its front, becoming more of an Italian power and
less of an ecumenical arbitrator and influence, just at the
moment when in England the clergy alone remained united
enough to withstand the royal will. The clerical estate did
not at first feel what was happening to it; for Henry VII
had no quarrel with it, and possibly had no design of
secularizing the powers that should have been, first of all,
moral and spiritual: he chose his ministers from churchmen,
and made bishops of his ministers; until the bishops forgot
that they were anything but ministers; sadly to the depression of religion, and sadly to the depression of learning,
as the revival showed when it threw the learning of the
country into the party of innovation, notwithstanding the
influence of such men as Morton, More, Warham, Colet,
and even Wolsey. The Church was sitting at the foot of a
dynasty which ere long was to kick it over and to trample
on it.

And fourthly, there was the people, weary of dynastic
parties and politics, and set on a new pursuit of money-
making, loving peace and hating taxation, and willing to
endure anything from kings who would so far humour them:
not altogether content, but discontented in a way that showed
that heart and treasure went together: for, true as some of
the charges of financial chicanery against Henry VII are,

they owe their real practical weight to the fact that the people who groaned under them were rapidly growing in acquisitive power and economic wisdom ; they knew they had something worth conserving.

Thus England, with her once turbulent baronage depressed and silent, her Church kept subservient by the bestowal of political influence to the loss of religious power, her people in good-humour so long as they were not overtaxed, was, under kings with determinate views, rich and ambitious, collected enough and manageable enough to enter as an efficient actor into the international drama.   If she wanted leaders, guides, dictators in the coming struggle, she found them in the race which Henry VII founded and impressed with a strong will, a strong policy, and a strong energetic activity that gave her unmistakeably her place in modern history.

It would be very difficult, more difficult than in the case of a reign which has a plot, or a dramatic complexity or unity, to attempt a chronological account of the development of any principle or principles in this reign.   I have said it is naturally divided into two great sections ; and those two are subdivided in their turn.

I am afraid that, having spent all my generalizations in the preamble, I must in the remainder of this and the following lecture descend to the level of tabular computations, pedigrees, Acts of Parliament, and treaties.   But we will hope for the best.   As I am not aware that there is anything in the statute under which I am lecturing which makes it incumbent on me to offer on these occasions a substantive original contribution to history, I shall not apologize for taking my hearers over well-known and well-trodden ground.

The first point, of course, that occurs to us in a survey of the reign is the nature of Henry VII's title to the throne. On this no little controversy has been raised, and yet very trenchant opinions are given.   We are not uncommonly told that Henry VII had not in his own person a shadow of hereditary right; that is a view not uncommonly taken in the schools; it is concise, and not hard to remember. But it is not exactly true. The whole question of the title of the house of Lancaster is a matter of dispute; and the title of the house of York has always, curiously enough, been a point on which extreme legitimists and extreme advocates of popular right have agreed. Edward IV was heir-general of Edward III, therefore he pleases the legitimists; he came to the throne by a revolution, therefore he satisfies their extreme opponents. From a legal point of view it is different; Henry VI was the heir, in the male line of succession, of Edward III, and also, by descent from Henry IV, was heir-male of a new purchaser under a new and parliamentary title. Henry VII's title was of course very debateable. With relation to Edward III, he was not heir-general, for that place belonged to the daughters of Edward IV: nor was he heir in the male line of succession, because the line was broken in the person of his mother. With relation to John of Gaunt, accepting the legitimation of the Beauforts by king, pope, and Parliament, he was heir-general; whilst with reference to Henry IV, he can hardly be said to have been heir by collateral descent or heir at all.

But a question arises, on what analogy does the royal succession proceed. If on the analogy of a private estate, then Henry VII, as the nearest kinsman to Henry VI on the side of the purchaser Henry IV, had a claim to succeed: that claim was barred, it is said, by reason of the half-blood; and to that the answer is given that the doctrine of the half-blood does not affect the royal succession. If, on the other hand, we take for analogy the descent of peerages limited to heirs male, there can be no question that the Earl of Warwick was the right heir through the line of York, irrespective of the line of Clarence; but Warwick's claim and that of all the

line of York was crossed by attainder: so also was the claim
of Lancaster.

Well, all this argument serves not to prove that Henry
VII had a hereditary claim, but to explain what he meant
when he said he had.   And, although not *very* important,
it is as well to try to understand it.   In truth, the law of
royal succession, except where it has been settled by Parliament, has never been very certain.   Mary I and Elizabeth
were akin by the half-blood only to Edward VI, yet they
claimed hereditary right: disputable perhaps in itself, that
position was strengthened by Henry VIII's will and acts
of settlement.   But Edward VI's will was set aside, and,
although conflicting opinions did conflict, the crown descended in the natural and legal order to James I.   There
can, I think, be no doubt that Henry VII was legitimately
Duke of Lancaster, if we suppose that such a title could pass
through a female, notwithstanding the half-blood.   It is
quite possible to maintain that he was King of England by
hereditary right.

Anyhow, he said he was.   In his first address to the
collected Parliament, Nov. 9, 1485, he declared that he had
come to the crown by just title of inheritance, and by the
true judgement of God in giving him the victory over his
enemy : the Parliament accepted the fact, and passed a statute,
in avoiding all ambiguities and questionings, ordaining,
establishing, and enacting that the inheritance of the crowns
of England and France, and so on, be, rest and remain, in
the person of our now sovereign lord and in the heirs of his
body.   You may think that this was enough, but the pope
clenched the matter in a bull of March 27, 1486, declaring
that Henry was king not only by the right of war, and by
the notorious and undoubted nearest title of succession, but
also by the choice and vote of all the prelates, peers,
magnates, nobles, and of the whole realm of England, and

by ordinance, decree, and statute of the three estates of the realm called the Parliament, for this purpose publicly and generally held. Perhaps the good old man swore a little too hard; the accumulation of reasons may show that Innocent VIII had some misgiving.

Trebly certain, however, as all this was, by a scale of verdicts rising from the king's own assertion, to the Parliament, to the pope, and to the judgement of the Almighty, the king would make assurance doubly sure by marrying the equally undoubted heiress of the rival line. He was espoused to Elizabeth of York on the 18th of January, 1486. He had not waited for her to be crowned with him; he himself had been crowned on the 30th of October: and he was in no great hurry to admit her to a share of his dignity. She was not crowned until the 25th of November, 1487, and a great deal had happened in the meantime. I am not sure that the marriage was a very happy one. *A priori*, there was no reason why it should, although I believe it is certain that husband and wife were faithful. But Elizabeth was a silly woman, and Henry was not a sympathetic man. It was said she would have married her uncle, and certainly her marriage with Henry was a marriage of convenience. Their family politics must have been very much opposed; that is if we suppose them to have had any family affections at all, which is rather a strong effort to suppose in the case of kings and queens in the fifteenth century. But it is still more certain that they both had mothers alive, and there would be, according to all analogies, no love lost. Henry was an affectionate and obedient son to a pious and noble mother: Elizabeth had a mother who had not much sense or discretion, and was constantly in disgrace. The Lady Margaret was strict and stately, and a woman of great experience, of many husbands and good advisers: the queen dowager may have learned, in the romantic seclusion to which her son-in-law consigned her, some lessons that would counteract the influences of the court in which she had reigned during her false, fair husband's lifetime, and she may have profited by the sweet uses of adversity; but she inherited the characteristic features of her mother Jacquetta, and her own early career was one of vanity and foolish ambition. Anyhow, the Lady Margaret had the upper hand; she kept her son straight and the court fairly pure, both during his wife's life and after her death, when the discipline was so close that poor Katharine of Aragon had to write home to her father that she could not get a mouthful of meat in Lent.

The history of the first half of the reign is the story of the struggle with which this trebly attested title to the throne was maintained; a bloody story, it is true, but, take it all in all, scarcely to be compared with what goes before and follows. The struggle is not altogether dynastic; it is not in all its details a contest of competitors; and, in fact, each of the incidents in it has a shade of its own, common as the colouring seems at a distance. There were dynastic rivalries, there were personal intrigues and party blood-feuds that made use of the dynastic rivalries to secure their victory or revenge, and there were administrative difficulties emerging in discontents, which had little to do with either dynastic or hereditary struggles, but lent aid to both and borrowed pretext from both.

It is hardly necessary for me perhaps to recall to your minds what roots of dynastic bitterness still subsisted: but for the sake of clearness I will enumerate them.. There was the Dowager Margaret of Burgundy, ready to say or do or believe anything for the sake of revenge; there was the son of Clarence, a prisoner in the king's hands; there were the De la Poles, the five sons of John, Duke of Suffolk, by Elizabeth of York, the eldest of whom had been recognized by Richard III as his presumptive heir; and there was the

doubt that hung over the death of Edward V and his brother
Richard. It is curious to trace the intertwining of these
really incompatible and inconsistent interests, and yet the
only conclusion at which we can fairly arrive is the utterly
desperate and unprincipled character of the Yorkist intrigues.

The first rising is perhaps the most desperate; in April
1486 the Viscount Lovel, and Humfrey and Thomas Stafford,
rose in Worcestershire; the king, as Bacon tells us, thought
it a mere rag of Bosworth: although at one time it seemed
to be becoming formidable, it collapsed before the king's offer
of pardon. Lovel escaped to the Duchess Margaret, Humfrey
Stafford was executed, and Thomas was pardoned. Whether
the original motive of the rising was the despair of the
attainted leaders, or an intrigue of the as yet unreconciled
Yorkist remnant, it is, by the agency of Lord Lovel, linked
on with the second rising, that of 1487, in the name of
Lambert Simnel. The idea of dethroning the new king by
setting up as claimant a person, who pretended to be another
person, who was well known to be a prisoner in the king's
hands, is not only desperate but unprincipled, and, if I can
say it without offence, not only unprincipled and desperate,
but Irish. Lambert Simnel, a boy of twelve years old, the
son of an organ-maker at Oxford, educated by a clever priest
named Symonds, a name still known here, was presented to
the world as Edward Earl of Warwick; was received in
Ireland in February 1487, crowned at Dublin in May, brought
to England in June, and taken prisoner at Stoke near Newark
on the 16th of that month. In this most extravagant imposture the Yorkist remnant was thoroughly implicated:
the Duchess Margaret was represented by Martin Swart and
his men; the Earl of Lincoln, the cousin of Warwick, was
slain fighting for Simnel; the Lord Lovel, 'the dog' minister
of Richard, disappeared on the field, and Henry's suspicions

were so strongly excited against his mother-in-law that he had to send her to a nunnery, and her son Lord Dorset to the Tower. The third rising, that in Yorkshire in 1489, was not directly connected with the dynastic quarrel, but was provoked by the taxation voted in the preceding Parliament: Egremont, however, the leader of the rioters who killed the Earl of Northumberland at Thirsk, was a Yorkist partisan, and found a refuge in his exile with the intransigent Duchess of Burgundy. After this we get on for three years without overt trouble. The year 1492 is marked by another Yorkshire battle, that of Acworth, between the Earl of Surrey and certain rebels, whose occasion of rising is not known; and it would therefore be of little use to argue whether or no it was connected with the imminent conspiracy for Perkin Warbeck, or a result of local discontent of which there may have been other cases not recorded at all.

Next comes the grand episode or tragedy of Perkin, which covers seven years of disturbance, and connects the Yorkist intrigues with the social discontents in a way more striking than any of the previous outbursts. I will only just indicate the dates and points of contact. Perkin, whose prompters, wiser than Lambert Simnel's, identified him with a claimant who could be more easily counterfeited, is said to have been educated by the Duchess Margaret to appear as her nephew Richard of York; as such he lands at Cork probably in 1491, certainly by February 1492. According to Bacon, he himself was not at first quite sure who he was, a sort of doubt that has affected the minds of his adherents ever since; but, if there was any hesitation on his part, it must have been assumed for the purpose of ascertaining under what title he would be most likely to make a good start. After having exhibited himself for some time in Ireland and France without much affecting the political feeling of England, he returned to Flanders in August, 1493, and his supporters for a while had to content themselves with intrigue. So thoroughly, however, was the scheme worked, that in 1494 the Yorkist lords in England sent over Sir Robert Clifford to ascertain the truth of the story that was put in Perkin's mouth; and Clifford, after having familiarized himself with the conditions of the party at home, was brought over to the king's side, turned against his employers, and gave up their names to the government. Several of these were of the old Yorkist connexion, and were executed in the autumn of 1494; the greatest victim, however, was Sir William Stanley the chamberlain, brother of the Lady Margaret's husband the Earl of Derby, and one of the most able of the adherents who had placed Henry of Richmond on the throne. He had, from some idea apparently that his own services were ill requited, entangled himself in the plot, and, although he must have been undeceived as to the identity of the impostor, was not therefore spared; he perished in February, 1495.

The increasing severity of the king's proceedings, and the success of his counter intrigues, thus warned the rest of the plotters that no time must be lost. In July of this year Perkin attempted a landing at Sandwich; this failing, he went again to Ireland, and then to Scotland, where he obtained full recognition and a noble wife. Henry was now pursuing the course which Edward IV had adopted with regard to himself in his boyhood, and endeavouring to obtain by diplomatic agencies the expulsion of the claimant from the territories of the neighbour princes. Early in 1496 he concluded a treaty with Burgundy, which forbade the entertainment of Perkin there; and in 1497, on the approach of a peace with Scotland, he negotiated for his surrender. The King of Scots, who in November 1496 had made a raid into the north in his behalf, was still prepared to support him and refused to betray him; but he thought it best to be rid of him: sent him to Ireland in July, and, after another invasion and defeat, concluded in September a truce for seven years, with which any overt support of the Pretender would have been incompatible.

Before the truce was actually signed Perkin's career was over. In its last act the plot connects itself with the social discontent. In the January Parliament a new subsidy had been voted, and this, when it came to be collected, provoked a rising in Cornwall. The men of Cornwall rose under the local hero Flammock, who, declaring the law on his side, and insisting on delivering a petition to the king, started them for London. Picking up as their leader a disaffected nobleman, Lord Audley, on the way, they pushed on to Blackheath, where they were defeated with great loss on June 22. The king's severity was somewhat arbitrary, but the effect was to quicken Perkin's movements and to point to the part of England where he was most likely to win support. He landed near Penzance in September, pushed to Taunton where he was put to flight, took sanctuary at Beaulieu, and on October 5 was surrendered to the king. Henry was inclined to spare him, possibly having some doubt as to his real identity; he was however imprisoned, and his escape in June, 1498, his recapture, and further involvement in the plot which was made an excuse for implicating the Earl of Warwick, ended in the execution of the two in November, 1499: a cruelty for which other motives and other influences, besides the sense of actual danger, are probably accountable.

After the extinction of these two, the false and the true competitors, the King had only the De la Poles to doubt about. The eldest of these, Edmund, who after his brother's death at Stoke had been the head of the branch, and who after his father's death in 1491 had been allowed to surrender his estate of Duke and subside into Earl of Suffolk, quitted England with his brother Richard, in August, 1501. What

intelligence they may have had of the means by which
Ferdinand the Catholic was likely to insure the succession of
his son-in-law Arthur; or whether Edmund, who had been
fairly well treated by the king, but had taken offence at a
humiliation which he had, so far as it was real, brought upon
himself, acted on mere impulse and carried his brother with
him, we cannot decide;—they fled together to their aunt
Margaret and constituted the dynastic bugbear for the rest
of the reign. It was not the first escapade. Edmund had
been indicted for murder in 1498; he had been pardoned,
but notwithstanding had run away to Flanders. He had,
however, then returned, apologized, and been received into
favour. Just before the celebration of the marriage of Arthur
he made this second flight; on the invitation of Maximilian,
who was engaged in one of his unaccountable intrigues, he
went from Flanders and joined him in Tyrol; the emperor
offering to put him at the head of a large force to secure his
rights, but really playing him as a card in his diplomatic
game with Henry and Ferdinand. In 1502 he was planning
an invasion of England to start from Denmark, and was implicated in the attempt on Guisnes which brought Sir James
Tyrrell to the block. The same year Henry, by promising
Maximilian 10,000 marks for his war against the Turks,
prevailed on him to expel the English malcontents, whilst
Ferdinand and Isabella as well as Lewis XII joined in urging
the proscription. Edmund fled then to the Count Palatine,
and in 1504, venturing into Guelders, was taken prisoner by
the duke. The same year he was attainted with fifty-two
of his adherents. The next year the duke gave him up to
the Archduke Philip, under whose care he made some very
brave show of claims against Henry VII for the estates and
dignities of his father. Unfortunately for him, when the
archduke, in 1506, was forced by the weather to land in
England, Henry made a point with him that Edmund should

be surrendered. Philip, who like his father was quite equal to playing a game of the sort that Henry loved, was on this occasion at the mercy of his host. He promised to surrender the prisoner on the strict understanding that his life should be spared. He was surrendered and his life was spared, so long as Henry VII lived. He came to the Tower in March, 1506. In 1513 he was beheaded by Henry VIII. According to Lord Herbert, Henry VII had left it in charge to his son that, although he had sworn not to execute him, his successor should and would be wise to do it. Whether or no this is true, Henry VIII's cruelty was no doubt stimulated by finding Richard De la Pole, the younger brother, fighting in the army of France against him. Richard continued to be a thorn in the side of England— the White Rose of York as he was called—until in 1525 he was killed fighting for Francis I at Pavia.

Margaret of Burgundy lived until 1503, but her power and wealth as well as her zeal had diminished, and after the failure of Perkin she had been almost innocuous. This finishes the dynastic complications of the reign of Henry VII. In the next lecture I shall devote myself chiefly to the constitutional points of importance in connexion with domestic and foreign history.

THE REIGN OF HENRY VII

(April 25, 1883.)

IN the first of these two public statutory lectures, I opened my subject with some vain remarks on the want of attractiveness which may be said to characterize the personal and political history of Henry VII : and then, having divided the reign into two portions, nearly coinciding with the change of century, I very briefly marked the series of dynastic quarrels, struggles, and disturbances, the interest of which belongs mainly to the first half of the reign. There remains to us some investigation of the constitutional and diplomatic history of a period which falls between two great constitutional periods, and lays the foundation of a great diplomatic, political, and commercial fabric ; or rather I should say opens a great diplomatic, political, and commercial period, which constitutes modern history in its general acceptation.

With regard to the constitutional history proper, nearly the same line may be drawn as in the other case, for, as only one Parliament was called between the year 1497 and the end of the reign, the greatest part of what little constitutional history there is belongs to the earlier half. It cannot however be said that, with the exception of two or three very distinct pieces of legislation, and a very distinct purpose of raising and storing money, there is much constitutional material to deal with. There is a great poverty of record. The Rolls of the Parliaments tell us scarcely anything more than the dates of opening, the subject of the chancellor's address, the name of the Speaker, and the titles of the Acts passed, including the subsidies. There are no details of deliberation, or discussions on petitions. There are no Journals of either House; there is nothing in the shape of writs or returns to indicate the composition of the House of Commons; and little, if indeed anything, to show how the composition of the House of Lords was able to influence legislation or administration. Not that we are entirely in the dark as to these matters: we know from the character of the Acts passed, and from the nature of the political measures of the reign, what sort of influences must have been at work: but we have no documentary details, nothing of personal or sensational import.

The ministerial changes of the reign are not in themselves important: the chancellorship, after having been held for a few months by Bishop Alcock, early in 1486 devolves upon Archbishop Morton, who is the minister of the reign: he retains the great seal as long as he lives, and during the rest of the reign it is held only by Dene and Warham, successively Archbishops of Canterbury. The treasury in the same way sees few alterations; whilst Alcock is chancellor, Sir Reginald Bray is treasurer; under Morton, Lord Dynham; and from 1500 to 1509 Thomas Howard, who, as Earl of Surrey and Duke of Norfolk, remains at the head of finance during his life and leaves the position to his son, who holds it until 1546.

The tenure of these great offices by prelates and magnates of this sort, of course, implies that a great deal of the business of the country was conducted by means of subordinate officials; it also means that the king and his council took such direct part in it, that the nominal ministers had a somewhat diminished responsibility; and it probably means further, under Henry VII at least, that the king dealt directly with the subordinate officials without much concert

with his nominal ministers. This is especially the case as
the reign proceeds; during the first half Archbishop Morton,
who was both a distinguished lawyer and, in popular opinion,
a too active financier, really did ministerial work. After his
death the king seems to have employed men like Empson
and Dudley for measures which men like Archbishop
Warham and the Earl of Surrey could certainly not have
approved, but which they were helpless to prevent, and
perhaps without courage to remonstrate about. There is not
then much to be said about ministerial history.

The next point to note is the composition of the House of
Lords. We are open to some risk of exaggeration in relation
to this, because of the slaughters and proscriptions connected
with the Wars of the Roses. But, great as were the effects
of those quarrels on the personality of the baronage, the
effect was far greater on the political status and influence of
the peerage. It was attenuated in power and prestige rather
than in numbers. Even the bloodshed and attainder fall
within a small circle; generation after generation perishes
out of a few great houses; the majority continue in succession and either escape ruin or soon recover. It is as well
to be particular as to this, because it has a real bearing on
the character of the Tudor despotism or dictatorship; and
we are liable to be misled both by striking catastrophes and
by untested generalizations. If we compare the last parliament of Edward VI with the first of Henry VII, we find a
great difference on the face of it: in 1483 there are forty-five
lords summoned to Parliament; in 1485 there are only
twenty-nine. But for this diminution the recent change of
dynasty is only very partially the cause: only six peers are
attainted as yet, three of whom, the late King Richard, the
Duke of Norfolk, and the Lord Ferrers, had fallen at
Bosworth field; and a fourth was Surrey, the son of the
Duke of Norfolk. Of the other missing lords, some had

perished under Richard's own tyranny, some two or three were now represented by minors, and about half-a-dozen seem to have had their summons suspended during either the whole reign or a great part of it. Of these suspended peers, who all reappear either in the later Parliaments or in the first Parliament of Henry VIII, the chief are the Ogle, Dacre, and Scrope lords, who rule in the north country, and whose absence, which is not necessarily to be accounted for on political grounds, is a point that has not been satisfactorily investigated. In this way, however, not by proscription or execution, the list is diminished. In the later Parliaments not only do many of these suspended peerages revive, the empty places being filled by the restoration of the heirs of Richard's victims, but even the attainders of 1485 are cancelled; the Howards return to favour and power in 1489, Ferrers in 1487, Zouch in 1495; Lovel perishes, the viscount himself who fell at Stoke leaving only coheiresses.

A proof of what I have been saying is seen also in the fact that during the whole reign only five new peerages were created; one of these, the earldom of Bath, held by a foreigner, does not seem to have entitled its possessor to a summons; another is an Irish earldom, Ormond; the other three are Daubeny, Cheney, and Burgh. Yet notwithstanding this economy and the later attainders of the reign, the subsequent Parliaments contain a lay peerage of forty members, which is not below the average of the century and was not increased materially until Henry VIII brought up the number of lay lords to that of the spiritual lords, before he finally reduced the latter to half their tale by getting rid of the abbots.

This point, like that of the composition of the House of Commons, on which we have no information, would be more important if we knew anything of the parliamentary history. As we do not, and find that the king in that august assembly had things very much as he pleased, we conclude, as we have other reasons for concluding, either that the assembled estates were cowed into complaisance, or else that they were too busy about other matters to care for the excitement of a quarrelsome debate.

There were seven Parliaments during the reign of twenty-four years; and of these seven, one had three sessions and another two; six of them fall before the close of 1497, and before the end of Archbishop Morton's life. I think that, if we had nothing else to judge by, we should infer from this, that so long as Morton was minister the king retained the Lancastrian idea of ruling mainly through Parliaments; whilst, during the nine years that followed the archbishop's death, he reigned chiefly through councils and held but one Parliament. Morton was indeed a thorough Lancastrian, though not of the type of Archbishop Arundel. He had been the mainstay of the party in evil times, and the leader of intrigue under Edward IV and Richard III; but the old political game of Lancaster had long been played out, and, although Morton probably retained the attachment to forms which marked it to the last, he, either as a politician or as overborne by the king, was not in his financial administration faithful to the constitutional principle. This matter touches, however, a point of character in which master and minister alike suffer. Henry VII is constantly accused of avarice, and Morton to the popular mind is best known as the inventor of the fork, Morton's fork, the dilemma by which he proved the necessity of the benevolences, to the great dissatisfaction of the payers: if you spend much you have plenty; if you spend little you must have saved; out of your plenty, or out of your savings, you must pay.

I do not know that I am concerned to defend Morton, who was certainly not an avaricious man himself, and who, if he incurs a part of his master's shame, incurs it as a too faithful servant; but it is worth while speculating on Henry's own character for avarice. He was a man who had a fair intelligence and a fair knowledge of history: he had been very poor himself, and he had learned that poverty and want of economic governance had ruined the great house to which Henry V had imparted so much glory. He knew, from the first, that he must save in order to get on at all; and when he had begun to save, and when, by the forfeitures of the early years, he had managed to save to some purpose, not only did the love of money increase as the money itself accumulated, but he found it pleasant to rule without having to ask Parliament for money; and finally found it pleasant, through Empson and Dudley, both to rule and to gather money without the trouble of Parliament. However that may have been, the seven Parliaments each had a subsidy or a budget; and the financial history is capable of a brief summary.

In the first Parliament Henry succeeded in obtaining a revenue for life; Bishop Alcock had made a moving speech on the text, 'Good luck have thou with thine honour, ride on;' in which he adduced the fable of the belly and members, the properties of bees, Isidore on the virtues of royalty, St. Ambrose in the Hexaemeron, and Ovid on the Golden Age; with the usual application. After the approval of the Speaker, the king addressed the Commons with a declaration of his title and promises of good government: and they responded with a liberal vote of tunnage, poundage, and the custom on leather for life; apportioning £14,000 to the household, £10,000 odd to Calais, and £2105 19*s*. 11*d*. to the wardrobe; there was likewise an act of resumption.

In the session of 1487 Morton preached on 'Cease to do evil, learn to do well:' a wonderful sermon in four heads, subdivided each into three arguments, illustrated from Cicero and other Gentile philosophers, the moral of which was the vote of two tenths and fifteenths, and a poll-tax upon aliens, payable at the next Easter. In 1489 the text was 'The eyes of the Lord are over the righteous;' the sermon a miracle of subdivision: the demand a lump sum of £100,000. To meet this, by a curious departure from the rule which is always supposed to have been long established, the Lords, by themselves, grant a tenth of their income from land; the Commons, with the advice and consent of the Lords, offer to raise £75,000 by a tenth on lands not belonging to the lords, and twenty-pence on every ten marks of goods. This must have been seen to be a dangerous experiment. An attempt to collect the tax caused the outbreak at Thirsk, in which the Earl of Northumberland was slain; the sums collected from the Commons only reached the amount of £27,000, and in the third session early in 1490 the grant of a tenth and fifteenth was substituted for the balance. The object of the budget was the maintenance of the army, which was being raised for the defence of Brittany against France, a design which culminates and terminates in the expedition to Boulogne in October, 1492. Before this expedition took place another Parliament in the autumn of 1491 and January of 1492 was asked for a vote. Morton chose his text from Jeremiah, and his illustrations from Sallust on the war with Jugurtha; the bill was two entire tenths and fifteenths, and a third if the king himself should go to the war. He did go to the war and made peace. And this carried him on to 1495.

I should say here that the parliamentary grants were each year supplemented by ecclesiastical grants made in the Convocations of the two provinces, and generally consisting of one entire tenth from each; the tenth of the Southern province was about £10,000 and that of York about £3,000, I think. In 1489, when the estates, as we have just seen, proposed separate grants, the share of the Canterbury clergy was fixed at £25,000, about the same sum as that offered by the House of Lords; but it finally took the form of two entire tenths.

Well, the grants of 1491, which extended over a year, proved insufficient for the king's needs, and he had recourse to the exaction of a benevolence; indeed the commissions for the benevolence were issued before the Parliament sat, and are supposed to have been authorized by a Great Council which sat in the June previous. This must have been a very liberal contribution, if the subscriptions of the country bore any proportion to the sum raised in London, which was £9682 17s. 4d. But I am not aware that any exact account of it exists. No doubt the commissions were executed in the usual way, but the authority given to the commissioners is only that they should intimate the king's purpose to the subjects, and move, exhort, and require them to assist him, in contemplation of the war with France. The commission was worked to some purpose, for the short expedition did not cost so much as might have been expected, and it was not until 1495 that the king found it necessary to call a Parliament. It is then to this period that we must fix the application of Morton's fork, and to it Lord Bacon assigns the beginning of the penurious or saving habits which later on grew so strong in the king. I will just add that, as it was the subsidy of 1489 that provoked the riot at Thirsk, it was in all probability the subsidy of 1491 and the exaction of the benevolence that caused the struggle at Acworth in 1492.

In the Parliament of 1495 no new tax was asked for; the archbishop's sermon was a lecture on law, which he divided into the law of Nature, the law of Nations, the Mosaic, Civil, Evangelic, and Canon law, with an application of the subject to the regulations of trade and commerce. These have a visible outcome in the sixty-five Acts that the Parliament passed. For our present point but one of these is important;

the tenth statute, on the benevolence: divers persons have granted benevolences for the expedition to France; some have paid what they promised, some have not; the crown is empowered to enforce the fulfilment of the promises. There can be little doubt after this as to the great value of the benevolence; no further demand is made of the Parliament, but the clergy grant an entire tenth.

The next session was not so happy. It was in January, 1497; the archbishop lectured this time on Roman history, Scipio, Curtius, Scaevola, Regulus, Julius Caesar and St. Augustine: the occasion was really pressing: the Scots king was making a succession of raids, and the invasion by Perkin was impending. And a very exceptional grant was made, two fifteenths and tenths first, and then another sum of the same amount, reaching, according to Lord Bacon, to £120,000, and no doubt contributing to the disaffection which brought the Cornishmen to Blackheath and encouraged Perkin to land at Penzance. The clergy are asked for £40,000, of which the king remits £10,000. This is the last great tax of the reign: peace is practically insured, and the king finds other ways of enriching himself. Nevertheless, in 1502 the clergy pay a tenth, or thereabouts, for the expedition against the Turks, that is to say, the subsidy promised to Maximilian for his expulsion of Edmund de la Pole; and in 1504 the Parliament granted £40,000 as an aid on the knighting of the king's eldest son and marriage of his eldest daughter. This was the last session of the reign. Morton had died four years before; and Archbishop Warham opened the Parliament with a discourse on moral philosophy from Aristotle and Cicero, of a much more florid and less scholastic type than the sermons of his predecessor, and probably in better Latin.

This closes the financial history of the reign except in one point. Henry VII is said to have left behind him £1,800,000 sterling, a great part of which must have been the result of savings from royal demesne and forfeitures, but which was partially, and in popular belief principally, accumulated by exactions made by Empson and Dudley. These two men, acting as members of the royal council and under the direct control of the king, had reduced to a system the extraction of money on false or exaggerated charges. They had revived old sentences and ancient worn-out claims, and had the king's connivance in exacting the pettiest sums. In the year 1504 so great was the outcry against them that the king, suffering at the time from illness and taking a spell of penitence, issued letters ordering that all who had any reason to complain of injury inflicted in the king's name should come forward and have a hearing. But no real good was done, and the abuses continued to the end of the reign : the culprits had imprisoned men without chance of hearing until they had paid their fines ; they had compelled others to recognize themselves as tenants in chief and so liable for feudal aids ; they had refused livery of seisin to wards, except on payment of enormous reliefs ; exacted two years' income from outlaws before they could sue for pardons ; they had heard and disposed of matters that belonged to the courts of law, and had imprisoned and fined a jury. These charges against them are in exact parallel with the abuses practised by William Rufus and remedied by Henry I and in Magna Carta. Yet they pleaded royal authority and the letter of the law, and, when the time of vengeance came, as it did at the very opening of the next reign, they perished on a charge of conspiring to govern the king and council, very much analogous to that which had been brought against the Despensers two centuries before, not on the ground of their real offences.

The next point to take is the legislation of the reign, on which I do not propose to say much, as it would be very tedious to repeat the dates and occasions of the Parliaments, whilst to go into the social questions touched by the new laws would be impossible. I will, however, take the principal measures in the order of time. It is not necessary to recur to the acts of attainder and restoration, which occupy so large a part of the pages of the statute book, further than to remark that, although it was doubtless a piece of legal pettifogging to antedate the beginning of the reign by a day in order to include Richard's supporters at Bosworth under the title of rebels, it can scarcely be said to have been an unreasonable proceeding in the new Conqueror to treat them as such. The large number of forfeitures, and the large sums exacted as fines on restoration, show that scarcely any amount of political guilt was beyond forgiveness, if the repentance were accompanied by a handsome sum down. On the whole, where society was just recovering from a condition in which nothing was certain for two days together, and nearly every household was divided against itself, anything like settled peace was worth paying for, and the people generally justified by acquiescence in fact, however much and rightly they might in words complain of the mercenary policy of the court. Parliament itself acquiesced without complaint.

Leaving then these acts out of sight, I will mention the most important laws of permanent interest. In the session of 1485 were passed the Act of Succession, establishing the king's title, an Act which allowed the bishops to imprison incontinent clergy without applying to the sheriffs to arrest them, and an Act against unlawful hunting. In 1487 the Act which founded the Court of Star Chamber was passed, as a remedy for the evils of maintenance, the misconduct of sheriffs, and riots and unlawful assemblies. The court so founded was to consist of the chancellor, treasurer and privy seal, taking to themselves a bishop, a lord temporal, and the two chief justices. This tribunal, which took its name from the Camera Stellata, the chamber in which the council generally sat, subsequently developed into a judicial meeting of councillors and peers

which has a great history of its own; but there is no reason
to question its historic identity throughout, or that this was
the occasion of its foundation. This is the great judicial
measure of the reign, and was intended to meet acknowledged evils.

Blackstone has recorded his impression that every Act of
the reign was intended for the benefit of the exchequer;
perhaps we may allow that, under certain conditions, there is
no price too heavy to pay for peace and order. The chief
Acts of 1489 and 1490 are commercial; cap. 13 limits the
benefit of clergy, which is to be allowed only once to persons
not in holy orders; murderers are to be marked with an M.,
other felons with a T.; and a second claim is not to be
admitted unless the Letters of Orders are produced. Cap. 19
forbids the pulling down of 'towns,' and laying to pasture
lands previously in tillage and tithable: Church and realm
are alike impoverished by the devastation that is going on;
owners of farm-houses, to which a holding of 20 acres is
attached, are bound to keep them in repair or forfeit half
the profits to the king. The importance of this matter
is the burden of the History of John Rous, the Warwick
historian, who does not otherwise add to our knowledge of
the reign. These two statutes are of great social significance; signs of the times of which men like Morton and
More took heed. Cap. 24, the Statute for Proclamation of
Fines, has had a reputation of greater importance than it
deserves, being supposed formerly to have given the power
of alienating entailed lands, and so allowing the great landowners to ruin themselves. This Hallam shows to be a
mistake, and the statute accordingly becomes a minor legal
detail.

Most of the Acts of the year 1491–2 are connected with
the expedition to France, which came off in the latter year;
the securing of the rights of absentees who took part in it,

and a number of restorations from attainder. Those of 1495
have a greater reputation in the law books, and especially
cap. 1, which enacts that persons going with the king for
the time being to war are not to be attaint of treason therefore; an Act passed in a true spirit of equity, but, I fear,
quite inadequate to secure its end in critical times. Perhaps
it has its chief importance as an historical landmark and as
enunciating a principle of public law; anyhow, it shows that
the king felt himself so secure that he need not speculate for
a fall. Cap. 2 is a law on the disposal of 'vacabunds and
beggars,' who are to be sent to their hundreds; if a university man is found begging he must produce a letter of
the chancellor identifying his status, or else must go as a
'vacabund.' Cap. 17 forbids the taking of pheasants and
partridges on other men's lands, an early definite game law
on which I will simply observe that a popular error makes the
introduction of pheasants much more modern than it was;
the Canons of Waltham had pheasants in the eleventh century, by Harold's ordinance, every festival day from Michael-
mas to Lent. Another Act, cap. 22, settled servants' wages,
and that at a rate which it would not be wise to mention to
modern economists, unless we presume there was a handsome
margin for perquisites; the wages, for instance, of a bailiff
are 26s. 8d. a year; and those of the agricultural labourer
4d. or 3d. a day according to the season, his meat and drink
being assumed to be worth 2d. or 1½d. a day: perhaps the
proportion was not so bad. Most of the other Acts of 1495
are what we should call private Acts; the exceptions dealing
with dishonesty in tradesmen, sheriffs' officers, and jurors.

The Acts of 1497 are few and not important; cap. 3 repeals
the Wages Act of the sessions of 1495; cap. 6 relieves the
merchant adventurers of England from the fines imposed by
the merchant adventurers of London, who claimed, under
colour of a fraternity of St. Thomas of Canterbury, to tax

them for dealing in foreign marts : the most significant Acts concern the money grants.

This brings us to the last Parliament, that of 1504. This assembly passed forty statutes, some of them comprehensive and historical enough, as cap. 34, which enumerates with names and dates the successive revolts and conspiracies which had been visited with attainder ; others are Acts of reconciliation and restoration. The most important statutes I can only name now; cap. 14 is on maintenance and livery, increasing penalties and extending the power of the Star Chamber; cap. 15 is on Uses, a step in the growth of the doctrine afterwards fully enunciated in the statute of Henry VIII; cap. 27 settles the custom on wool taken at Calais for the payment of the garrison, to the amount of £10,022 4s. 8d. for the next sixteen years.

Other statutes are interesting mainly in relation to details of trade and to minute points of legal proceedings, and do in their particulars throw light on a few social questions on which light is much needed. Still, on the whole, the survey of the legislation of the reign does not much impress us ; in spite of the one or two really important notes we have marked, there is no trace of a grand or constructive genius such as might be looked for in the opening of a new era ; it is really business-like and humdrum, the work of men who welcomed legislation only just so far as it helped them to get on steadily in the course, the quiet course which they had marked out for themselves. There is nothing, moreover, in the record, either of financial or of legal proceedings, that suggests any political struggles in the Parliament itself ; the story that Sir Thomas More in a Parliament in 1502 prevented the Commons from granting an aid for the marriage of Margaret, although told on good authority, falls to the ground, for the good reason that no Parliament was held in 1502 and that in 1504 the grant was actually made.   More

probably was instrumental in limiting the sum. Outside of
the circle of attainders and restorations very little was done
which was likely to excite opposition or obstruction ; and as
to the little that was done at all, it seems that Lord Bacon's
dictum is too much to say for it : that such was the excellency
of the king's laws that he may be justly celebrated for the best
lawgiver to this nation after King Edward I. It is not well
to analyse the words of an express panegyric, but Bacon's
theory of government must have been, to say the least,
peculiar, if he overlooked the great statutes of Edward III on
taxation and on Church liberties, not to speak of the elaborate
legislation of the next reign. Richard II was, however, no
great lawgiver, and Edward III's good laws were mainly concessions to popular demands; if the words I have quoted
refer to the king's possible personal agency in legislation,
they may have a meaning, otherwise not. I have already
mentioned Blackstone's very different opinion, that all the
laws were calculated for the benefit of the exchequer.

I must now pass on to the foreign transactions and negotiations of the reign, which are most important and most
tedious ; most important because they are closely connected
with the opening of the new drama, the equipment of
England for her part on the stage ; most tedious because
they go on without crisises and without issues, like a game
at chess which has a charm only for an adept, or a well-
contested game at croquet which never comes to an end.
If I cannot help being tedious about this, I will at all risks
be brief.

At the opening of the reign of Henry VII there were, I
think, only two points at which English foreign politics
touched the interests of the continent, Brittany and Burgundy.
Brittany Henry was, for substantial reasons of personal
gratitude, bound to help ; and a marriage with the heiress
Anne, supposing that he was not obliged to marry Elizabeth

of York, was a conceivable contingency. Burgundy under Maximilian was likewise involved in the alliances of Brittany; both were hostile to, or afraid of France, which, under Anne of Beaujeu and Charles VIII, was rather preparing for than actually engaged in her scheme of aggrandisement. From 1485 to 1491 Brittany is the point round which English diplomacy moves. Maximilian is unable to go to war: Henry is unwilling to go to war; France is able and willing; but it requires at least two combatants to fight a respectable battle. Duke Francis, who had been Henry's friend in his exile, had been constantly opposed to Lewis XI, and was intent on securing the succession for his daughter. By receiving Orleans and Dunois in 1485, he had set himself against Anne of Beaujeu; in 1486 he had prevailed on the estates to settle the succession; in 1487 he had been openly attacked by Charles VIII, and had betrothed his daughter to Maximilian. Henry had not as yet moved; he was busy in negotiations all round, but he did allow Edward Wydville to collect volunteers for a campaign in 1488 against the French, followed, as Henry's few campaigns always were, by an immediate truce. That year Duke Francis died. For the three following years Henry talked of war, and war really went on occasionally as if it was stimulated by the little peaces that interrupted it. In 1489, Charles and Maximilian made peace at Frankfort, and Brittany joined. In 1490, Henry made a league with Maximilian and the Catholic Sovereigns to defend Brittany if it were attacked; in 1491 it was attacked and they did not defend it. That year Charles VIII took Nantes and married Anne of Brittany. Then, in fulfilment of his engagements, as well as in compliance with the wish of the nation, Henry, in good time, made his expedition to Boulogne in the Autumn of 1492, which ended in the peace of Etaples concluded in November.

The peace of Etaples is an epoch in more senses than

one; it was the most definite peace that had been made between England and France since the reign of Edward I. It was the closing of the Brittany business which had been the door by which England entered the arena of the new politics; and it allowed Charles VIII to begin his Italian expedition, which usually is regarded as the starting-point of the new drama. Henry, moreover, made a great deal of money by it. It was to last during the lives of both kings, and practically did so. For, in 1498, after Charles' death, it was renewed with Lewis XII, and notwithstanding jealousies, intrigues and counter intrigues, remained unbroken until the next reign.

Scotland, which had been and was still to be the facile tool of France, had a policy of her own during these years. James III, who recognized in Henry VII a friend and kinsman representing the Lancaster interest, which he had always supported, perished in 1488, and from that year to 1498 the relations of the two countries consisted of an uneasy succession of truces broken by inroads of the Scots into the north, which, during the period of the activity of Perkin Warbeck, threatened to develop into active warfare.

In 1491, we find Henry intriguing to get the young king James IV into his own hands, as Henry IV had James I: in 1493, a treaty for seven years was concluded but not kept: in 1495, the marriage of James with the king's daughter Margaret was proposed. In 1498, by the good offices of the Spanish ambassador, a treaty for seven years was concluded which was shortly turned into a peace for life, cemented by the marriage which really came off in 1502. Thus, about the same time, although by a different process, the king secured himself, so far as negotiations could secure him, in peace for life with his two national and ancestral foes. In 1502 was made a treaty of perpetual peace with both.

The direct negotiations between England and Spain,

which, like those between Henry and Maximilian, arose on the Brittany business, began, in 1489 and 1490, with the alliance for the defence of the duchy, and so early comprised a purpose of marriage between Arthur and Katharine of Aragon. The marriage itself was not concluded until 1501 ; and, on Arthur's death early in 1502, the scheme for her marriage with his brother Henry was set on foot; out of which so great results were to come. The design was not, however, carried into effect until the next reign; and the intervening years are full of correspondence on points connected with dowry and dispensation. The earlier years of the Spanish negotiations contain no incidents independent of the general action of Europe, in which Henry, like Ferdinand and Isabella, was content to play a waiting game.

I have left to the last the negotiations with Flanders, first under Maximilian, and after the year 1494 under his son Philip. These, so far as they concerned the dynastic quarrels, are so closely interwoven with the French and Breton relations, that I need not recur to them.

In 1496 was concluded the great commercial treaty called *Intercursus magnus*, which was intended to secure the freedom of trade intercourse between England and the Netherlands, as well as the exclusion of Perkin Warbeck. The peaceful relations were not broken whilst Maximilian and Philip were lending questionable support and making promises to Edmund de la Pole. The network of the family alliance, by which Ferdinand and Maximilian were uniting the great inheritances, might have led to a wavering of the balance under a more energetic hand than that of Henry ; but, even if it had been endangered, the danger would have been averted by the arrangement concluded by the archduke on his forced visit to England in 1506 ; this, besides some advantage gained in the way of commerce which led the Flemings to call it *Intercursus malus*, not only secured the surrender of Edmund de la Pole, but opened a series of fresh marriage schemes, which entertained the king during the short remainder of his life. The most important of these was the engagement of the Lady Mary to the Archduke Charles; but the king himself, who had lost his wife in 1503, was in the matrimonial market, and his adventures contribute the one semi-comic element to this severely business-like reign.

The death of the Archduke Philip in 1506, the advanced years of Ferdinand, and the proved impracticability of Maximilian, seemed to be opening out a career for a new leader in Europe; and many eyes were turned on Henry. He was willing enough to marry, perhaps the Queen Dowager of Naples; perhaps the Archduchess Margaret; the latter marriage would have given him a direct hold on the Netherlands and a possible claim on the regency of Castile, especially if the young Charles should become his son-in-law. With two such competitors, however, as Ferdinand and Maximilian the diplomatic game was slow and cautious. And in the midst of it Henry died, on April 21, 1509.

I cannot now presume to enter upon two remaining aspects of the reign, the social and the religious, although both of them furnish us with details not less important, and scarcely more entertaining than those which we have now gone through. As for the social history, I can only say that it must be read chiefly in the Statutes concerning trade, labour, and agriculture, and the slightly increasing store of such letters as we have in the Paston and Plumpton collections. The letters of Erasmus and the scholars of the time, More's Utopia, and a very few other sorts of materials, add a little to the light that is beginning to shine towards the close of the reign. Ecclesiastically Archbishop Morton's design of visiting and reforming the monasteries was a partial anticipation of the much greater scheme of Cardinal Wolsey. There is little or no religious persecution; there is little or no literary or ecclesiastical activity, although there are, now and then, small flashes of anticipation of what is coming: the reign of Henry VIII would not in any respect have been what it was, if he had not had a predecessor like Henry VII; but, such as it was, it gathers up and concentrates in itself all the interest that would properly belong to that of his father.

I have said enough about the political importance of the reign, and perhaps in the last lecture more than enough about personal incidents and characteristics. To the last, however, Henry VII remains somewhat of an enigma to us. Was he a great king? If it be enough to constitute a great king, to have reigned twenty-four years without a single important war, and to have united in apparent peace a number of dynastic forces that had been struggling for a century; to have found England weak and poor, and divided against herself and isolated in Europe, drenched in blood and impotent in internal government; and to have left her rich, and at peace with herself, and growing in contentment, and well administered; having a place in the councils of Europe second to none, courted on every side and able to make her weight felt perceptibly in the balance; to leave a full treasury and an uncontested title to his successor, and a reputation stained by nothing that in the eyes of his contemporaries bore the guilt of crime; then the reign of Henry VII was a great reign, and perhaps Henry VII himself was a great king.

If we look rather on the moral of the reign we may somewhat modify our opinion. We look in vain for anything that would constitute him a hero or a benefactor. We find no great fault except his avarice, but even that cannot be regarded as the vulgar appetite for hoarding: and avarice, in a king who keeps within the letter of the law and the constitution, is perhaps really, and certainly in a land which had

suffered from royal prodigality for three centuries, a less
fault than extravagance. Even avarice is not always fatal to
the heroic character, if there be the rudiments of the true
heroic character there at all.   Henry VII was a virtuous
man, sober, temperate, and chaste, withstanding great temptations to vice and an abundant store of loose example.   His
household was kept frugally and severely; all his advisers,
except Empson and Dudley, were men of character unstained,
if not energetic for good.   For one better or greater king,
there are in European history fifty smaller and worse.   But
still—is there any of that self-denying devotion which gives
itself for the people?   Is there any true conception of the
duty of a shepherd of the host?   Is there any impulsive
well-doing?   I can see none.   I see a cold, steady, strongly-
purposed man, patient, secret, circumspect; with not many
scruples, yet not regardless of men's opinions; very clear-
sighted; very willing to wait for reconciliation where there
is a chance, and not hasty where vengeance is the only
course; but ruthless where his own purpose is directly endangered, and sparing neither friend nor foe where he is not
strong enough to rely on himself alone.   It may have been
a nature too cold to care for popular love; or too self-
contained to condescend to court it; there is no evidence
that Henry VII ever dreamed of winning it.   In his domestic
life there is little that calls for remark.   He cannot have
cared much about his wife or any of her relations: he
honoured and trusted his mother, and may have been in
some matters guided by the advice which natural acuteness
and varied experience helped her to give him.   But this is
a minor matter, and would count for little in the picture of a
man of whose real character we knew enough to enable us to
judge of him.   I said in the former lecture there is nothing
attractive about him, with all his virtues and all the great
consequences of his work.   There is surely always something

attractive about either greatness or goodness, unless they fall in an age so lost to itself as to be unable to appreciate either. And the opening century, whilst to some extent it shared the king's character, was scarcely so lost as that.

I conclude : like many other things on which it has been my lot all these years to give public statutory lectures, this reign and this king, the more we study them, give the more ground for questioning our own judgements, and the extent and character of our knowledge : the Cheshire cat in Alice's adventure faded away into a grin; we grow more and more impatient of generalizations and idealizations, and more and more intolerant of dogmatic assumptions, the longer we study them. Perhaps this may be the whole lesson, and if it is, it is a lesson that can never be too thoroughly learned or too often repeated.

XVII

A LAST STATUTORY PUBLIC LECTURE

(May 8, 1884.)

A LAST statutory public lecture ought, I suppose, to combine the characteristics of an *Apologia* and a *Symposium ;* or perhaps, in more modern fashion, as befits a Professor of Modern History, the qualities of an after-dinner speech, of the defence and confession of a penitent, of the last will and testament of one who has something to leave. I do not know that, in what I am going to say, I shall strike exactly on any one of such notes ; but there are some things that I ought to say, some that I wish to say, and some that I can say to fill up the prescribed three-quarters of an hour. I will ask for your tolerance and sympathy for what I have to say, whether in jest or in earnest; for you will believe me when I say that even the last statutory public lecture is a matter which mingles pleasure with pain, in no slight measure of both.

Seventeen years ago, in the address which I delivered in this room by way of inaugural lecture, and eight years ago, when I was approaching the end of my first decade of office, I ventured to make the statutory public lecture an opportunity of stating what seemed to me to be points of interest touching the study of History, in relation to persons, subjects and methods of teaching. The inaugural lecture contained, as was very natural, some crude and carelessly treated material; I said some things which were misunderstood, and some which I had better not have said at all ;

probably both are forgotten by this time. But, as to the main object of the lecture, the stating of the proper part which the teaching of History has in mental education, I have not changed my mind, nor am I inclined to do so now. I still think that the aim of Historical teaching is the training of the judgement to be exercised in the moral, social and political work of life; and that, as an instrument of education, such teaching will seek its fittest material in those portions of History which have enough of living interest to stimulate research, but have not enough of immediate practical importance to rouse political partisanship; that accordingly we do best when we begin at the beginning of the history of the forces and materials out of which modern life has grown, and that, in so doing, we have a distinct advantage over those who start to work backward from the immediate interests of to-day. I do not now wish to enter on controversy about this; I know that it is not uncontroverted; I state it, however, as a principle on which I have taught, and have believed myself justified by results. As I stated it in my first, I stand by it in my last lecture.

The lectures of 1876 were given after several years or experience, during which I had learned my own weakness, and begun to find the way in which I trusted that I might be really helpful: years during which the study of History has greatly developed here, and in which we had tried to frame, and I think had succeeded in organizing a method of combined teaching, which brought into play the ability of a considerable number of enthusiastic and laborious tutors, and which resulted not only in enlarged and improved schemes of reading, and enlarged and more highly valued distinctions in the way of class and prize, but also in very valuable and important work done for History in the way of research and in the production of books. At that time too, the University was engaged in taking stock of its means and requirements, in preparation for meeting the Commission which was understood to be impending, and which has since worked changes in our constitution, collegiate and academic, which are now only beginning to develop results. I attempted, in the two lectures which I delivered then, to take a comprehensive survey of the condition of Historical Study, so far as it affected our own material and method, both within and outside of our own borders, and to express certain views which I hoped might find favour in the expected reforms.

Without following the same plan, I propose now to take up, and, in the desultory way which is almost necessary under the circumstances, to remark upon some of the more important points which have varied our own history, as academic and historic workers, since that time. If I speak too much of myself, I will ask you to believe that it is not because I set an especially high value on my own services, for none knows or feels better than I do how much more I ought to have done, or how little my share has been in what has been done; still less because I undervalue the labours of my fellow-workers, who have had far more personal anxiety and more direct and more measurable responsibilities than I have had; it is mainly because the retrospect of my own work is forced upon me by the circumstances of my departure from Oxford ; also because, not only as Professor, but in several other capacities, as Delegate of the Press, Curator of the Bodleian, a Member of Council, and as having a share too of the representation of our Oxford School of History before the outside world, I have had work to do and a place to fill which it would be very mock humility on my part to leave out of sight now that I am parting from such a home as this. You will pardon me, I hope and trust, because it is the last time.

A word first on our losses and our gains : and our losses and gains are so intimately bound together that I must take them in the order in which they most naturally occur to me, balancing one another by a law of compensation inseparable from all progress : it is surely a matter of congratulation that since 1876 we have so much enlarged the number of our students that our class lists contain nearly double the tale of names, and that, as a road to an honourable degree in arts, our study is now followed by nearly, if not quite, as large a body of pilgrims as any of the other honour schools. This is the result of no lowering of the standard of the History Examination, but of the greater educational vivacity of the University, of the increased interest felt in the country at large in historical work, of the efforts of some of the Public Schools to make a beginning of such work a part of elementary education, but chiefly I think to the zeal, and self-denial, and labour, and personal sympathy of the History tutors. The work is, so far as it is the bringing to bear of historical influences, interests, and inducements on the individual students, entirely their work ; and their work also mainly in the other bearings of our common design, in which professorial teaching or other professorial working could be at all utilized. I wish to say this distinctly, and shall say it again before I close ; all the more distinctly, because I, for my part, am well aware that, in many details of organization and division of labour, my opinions have differed from theirs, and I would like them to remember that, where we have differed, it has not been for want of sympathy on my part, or for any wish to spare myself.

Since 1876 in the body of tutors we have had some few losses ; our dear friend the Dean of Winchester has left us for a place of more dignity, and more freedom for the working of his unrivalled and peculiar gifts : we are sure that he will never be idle, and whatever he does will be done well. Mr. Jayne has left us, also for a place of honour and responsibility, where his presence will be to us the earnest of sound work in our own as well as in the other departments of clerical education, and where he has already enlisted the help of one of the most successful and zealous of the younger men who have followed our line here. Of our dear friend Laing, whose absence we feel more and more every term, what can I say, but that we trust and hope that one day he may be restored to us and to the studies that he was so wonderfully qualified to develop and adorn? Well, with these home losses we have counterbalancing gains in the enlisting of new men. The continued vigour of our veterans is hardly to be called a gain, but it is a matter of profound congratulation: I rejoice to think that the Chichele Professor, Mr. Owen, and Mr. Boase are as young, and zealous and kind, and sympathetic as they ever were, and that is as much as the best and kindest of men can be; seventeen years of a very trying Regius Professor have not worn out their goodwill.

Another point I will mention, though I need not tell too much of the secrets of the Seminar: there is a great gain to us in the spontaneous working of the little clubs of Historical debate which have sprung up within the last few years, collegiate and inter-collegiate. I will not talk of comparing great things with small, but I rejoice to see in these a continuity, with differentiation, of the old circles which I remember when I was an undergraduate and a bachelor: I was always proud of having been for a little time secretary of the Hermes, which Archdeacon Palmer, and, alas! how few besides, must recollect as a very small and earnest and affectionate literary brotherhood, well to be remembered as a seed-bed in the sowing time, not only of germinating ideas that spring and die with or without fruit-bearing, but of high sympathies and dear friendships that grow stronger and immortal by age. I would augur for our little History clubs as fair a future.

Another gain, which is still perhaps a matter for augury, is the formation of the Oxford Historical Society; if the choice of subject, singularly and universally attractive, rich in materials and full of varied interest, if the zeal, ability and perseverance of the promoters, and the sympathy of all historical students, can secure success, the Society has a most happy future in prospect.

But the mention of it suggests irrepressibly the memory of the man whose genius inspired the idea, and of whom the Society is in this place the fittest possible monument. John Richard Green, the dear friend of many amongst us, has left behind him a name which cannot soon be forgotten. His books are by themselves the warrant of the fame which he so widely gained; the extent of his reading, the power of his grasp, the clearness of his insight, the picturesque reality of his narration, are patent to all who are capable of judging. We, who knew him better than the world of his readers, know too of his unwearied industry, his zeal for truth, and the inspiring force of his conversation. For twenty years he and I were close friends; with countless differences of opinion, we never quarreled; with opposite views of the line of history and of the value of character, we never went into controversy; his letters were a delight and honour to me; I believe that my visits were a pleasure and in some way a comfort to him. In the joint dedication of his book I confess that I received a compliment which I place on a level with the highest honours I have ever received.

I am tempted to modify the excessive dryness, as the Edinburgh Reviewer puts it, of my discourse, by telling the story of our first introduction to one another, chiefly because it has been made the subject of a myth which has made us both a little, or not a little ridiculous. Some of you I dare say remember a paragraph that went the round of the September papers years ago; and told how two persons, a stout and pompous professor and a bright ascetic young divine, met in a railway carriage; how the burly professor aired his erudition by a little history lecture (an anticipation of the informal instruction of the Commissioners) on every object of interest that was passed on the road, and how each of his assumptions and assertions was capped by an answer from the ascetic divine which showed that he knew it all and knew it better. The professor at last, exasperated by the rejoinders, broke into a parody of the famous address of Erasmus, 'aut Morus aut diabolus,' substituting for Morus ' Johnny Green.' Could this be true? It was in 1863 that we met; I was not yet a professor, he had not begun to wear the air of an ascetic. We were invited to Wells, to a meeting of the Somerset Archaeological Society, to stay with a common friend whom you will have no difficulty in iden-tifying. I was told, 'if you leave the station at two you will meet Green, and possibly Dimock,' the biographer of St. Hugh, whom I knew already. I knew by description the sort of man I was to meet; I recognized him as he got into the Wells carriage, holding in his hand a volume of Renan. I said to myself, 'if I can hinder, he shall not read that book.' We sat opposite and fell immediately into con-versation. I dare say that I aired my erudition so far as to tell him that I was going to the Archaeological meeting and to stay at Somerleaze. ' Oh then,' he said, ' you must be either Stubbs or Dimock.' I replied, 'I am not Dimock.' He came to me at Navestock afterwards, and that volume of Renan found its way uncut into my waste-paper basket. That is all; a matter of confusion and inversion; and so, they say, history is written. Well, perhaps a friendship between two historical workers may be called a historic friendship and, to be historical, should gather some of the mist of fable about its beginning: anyhow it was a friendship that lasted for his life, and the loss of which I shall never cease regretting.

Mr. Green's death is one of our greatest losses, but not the only one. In Sir Thomas Hardy the whole world of histori-cal students lost a leader, a counsellor, and a friend; whose services it is impossible to overrate. Practically the founder of the series of national Chroniclers to which I at all events, and our school here, owe so much; a man full of carefully stored and readily imparted knowledge; full of business and as full of kindliness, to every Oxford student, of record or of chronicle, he was a most willing and ready helper. Soon after him we lost Mr. Brewer, who shared with him some of the most important sections of his work, and who added to his labours as a collector and arranger of record, those of an indefatigable writer and faithful, energetic, and stimulating teacher. Then we lost Dr. Pauli, the man who made English History a living study on the continent; the most faithful and fair-minded of investigators, bound to me by peculiar bonds of friendship, and to Oxford by a number of ties; an honourable recognition on our part, and a grateful affection on his. In Dr. Guest we have lost not indeed an Oxford man, but an Oxfordshire scholar, whose devotion to our studies, and whose only half-completed labours, are well deserving to be had in remembrance. If I were able now to go beyond our immediate limits, I should say a word about Mr. Carlyle, but it would take me too far afield, and it is perhaps even a presumption in me to name him at all, or to claim for History a champion whose exploits are in all the regions of literary life.

But, although we grieve over personal and special losses, the work in which we are engaged goes on without flagging. The accumulation of historical literature since 1876, within and without our own particular range, has been remarkable for extent and interest. I cannot attempt to enumerate even the more conspicuous additions to our store, and it would be invidious to make a selection except in reference to our own share in the work. The Government publications, however, I may say, continue to maintain and even increase their value and interest: Mr. Gairdner, who has succeeded to Mr. Brewer's position, is giving us annual instalments of the history of Henry VIII, full of extraordinary revelations: before the year 1900 it may be possible that some one of us, gifted with strength, sight and perseverance, may write a complete history of the most critical of all reigns. Mr. Rawson Gardiner, a man who should be claimed and must be reclaimed for Oxford, is working, like a great constructive historian as he is, at the next most critical epoch. Mr. Creighton, even more entirely our own, has given us a splendid instalment of a great work which places him at once in the forefront of our phalanx. Mr. Freeman has completed his History of the Norman Conquest by the addition of the History of William Rufus. Mr. Fyffe has begun what will be a standard book on later history. I myself have finished my contributions, in a third volume, to Constitutional History; have edited six stout volumes of Chronicles in the Rolls series; and in the Appendices to the Report of the Ecclesiastical Courts Commission have put together a mass of matter, which, whether or no it is worth the paper on which it is printed, is both true history and the result of hard work: of other designs, the accomplishment of which my removal from Oxford will probably prevent, I can scarcely speak: but I hope that I may find time to complete two or three things on which I have made considerable progress, a fourth volume of Councils, an edition of William of Malmesbury, a second series of Select Charters, and possibly a sketch of the Constitutional History of the Reformation. I am, as I warned you, running off into my own concerns. Mr. Tozer's beautiful edition of Finlay's Greece, Mr. Hodgkin's Italy and her Invaders, Professor Rogers' Extracts from Gascoigne, and two new volumes of the History of Agriculture, the collections and comments of Dr. Vigfusson and Mr. York Powell, Mr. Kitchin's third volume of French History, Mr. Sidney Owen's Selection of Wellesley and Wellington Dispatches, not to speak of the works in which History claims an equal share with Language or Law, testify to the zeal which the Delegates of the Press have encouraged in the same direction. Outside of our lines, time would fail me to tell of Mr. Skene's completed labours on Early Scotland, of the interesting and suggestive work of Mr. Seebohm, of Mr. Elton's searching and comprehensive examination into the history of Primitive Britain; or going further ahead, of the immensely valuable editions and re-publications of the Laws and Chronicles of Germany, now proceeding under the management of Dr. Waitz, and full of illustration of the history of the common institutions of the German races.

It is most gratifying to a student of the institutions of England to find that in the literature of more distant nations the study of our constitution is taking an important place. I cannot refrain from expressing the great pleasure which it gives me to receive, from time to time, heavy volumes and light pamphlets of dissertations on the subjects at which we have been at work here, from scholars in Germany, Russia, Denmark, France, Italy and America, who read and criticize and utilize our books. From Berlin we hear of Dr. Gneist, reissuing and rewriting on his old subject; from Munich, of Dr. Liebermann re-editing the Anglo-Saxon Laws for the Bavarian Academy; from Vienna we have Dr. Budinger's lectures on the Englische Verfassungs-Geschichte; from Parma Signor Cardon's Svolgimento Storico; from Würzburg Dr. Schanz's Handelspolitik; Sickel doing the same work at Göttingen; Brunner at Berlin; Kovalefski and Vinogradoff in Russia; Steenstrup in Denmark; and in America, where our study has taken root with remarkable and most promising vigour, the clusters of searchers, such as the men of the Johns Hopkins University, and to specify particularly, Mr. Bigelow, the author of the work on *Anglo-Norman Procedure*, and the collector of the *Placita Anglo-Normannica*.

Well, and let me confess—I hope that I have not been guilty of dishonestly receiving honours meant for other people—let me confess, that it has been exceedingly pleasant to me to receive from the Academies of Germany their recognition that the labours of the Oxford school have not been thrown away. I am very proud to be the recipient of diplomas signed by Döllinger and Giesebrecht, by Curtius, Pauli, Ritschl, and Dove, and to be numbered among the members of the American Academy.

But it is time that I should go on to another point. Since 1876 we have gone through the throes of a Commission and begun the struggles of a reorganization. There is no reason why I should either speak or be silent about the general conduct of the Commission or the probable working of its results, except in relation to our own study and to the character of Professorial work as likely to be affected by the changes that are coming or come. I could have wished that the Commission had had more sympathy with literary and historical studies, that it had shown more appreciation of the true character of Professorial teaching, that it had seen, more distinctly than the new statutes seem to show that it did see, the imprudence of arranging the duties of Professors, the number and character of their lectures, not according to the nature of the subject but according to the amount of stipend forthcoming in the several cases. It surely was not necessary to treat the idle Professor as the typical Professor; it surely might have been enough to take the best means to secure a good Professor and have left him to work, not nominally but really, in the way in which he knew he could do the most good. Surely the idle professor, the *chimaera bombinans in vacuo comedens secundas intentiones*, should have been caught before he was tortured. No man has a greater capacity for idleness than I have, nor a greater desire of rest; sometimes I think the love of idleness is the greatest spur to exertion :

anyhow I have been made to work, even without the Visitatorial Board. But what I want to say is this: it is possible in certain subjects to carry on research and elementary teaching together; it must be so in logic and grammar; in mathematics, possibly, although there it must be more difficult; in language, if the pupils are forward, it must be feasible: but in abstruse philosophy and in minute historical research it is not possible to do both things easily and at once. An arrangement of occasional epideictic lectures, ordinary elementary teaching in class, and informal instruction out of class, is symmetrical enough and useful enough where it can be applied, but it is not of universal application, or suited to Professors of all calibres. Restricting my remark to my own study, I will say, if an Oxford Professor of History is to be a man to be trusted to maintain the reputation of his University, to keep abreast with foreign scholars, and to conduct research on his own account, he ought to have been left with some discretion as to the management of his teaching. I have often felt, when I was busy with some matter that required concentration of thought and continuity of investigation, that I would rather have broken into my line of work by going and giving a lecture in Euclid or Algebra, than by coming down to an elementary discourse, in which, from the very affinity of the subjects, I should be constantly tempted to revert to the minute point on which my special labours in my study were fixed, to the confusion of the class and to the damage of the subject that I had to treat before them. It was in order to avoid this that for some years I wrote out my lectures before term began; a plan which has obvious drawbacks, chiefly in what is called losing touch with the class. Afterwards I lectured on texts rather more freely; latterly, as my classes regularly diminished, I took up more out-of-the-way subjects, and very nearly succeeded in getting rid of my classes altogether; in the end I have reverted to my first plan.

Well, perhaps I never was fit for the place; anyhow, on the now stereotyped plan of the Professoriate, it is as well that I should go. I am told that the great historical works of the great foreign professors have been accomplished by men who have done much elementary lecturing and much informal instruction. That is true, but it is to be remembered that the great German professors have the power and the right to direct the studies of their pupils, classes and individuals, to the specialized and differentiated details of their own subject, not merely to general class examinations in which all the candidates are expected to show the same sort of knowledge derived from the same sort of books. What I wanted from the Commission was not less work but more liberty; what I succeeded in getting was a little more elasticity of tether. But I will not grumble any more: it is over; both the evidence, voluminous and appreciative, the formal audience, so redolent of sympathy and profound attention on the part of the Commissioners, the lively meetings of council and committee, and the truly charming debates of the professors and tutors: let them have the light that never was on sea or land, in the sweetness of memory—a consecration, a professor's dream; at all events we have a system of faculties, informal instruction, and a Visitatorial Board.

But let us go on to more serious things than these. I have spent nearly eighteen very happy years in Oxford: holding the office for a longer period than any of my predecessors except Spence, who was professor for twenty-six years, Nowell, who was professor for thirty years, and Dr. Nares, who occupied the chair for twenty-eight years. The principal event that touches the constitutional position of the Professorship during my occupation is its final and complete connexion with Oriel College. Of the professors before me, three, Dr. Beeke, who was in office during the early years of this century, and two better known men, Dr. Arnold and

Mr. Halford Vaughan, had been Fellows of Oriel. The Ordinance of 1857, passed nearly at the end of Mr. Vaughan's tenure of office, allowed Oriel College to undertake the payment of a considerable sum in augmentation of the annual income provided by King George II, which augmentation might be exchanged for a fellowship of the College : and by a University Statute of 1859 a new body of regulations was provided for the conduct of the professor. Under these Mr. Goldwin Smith and I have held office ; he being, as Fellow of University, ineligible for the Oriel Fellowship, became by election after his resignation an honorary fellow, and I was in 1868 elected to the fellowship which I still hold : henceforth the Regius Professor will, under the Commissioners' Statutes, be a Professor-Fellow. Whilst I look back with pride and gratitude on the honour which the College conferred on me so early in my career as professor, and with a lifelong pleasure on the friendships that my connexion with Oriel enabled me to form, I fear that I have been a very unprofitable member of governing body and educational staff : I console myself with the reflexion that there are some minds, which, in some situations, acquit themselves of their responsibilities most satisfactorily by never getting in the way. Non-obstructiveness is not the highest degree of efficiency, but there are worse faults. Anyhow my successor will have a chance in this line of work of approving his superiority to what has gone before.

The fact that two of my predecessors are alive and well is a matter of congratulation : Mr. Halford Vaughan and Mr. Goldwin Smith have both conferred on the Professorship an honour which I am glad to recognize. Both, eminent as scholars and political thinkers, lectured during the sixteen years of my absence from Oxford ; there are some, however, left who remember Mr. Vaughan's lectures under the old system, the soundness and learning displayed in them and the

stimulus which they supplied to the study of Modern History
at the moment that it was taking its place among the recognized subjects of the Schools. It was whilst Mr. Vaughan
was Professor that the School of Law and History was
organized; Mr. Goldwin Smith, as I said, lectured under the
new arrangements of 1859 and was examiner in 1862. I
rejoice to know that on neither of these gentlemen has the
study of the subject, that I have lived and worked for, produced any exhausting or debilitating effects; and, when I
consider the case of my successor designate, 'the Regius
Professor elect,' and think how many books he has written,
and in how many fields he has shown his prowess, and how
now, some few years my senior in standing, he is preparing
to take my work on his shoulders, to go on writing, to give
public statutory lectures, ordinary lectures, informal instruction,
and to face the Board of Faculty and the Visitatorial Board,
I flatter myself that the energy with which he will go to work
will not be damped with the reflexion that his predecessors
ever broke down. I am very glad to welcome him back to
Oxford, to the home and the studies that he has loved so
well, as the great champion and representative of that branch
of historic literature on which I believe the success of the
study here to depend. Not that he is eminent in this alone.
But I am now flattering myself and not him.

And so I come to my parting words. I am going to leave
Oxford, not for a place of rest, but for a post of work. I
frankly confess that I have always worked towards an ideal of
rest; my own anticipations have been, after a few years more
here, during which I might see some of my boys started in
the world, I might have retired, we will say, to the Parks, and
have given no more lectures. But I have always believed, in
the case of other people, that the reward of good work is to
have more work given you; and I do trust that it may be so with
myself. If the gifts that I have done my best to make useful

here are such as can for a little time be made useful elsewhere, I am grateful and hopeful in the change, although it is so very different from anything that I thought I was working for.

I am going to leave with Oxford many, very many friends; to leave but not I trust to lose them. I hope that I have made no enemies, I have more dread of making enemies than is at all consistent with a properly constituted moral courage. I hope that I have succeeded. At all events I have never reviewed the books of ally or opponent, or any one else ; I have never given pain or incurred hostility in that way. I have abstained from controversy, religious, political or historical, for I have tried to live up to my own ideal of a strong position, that it consists far more in proved confidence in your own cause, in the vigilant maintenance of your own defences, in the thorough realization of your sources of strength and weakness, than in the most adroit use of weapons or the most energetic tactics of aggression. I have never scrupled to correct my own mistakes, and I have never made a captious use of the mistakes of other men. I trust that I have never plucked a candidate in the Schools without giving him every opportunity of setting himself right. I hope that I have never intrigued or bullied : I do not say this with any wish to imply that such things are ever done here ; although the popular idea of the professorial character might suggest the need of a disclaimer ; but, if there was temptation to do so, I claim to have resisted it. So much I trust that you will let me take credit for. I know that I have great faults ; I have a good deal of sympathy but too little zeal : sometimes I have feared that, in my lack of zeal, my fellow-workers have detected or suspected a lack of sympathy : somehow the adage ' melior est conditio prohibentis ' does come to be confused with or to be interpreted into the policy of ' How not to do it ' : perhaps I have tried to work too much in my own way and too little in theirs. Then too, I have never been able to reconcile

myself with smoking, late hours, dinner parties, Sunday break-
fasts, or University sermons: nor is Joe Pullen's tree such a landmark in my life as it might very well be to the benefit of my
constitution.   I will say no more about informal instruction ;
I think that need not be remembered against me ; if I am
not mistaken, I have read over many proof-sheets and my
name appears as the name of a helper in many prefaces.

Well, so much for my *apologia* and confession ! for want
of zeal, for weakness of temper, for occasional absence of
discretion, I do ask pardon of all whom I may have offended,
or disappointed or misunderstood.   I do not mind under the
circumstances being called sentimental ; I feel sentimental.
I confess that I do hope that you will remember me kindly ;
and I wish to be judged, as I have tried to judge other
historical personages, according as I have acted or have not
acted up to my lights.   I know that I have not been much
of an organizer ; I dislike to organize for other people, I still
more dislike other people to organize for me ; I have a great
dislike of hard and fast rules, I would not so rule other
people, I should still more dislike to have such rules made for
me.   If there is any virtue in this love of freedom, do not
think that I am blind to the drawbacks which beset it.   Only
all men have not the same gifts, and happily all men are not
set to the same tasks, even Professors under schedules.
Please to think of me as of one who, very conscious of his own
shortcomings, and wanting, consciously wanting, in many
of the instincts of the successful Academic administrator, still
tried to do his duty ; tried to maintain for History its proper
place among the studies of Oxford, and to maintain the
reputation of Oxford as a nursery of historical study among
the Academies of Europe ; tried and worked hard to do
honour to the University, to Christ Church, and to the
Colleges, to which he owes, humanly speaking, all that he
has and is, and his capacity for doing better.

ADDRESS ON CHURCH HISTORY

To the Oxford Diocesan Church History Society

(Jan. 10, 1890.)

I SHOULD not have undertaken to give an address on
the great subject on which our common interests and
sympathy bring us together to-day, if I had not felt that any
contribution, however small, in support of the scheme would
have a certain value as expressive of such interest and
sympathy. And, when I speak of my own possible contribution as a very small one, do not think that I am laying
myself out for a compliment in false humility. I have read
and written a good deal on the subject; read a great deal
more than I can remember, and written a great deal more
than any one is ever likely to read; I do not ask you to
excuse me as a novice. But I am very sensible that, with
the innumerable and distracting claims on mind and body
which my present position entails, any attempt at the
illustration of so great a topic as this proposed to me, can
only end in a futile putting together of old and perhaps
somewhat irrelevant considerations. At the best, any address
from me on Church History would have to be more or less
of the nature of a sermon. Perhaps, however, the fact that it
is not pronounced *ex cathedra* will have the effect of rescuing
what I have to say from the fate which attends so many
sermons worthy of far more attention than anything that
I can put together now.

For the subject is a very great subject; embracing every

sort and department of details and principles, philosophic, theological, moral as well as historical; it is a subject that has a hold on us, not only through our minds but on our heart and affections; it is one on which there is a desperate, almost internecine conflict between schools and sects; in which what to one set of men are principles to another are prejudices; what to one are fundamental truths are to the other fables little less than blasphemous: and it is one of itself full of stumbling-blocks and pitfalls, dangerous to all, most dangerous to those who, in soundness of heart and sincerity, think that the balance of truth and virtue and infallibility must always be on their own side. Like all History it has its grand lessons of patience, of suspended judgements, of tolerance and humility; and, like our own national history, it is full of temptations to read it always in our own sense of political fitness. The wisest man, accordingly, considering the subject-matter, has need to approach it with prayer and in faith: the earnest petition for guidance and that certain confidence, in which humility rests, waiting for the solution of hard questions; not dictating the way in which they must be answered but certain that they will be answered in the appointed time:—and yet not the patience which, because the questions cannot be answered, will not deign to ask them; such is rather impatience or contented ignorance; but that which will try, as the law of the Church's life and progress reveals itself, in experience and development, to justify the wisdom of the Lawgiver, and, without anticipating consummation, accept, as sufficient for the day, the day's instalment of growing knowledge.

And what is Church History, and what is the Church? Is that second question too hard a one for present discussion, so that we had better confine ourselves to the form, 'What is the Church in the sense in which we speak of it as the subject of Church History?' Probably that will be safer.

And yet, I think, we should not, as Churchmen, shirk the higher question; for to us the Church is identical with the subject-matter of Church History: even our own national Church is the presentment, to us, of the reality of the great Church of God; whose character and limits we do not attempt to fix by any definition of exclusion, but which, we claim a right to believe, becomes visible and tangible, and susceptible of investigation and testing, of searching out and tracing into detail, as well as of moral and spiritual and social and intellectual handling, in the historical community in which we have been brought to the knowledge of the Truth.

We believe that our Lord founded a community, we do not believe that He merely promulgated an idea. We believe that He founded a community, a body corporate, not merely a school of thinkers or even of believers. We believe that He founded a community, a body corporate, with law, order, system of government, doctrines, sacraments and ministries ; and that, by historical continuity, not merely by philosophic agreement, that community goes on existing, and reaches us, and includes us, in the community of our own National Church ; the wing of the Militant Church that covers our own land, and of which our forefathers and our children, our friends, neighbours, all who, whether they recognize the corporeity or not, come within the range of our corporate action, are in flesh and blood, or in heart and memory, partakers with us.

This community, as an institution among men, and matched with, and in many ways included among, the run of human institutions, has no present immunity from the variations of institutions that are worked by men; it must have its times of prosperity and adversity, of poverty and riches, of decline and recovery, of division and reunion ; but its existence is a matter of historic knowledge, and its final destiny an article of historic and religious faith. We have no doubt about the past, no misgiving about the future, which is in the Hand of Him in whom we have trusted.

It is needless now to characterize the idea and belief of those who either reject this as an unproved and unproveable theory; or who attenuate it down to an irrelevant and absolutely unpractical phase of thought; or who declare that it is an extravagant imposture; or who, recognizing its historical existence, declare it to be an enemy and a counter-feit of the true ideal of the founder. As long ago as St. Paul's time there were believers, who said that they were not of the body; we may ask as he did 'are they not of the body?' It is not for us to judge, certainly not for us to exclude; not for us to think of shutting the ears of God, or telling to our severest adversaries that He is not theirs as well as ours. We do well to content ourselves with affirming our own position, and not usurping as a right that which we have no claim or power of enforcing.

I know that there are many people to whom this very affirmation of our own position sounds like an assumption of superiority over those who either do not claim the like position, or claim a position which is based on altogether different principles and assumptions : that we cannot help. It is not we that exclude or expropriate, we do not even hold fast that which we have received in such a spirit as to refuse to them a share.

That to my mind is the account of the matter; if it commends itself to me intellectually, morally, spiritually and historically, it certainly does not preclude criticism or con-tradiction, but as certainly it is the conception which I am bound to try to realize; and, where it is a matter of History, I know what to look for and where to look for it, and I am obliged to be content with that which I am guided to find.

I have dwelt thus at length upon this initial point rather with reference to our general position and attitude on the great question, than in direct connexion with our special subject, because to my mind it underlies the whole doctrine of Church History, and, where it is not recognized, the study is apt to degenerate into merely philosophical disquisition on the one hand, or to antiquarian research on the other, not to speak of the more hazardous region of controversial criticism. This, however, being accepted, the pursuit of the knowledge that illustrates, and realizes it, becomes, perhaps, the most seriously and intrinsically interesting pursuit within the whole range and area of human experience.

Whether we begin with the scene in the Upper Chamber on the Day of the Resurrection, and trace the development of the Historic Body for nineteen centuries onwards; or begin with the infinitely differentiated details of our own Church life at this moment, and work backwards step by step, link by link, to the same point of initiation; what are we doing but trying to connect the spiritual condition, the life and belief, the memory and the hope, the fellowship and the experience, the duties and the privileges of our souls and bodies, and of the souls and bodies of those whom with us our Lord died for, with the great truth of the Incarnation of God, the Atonement, and the Corporate Life of His Mystical Body! History is the investigation of how that which is comes to be what it is; things spiritual and things natural are to my mind the same things in two aspects, the one seen through the other: the Church is, I repeat, no idea, but a reality of flesh and blood, wood and stone, books and words, souls and bodies, hopes and memories, loves and longings, sorrows and joys, sins and repentances, wanderings and returnings, experiences of example and accumulations of influences, developments and differentiations; a reality of men and women, a body with a life and limbs, nerves, sinews, fibres, joints and circulation; of heart and brain;

a body 'growing up into Him in all things, which is the head, even Christ: from whom the whole body fitly joined together and compacted by that which every joint supplieth, according to the effectual working in the measure of every part, maketh increase of the body unto the edifying of itself in love.' Church History then becomes the tracing out of the 'working in the measure of every part,' in the past and in the present. Need I say more in illustration of the dignity and vital interest of the study to all who have the instinct of searching?

Did I not say truly that I could not help making so much of my address a sermon? Well! ideas, doctrines, dogmas; institutions, constitutions, revolutions; partial views growing into exclusive infallibilities; reasonable doubts growing into universal negations; reactions without balance; reforms undistinguishable from destructions; variations of opinion developed into internecine schisms; the lives and experiences of Saints and Sinners; the conversion and apostasy of nations; the rise and fall of learned and noble Churches; literature, arts and arms; 'quidquid agunt homines, votum, timor, ira, voluptas, gaudia, discursus, nostri est farrago libelli'; it may be the motto of the Church Historian as well as of the satiric poet: only, in and through all, the errings and strayings and returnings, we would trace the law of the revelation of progress towards the perfect man, the measure of the stature of the fulness of God incarnate, and the mighty working whereby He is able even to subdue all things unto Himself.

Here then comes the first and greatest question regarding the study of the subject: Can we study Church History under the same conditions as secular history? Can we, where there is so much that is of faith, so much that turns on the spiritual things which faith can only just touch, and certainly neither faith nor present knowledge can gather into the hand, can we approach with the same fearlessness, and handle with the same impartiality, and frame conclusions with the same confidence, and exercise judgement with the same contented scepticism, or the same ardent partisanship it may be, that we apply to historical research in regions in which we are less vividly, less personally, less seriously interested? Can we read Church History for the same purposes, for the educational training of the judgement, for the independent acquisition of knowledge, for the mere profit and delight of mental culture?

You see what a variety of branches the great question takes. And it is no answer to the question to point to the shelves of the Bodleian, to count the folios of the 'Acta Sanctorum,' or the 'Concilia.' It is no answer to say it has been done and may be done again; no doubt immense stores have been and are being accumulated: no doubt a vast armoury of controversial weapons has been collected; no doubt a magnificent array of record of devout experiences has been marshalled: and we have no right to question that the men who stored the fruit of their researches on those shelves were true men, and honest, and earnest, politic, and therefore straightforward, advocates of causes of the justice of which they were convinced: humble and industrious admirers of the virtues which their labours enable us to contemplate. But the question of the result remains: how did they do it, what did they contribute to the result; how did the research affect them themselves; did they start as re- searchers or as partisans, as judges or as advocates; did they end their study as patient, faithful, trusting men, or as sceptics impatient of difficulties that they had failed to solve, and incredulous of holiness that could not be shown to be without a flaw?

I have stated the question more strongly than clearly, I am fully aware: but I have stated it rather as suggestive of thought than as capable of a summary answer. To a certain extent, just as the Bible may be read as any other book, so the history of the Church may be read as the history of any other institution. To a certain extent it is impossible to read the Bible as any other book, or the History of the Mystical Body of the Lord as the History of a Nation or a Parliament. The whole interest of both lies too close to our hearts to suffer it. Yet why should it be so, if the natural and the spiritual, as I have said, do represent the same thing in two aspects and relations only, so far as our present powers of comprehension reach? There is a natural body and there is a spiritual body, an identity persistent in the diversity and in spite of all the changes of growth, decay, renewal, consummation. The Church whose History we study is an association of men, to our eyes undistinguished by any immunity from temptation, error, sin, or sorrow : its ministrations are carried on through the medium of the senses, touch and taste and sight and hearing : its counsels are determined by the pleas of law, of justice and equity, policy and expediency : its fabrics are of wood and stone arranged by human art and man's device ; its records are written and printed with ink and pen and type on paper and parchment : its language is the grammatical and intelligible language of the dictionaries ; its discipline is exemplified in the behaviour of its members to the men, women, and children of their own town or village, street, or lane, or house. Its very continuity of life can be measured by the overlapping of the years of the fathers and the children. In all this, within these certain conditions, we may read its History as we read any other History : and the mental discipline that results is much the same as that which results from the honest and patient study of other History. And I do not think that it is too much to say that exactly in proportion as it is read as other history so will the benefit be, on the understanding that the reading be

patient and honest, and in a mind waiting for the Justification of the Eternal wisdom that rules among the kingdoms
of men as certainly as in the Kingdom of Christ.

It will be familiar to those who in former years attended
my lectures, and to those who have read what I have written
on Historic Study, that one point which I have constantly
enforced on teachers in political History is that, as they
cannot prevent people from being partisans, they should
try to make them honest and judicious partisans: make
Tories good Tories, and Whigs good Whigs, and Radicals
good Radicals. Men are partisans by nature, inheritance,
education, experience, success or disappointment; but they
may be partisans without being led by party spirit; seeing
one side of the shield and not the other, they may still read
and argue and contend about things of contention, by lawful
methods and with just and honest weapons. And this principle will run into religious controversy also, and, as religious
controversy must colour Church History, by reason of the
very vitality of religious dogma and the vivacity of religious
dogmatists, Church History affords an ample arena for the
struggles of parties and schools.

I will not waste your time with the very, very commonplace commonplaces about mutual goodwill, and tolerance
of opposing views, and largeness of mind and openness of
view; principles which, however liberally laid down, are
far less commonly acted upon than they are asserted.
Rather let me revert to the line of thought from which
I have diverged.

I would place our duty in this respect on a higher basis
than the mere common ground of prudence in controversy.
If the Church is the Lord's Body, the divisions of opinion
and of belief are divisions among the members of the body,
the prayers and hopes and earnest desires of which are that
divisions may cease in the body; whether the ceasing of the

divisions shall be in the increased light which shows that the opposite views are complementary colours rather than contradictory ideas; or in the growth of a patience and loving forbearance which is content to wait for such revelation. To speak the truth in love, to read the truth in love: to keep indignation for real sin, to expect perfection in no human character or theory; to recognize as a fact that many questions may be asked that cannot be answered, and many legal doubts be raised that cannot in reason hope for a solution; to face the truth that if the merit of a cause is to be judged by the merit or policy of its defenders, no good cause could stand; the truth that although more sins have been committed in the name of liberty and in defence of it, than in suppression of it, περὶ παντὸς τὴν ἐλευθερίαν—so too more sins may have been committed in defence of truth than in opposition to it, and yet Truth is of all things the holiest, the purest, and the strongest: and, as a resultant of all such considerations, there must be charity for those who oppose us, and just judgement for those who are on our side. The controversialist on Church History cannot afford to be ungenerous, the very use of unchristian weapons is a desertion of the principle of charity in which is contained all that is worth contending for. We do not admire the advocate who is to be called on to beat Satan with his own weapons, and we do not believe in his advocacy either.

But I am getting too controversial myself, it may be, it may well be; if so, act by me on my own law, and credit the cause as better than the counsel. Let us go on. I have spoken of the dignity of the subject and of the disciplinary value of the study. A third question is of the real and material value of the knowledge acquired or acquirable by it: the value of the truths that are made out by the research. Now here I think I am getting myself into difficulty, and a temptation to talk big as the saying is. For the direct answer that I want to get at is this : the real value of the knowledge acquired by the Study of Church History, apart from the general value that all real knowledge on any subject whatever does possess, must surely lie in this, that it enables us to understand practical questions that come before us as Church-men and Church-women, and helps us not only to judge but to act upon our judgement of what is right and advisable when and where we are called on to act. That surely is the answer to the question; but it looks as if it were going to land us in the midst of those very con-troversial quicksands of which I wanted to steer you clear. What does it mean ? Well, what are the practical questions of to-day ? What are the points on which men and women are now deciding, or are likely to be called upon to decide by their votes ? What are the subjects that people are constantly writing letters about in the religious newspapers? Now, please, do not mistake what I am going to say, and go out of this room saying either that I justify the existence of religious newspapers, or that I deprecate all the letters of all correspondents on subjects of Church History. I say neither the one thing nor the other. But I do say that as these things do exist, for good, evil, or indifferent as you—not I, for I have taken up the agnostic attitude on this point—may judge them, I do say that as these things do exist, these questions are in the air, the children of the Church, the children of the Church of England should try to inform themselves of the facts of the cases; and that it is of the very highest prac-tical importance, not merely of moral and religious duty, that they should do so.

Now I will not adduce, or at least I will not do more than adduce such burning questions as Ornaments Rubrics —perhaps I need only advert momentarily to the Tithe Question, or the large controvertible departments of Eccle-siastical jurisdiction. There is a great deal of current and dangerous ignorance on these matters, and that ignorance which is wilful. On the first of the questions there is great obscurity; the utmost that I can recommend to you is to make yourselves acquainted with the contending views and reserve your judgement. But the other questions are capable of fairly easy historical determination, are settled in books of first-rate authority, and are only capable of controversial treatment for one or both of two reasons: the unhappy habit of politicians, who will not read history, of mixing up every conceivable question, even vaccination, vivisection, and the muzzling of dogs, with the partisanships of political colours; and the unhappy habit of others, besides politicians, of contenting themselves with research into the most accessible books of reference that tell them what they want to believe, or as much as they care to know.

Well, so much for them. There are authoritative books; one object of the association in which we are binding ourselves is to direct our members to such books and to help them to understand them: but they are not on the shelves of the popular Libraries of Reference—I wish that I could believe the reason to be that they are always in the hands of readers. Now I do not tell you that the reading up of the ecclesiastical subjects of the day even in authoritative books is the great utilitarian (and 'real' as opposed to educational) object of your study of Church History, or that the only arena in which you have to learn to act as Church-men and Church-women is in vestry-meetings or polling-booths; I adduce these matters as telling instances of cases in which sound information ought to be acquired before men can conscientiously and honestly act in support of or in opposition to public measures of interest. I could easily point you to illustrations of very considerable miscarriages of both policy and justice which have arisen from the ignorance of statesmen and public men, who were acting as they believed and hoped for the benefit of the Church, in what they did, because they either had not the means or would not take the pains to inform themselves adequately. And such is the infallibility of ignorance, that you will find even now men of acute minds and earnest desire of good, who will defend conclusions and policies which are historically untenable on the very principles to which in the first instance those conclusions and policies belong—who will defend, I say, the historical fallacies as truths, because of the practical reform that has followed the misapplication of them. I could point this extremely involved remark with modern instances; but we need not look further back than the Reformation, knowing that there are still people who believe that Gospel truth lived in Anne Boleyn's eyes, and that Edward VI was a second Josiah. However, here I am in hot water again.

Well, I say, inform yourselves about the practical questions, even if the result be only to make you hesitate on which side you shall decide: ignorance is a worse evil than indecision; and if there is anything worse than party spirit it is contented supercilious apathy. Here apathy is traitorous; but patience is not indifference. Happily the arena of party questions is not the only one in which we are called upon to act: our study has other fields for practical work in which its lessons may be read with advantage; it has great lessons of good works, great examples of faithful virtue, great patterns of patience, sympathy, hope and self-denial. But I will not enlarge on these further than to say how large an element of Church History is the biography of good men and women, and how by the lessons of their lives the great example of the Saints and of their and our own great Exemplar is brought down to the level of our simple lives, so that we feel that, with all our shortcomings and misgivings, our membership of the mystical body of the Lord is a really intelligible and sensible truth. Here I am verging on matters that are perhaps beyond the last of a lecturer; perhaps I have indicated with sufficient clearness what the line of my thought would be, and what is really the link of connexion or transition to the last, the fourth and last section of my essay, if I may modestly call it one.

And this section of the subject is the widest and the largest in each dimension, although in my treatment of it I must make it very brief. It concerns the subsidiary or subordinate advantages of the study, a range that extends from the highest spiritual and moral edification to the smallest and most minute department of antiquarian research. It has in common with all historical study, an unlimited field of material for the investigatory instinct. Whether you study the growth of ideas or the minutiæ of architecture; the development of institutions or the succession of officials; the character of saintly men or the geography of ecclesiastical administration; it offers an enormous area for the wholesome exercise of intelligent curiosity. And I do not speak lightly of this, although it is, as you may well imagine, the most superficial and shallowest aspect of the matter. Many a man has been led up by local or genealogical, or even what is called folklore questions, first to a more distinct personal realization of his own connexion with History, and afterwards to a real love of his subject for its own sake. It is not always so: there are men whose homes are on the great battlefields of the world, to whom the whole interest of their home is in its capacity for growing wheat or vegetables for the market; as there are those who, living in the midst of the fairest woods and sweetest waters, regard their surroundings only with a view to the available timber, or the force utilizable for the milling interest. But they are not all. And so there are some to whom the parish church where for generations their fathers have been baptized, married and buried; where the prayers of the parents have stored up blessing for the children and children's children; and where the loving care of generation after generation has bestowed with no sparing hand all that the loving mind could devise of beauty befitting the house of God; there are, I say, some to whom the parish church is as much a mere matter of course as a hill-side or a plantation, not quite so vividly interesting as a well-thatched haystack. But it is not so with all, and we may thankfully say that it is ceasing to be so with the majority. There are many who, beginning with the home interests of their own parish churches; with minds stimulated to some sense of beauty by its difference from commonplace surroundings, beginning with the question why are churches distinguished in style and furniture from schools and dwelling-houses; and forming some sort of taste in the realization of the difference, are led on to the question who were the men who built them, and why did they build, and did they build them for us, and what moved them to build them so? And then by the very attraction of the love, of which like the higher Wisdom they that eat are yet hungry and they that drink are yet thirsty, they are led on to the higher aspects of the subject-matter, and into new vistas of intelligent and loving study: and these things have their reward, like every other subject of thought that is lovely and honest and true and pure and just and of good report. There are, I say, minds that are led on so, just as there are minds that, beginning at the other end of the scale, find a relief and pleasure in descending step by step, from the great and eternal verities which they apprehend by faith, down to the details of modern life, and material surroundings, in the midst of which the natural grows out of the spiritual, and the highest lessons of faith are translated into tangible duty, person, place and relation, faith justifying itself by work.

There are many other branches of this line of thought : there is for instance the question which may some day be worked out with advantage—for it certainly has not yet —of the result on the development of national character arising from the peculiar history of the Church of England : its early and late isolation ; its escape in the mediaeval period from the worst dangers of the imperial-papal rivalry ; the mixed character of its reformation struggles, its action upon, and the reflex effect of, the constitutional struggle of the Stewarts : what the Duke of Wellington meant when he said : 'It is the Church of England that has made England what she is—a nation of honest men[1].' Or quite on another tack, there is a question of the distinctive features of our insular Church History, distinctive outside in relation to the continental Churches ; and within the British seas in reference to Irish, Scottish, and Welsh religious life : I scarcely recommend that latter branch at this moment, but it is one on which much pains might be spent and some results obtained. Then there is a great and most interesting field in the History of Missions ; the cause of the delay and frustration of the spread of the Gospel after a certain date ; the marvellous efforts of the mediaeval missionaries, before Eastern Europe and Asia, under the deadening hand of Islam, had shut in Christendom with walls that her internal divisions gave her no time to break through ; the widening of men's thoughts by the discovery of America and the sea-way to India ; the paralysis of Missionary work as compared with colonial and mercantile enterprise down to the middle of the last century ; the causes of the revival, and of the extremely varied achievements of spiritual energy since the revival began, and so on.

I am not a sufficiently strong believer in the Science of

[1] Lord Stanhope's Conversations with the Duke of Wellington, Ed. 3, p. 282.

History to tell you that I think that you may, from an estimate of the forces at work in past times, come to a useful conclusion as to the results of present energies at least in the immediate distance; but I am sure that the study of these things will teach you many lessons that will help you to justify the wisdom of God and stimulate your desire to emulate the good deeds of the past, and to help the good efforts of present workers.

But now, to say the truth, are we not both getting tired? and do not you think that I have left out a great branch of the subject, the elaborate character-drawing and word-painting, the pictorial side, the polychrome and stained-glass windows of Church History? I confess that, until I was writing the words that I am now saying, I never once thought of it. And it is an important thing; and a thing which, if it has been made too much of on one side, has perhaps been underrated on the other; but it is a thing that belongs for practical consideration to the writers and not to the students of the subject; let the Mosheim and the Burton, and the Gieseler and even the Robertson be set on one side; and the Milman, the Stanley, the Milner, the Neander, on the other; and let our dear Professor of Ecclesiastical History strike the balance between them, as he well can, mixing the *utile* of the one view with the *dulce* of the other.

Dear friends, when I remember what a terrible bore I used to think a public lecture was, when I was statutably bound to give one, I am lost in astonishment at the bracing effect that episcopal character, and the liberty of true genius, and the pressure of the care of a thousand clergymen have had upon me, and I find myself giving a lecture again in Oxford and not knowing when to stop. Shall I thank you for listening?

ADDRESS ON THE OPENING OF A COURSE OF LECTURES ON ENGLAND UNDER THE STEWARTS

(Reading, Oct. 8, 1889.)

WHEN the Provost of Queen's asked me to undertake the inauguration of a term's course of History Lectures, I accepted the invitation, perhaps too rashly, but certainly with a good will. For such a function would, I thought, enable me to reiterate some of the lessons which I have been accustomed to give on the same subject to other audiences; to repeat, with even more imperious insistence than of old, the lessons of which longer experience has made me even more confident; to hold in solution more modestly the conclusions that have less certainly borne wear and tear; and possibly to recant some small matters that needed to be unsaid, or, if I put it more gently, to be explained.

Whilst I was in this happy frame of mind, I heard from Mr. Butler that the course for the term was to be on the History of England under the Stewarts, and that my introductory effort ought *prima facie* to be an introduction to the same. Now this alarmed me : what was I to do? to hold by my first intention or to adapt myself to the sectional topic? Possibly I might shirk the difficulty, for there was, as I will confess, a difficulty : not only had I never lectured on the History of England under the Stewarts, but I had formulated a set of reasons why I did not, and another why I thought that the Stewart period was too full of controversy, of living controversial material, to allow it to be a meet subject for educational lectures. That opinion I am still strongly inclined to, as you will probably discover as I proceed; but, as an opinion, it might be waived, and I might come before you as an historic agnostic, pretending that I thought one side as good as the other, with the mental reservation, yes, quite so, and rather better.

It then occurred to me, could you not do it in this way? The course of lectures is introductory to the Stewart period, could you not make your lecture introductory too; that is, lead up the class through the preceding stage and bring them quite to the door, but avoid, for your own part, strictly avoid crossing the threshold? Well, I might do that; I might treat the matter like the tutor who, preparing a course on the French revolution, spent a couple of terms in bringing his class up to the point of the building of the pyramids. However, edifying though such a proceeding might have been, it was, I thought, hardly either one thing or the other. I had better make my choice and hold by it, apologizing to you, if I should come and do what you did not want me to do, and rejoice in the consciousness that the world has always profited much more by the failures than by the successes of ambitious men. So I determined to abide by my first idea: lecture to you on the study of History, its dignity, its discipline, its material value, and its adventitious advantages; a set of topics quite sufficient for an hour's friendly talk in an autumn evening, and quite suggestive enough to satisfy the most thirsty inquirer into the History of England during the Stewart period; suggestive enough of topics, principles, prejudices, premises and conclusions, views of character, incidents of picture, thoughts solemn, thoughts humorous, and thoughts both solemn and humorous, that occur to us in the examination of what to many minds reads as the crucial period of our national History.

If it *is* a crucial period, the generalities which I shall propound to you must find illustrations of their applicability in it; and if they are true, as they are to my mind, there will be no lack of opportunities of bringing them to bear. I shall, however, not think it necessary to be harping on that one string; rather I will try to explain to you what are the four points that I have specified and trust you to apply them where you think them capable of apposite illustration.

So we can begin at the beginning, what is History, and what is the study of History, what is its dignity, what is its discipline, what the material value of its results, what the interest and the pleasure, the adventitious advantages, as I called them, of its pursuits?

You are no doubt prepared to hear me say that the object of History is the discovery how that which is comes to be as it is, and to ask me the resulting question, what do you mean by that which is? and to propose that I should limit it to something less transcendental, less ecumenical, less impracticable. I do not suppose that you will be satisfied with my first answer that, to my mind, the study of History is coextensive with all pursuit of human knowledge : 'Homo sum, humani nihil a me alienum puto'; the historic Muse replies, ' I am a lady of condition, and there is nothing connected with the welfare of the human race in which I do not take a lively interest.' Perfect History must be coincident, and therefore coextensive with perfect knowledge. But we can never have perfect knowledge in this life, if ever; nor can we ever know anything, any one thing, perfectly, because such is the wonderful interpenetration of causes and consequences, in all things small and great, that to know one thing in every relation we must know all : which, as Euclid would remark, is absurd, as being impossible. Well, I do not grant that, because a thing is impossible we should never try to get as near to it as possible; nor because a height of knowledge is too wonderful and excellent for us, we should never try to attain unto it; if that had been the rule with searchers no great discovery would ever have been made. But I will grant that knowledge has to be acquired bit by bit, and that the pursuers of knowledge have to conduct their pursuit in detached parties, and that special departments require special preparation; and if there are to be co-operative searchers and special fields of inquiry, the fields must be mapped out and the searchers know their allotted tasks. Let us grant that History, as it comes within the compass of our hands, is the knowledge of how the present state of the world, the present state of England, the present state of Berkshire, the present state of Reading if you like, comes to be what it is:—how God has dealt with us, how our fathers dealt for us, how it is that we have come to look on and to deal with one another as we do, and, further, how we are going to guide our children by our advice, our successes or our failures, to deal with God, and with our memories, and with one another, and with their own children in their turn:—the knowledge of the good and evil that is mixed in the growth of human nature, the ebbs and flows in the tide of progress, the gradual revelation of eternal truths, and the gradual elimination of all that is less than eternal, in the great progress to the glorious consummation for which we are bidden to strive and struggle to do our part. Here is a study of no small dignity, a study with the most glorious subject-matter, for, if man is to man God's greatest work, there is none other that comes into competition with it; and it is a growing study, as it has an ever-expanding and exalting influence on the mind that gives itself to the search, self-correcting and self-denying, patient, tolerant, and, above all things, confident in the moral government that is ever leading on the world to that which is better.

But I am not to be, I am not really, transcendentalizing. History is a very patient study; and in that respect it has its advantage over both the study of science and the study of law. And this is worth noting, although I shall have to recur to it under my second head. History does not insist like science on absolute demonstration; History does not insist like law on practical decision. Like life, according to Butler, probability is the very guide of History, and its conclusions are moral and not mathematical inferences. History, unlike law, does not assert its infallibility simply because it must have perfection in decisive action. Science, indeed, suspends its determinations until it is sure of them, and law makes the best of its evidences before it gives verdict or passes sentence. But History knows that it can wait for more evidence and review its older verdicts; it offers an endless series of courts of appeal, and is ever ready to reopen closed cases. And in that light I claim for it a special dignity of its own, the dignity of being able freely to accept new lights and correct old prejudices. And perhaps this is enough for the first head. Only let me urge on you the importance of recognizing this in your approach to its study. You must come as willing to work, willing to learn, and willing to wait.

And so now come to the discipline of the study, its educational value, as we say, its position as a section of culture, of the training of the judicial and moral side of the intellect. And here perhaps I may descend a step or two, and let you ask me what is the special, moral or judicial training that you may expect to obtain from the study of the History of your own people and country, modern History, English History, the History of the Stewart period if you will have it so. Well, if you really wish it, I will repeat that I believe the disciplinary force of the study of History is to make people honest and intelligent politicians; yes, you may well stare at such a sentiment from one who is by the very nature of his position bound to be unpolitical. Perhaps I might say that is the very reason why you should value my advice and perhaps profit by my experience ; but I will guard myself further by saying that, by speaking of politicians, I do not mean primarily political partisans. A man may be a very good politician without belonging to a party, as a man may be a very good lawyer and never have a brief; but further than that, a political partisan will be a better partisan for being a good politician, a safer friend, a more honest enemy, a wiser adviser, a more conciliatory diplomatist.

However, I think I used the word in a more philosophic sense, in the sense in which a sound peripatetic would comprehend pretty nearly all that is comprehended in the duty towards your neighbour. So I repeat the disciplinary benefit of the study of History is to make people honest and intelligent in their view of public events, and of public measures and duties, as well as of men and parties : it is a training of the judgement, and it helps to train it for other than public duties too, for the patient consideration of private as well as public opinion, and for individual as well as corporate consciousness. How does it do this, say you ? Why by accustoming us to trace events to their causes, to trace opinions to their roots, to trace narratives to their authorities, institutions to their germs; it trains us to the pursuit of origins. Next by accustoming us to balance evidence, to accept all testimony for what it is worth, and to weigh not only books but the moral qualifications of book-makers, to count charters and analyse their attestations, to piece together detached segments of the circle of truth, and to cast away the pieces that will not fall into the places which they were forged to fill.

Next, by teaching us temperance in estimating character,

and even in calculating the curve of developing progress. Such lessons it impresses, that the evil is always mixed with the good in human affairs; that no school or party or leader ever was so entirely in the right that to oppose him was an infallible proof of falsehood or insanity or idiocy : that right and wrong are often so disguised, that it is only by the resulting outcome that the next age is able to discover which was right and which was wrong, and so many a time the best men are found fighting on the wrong side, and the advantage of the world and mankind, and perhaps of the particular nation whose history we are investigating, was secured by the victory of men whose very names provoke a curse rather than evoke a blessing from those who examine their principles and their purposes.

I might go further in the details of this education, and point out to you how, in the portion of History which you are going to read, what I have said applies : the royalist partisan historically trained, will not regard Cromwell as a monster ; the republican partisan historically trained will not sneer at Charles as a liar or as a pseudo-martyr : both, abhorring falsehood, will refrain from judging seventeenth-century diplomacy by the standards of that ideal which the nineteenth century with all its aspirations has as yet found it impossible to realize. I may like Charles, and believe that he died for a cause which I ought to die for if I were called on to die for any, and yet not believe him faultless : you may honour Cromwell and yet not believe him to have been a free and farsighted politician. And, further on, I may be thankful for the results of a contest in which I should have taken, and indeed would even now take, the losing side; you may regret the loss of some things that were lost as a part of the price that had to be paid for the liberating and developing of the national life.

So even more certainly we may look at the history of

the French Revolution, or of the Civil War in the United States : not all the good men were on the same side, not all the advantages were unbalanced by losses ; the result justifies the moral government of the world, but it does not justify the acts, if they are otherwise unjustifiable, of the victors, or condemn the characters, if they are otherwise uncondemnable, of the conquered. And do not think that I am trifling with you, if I say that it would be a good thing if, by training our judgement on such periods, periods in which our prejudices, strong as they may be, are not so strong as to pervert our ideas of truth, we could qualify that same judgement for a similar relation to the events, parties, champions of our own day, and for a like judicial relation to other matters, private as well as public, upon which independent honest counsel is required. But you will see, if you will think it over, how all this may be expanded in many directions of work and thought also.

And there is one lesson more, a lesson which I have already adverted to, which the impatient human mind is very slow to learn, and the necessity of which it is very loth to admit. It is the lesson that there are many questions in History, and in human life also, which cannot be decisively answered; many which need never be answered at all, and yet which it is well to have asked. We learn to suspend as well as to use our judgement for decision; and the moral effect of that is, not to make us sceptical, but first to make us tolerant, and then to make us hopeful; as I said before, patient, enduring contradiction, and enduring suspension and expectation, and even that which maketh the heart sick. Do you think that I am making too much of my favourite study ? that I am ascribing to it results that should be referred to the religious Graces of Faith, Hope and Charity ? I wish indeed that the other of the nine Muses were as certainly servants of the soul to edification, as I believe this one of my choice to be.   But I am not one of those who would draw a sharp and hard fast line between things natural and things spiritual; I believe and know that in all ways the Eternal Wisdom is justified of her children.

And now in the third place, I ought to explain what is the material value of the knowledge acquired by our study as distinguished from the disciplinary virtue that is developed in the pursuit of it.   Well, I will answer this question in the same general, or loose, if you prefer to call it a loose way, in which I have discussed the others.   The knowledge of History enables you, first, to understand what is going on around you in the great world; and second, to understand what it is your duty to understand, and to do what it is your duty to try to do in the most intelligent way, in the little share of administration of the little world around you, that falls to your share.   You all read your newspapers : you read of the political struggles that are going on, we will say on the continent, possibly the strife that is going on at this moment within our own kingdom.   You take an interest in it : you take a side in it, perhaps the side your father took or takes, perhaps the opposite one.   But do you not feel first that you ought to understand something of the rights and wrongs of the struggle, the principles of the combatants, the course of events that have brought on the present complications, and to be able to defend, not only honestly and manfully but intelligently, the side you take?   Even boys and girls are politicians; yes, even in the narrower sense to which we have in common language filed down the word. I am not ashamed to address you, who are listening to me, as such; I do not expect you all to qualify as secretaries of state, or to know as much about foreign affairs as my Lord Salisbury or my Lord Rosebery.   But I say that people, young people too, who have gone to work at their Modern History with a good will, will not long be content to say, I sympathize with Germany and against Russia because this minister does, or with France and Russia against the other European powers (I am merely putting the case), because some other politician, whom I like, says that they are in the right; much less will they take their impressions without examination from the leading papers on the contending sides. They know that the complications have causes, and the parties have principles, and the particular points that are at issue to-day have their roots and determining forces in a past, more or less distant as it may be, the knowledge of which lies open to him or her who is minded to be trained to seek it.

Now if we would wait until we have learned so much, we should not care so much for the voice of the press, or the voice of the people as the cant goes, as we do, and we should be instrumental, yes, in no small way, in helping the press and the people to know what they are dogmatizing about. We should not long have to listen to sneers about the uselessness of historic inquiry, when action not argument is the thing that is required : of course if historical inquiry is postponed until action is required, it is useless, for before it can be instituted, action has taken place and the greatest fools can be wise after the event; but historical knowledge should be a ready fund, ready to be used at once and in abundance ; and so the study will help to make a man a ready and well furnished, as well as an honest and patient and tolerant judge of affairs and characters. A good historical student should be in the way of becoming a sound practical man. And this I insist on more strongly, because I have lately seen essays and articles in which this aspect of our study is distinctly disparaged. I insist on it strongly, and I will adduce as an illustration the fact that the nation of Modern Europe in which the study of History has long most conspicuously flourished is the most practical, and at this moment the most successful; notwithstanding its character for sentiment and its too great addiction to the Gospel of Force. But in these days we want even more than to understand what is going on around us, we want to know how to take our own part; and perhaps it is not too much to say that every day now brings us nearer the condition of affairs in which every man, woman and child, will be made to feel that he, she, and it, have a part to play in local administration and even as units of a still higher scale. Every man almost has a vote for members of parliament, and there are regions in which women also have a direct vote as well as that mediate influence which they exercise on and through men. School boards, local boards, county councils, district councils—others too which, like the offices under the new local government act, would have been better named, and perhaps better organized, if their originators had read constitutional history as they ought to have done, are placing the management of many important branches of public work within the reach of all who will take the trouble to qualify themselves. And for so qualifying ourselves the first requisite may be the formation of a judicial habit such as we have spoken of already: a second is assuredly the knowledge of the institutions of our own country; and a third the intelligent perception of the ideas that underlie the changes which have brought things into their present state. The relation of the State to the Church, of the Church to the State, of the legislative to the executive, of the crown to the parliament, of the several courts of justice, and of the several estates of the realm to one another, should really be at least attempted to be understood by all who undertake public office; not only, that is, what is the condition of things under which they undertake to serve, but as I have said, how that state of things comes to be what it is.

And when I say that the study of our national institutions

will help us, nay is indispensable to us if we want to do our duties decently, I mean more than that it will enable us to talk about them, or even to correct popular mistakes about them. Those who read History intelligently do not speak of the present condition of England as being under a democracy, although they do not shut their eyes to the fact that many public men are to all intents and purposes democrats, or that democratic principles are largely leavening legislation. Some of us may think that the sooner the state of things thus indicated comes about the better; others may think, so much the worse; others will be satisfied if when the time comes we or our children shall be duly prepared and equipped to take our part in it; but whichever view we hold, if we try to read the state of the world honestly we shall hate claptrap, and assumption of infallibility, and decline to listen to the dictation of party war-cries, or to admit by anticipation the incoming of influences which must be safely tempered before they can become supreme.

But I am becoming too peremptory I fear; let me go on to the last of my four heads, which may perhaps for you in your present stage be the most interesting if not also the most remunerative. I said that this head should be the adventitious advantages of the study of History, that is generally the benefit of wholesome and entertaining exercise of the historical instinct. Now I think that in what I have been saying you will see that in coming down from my transcendental perch I have arrived at the ground on which we are all common workers. We are not all philosophers, we are not all judges, or we are not all, thank goodness, members of local boards or county councils, but we do live in homes, county towns, villages, old houses or new neighbourhoods, we all have had parents, who had their homes and their family traditions. We have none of us, thankful we may be for it, had to make ourselves, and such of us as have made or are in the way of making our fortunes, know that if it had not been for what the elders, our parents, our helpers, our early friends, the companions and associates of our mature life have done for us, we might have been, must have been, something very different from what we are pleased to think ourselves now. That means that we all have personal and local interests and connexions that are worth exploring, and that when they are explored fasten us on to the past history of our country in ways that are surpassingly attractive to minds that love History.

There is not an acre I think I may say in England, certainly there is not a parish or a manor, that has not its place in English History, either as the scene of some considerable act, or as the home of some considerable man ; and there is not, I think, an intelligent person in England who is not in one way or another a sharer in such interests of tradition if he would or could realize it. By realizing your own personal connexion with these, you realize your historical relation to the progress of your country, and, by working out the details of the local or personal history in which you are so interested, you may yourselves largely contribute to the ascertaining of historical truth in detail. Every parish must have a history, every parish has a register, every person has a parish. Every manor has a lord, and every lord has had a share in the struggles by which our national life has become what it is ; and every lord has had a following of his tenants whose blood, shed for him, as it may have been, quite as certainly as for the cause in which he was enlisted, may constitute for us, who are not descended from lords of manors, our personal link with the past. Of course some parts of England have been the scenes of more bloody battles and keener political conflicts than others ; but it is very rare to find any district which has not its own special traditions and local affections.

In illustrating this point, you will excuse me if I take an illustration from my own life, and it may indicate to you perhaps some of the influences which have made me so devout an admirer of my study. I was born under the shadow of the great castle in which Becket's murderers found refuge during the year that followed his martyrdom, the year during which the dogs under the table declined to eat their crusts. There, too, as customary tenants of the Forest, my forefathers had done suit and service to Richard, King of the Romans, and after him to Queen Philippa and John of Gaunt long before poor King Richard was kept a prisoner in the king's chamber. My grandfather's house stood on the ground on which Earl Thomas of Lancaster was taken prisoner by Edward II, on the very site of the battle of Boroughbridge; he too was churchwarden of the chapel in which the earl was captured. The first drive that my father ever took me led us across Marston Moor; one great-grandfather lived in an old manor house of the Monks of Fountains; another had a farm in the village where Harold Hardrada fell before the son of Godwin. Then, within a radius of ten miles we returned ten members to Parliament from five boroughs, two lying in the same parish, and one or other, and all together using every different franchise known to the law before the Reform Act. That Act, and the agitation that preceded it, are among my very earliest recollections, and the question of the franchise was made familiar by the fact that another grandfather was prosecuted by order of the House of Commons for a riotous attempt to defeat the right, exercised by the duke of Devonshire, of returning two members for the town by the votes of forty of his tenants, not one of whom was resident or had any other qualification than a deed of feoffment of a burgage, given him as he entered the polling booth and returned when he left it. Nay, if I might boast of my own exploits,

I could tell you how I myself, before the passing of the Act, was privileged to wave the True blue Tory flag in the face of Henry Brougham, one of the last representatives of the pocket borough.

Well, I am not telling you these things to account for my political views which, even if I had not been born and brought up in a centre of Lancastrian traditions, would, I dare say, have been as reactionary and obstinate as I feel them to be; for I do not believe that the views of the Cliffords and the Percies, or even of John of Gaunt himself, had much currency fifty years ago in the heart of the West Riding; but that having an historic taste, I found it constantly drawn out by historic surroundings. These things must have had, bad or good, some share in making my forefathers, and so in making me.

Forgive me this detail, but let me urge on you to try to awake the historic instinct in yourselves which shall meet its true correlative in your own surroundings. Berkshire has a history, not quite so big a one as Yorkshire, but quite as living to Berkshire people and as historical to the historic interest. The interest is perhaps more equally diffused, but it is diffused all over. I will not indicate particulars, even though the name of Alfred occurs to me as the theme of even a longer lecture than the present. Nor will I insist that every one of you should send in to the Oxford Historical Society a memoir of your own parish, at once, although I think that by putting your heads together and comparing your papers and registers you might soon collect a very seriously valuable stock of memoranda for the Society. But I will advise you to add to your still more serious study of general, national and constitutional History, the delightful annex of personal and local research. Bring yourself, your home, your family, your school, into direct connexion with the greater and wider processes—war, peace, administration, religion, reform, local government, or whatever you like that has an historical meaning to you, and you will find the appetite increase upon what it feeds on, and the accumulation of the store, as well as the store accumulated, an abundant stock of pleasant associations, an abundant opportunity for making delightful discoveries, and perhaps valuable additions, links in detail of great price.

Well, I have gone on for a long time; how about the History of England under the Stewarts? As I am not going to give the course, I will not commit myself to any conclusions, but let me just recommend you to keep a few of the points in view that I have urged under the four heads now happily dismissed. First, carry through the course the recollection that the great struggle was a struggle of principles, authority and liberty; authority which had been overstrained, liberty which did not as yet realize its own laws or its own destiny; principles which had been long in growing into such form that they could struggle, and must be traced backward; principles which continued to grow long after they had shed the outward garb in which they first stood up in irreconcileable opposition, and which must therefore be traced forward : back to the Reformation; back to Magna Carta; on to the Revolution, and on to the Reforms of the present reign.

Remember, secondly, that the struggle was a struggle of men who did not altogether realize the strength or weakness of their own cause, and that on both sides their cause was encumbered with religious as well as political complications which have not now, after two hundred years, ceased to affect public affairs. Do not believe those who tell you that the essential of puritanism is in the directness of personal consciousness of relation with God, and the essence of churchmanship in the exclusive claim of corporate religion. Bishop Andrewes was as directly conscious of the personal relation as Howe and Baxter, and Howe and Baxter as insistent on the corporate relation as Whitgift or Hooker. Do not be misled by loose generalizations.

Lastly, remember that the men who fought the battle were your own forefathers, and be kind and gentle to their memories. You may, like the Americans, like to trace your pedigree to the army lists of one side or other; you must learn on which side the men of the counties to which you belong, the parishes to which you belong, the families to which you belong, ranged themselves in the conflict, and so doing, you may add to the memorials of a most striking age, and add, as I have tried to show you, the adventitious advantage of strong personal interest to the more ideal, if loftier, interest that you will feel yourselves growing into, as illuminated politicians. And so I will wish you good night and pleasant dreams; happy if the hour that we have spent together has had the effect of putting before any one of you wholesome thoughts, and temperate ambitions, that you have not had before, or turning you to sources of useful and entertaining employment of the few leisure hours which the increasing rate of the world's progress, its unmeaning competitions and the exasperation of its party conflicts, seem likely to make the last few leisure hours of your and the next generation.

INDEX

THE END.

Date Due